AN OBJECT-ORIENTED APPROACH TO PROGRAMMING LOGIC AND DESIGN

Joyce Farrell

An Object-Oriented Approach to Programming Logic and Design

by Joyce Farrell

Executive Editor:
Mac Mendelsohn

Senior Product Manager:
Tricia Boyle

Development Editor:
Lisa Ruffolo

Technical Editor:
John Bosco and Nicole Ashton,
Green Pen Quality Assurance

Product Marketing Manager:
Brian Berkeley

Associate Product Manager:
Sarah Santoro

Editorial Assistant:
Jennifer Smith

Production Editors:
Melissa Panagos and Brooke
Booth

Cover Designer:
Nancy Goulet

Interior Designer:
Betsy Young

Compositor:
GEX Publishing Services

Manufacturing Coordinator:
Laura Burns

Copyeditor:
Susan Forsyth

Proofreader:
Robin Flynn

Indexer:
Liz Cunningham

BRIEF CONTENTS

TABLE OF CONTENTS

CHAPTER THREE
Using Methods and Parameters   55

CHAPTER FOUR
Understanding Structure

CHAPTER FIVE
Making Decisions

CHAPTER SIX

CHAPTER SEVEN
Arrays 217

CHAPTER TEN
Modeling With UML   303

CHAPTER ELEVEN

Object Concepts: Polymorphism and Inheritance 329

CHAPTER TWELVE

Exception Handling 363

■■■■■ PREFACE

An Object-Oriented Approach to Programming Logic and Design provides the beginning programmer with a guide to developing object-oriented program logic. This textbook assumes no programming language experience. The writing is non-technical and emphasizes good programming practices. The examples are business examples; they do not assume mathematical background beyond high school business math. Additionally, the examples illustrate one or two major points; they do not contain so many features that students become lost following irrelevant and extraneous details.

The examples in *An Object-Oriented Approach to Programming Logic and Design* have been created to provide students with a sound background in logic no matter what programming languages they eventually use to write programs. This book can be used in a standalone logic course that students take as a prerequisite to a programming course, or as a companion book to any object-oriented programming language text using any language such as Java, C++, or C#.

ORGANIZATION AND COVERAGE

An Object-Oriented Approach to Programming Logic and Design introduces students to programming concepts, enforcing good style, and logical thinking. General programming concepts are introduced in Chapter 1. Chapter 2 discusses the key concepts of object-orientation, including classes, objects, behaviors, and attributes. Chapter 3 extends the information on structured programming to the area of data hiding, particularly how to create methods and pass parameters to them and how public methods are used to access the private data of class objects. In Chapter 4, students are introduced to the advantages of structured programming, creating methods that include sequence, selection, and loop structures. Chapters 5 and 6 further explore the intricacies of decision-making and looping. Students learn to develop sophisticated programs that use arrays in Chapters 7 and 8.

The later chapters in the book provide the student with a background in a wide variety of programming techniques used in modern object-oriented applications. Chapter 9 describes programming with graphical user interface (GUI) objects and handling the events they generate. Chapter 10 teaches the basics of system design, introducing the Unified Modeling Language, Chapter 11 provides background in the object-oriented concepts of inheritance and polymorphism, and Chapter 12 describes managing program errors using the object-oriented technique called exception handling.

In addition to the 12 chapters, three appendices allow students to gain extra experience with structuring large unstructured programs, using the binary numbering system, and working with large decision tables.

An Object-Oriented Approach to Programming Logic and Design combines text explanation with flowcharts and pseudocode examples to provide students with alternative means of expressing structured logic. Numerous detailed, full-program exercises at the end of each chapter illustrate the concepts explained within the chapter, and reinforce understanding and retention of the material presented.

An Object-Oriented Approach to Programming Logic and Design is a language-independent introduction to programming logic beginning with object-oriented principles. It distinguishes itself from other programming logic texts in the following ways:

- Objects are covered first so that students who intend to write programs in object-oriented programming languages do not learn procedural logic first, and then unlearn it to write in an object-oriented fashion. Instructors whose students will begin their programming careers using Java, Visual Basic, C++, or C# will appreciate this approach.

- Object-oriented programming terminology is explained in easy-to-understand language, using every-day real-life examples as well as programming examples. Object-oriented concepts such as static and instance methods, and private and public access methods are learned before being burdened with the syntax of a specific language.

- Object-oriented terminology is explained as it refers to GUI objects used in visual languages as well as to business objects.

- No programming experience is assumed.

- Examples are language-independent. This book can be used alone in a logic course or as a companion text in courses in any object-oriented programming language such as Java, Visual Basic, C++, or C#.

- Examples are everyday business examples; no mathematics beyond high school algebra is required. This is not a computer science text; it is an introduction to logic for CIS students who want to get up to speed quickly developing useful programs.

- Examples are simple; the point under discussion is not lost in examples with too much detail.

- The student will understand data types and gain a solid foundation in the declaration, definition, and use of variables, arithmetic operations, and other basic programming concepts. Within methods, structure is stressed; students will become proficient in recognizing and using sequences, selections, loops, and arrays.

FEATURES OF THE TEXT

An Object-Oriented Approach to Programming Logic and Design is a superior textbook because it includes the following features:

- Objectives: Each chapter begins with a list of objectives so the student knows the topics that will be presented in the chapter. In addition to providing a quick reference to topics covered, this feature provides a useful study aid.

- Flowcharts and pseudocode: This book has plenty of figures and illustrations, including flowcharts that provide the reader with a visual learning experience, rather than one that involves simply studying text.

- Complete class example: Provides a complete class example in most chapters to demonstrate the application of the topics learned.

- Tips: These notes provide additional information—for example, another location in the book that expands on a topic, or a common error to avoid.

- Chapter summaries: A summary recaps the programming concepts and techniques covered in the chapter. This feature provides a concise means for students to review and check their understanding of the main points in each chapter.

- Key terms: A collection of all the key terms ends each chapter. Definitions are also included in sentence format and in the order in which they appear in the chapter.

- Review questions: Twenty review questions at the end of each chapter reinforce the main ideas introduced in the chapter. Successfully answering these questions will demonstrate mastery of the concepts and information presented.

- Exercises: Each chapter includes meaningful programming exercises that provide students with additional practice of the skills and concepts they learned in the lesson. These exercises increase in difficulty and are designed to allow students to explore logical programming concepts. Each exercise can be completed using flowcharts or pseudocode; in addition, instructors can choose to assign the exercises as programming problems to be coded and executed in an object-oriented programming language.

- Case project: Each chapter concludes with a running case project involving a hypothetical business. By applying the current chapter's concepts to the continuing business example, the student discovers that the concepts learned in each chapter contributes to the development of a complete business system.

TEACHING TOOLS

The following supplemental materials are available when this book is used in a classroom setting. All of the teaching tools available with this book are provided to the instructor on a single CD-ROM.

Electronic Instructor's Manual. The Instructor's Manual that accompanies this textbook includes additional instructional material to assist in class preparation, including Sample Syllabi, Chapter Outlines, Technical Notes, Lecture Notes, Quick Quizzes, Teaching Tips, Discussion Topics, and Key Terms.

ExamView®. This textbook is accompanied by ExamView, a powerful testing software package that allows instructors to create and administer printed, computer (LAN-based), and Internet exams. ExamView includes hundreds of questions that correspond to the topics covered in this text, enabling students to generate detailed study guides that include page references for further review. The computer-based and Internet testing components allow students to take exams at their computers, and also save the instructor time by grading each exam automatically.

PowerPoint Presentations. This book comes with Microsoft PowerPoint slides for each chapter. These are included as a teaching aid for classroom presentation, to make available to students on the network for chapter review, or to be printed for classroom distribution. Instructors can add their own slides for additional topics they introduce to the class.

Solutions. Solutions to Review Questions and Exercises are provided on the Teaching Tools CD-ROM and may also be found on the Course Technology Web site at **www.course.com**. The solutions are password protected.

Distance Learning. Course Technology is proud to present online test banks in WebCT and Blackboard, as well as MyCourse 2.0, Course Technology's own course enhancement tool, to provide the most complete and dynamic learning experience possible. Instructors are encouraged to make the most of the course, both online and offline. For more information on how to access the online test bank, contact your local Course Technology sales representative.

ACKNOWLEDGMENTS

I would like to thank all of the people who helped to make this book a reality, especially Lisa Ruffolo, Development Editor, whose hard work, attention to detail, sense of humor, and perceptive appreciation for the methodology required to teach this subject matter have made this a quality textbook. Thank you, Lisa, for making my job easier. Thanks also to Tricia Boyle, Senior Product Manager; Drew Strawbridge, Senior Acquisitions Editor; Melissa Panagos and Brooke Booth, Production Editors; and John Bosco, Technical Editor. I am grateful to be able to work with so many fine people who are dedicated to producing quality instructional materials.

I am grateful to the many reviewers who provided helpful and insightful comments during the development of this book, including Nelson Capaz, Pasco Hernando Community College; Bob Husson, Craven Community College; Sara Mathew, Oklahoma City Community College; Herbert Rebhun, University of Houston–Downtown; Ronald Schwartz, Florida Atlantic University.

Thanks, too, to my husband, Geoff, who provides encouragement and drives the car so I can write on the laptop. This book is dedicated to him and to our daughters, Andrea and Audrey.

Joyce Farrell

AN OVERVIEW OF COMPUTERS AND LOGIC

After studying Chapter 1, you should be able to:

- ☐ Understand computer components and operations
- ☐ Understand the evolution of programming techniques
- ☐ Describe the steps involved in the programming process
- ☐ Understand flowcharts and pseudocode statements
- ☐ Create an application class with a main( ) method
- ☐ Use and name variables
- ☐ Assign values to variables
- ☐ Describe data types

UNDERSTANDING COMPUTER COMPONENTS AND OPERATIONS

The two major components of any computer system are its hardware and its software. **Hardware** is the equipment, or the devices, associated with a computer. For a computer to be useful, however, it needs more than equipment; a computer needs to be given instructions. The instructions that tell the computer what to do are called **software**, or programs, and are written by programmers. This book focuses on the process of writing these instructions.

 Software can be classified as application software or system software. **Application software** comprises all the programs you apply to a task—word-processing programs, spreadsheets, payroll and inventory programs, and even games. **System software** comprises the programs that you use to manage your computer—operating systems such as Windows or Unix. This book focuses on the logic used to write application software programs, although many of the concepts apply to both types of software.

Together, computer hardware and software accomplish four major operations:

1. Input
2. Processing
3. Output
4. Storage

Hardware devices that perform input include keyboards and mice. **Input devices** provide the ways that **data**, or facts, enter the computer system. **Processing** data items may involve organizing them, checking them for accuracy, or performing mathematical operations on them. The piece of hardware that performs these sorts of tasks is the **central processing unit**, or **CPU**. After data items have been processed, the resulting information is sent to a printer, monitor, or some other **output device** so that people can view, interpret, and use the results. Often, you also want to store the output information on **storage devices**—hardware such as magnetic disks, tapes, or compact discs. Computer software consists of all the instructions that control how and when the data are input, how they are processed, and the form in which they are output or stored.

 Data includes all the text, numerical information, or other information that is processed by a computer. However, many computer professionals reserve the term "information" for data that has been processed. For example, your name, Social Security number, and hourly pay rate are data items, but your paycheck holds information.

Computer hardware by itself is useless without a programmer's instructions, or software, just as your stereo equipment doesn't do much until you provide music on a CD or tape. You can buy prewritten software that is stored on a disk, or you can write your own software instructions. You can enter instructions into a computer system through any of the hardware devices you use for data; most often, you type your instructions using a keyboard and store them on a device such as a disk or CD.

You write computer instructions in a computer **programming language** such as Visual Basic, C#, C++, Java, Pascal, COBOL, RPG, or Fortran. Just as some people speak English and others speak Japanese, programmers also write programs in different languages. Some programmers work exclusively in one language, while others know several and use the one that seems most appropriate for the task at hand.

No matter which programming language a computer programmer uses, the language has rules governing its word usage and punctuation. These rules are called the language's **syntax**. If you ask, "How the get to store do I?" in English, most people can figure out what you probably mean, even though you have not used proper English syntax. However, computers are not nearly as smart as most people; with a computer, you might as well have asked, "Xpu mxv ot dodnm cadf B?" Unless the syntax is perfect, the computer cannot interpret the programming language instruction at all.

Every computer operates on circuitry that consists of millions of on-off switches. Each programming language uses a piece of software to translate the specific programming language into the computer's on-off circuitry language, or **machine language**. The language translation software is called a **compiler** or **interpreter**, and it tells you if you have used a programming language incorrectly. Therefore, syntax errors are relatively easy to locate and correct—the compiler or interpreter you use highlights every syntax error. If you write a computer program using a language such as C++, but spell one of its words incorrectly or reverse the proper order of two words, the compiler lets you know it found a mistake by displaying an error message as soon as you try to run the program.

Although there are differences in how compilers and interpreters work, their basic function is the same—to translate your programming statements into code the computer can use. When you use a compiler, an entire program is translated before it can execute; when you use an interpreter, each instruction is translated just prior to execution. Usually, you do not choose which type of translation to use—it depends on the programming language.

For a program to work properly, you must give the instructions to the computer in a specific sequence, you must not leave any instructions out, and you must not add extraneous instructions. By doing this, you are developing the **logic** of the computer program. Suppose you instruct someone to make a cake as follows:

```
Stir
Add two eggs
Add a gallon of gasoline
Bake at 350 degrees for 45 minutes
Add three cups of flour
```

Even though you have used the English language syntax correctly, the instructions are out of sequence, some instructions are missing, and some instructions belong to procedures other than baking a cake. If you follow these instructions, you are not going to end up with an edible cake, and you may end up with a disaster. Logical errors are much more difficult to locate than syntax errors; it is easier for you to determine whether "eggs" is spelled incorrectly in a recipe than it is for you to tell if there are too many eggs or they are added too soon.

Programmers often call logical errors **semantic errors**. For example, if you misspell a programming-language word, you commit a syntax error, but if you use a correct word that does not make any sense in the current context, you commit a semantic error.

Just as baking directions can be given correctly in French, German, or Spanish, the same logic of a program can be expressed in any number of programming languages. This book is almost exclusively concerned with the logic development process. Because this book is not concerned with any specific language, the programming examples could have been written in Japanese, C++, or Java. The logic is the same in any language. For convenience, the book uses English!

Once instructions have been input into the computer and translated into machine language, a program can be **run**, or **executed**. You can write program instructions that take a number (an input step), double it (processing), and provide you with the answer (output) in a programming language such as Java or C++, but if you were to write it using English-like statements, it would look like this:

```
Get inputNumber.
Compute calculatedAnswer as inputNumber 2.
Print calculatedAnswer.
```

TIP □ □ □ □ | You will learn about the odd elimination of the space between words like "input" and "Number" and "calculated" and "Answer" in the next few pages.

The instruction to `Get inputNumber` is an example of an input operation. When the computer interprets this instruction, it knows to look to an input device to obtain a number. Computers often have several input devices, perhaps a keyboard, a mouse, a CD drive, and two or more disk drives. When you learn a specific programming language, you learn how to tell the computer which of those input devices to access for input. Logically, however, it doesn't really matter which hardware device is used, as long as the computer knows to look for a number. The logic of the input operation—that the computer must obtain a number for input, and that the computer must obtain it before multiplying it by two—remains the same regardless of any specific input hardware device. The same is true in your daily life—if you follow the instruction "Get eggs from store," it does not really matter if you are following a handwritten instruction from a list or a voice mail instruction left on your cell phone—the process of getting the eggs, and the result of doing so, are the same.

TIP □ □ □ □ | Many computer professionals categorize disk drives and CD drives as storage devices rather than input devices. Such devices actually can be used for input, storage, and output.

Processing is the step that occurs when the mathematics is performed to double the `inputNumber`; the statement `Compute calculatedAnswer as inputNumber times 2` represents processing. Mathematical operations are not the only kind of processing, but they are very typical. After you write a program, the program can be used on computers of different brand names, sizes, and speeds. Whether you use an IBM, Macintosh, Linux, or Unix operating system, and whether you use a personal computer that sits on your desk or a mainframe that costs hundreds of thousands of dollars and resides in a special building in a university, multiplying by 2 is the same process. The hardware is not important; the processing will be the same.

In the number-doubling program, the `Print calculatedAnswer` statement represents output. Within a particular program, this statement could cause the output to appear on the monitor (which might be a flat panel screen or a cathode-ray tube), or the output could go to a printer (which could be laser or inkjet), or the output could be written to a disk or CD. The logic of the process called "Print" is the same no matter what hardware device you use.

Besides input, processing, and output, the fourth operation in any computer system is storage. Storage comes in two broad categories. All computers have **internal storage**, probably referred to more often as **memory**, **main memory**, or **primary memory**. This storage is inside the machine and is the type of storage most often discussed in this book. Computers also have **external storage**, which is permanent storage outside the main memory of the machine, on a device such as a floppy disk, hard disk, or magnetic tape. In other words, external storage is outside of the main memory, not necessarily outside the computer. Both programs and data sometimes are stored on each of these kinds of media.

To use computer programs, you must first load them into memory. You might type a program into memory from the keyboard, or you might use a program that has already been written and stored on a disk. Either way, a copy of the instructions must be placed in memory before the program can be run.

A computer system needs both internal memory and external storage. Internal memory is needed to run the programs, but internal memory is **volatile**—that is, its contents are lost every time the computer loses power. Therefore, if you are going to use a program more than once, you must store it, or **save** it, on some nonvolatile medium. Otherwise, the program in main memory is lost forever when the computer is turned off. External storage (usually disks or tape) provides a nonvolatile medium.

TIP □ □ □ □ Even though a hard disk drive is located inside your computer, the hard disk is not main, internal memory. Internal memory is temporary and volatile; a hard drive is permanent, nonvolatile storage. After one or two "tragedies" of losing several pages of a typed computer program due to a power failure or other hardware problem, most programmers learn to periodically save the programs they are in the process of writing, using a nonvolatile medium, such as a disk.

Once you have a copy of a program in main memory, you want to execute or run the program. To do so, you must also place any data that the program requires into memory. For example, after you place the following program into memory and start to run it, you need to provide an actual `inputNumber`—for example, 8—that you also place in main memory.

```
Get inputNumber.
Compute calculatedAnswer as inputNumber times 2.
Print calculatedAnswer.
```

The `inputNumber` is placed in memory in a specific memory location that the program will call `inputNumber`. Then, and only then, can the `calculatedAnswer`, in this case 16, be calculated and printed.

TIP □ □ □ □ Computer memory consists of millions of numbered locations where data can be stored. The memory location of `inputNumber` has a specific numeric address, for example, 48604. Your program associates `inputNumber` with that address. Every time you refer to `inputNumber` within a program, the computer retrieves the value at the associated memory location. When you write programs, you seldom need to be concerned with the value of the memory address; instead, you simply use the easy-to-remember name you created.

TIP □ □ □ □ Computer programmers often refer to memory addresses using hexadecimal notation, or base 16. Using this system, they might use a value like 42FF01A to refer to a memory address. Despite the use of letters, such an address is still a number. When you use the hexadecimal numbering system, the letters A through F stand for the values 10 through 15.

UNDERSTANDING THE EVOLUTION OF PROGRAMMING TECHNIQUES

People have been writing computer programs since the 1940s. The oldest programming languages required programmers to work with memory addresses and to memorize awkward codes associated with machine languages. Newer programming languages look much more like natural language and are easier for programmers to use. Part of the reason it is easier to use newer programming languages is that they allow programmers to name variables instead of using awkward memory addresses. Another reason is that newer programming languages provide programmers with the means to create self-contained modules or program segments that can be pieced together in a variety of ways. The oldest computer programs were written in one piece, from start to finish; modern programs are rarely written that way—they are created by teams of programmers, each developing his or her own reusable and connectable program procedures. Writing several small modules is easier than writing one large program, and most large tasks are easier when you break the work into units and get other workers to help with some of the units.

TIP □ □ □ □   You will learn more about program modules in Chapters 2 and 3.

Currently, there are two major techniques to use to develop programs and their procedures. One technique, called **procedural programming**, focuses on the procedures that programmers create to manipulate data. That is, procedural programmers focus on the actions that are carried out—for example, getting input data for an employee and writing the calculations needed to produce a paycheck from the data. Procedural programmers would approach the job of producing a paycheck by breaking down the paycheck-producing process into manageable subtasks.

The other popular programming technique, called **object-oriented programming**, or **OOP**, focuses on objects, or "things," and describes their features, or attributes, and their behaviors. The **attributes of an object** are the features it "has"; the values of an object's attributes constitute the object's **state**. For example, an attribute of a paycheck is the monetary value of the check, and the state of one paycheck's monetary value might be $400. The **behaviors of an object** are the things it "does"; for example, a paycheck object can be written and cashed, and it contains calculations that result in the check amount. Object-oriented programmers might design a payroll application by thinking about all the objects needed such as employees, time cards, and paychecks, and describing their attributes and behaviors.

TIP □ □ □ □   Programmers use the term "OO," pronounced "oh oh," as an abbreviation for "object oriented." When discussing object-oriented programming, they use "OOP," which rhymes with "soup."

With either approach, procedural or object-oriented, you can produce a correct paycheck, and both techniques employ reusable program modules. The major difference lies in the focus the programmer takes during the earliest planning stages of a project. Taking an **object-oriented approach** to a problem means defining the objects needed to accomplish a task and developing the objects so that each maintains its own data and carries out tasks when another object requests them. The object-oriented approach is said to be "natural" because it is more natural to think of the world as consisting of objects and the ways in which they interact than it is to think of systems in terms of data items and the logic required to manipulate them.

TIP □ □ □ □   Object-oriented programming employs a large vocabulary; you can learn much of this terminology in Chapter 2 of this book.

Originally, object-oriented programming was used most frequently for two major types of applications—computer simulations and graphical user interfaces (**GUIs**). Thinking about objects in these two types of applications makes sense. For example, a city might want to develop a program that provides a simulation of traffic patterns so as to better prevent traffic tie-ups. By creating a model with objects such as cars and pedestrians that each contain their own data and rules for behavior, the simulation can be set in motion. For example, each car object has a specific current speed and a procedure for changing that speed. By creating a model of city traffic using objects, a computer can create a simulation of a real city at rush hour.

Creating a GUI environment for users also is a natural use for object orientation. It is easy to think of the components a user manipulates on a computer screen, such as buttons and scroll bars, as similar to real-world objects. Each GUI object contains data—for example, a button on a screen has a specific size and color. Each object also contains behaviors—for example, each button can be clicked and reacts in a specific way when clicked. As a matter of fact, some people consider the term "object-oriented programming" to be synonymous with GUI programming, but object-oriented programming means more, and modern businesses use object-oriented design techniques when developing all sorts of business applications.

UNDERSTANDING THE PROGRAMMING PROCESS

When a business develops a system, such as payroll, inventory, or billing, using an object-oriented approach involves three separate tasks:

- Analyzing the system using an object-oriented approach (**object-oriented analysis**, or **OOA**)
- Designing the system using an object-oriented approach (**object-oriented design**, or **OOD**)
- Writing the programs using an object-oriented approach (object-oriented programming, or OOP)

Often a programmer performs all of these tasks; sometimes a systems analyst analyzes and designs the system and programmers simply write the programs. Although these three tasks are often intertwined, this book focuses on the process of writing programs that have already been designed. Writing programs involves the following steps:

1. When object-oriented programmers write programs, they envision the objects they need. For example, one necessary object for an application might be a form on a computer screen in which a user can enter data. The programmer then writes instructions in a programming language to create the objects. Perhaps a user will use a form to enter a number and view its double value (such as in the three instructions in the doubling program in the preceding section). A professional programmer usually does not just sit down at a computer keyboard and start typing the instructions in a programming language. The object-oriented programmer's job consists of several distinct steps. You identify all the objects you want to manipulate and how they relate to each other; this is known as **data modeling**. After you have identified an object, you create a general category for the object; this general category is called a **class**. Very often, someone has already created the class—for example, many object-oriented languages already contain a class you can use to create a form on the screen—you do not have to build this class from scratch. However, your form might have a size, contain words, or be a color that is different from any existing form, so you have to write those instructions. Whether you use prewritten classes or need to create some from scratch, you also establish the ways you will communicate with the objects in your program, and how they will communicate with each other.

TIP □ □ □ □ | You will gain a much more thorough understanding of the concept of "class" in Chapter 3.

2. You code the statements you need in a programming language. That is, you write the class definitions including describing all the data in each class and all the operations that will be performed with the data in each class.

3. You translate the program statements into machine language.

4. You test the program.

5. You put the program into production.

IDENTIFYING OBJECTS, CREATING CLASSES, AND ESTABLISHING COMMUNICATION

The heart of the object-oriented programming process lies in the design of the objects and classes you need. Chapter 2 will get you started in planning these features.

CODING THE PROGRAM

Once the programmer has identified the objects needed, only then can he or she write the definitions for the objects in a programming language. Well-known object-oriented programming languages include C++, C#, Java, SmallTalk, OO COBOL, and Simula. Despite their differences, these programming languages are quite alike—each can handle creating objects and establishing communication between them. The objects a program requires and logic needed to work with the objects can be executed using any number of languages. It is only after a language is chosen that the programmer must worry about each command being spelled correctly and all of the punctuation getting into the right spots—in other words, using the correct *syntax*.

Some very experienced programmers can successfully combine the planning and the actual instruction writing, or **coding** of the program, in one step. This may work for planning and writing a very simple program, just as you can plan and write a postcard to a friend using one step. A good term paper or a Hollywood screenplay, however, needs planning before writing, and so do most programs.

Which step is harder, planning the objects and classes or coding them? Right now, it may seem to you that writing in a programming language is a very difficult task, considering all the spelling and grammar rules you must learn. However, the planning step is actually more difficult. Which is more difficult, thinking up memorable characters and how they interact and navigate the twists and turns to the plot of a best-selling mystery novel, or writing a translation of an already written novel from English to Spanish? And who do you think gets paid more, the writer who creates the characters and plot or the translator? (Try asking friends to name any famous translator!)

TRANSLATING THE PROGRAM INTO MACHINE LANGUAGE

Even though there are many programming languages, each computer knows only one language, its machine language, which consists of many 1s and 0s. Computers understand machine language because computers themselves are made up of thousands of tiny electrical switches, each of which can be set in either the on or off state, which is represented by a 1 or 0, respectively.

Languages like Java or Visual Basic are available for programmers to use because someone has written a translator program (a compiler or interpreter) that changes the English-like **high-level programming language** in which the programmer writes into the **low-level machine language** that the computer understands. If you write a programming language statement incorrectly (for example, by misspelling a word, using a word that doesn't exist in the language, or using "illegal" grammar), the translator program doesn't know what to do and issues an error message identifying a **syntax error**, or misuse of a language's grammar rules. You receive the same response when you speak nonsense to a human language translator. Imagine trying to look up a list of words in a Spanish-English dictionary if some of the listed words are misspelled—you can't complete the task until the words are spelled correctly. Although making errors is never desirable, syntax errors are not a major concern to programmers because the compiler or translator catches every syntax error, and the computer will not execute a program that contains them.

A computer program must be free of syntax errors before you can execute it. Typically, a programmer develops objects, writes the code the objects need, and then compiles the program, receiving a list of syntax errors. The programmer corrects the syntax errors, and compiles the program again. Correcting the first set of errors frequently reveals a new set of errors that originally were not apparent to the compiler. For example, if you could use an English compiler and submit the sentence `The grl go to school`, the compiler at first would point out only one syntax error to you. The second word, `grl`, is illegal because it is not part of the English language. Only after you corrected the word `girl` would the compiler find another syntax error on the third word, `go`, because it is the wrong verb form for the subject `girl`. This doesn't mean `go` is necessarily the wrong word. Maybe `girl` is wrong; perhaps the subject should be `girls`, in which case `go` is right. Compilers don't always know exactly what you mean, nor do they know what the proper correction should be, but they do know when something is wrong with your syntax.

When writing a program, a programmer might need to recompile the code several times. An executable program is created only when the code is free of syntax errors. Figure 1-1 shows a diagram of this entire process.

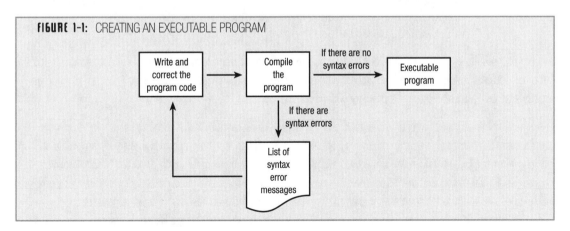

FIGURE 1-1: CREATING AN EXECUTABLE PROGRAM

TESTING THE PROGRAM

A program that is free of syntax errors is not necessarily free of **logical errors**. For example, the sentence `The girl goes to school`, although syntactically perfect, is not logically correct if the girl is a baby or a dropout.

Once a program is free of syntax errors, the programmer can test it—that is, execute it. Many programs require that you enter some sample data to see whether the results are logically correct. Recall the number-doubling program segment from earlier in the chapter:

```
Get inputNumber.
Compute calculatedAnswer as inputNumber times 2.
Print calculatedAnswer.
```

If you write a program containing these statements, execute it, provide the value 2 as input to the program, and the answer 4 prints out, you have executed one successful test run of the program.

However, if the answer 40 prints out, maybe it's because the program contains a logical error. Maybe the second line of code was mistyped with an extra zero, so that the program reads:

```
Get inputNumber.
Compute calculatedAnswer as inputNumber times 20.
Print calculatedAnswer.
```

The error of placing 20 instead of 2 in the multiplication statement caused a logical error. Notice that nothing is syntactically wrong with this second program—it is just as reasonable to multiply a number by 20 as by 2—but if the programmer intends only to double the `inputNumber`, then a logical error has occurred.

Programs should be tested with many sets of data. For example, if you write the program to double a number and enter 2 and get an output value of 4, that doesn't mean you have a correct program. Perhaps you have typed this program by mistake:

```
Get inputNumber.
Compute calculatedAnswer as inputNumber plus 2.
Print calculatedAnswer.
```

An input of 2 results in an answer of 4, but that doesn't mean your program doubles numbers—it actually only adds 2 to them. If you test your program with additional data and get the wrong answer—for example, if you use a 3 and get an answer of 5—you know there is a problem with your code.

Selecting test data is somewhat of an art in itself, and it should be done carefully. If the Human Resources Department wants a list of the names of five-year employees, it would be a mistake to test the program with a small sample file of only long-term employees. If no newer employees are part of the data being used for testing, you don't really know if the program would have eliminated them from the five-year list. Many companies don't know that their software has a problem until an unusual circumstance occurs—for example, the first time an employee has more than nine dependents, the first time a customer orders more than 999 items at a time, or when (in an example that was well-documented in the popular press), a new century begins.

PUTTING THE PROGRAM INTO PRODUCTION

Once the program is tested adequately, it is ready for the organization to use. Putting the program into production might mean simply running the program once, if it was written to satisfy a user's request for a special list. However, the process might take months if the program will be run on a regular basis, or if it is one of a large system of programs being developed. Perhaps data-entry people must be trained to prepare the input for the new program, users must be trained to understand the output, or existing data in the company must be changed to an entirely new format to accommodate this program. **Conversion**, the entire set of actions an organization must take to switch over to using a new program or set of programs, can sometimes take months or years to accomplish.

You might consider maintaining programs as a sixth step in the programming process. After programs are put into production, making required changes is called maintenance. Maintenance is necessary for many reasons: for example, new tax rates are legislated, the format of an input file is altered, or the end user requires additional information not included in the original output specifications.

You might consider retiring the program as the seventh and final step in the programming process. A program is retired when it is no longer needed by an organization—usually when a new program is in the process of being put into production.

USING FLOWCHARTS AND PSEUDOCODE STATEMENTS

When programmers plan the logic for a solution to a programming problem, they often use one of two tools, flowcharts or pseudocode (pronounced "sue-doe-code"). A **flowchart** is a pictorial representation of the logical steps it takes to solve a problem; **pseudocode** is an English-like representation of the same thing. When you create a flowchart, you write program steps in boxes that you connect with arrows, or **flowlines**, to show the order in which steps will be processed. Figure 1-2 shows a flowchart of the number-doubling problem.

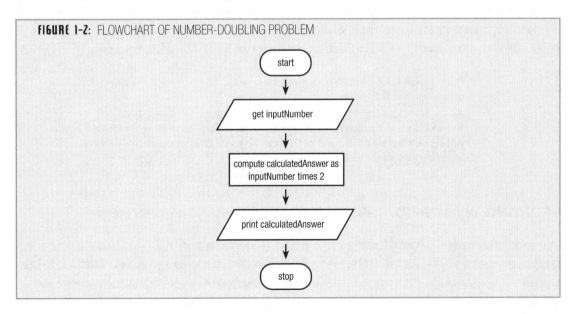

FIGURE 1-2: FLOWCHART OF NUMBER-DOUBLING PROBLEM

Figure 1-2 shows the input and output statements in parallelograms and the processing statement in a rectangle. Parallelograms and rectangles are conventionally used for these respective purposes by flowchart creators. Additionally, the figure shows the conventional shapes for start and stop symbols; this shape is called a lozenge.

Pseudocode provides an alternative to flowcharting. *Pseudo* is a prefix that means "false," and to *code* a program means to put it in a programming language; therefore *pseudocode* simply means "false code," or sentences that appear to have been written in a computer programming language but don't necessarily follow all the syntax rules of any specific language.

You have already seen examples of statements that represent pseudocode earlier in this chapter, and there is nothing mysterious about them. The following three statements constitute a pseudocode representation of a number-doubling problem:

```
get inputNumber
compute calculatedAnswer as inputNumber times 2
print calculatedAnswer
```

The steps in the pseudocode statement are identical to those between the start and stop symbols in the flowchart shown in Figure 1-2. Using pseudocode simply involves writing down all the steps you will use in a program. Most pseudocode writers do not bother with punctuation such as periods at the end of pseudocode statements, although it would not be wrong to use them if you prefer that style. Similarly, there is no need to capitalize the first word in a sentence, although you might choose to do so. This book follows the conventions of using lowercase letters for verbs that begin pseudocode statements and omitting periods at the end of statements.

Some professional programmers prefer writing pseudocode to drawing flowcharts because using pseudocode is more similar to writing the final statements in the programming language. Others prefer drawing flowcharts to represent the logical flow because flowcharts allow programmers to more easily visualize how the program statements will connect. Especially for beginning programmers, flowcharts are an excellent tool to help visualize how the statements in complicated portions of a program are interrelated; you will use flowchart symbols in Chapters 5 and 6 when you learn to write decisions and loops.

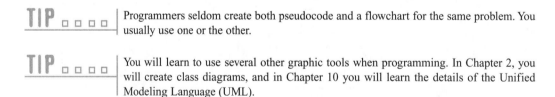 Programmers seldom create both pseudocode and a flowchart for the same problem. You usually use one or the other.

TIP □ □ □ □ You will learn to use several other graphic tools when programming. In Chapter 2, you will create class diagrams, and in Chapter 10 you will learn the details of the Unified Modeling Language (UML).

CREATING AN APPLICATION CLASS WITH A MAIN() METHOD

In purely object-oriented programming languages, such as Java, every statement you make must be part of a class. In other languages, such as C++, you can write programs that contain class objects, yet are not classes themselves. This book will use the "pure view"—that every application is a class. An **application** is a program that accomplishes some task. The pseudocode for every application you create will begin with the word `class` and end with `endClass`.

Although no object-oriented programming language uses exactly this statement, this book will use it to make clear to you where a class ends. In every object-oriented language, all the program actions must take place within a method. A **method** is a set of statements that performs some task or group of tasks. In most object-oriented programming languages, if a class contains only one method that executes, the method is named `main()`. Just about the simplest program you can write is one that prints a message on the screen. Figure 1-3 shows the pseudocode for a simple application that prints the word "Hello".

FIGURE 1-3: PSEUDOCODE FOR THE `Hello` CLASS

```
class Hello
   main()
      print "Hello"
   return
endClass
```

In Figure 1-3, the class begins with the word `class`, followed by the class name. A class name can be any legal identifier you choose. An **identifier** is the name of a programming object—a class, method, or variable.

Every computer programming language has its own set of rules for naming identifiers. Most languages allow both letters and digits within identifiers. Some languages allow hyphens, underscores, dollar signs, or other special characters in identifiers, others allow foreign alphabet characters such as π or Ω. You must learn the rules for creating identifiers in each programming language you use.

TIP ▫ ▫ ▫ ▫ | You also can refer to an identifier as a **mnemonic**. In everyday language, a mnemonic is a memory device, like the sentence "Every good boy does fine," which makes it easier to remember the names of the lines on a musical staff. In programming, an identifier makes it easier to remember class and variable names than if you had to remember their memory addresses.

Different languages put different limits on the length of identifiers, although in general, newer languages allow longer names. For example, in some very old versions of BASIC, an identifier could consist of only one or two letters and one or two digits; this caused programmers to create some cryptic identifiers like `hw` or `a3` or `re02`. In other languages, identifiers can be very long; many modern languages allow more than two hundred characters in an identifier, and in the newest versions of C++, C#, and Java, the length of identifiers is virtually unlimited. These languages are case sensitive, so `Hello, hello, and HELLO` represent three separate classes. Most programmers who use the more modern languages employ the format in which class names begin with an uppercase letter. Multiple-word identifiers names are run together, and each new word within the identifier begins with an uppercase letter.

TIP ▫ ▫ ▫ ▫ | When an identifier begins with a lowercase letter, but contains uppercase letters within it, as in `studentGrade`, the format is called **camel casing**, because such class names have a "hump" in the middle. When the first letter is uppercase, as in `HelloClass`, then the format is known as Pascal casing. The identifiers in this text are shown using these formats.

Even though every language has its own rules for creating identifiers, when designing the logic of a computer program, you should not concern yourself with the specific syntax of any particular computer language. The logic, after all, works with any language. The identifiers used throughout this book follow only two rules:

1. *Identifier names must be one word*. The name can contain letters, digits, hyphens, underscores, or any other characters you choose, with the exception of *spaces*. Therefore `H` is a legal identifier, as is `Hello`, as is `MyHelloClass`. The identifier `My Hello Class` is not allowed because of the spaces.

2. *Identifiers should have some appropriate meaning*. This is not a rule of any programming language. When you write a class that prints the word "Hello", the computer does not care if you call the class `G`, `U84`, or `Fred`. As long as the correct result appears, the name of the class doesn't really matter. However, it's much easier to keep track of classes that have reasonable names. When you look at an application several months after completing it, you and other programmers working with you will appreciate clear, descriptive identifiers.

The first line in Figure 1-3, `class Hello`, is the **class header**. The `endClass` statement in the last line of Figure 1-3 shows where the class ends. The class header and the `endClass` statement align vertically to show they are a pair—there will always be only one `endClass` statement for each class.

In Figure 1-3, the class contains one method, the `main()` method. The statement `main()` is the **method header**. By convention, most object-oriented programmers begin their method names with a lowercase letter, and this book follows that convention. Method names are always followed by a set of parentheses. As you learn more about programming, you will discover that sometimes it is necessary to place statements called declarations within these parentheses. Additionally, you frequently will need to add information in front of the `main()` header.

TIP ▫ ▫ ▫ ▫ | In C#, the main( ) method begins with an uppercase M, but in C++ and Java, it begins with a lowercase m.

When a class contains a `main()` method, the class is an application—or executable program. You will learn in Chapter 2 that not all classes contain a `main()` method, but those that do are runnable programs.

In this book, every method will end with a `return` statement. In many programming languages, a `return` statement marks the end of every method. Sometimes you will need to add more information after the `return` statement, but in this case nothing else is needed. The `main()` method header and the method's `return` statement vertically align to show they are a pair.

Within the `main()` method of the `Hello` class, between the `main()` method header and the method's `return` statement, you place all the action statements of the `main()` method. In this case, the desired action is to print "Hello".

Figures 1-4 and 1-5 show how the `Hello` class looks when implemented in Java and C++, respectively. Although each of these programs contains confusing syntax and punctuation not used in the pseudocode, see whether you can discern the pieces of code that correspond to each part of the pseudocode in Figure 1-3.

FIGURE 1-4: THE `Hello` CLASS WRITTEN IN THE JAVA PROGRAMMING LANGUAGE

```
class Hello
{
   public static void main(String[] args)
   {
      System.out.println("Hello");
   }
}
```

FIGURE 1-5: THE `Hello` CLASS WRITTEN IN THE C++ PROGRAMMING LANGUAGE

```
class Hello
{
  public:
    static void mainMethod();
};
void Hello::mainMethod()
{
    cout<<"Hello";
}
```

USING AND NAMING VARIABLES

Programmers commonly refer to the locations in computer memory as variables or fields. **Variables** or **fields** are memory locations, whose contents can vary or differ over time. Most of the objects you create in programs contain variables that hold the objects' attributes. For example, a GUI form that appears on the screen has a height, and a bank account has a balance. The height of a form and the balance of an account are different at different times. As another example, when you name a memory location `inputNumber`, as in the last section, sometimes it can hold a 2 and `calculatedAnswer` will hold a 4; at other times, `inputNumber` can hold a 6 and `calculatedAnswer` will hold a 12. It is the ability of memory variables to change in value that makes computers and programming worthwhile. Because one memory location can be used over and over again with different values, you can write program instructions once and then use them for thousands of separate calculations. *One* set of payroll instructions at your company produces each individual's paycheck, and *one* set of instructions at your electric company produces each household's bill.

The number-doubling example requires two variables, `inputNumber` and `calculatedAnswer`. These can just as well be named `userEntry` and `programSolution`, or `inputValue` and `twiceTheValue`. As a programmer, you choose reasonable identifiers for your variables. The language interpreter then associates the names you choose with specific memory addresses.

TIP ▫ ▫ ▫ ▫ As a convention, this book will begin variable names with a lowercase letter.

TIP □ □ □ □ When you write a program, your compiler may show variable names in a different color from the rest of the program. This visual aid helps your variable names stand out from words that are part of the programming language.

You use the same rules for naming variables as you do for naming classes. Variable identifiers must be one word containing no spaces and must have a reasonable meaning. Some programmers have fun with their variable names by naming them after friends or creating puns with them, but such behavior is unprofessional and marks those programmers as amateurs. Table 1-1 lists possible variable names that might be used to hold an employee's last name and provides a rationale for the appropriateness of each one.

TIP □ □ □ □ Another general rule in all programming languages is that variable names may not begin with a digit, although usually they may contain digits. Thus, in most languages budget2013 is a legal variable name, but 2013Budget is not.

TABLE 1-1: VALID AND INVALID VARIABLE NAMES FOR AN EMPLOYEE'S LAST NAME

Suggested Variable Names for Employee's Last Name	Comments
employeeLastName	Good
employeeLast	Good—most people would interpret Last as meaning last name
empLast	Good—emp is short for employee
emlstnam	Legal—but cryptic
lastNameOfTheEmployeeInQuestion	Legal—but awkward
last name	Not legal—embedded space
employeelastname	Legal—but hard to read without camel casing

ASSIGNING VALUES TO VARIABLES

When you create pseudocode for a program that doubles numbers, you can include the statement `compute calculatedAnswer as inputNumber times 2`. This statement incorporates two actions. First, the computer computes the arithmetic value of `inputNumber` times 2. Second, the computed value is stored in the `calculatedAnswer` memory location. Most programming languages allow a shorthand expression for **assignment statements**, statements that assign values to variables. For example, `compute calculatedAnswer as inputNumber times 2` is an assignment statement, and the shorthand takes the form `calculatedAnswer = inputNumber * 2`. The equal sign is the **assignment operator**; it always requires the name of a memory location on its left side—the name of the location where the result will be stored.

TIP □ □ □ □ In Pascal, the same expression is calculatedAnswer := inputNumber * 2. You type a colon followed by an equal sign to create the assignment symbol. Java, C++, C#, Visual Basic, and many other languages all use the equal sign for assignment.

TIP □ □ □ □ | Most programmers use the asterisk (*) to represent multiplication. When you write pseudocode, you can use an X or a dot for multiplication (as most mathematicians do), but you will be using an unconventional format. This book will always use an asterisk to represent multiplication.

According to the rules of algebra, a statement like `calculatedAnswer = inputNumber * 2` should be exactly equivalent to the statement `inputNumber * 2 = calculatedAnswer`. That's because in algebra, the equal sign always represents equivalency. To most programmers, however, the equal sign represents assignment, and `calculatedAnswer = inputNumber * 2` means "multiply `inputNumber` by 2 and store the result in the variable called `calculatedAnswer`." Whatever operation is performed to the right of the equal sign results in a value that is placed in the memory location to the left of the equal sign. Therefore, the incorrect statement `inputNumber * 2 = calculatedAnswer` means to attempt to take the value of `calculatedAnswer` and store it in a location called `inputNumber * 2`, but there can't be a location called `inputNumber * 2`. For one thing, `inputNumber * 2` can't be a variable because it has spaces in it. For another, a location can't be multiplied. Its contents can be multiplied, but the location itself cannot be. The backwards statement `inputNumber * 2 = calculatedAnswer` contains a syntax error, no matter what programming language you use; a program with such a statement will not execute.

TIP □ □ □ □ | When you create an assignment statement, it may help to imagine the word "let" in front of the statement. Thus, you can read the statement calculatedAnswer = inputNumber * 2 as "Let calculatedAnswer equal inputNumber times two." Both the BASIC and Visual Basic programming languages allow you to use the word "let" in such statements. You also might imagine the word "gets" or "receives" in place of the assignment operator. In other words calculatedAnswer = inputNumber * 2 means calculatedAnswer gets inputNumber * 2.

Computer memory is made up of millions of distinct locations, each of which has an address. Fifty or sixty years ago, programmers had to deal with these addresses and had to remember, for instance, that they stored a salary in location 6428 of their computer. Today we are very fortunate that high-level computer languages allow us to pick a reasonable "English" name for a memory address and let the computer keep track of where it is. Just as it is easier for you to remember that the president lives in the White House than at 1600 Pennsylvania Avenue, Washington, D.C., it is also easier for you to remember that your salary is in a variable called `mySalary` than at memory location 6428104.

Similarly, it does not usually make sense to perform mathematical operations on names given to memory addresses, but it does make sense to perform mathematical operations on the *contents* of memory addresses. If you live in `blueSplitLevelOnTheCorner`, adding 1 to that would be meaningless, but you certainly can add one person to the number of people already in that house. For our purposes, then, the statement `calculatedAnswer = inputNumber * 2` means exactly the same thing as the statement `calculate inputNumber * 2 and store the result in the memory location named calculatedAnswer`.

TIP □ □ □ □ | Many programming languages allow you to create named constants. A named constant is a named memory location, similar to a variable, except its value never changes during the execution of a program. If you are working with a programming language that allows it, you might create a constant for a value like pi = 3.14 or countySalesTaxRate = .06.

UNDERSTANDING DATA TYPES

Computers deal with two basic types of data—text and numeric. When you use a specific numeric value, such as 43, within a program, you write it using the digits and no quotation marks. A specific numeric value is often called a **numeric constant** because it does not change—a 43 always has the value 43. When you use a specific set of characters, or a **string constant**, such as "Chris," you enclose the string within quotation marks. Many programming languages, including C++, C#, Java, and Pascal, use single quotes surrounding a **character constant**, such as 'C' and double quotes for a string such as "Chris".

Similarly, most computer languages allow at least two distinct types of variables. One type of variable can hold a number, and is often called a **numeric variable**. In the statement `calculatedAnswer = inputNumber * 2` both `calculatedAnswer` and `inputNumber` are numeric variables; that is, their intended contents are numeric values such as 6 and 3, 150 and 75, or −18 and −9.

Most programming languages have separate types of variables that can hold letters of the alphabet and other special characters such as punctuation marks. Usually, variables that hold a single character are called **character variables**, and those that hold a group of characters are called **string variables**. If a working program contains the statement `gradeInTheClass = 'A'`, then `gradeInTheClass` is a character variable. If a working program contains the statement `lastName = "Lincoln"` then `lastName` is a string variable.

Programmers must distinguish between numeric and character variables because computers handle the two types of data differently. Therefore, means are provided within the syntax rules of computer programming languages to tell the computer which type of data to expect. How this is done is different in every language; some languages have different rules for naming the variables, but with others you must include a simple statement (called a declaration) telling the computer which type of data to expect. A **variable declaration** consists of the data type and the identifier. Optionally, you can provide an initial starting value for the variable—doing so is **initializing** the variable.

Some languages allow for several types of numeric data. Languages such as Pascal, C++, C#, and Java distinguish between **integer** (whole number) numeric variables and **floating-point** (fractional) numeric variables that contain a decimal point. Thus, in some languages, the numbers 4 and 4.3 would have to be stored in different types of variables.

Some programming languages allow even more specific variable types, but the distinction between character and numeric data is universal. For the programs you develop in this book, assume that each variable is one of three broad types—numeric, character, or string. If a variable called `taxRate` is supposed to hold a value of 2.5, assume that it is a numeric variable. If a variable called `middleInitial` is supposed to hold a value of 'M', assume it is a character variable. And, if a variable called `inventoryItem` is supposed to hold a value of "monitor", assume that it is a string variable. You would declare these three variables as follows:

```
numeric taxRate
character middleInitial
string inventoryItem
```

When you declare variables using the preceding statements, you have not provided any initial values. Although some languages provide automatic, or **default values**, for uninitialized variables, this book will assume any uninitialized variable contains an unknown value, sometimes called a **garbage value**.

> TIP □ □ □ □ Some compilers will warn you when you attempt to use a variable that has not been provided with a value. Such variables are called **undefined variables**. An undefined variable has been declared, that is, provided with a type and identifier; it just does not contain a useable value. On the other hand, an **undeclared variable** is one that has not been provided with a data type and identifier.

To provide values for the variables `taxRate`, `middleInitial`, and `inventoryItem`, you have two options. First, you can declare the variables, and then assign values later, as follows:

```
numeric taxRate
character middleInitial
string inventoryItem
taxRate = 2.5
middleInitial = 'M'
inventoryItem = "monitor"
```

Notice that in the preceding example, the identifier is associated with its data type just once. A declaration such as `numeric taxRate` establishes a memory location named `taxRate`. Later, when you assign a value to it, you do not establish the memory location again.

Alternatively, you can initialize the variables when you declare them, as follows:

```
numeric taxRate = 2.5
character middleInitial = 'M'
string inventoryItem = "monitor"
```

> TIP □ □ □ □ Values such as "monitor" and 2.5 are called constants or literal constants because they never change. A variable value *can* change. Thus, inventoryItem can hold "monitor" at one moment during the execution of a program, and later you can change its value to "modem".

> TIP □ □ □ □ Any values can be characters or contained within strings. Besides letters of the alphabet, punctuation marks, spaces, and even digits can be treated as characters. If you intend a variable to be used in arithmetic statements, you declare it to be numeric. However, if it is all digits but will not be used in arithmetic statements, such as an ID number or telephone number, then you can declare the variable to be a string.

By convention, this book encloses string data like "monitor" within quotation marks to distinguish the characters from yet another variable name. Character data, such as 'W' is contained in single quotation marks, following the syntax of Java, C++, and C#. Also by convention, numeric data values are not enclosed within quotation marks. According to these conventions, `taxRate = 2.5` and `inventoryItem = "monitor"` are both valid statements. The statement `inventoryItem = monitor` is a valid statement only if `monitor` is also a string variable. In other words, if `monitor = "color"`, and subsequently `inventoryItem = monitor`, then the end result is that the memory address named `inventoryItem` contains the string of characters "color".

Every computer handles text or character data differently from the way it handles numeric data. You may have experienced these differences if you have used application software such as spreadsheets or database programs. For example, in a spreadsheet, you cannot sum a column of words. Similarly, every programming language requires that you distinguish variables as to their correct type, and that you use each type of variable appropriately. Identifying your variables correctly as numeric, character, or string is one of the first steps you have to take when writing programs in any programming language. Table 1-2 provides you with a few examples of legal and illegal variable assignment statements.

TABLE 1-2: SOME EXAMPLES OF LEGAL AND ILLEGAL ASSIGNMENTS

Assume lastName and firstName are string variables.

Assume middleInitial is a character variable.

Assume quizScore and homeworkScore are numeric variables.

Examples of Valid Assignments	Examples of Invalid Assignments
lastName = "Parker"	lastName = Parker
firstName = "Laura"	"Parker" = lastName
lastName = firstName	lastName = quizScore
middleInitial = 'P'	middleInitial = P
middleInitial = ' '	middleInitial = lastName
quizScore = 86	homeworkScore = firstName
homeworkScore = quizScore	homeworkScore = "92"
homeworkScore = 92	quizScore = "zero"
quizScore = homeworkScore + 25	firstName = 23
homeworkScore = 3 * 10	100 = homeworkScore

Figure 1-6 shows a complete `DoubleNumber` class that allows the user to enter a number and see the result when the value is doubled. The class name is `DoubleNumber` and it contains one method, the `main()` method. Two variables, `inputNumber` and `calculatedAnswer`, are declared; there is no need to provide initial values for these variables because one will be provided by a user and the other will be calculated based on the user's input. The three statements that perform the action of the `main()` method follow the variable declarations.

FIGURE 1-6: THE `DoubleNumber` CLASS

```
class DoubleNumber
   main()
        numeric inputNumber
        numeric calculatedAnswer
        get inputNumber
        compute calculatedAnswer as inputNumber times 2
        print calculatedAnswer
   return
endClass
```

As you work through this book, you will create increasingly complicated classes. However, the format for the pseudocode for all your classes will be similar to that shown in Figure 1-6.

CHAPTER SUMMARY

☐ Together, computer hardware (equipment) and software (instructions) accomplish four major operations: input, processing, output, and storage. You write computer instructions in a computer programming language that requires specific syntax; the instructions are translated into machine language by a compiler or interpreter. When both the syntax and logic of a program are correct, you can run, or execute, the program to produce the desired results.

☐ Procedural programming focuses on the procedures that programmers create to manipulate data. The other popular programming technique, called object-oriented programming, or OOP, focuses on objects, or "things," and describes their features, or attributes, and their behaviors.

☐ A programmer's job involves identifying objects and classes, coding the program, translating the program into machine language, testing the program, and putting the program into production.

☐ When programmers plan the logic for a solution to a programming problem, they often use flowcharts or pseudocode.

☐ Variables are named memory locations, the contents of which can vary. As a programmer, you choose reasonable names for your variables. Every computer programming language has its own set of rules for naming variables; however, all variable names must be written as one word without embedded spaces, and should have appropriate meaning.

☐ Most programming languages use the equal sign to assign values to variables. Assignment always takes place from right to left.

☐ Programmers must distinguish between numeric, character, and string variables because computers handle the types of data differently. A variable declaration tells the computer which type of data to expect.

KEY TERMS

Hardware is the equipment of a computer system.

Software is the instructions written by programmers that tell the computer what to do; software is computer programs.

Application software comprises all the programs you apply to a task.

System software comprises the programs that you use to manage your computer—operating systems such as Windows or Unix.

Input devices include keyboards and mice; through these devices, data enter the computer system. Data can also enter a system from storage devices such as magnetic disks and CDs.

Data are facts.

Processing data items may involve organizing them, checking them for accuracy, or performing mathematical operations on them.

The **central processing unit**, or **CPU**, is the hardware component that processes data.

Information is sent to a printer, monitor, or some other **output device** so that people can view, interpret, and work with the results.

Storage devices are hardware such as magnetic disks, tapes, or compact discs, on which you can store output information.

Programming languages, such as Visual Basic, C#, C++, Java, Pascal, COBOL, RPG, or Fortran, are used to write programs.

The **syntax** of a language consists of its rules.

Machine language is a computer's on-off circuitry language.

A **compiler** or **interpreter** translates a high-level language into machine language and tells you if you have used a programming language incorrectly.

You develop the **logic** of the computer program when you give instructions to the computer in a specific sequence, without leaving any instructions out or adding extraneous instructions.

Programmers often call logical errors **semantic errors**.

A program is **run** or **executed** when the computer actually uses the written and compiled program.

Internal storage is called **memory**, **main memory**, or **primary memory**.

External storage is permanent storage outside the main memory of the machine, on a device such as a floppy disk, hard disk, or magnetic tape.

Internal memory is **volatile**—that is, its contents are lost every time the computer loses power.

You **save** a program on some nonvolatile medium.

Procedural programming focuses on the procedures that programmers create to manipulate data.

Object-oriented programming, or **OOP**, focuses on objects, or "things," and describes their features, or attributes, and their behaviors.

The **attributes of an object** are the features it "has".

The values of an object's attributes constitute the object's **state**.

The **behaviors of an object** are the things it "does".

Taking an **object-oriented approach** to a problem means defining the objects needed to accomplish a task and developing the objects so that each maintains its own data and carries out tasks when another object requests them.

A **GUI** is a graphical user interface.

Object-oriented analysis, or **OOA**, is analyzing a system using an object-oriented approach.

Object-oriented design, or **OOD**, is designing a system using an object-oriented approach.

Data modeling is the act of identifying all the objects you want to manipulate and how they relate to each other.

A **class** is a general category of objects.

Coding a program means writing the statements in a programming language.

High-level programming languages are English-like.

Low-level machine language is the statements made up of 1s and 0s that the computer understands.

A **syntax error** is an error in language or grammar.

Logical errors occur when incorrect instructions are performed, or when instructions are performed in the wrong order.

Conversion is the entire set of actions an organization must take to switch over to using a new program or set of programs.

A **flowchart** is a pictorial representation of the logical steps it takes to solve a problem.

Pseudocode is an English-like representation of the logical steps it takes to solve a problem.

Flowlines are the arrows in a flowchart that show the sequence of steps carried out.

An **application** is a program that accomplishes some task.

A **method** is a set of statements that performs some task or group of tasks.

An **identifier** is the name of a programming object—a class, method, or variable.

A **mnemonic** is a memory device; variable identifiers act as mnemonics for hard-to-remember memory addresses.

Camel casing is the format for naming variables in which multiple-word variable names are run together, and each new word within the variable name begins with an uppercase letter.

A **class header** contains the word class and the class identifier; it is the first line written in a class definition.

A **method header** is the first line in a method.

Variables or **fields** are memory locations, whose contents can vary, or differ, over time.

An **assignment statement** stores the result of any calculation performed on its right side to the named location on its left side.

The equal sign is the **assignment operator**; it always requires the name of a memory location on its left side.

A **numeric constant** is a specific numeric value.

A **string constant** is a literal set of characters enclosed within quotation marks.

A **character constant** is a single character enclosed in single quotation marks.

Numeric variables hold numeric values.

Character variables hold single character values.

String variables hold a series of characters.

A **variable declaration** is a statement that names a variable and tells the computer which type of data to expect.

Initializing a variable declares it and provides an initial value.

Integer values are whole number numeric variables.

Floating-point values are fractional numeric variables that contain a decimal point.

Default values are automatically supplied values.

A **garbage value** is an unknown value in an uninitialized variable.

Undefined variables are those that have not been provided with a value before you attempt to use them.

Undeclared variables have not been provided with a data type or identifier.

REVIEW QUESTIONS

1. **The two major components of any computer system are its _____.**
   a. input and output
   b. data and programs
   c. hardware and software
   d. memory and disk drives

2. **The major computer operations include _____.**
   a. hardware and software
   b. input, processing, output, and storage
   c. sequence and looping
   d. spreadsheets, word processing, and data communications

3. **Another term meaning "computer instructions" is _____.**
   a. hardware
   b. software
   c. queries
   d. data

4. **Visual Basic, C++, and Java are all examples of computer _____.**
   a. operating systems
   b. hardware
   c. machine languages
   d. programming languages

5. **A programming language's rules are its _____.**
   a. syntax
   b. logic
   c. format
   d. options

6. **The most important task of a compiler or interpreter is to _____.**
   a. create the rules for a programming language
   b. translate English statements into a language such as Java
   c. translate programming language statements into machine language
   d. execute machine language programs to perform useful tasks

7. **Which of the following is not associated with internal storage?**
   a. main memory
   b. hard disk
   c. primary memory
   d. volatile

8. **Object-oriented programming focuses on _____.**
   a. data
   b. objects
   c. procedures
   d. all of the above

9. **The attributes of an object are the things that it _____.**
   a. has
   b. does
   c. influences
   d. understands

10. **In object-oriented programming, each object _____.**
    a. maintains its own data
    b. carries out tasks when another object requests them
    c. both of these
    d. none of these

11. **Originally, object-oriented programming was used most frequently for two major types of applications. These were _____.**
    a. payroll and inventory
    b. input and storage
    c. computer simulations and graphical user interfaces
    d. public and private applications

12. **Using an object-oriented approach involves all of the following except _____.**
    a. analyzing the system using an object-oriented approach (object-oriented analysis, or OOA)
    b. designing the system using an object-oriented approach (object-oriented design, or OOD)
    c. writing the programs using an object-oriented approach (object-oriented programming, or OOP)
    d. testing the programs using an object-oriented approach (object-oriented testing, or OOT)

13. **Identifying all the objects you want to manipulate and how they relate to each other is known as _____.**
    a. object orienting
    b. data modeling
    c. method manipulation
    d. relating

14. **The two most commonly used tools for planning a program's logic are _____.**

    a. flowcharts and pseudocode

    b. ASCII and EBCDIC

    c. Java and Visual Basic

    d. word processors and spreadsheets

15. **Writing a program in a language such as C++ or Java is known as _____ the program.**

    a. translating

    b. coding

    c. interpreting

    d. compiling

16. **A compiler would find all of the following programming errors except _____.**

    a. the misspelled word "prrint" in a language that includes the word "print"

    b. the use of an "X" for multiplication in a language that requires an asterisk

    c. a `newBalanceDue` calculated by adding a `customerPayment` to an `oldBalanceDue` instead of subtracting it

    d. an arithmetic statement written as `regularSales + discountedSales = totalSales`

17. **Which of the following is not a legal variable name in any programming language?**

    a. `semester grade`

    b. `fall2005_grade`

    c. `GradeInCIS100`

    d. `MY_GRADE`

18. **The broadest types of data are _____.**

    a. internal and external

    b. volatile, constant, and temporary

    c. string, character, and numeric

    d. permanent and temporary

19. **Assuming `address` is a string variable, which of the following is a legal assignment statement?**

    a. address = "23 Elm"

    b. "23 Elm" = address

    c. address = 23 Elm

    d. address = 23

20. **Assuming `salary` is a numeric variable, which of the following is a legal assignment statement?**

    a. salary = "not enough"

    b. salary = "23.45"

    c. both of these

    d. none of these

EXERCISES

1. **Match the definition with the appropriate term.**

    1. Computer system equipment   a. compiler

    2. Another word for programs   b. syntax

    3. Language rules   c. logic

    4. Order of instructions   d. hardware

    5. Language translator   e. software

2. **In your own words, describe the steps to writing a computer program.**

3. **Lakeview Towers is being constructed as a high-rise apartment building in a downtown urban district. The managers of the building want to create a simulation of daily elevator use to plan for the optimum number of elevators so that elevators are neither idle too frequently nor cause more than a one-minute wait for any resident. What sorts of objects should be created to use in a simulation of potential elevator activity?**

4. **Which of the following names seem like good variable names to you? If a name doesn't seem like a good variable name, explain why not.**

    a. c
    b. cost
    c. costAmount
    d. cost amount
    e. cstofdngbsns
    f. costOfDoingBusinessThisFiscalYear
    g. cost2004

5. **If myAge and yourRate are numeric variables, and departmentCode is a string variable, which of the following statements are valid assignments? If a statement is not valid, explain why not.**

    a. myAge = 23
    b. myAge = yourRate
    c. myAge = departmentCode
    d. myAge = "departmentCode"
    e. 42 = myAge
    f. yourRate = 3.5
    g. yourRate = myAge
    h. yourRate = departmentCode
    i. 6.91 = yourRate
    j. departmentCode = Personnel
    k. departmentCode = "Personnel"
    l. departmentCode = 413
    m. departmentCode = "413"

    n. departmentCode = myAge

    o. departmentCode = yourRate

    p. 413 = departmentCode

    q. "413" = departmentCode

6.   **Write the pseudocode for an application that allows a user to enter the price of an item and computes 5 percent sales tax on the item.**

7.   **Write the pseudocode for an application that allows a user to enter the cost of home maintenance in each of the four seasons—summer, fall, winter, and spring—and displays the total.**

8.   **Write the pseudocode for an application that allows a user to enter a credit card balance. Assuming the interest rate is 1 percent per month and that the user makes no payments, display the amount that will be due after one month and after two months.**

CASE PROBLEM

Cost Is No Object is a car rental service that specializes in lending antique and luxury cars to clients on a short-term basis. A typical customer might rent a vintage convertible for a high school reunion weekend, or a luxury car to transport a wedding party. The service currently has three employees and ten vehicles that it rents. List the objects needed to write a program that could provide a simulation of one day's business activity.

2

OBJECT-ORIENTED PROGRAMMING CONCEPTS

After studying Chapter 2, you should be able to:

- ☐ Understand the basic principles of object-oriented programming
- ☐ Define classes and create class diagrams
- ☐ Understand public and private access
- ☐ Instantiate and use objects
- ☐ Understand inheritance
- ☐ Understand polymorphism
- ☐ Understand protected access
- ☐ Describe GUI classes as an example of built-in classes
- ☐ Understand the advantages of object-oriented programming

AN OVERVIEW OF OBJECT-ORIENTED PROGRAMMING

Object-oriented programming is a style of programming that focuses on an application's data and the methods you need to manipulate that data.

Objects both in the real world and in object-oriented programming are made up of attributes and methods. **Attributes** are the characteristics that define an object as part of a class. For example, some of your automobile's attributes are its make, model, year, and purchase price. Other attributes include whether the automobile is currently running, its gear, its speed, and whether it is dirty. All automobiles possess the same attributes, but not, of course, the same values for those attributes. Similarly, your dog has the attributes of its breed, name, age, and whether his or her shots are current.

TIP □ □ □ □ | In grammar, a noun is equivalent to an object and the values of a class's attributes are adjectives—they describe the characteristics of the objects. Programmers also call the values of an object's attributes the **states** of the object. Later in this chapter you will learn about methods, which are equivalent to verbs.

In object-oriented terminology, a **class** is a term that describes a group or collection of objects with common properties. An **instance** of a class is an existing object of a class. Therefore, your `redChevrolet Automobile` with the dent can be considered an instance of the class that is made up of all automobiles, and your Golden Retriever dog named Ginger is an instance of the class that is made up of all dogs. Thinking of items as instances of a class allows you to apply your general knowledge of the class to individual members of the class. A particular instance of an object takes its attributes from the general category. If your friend purchases an `Automobile`, you know it has a model name, and if your friend gets a `Dog`, you know the dog has a breed. You might not know the current state of your friend's `Automobile`, such as its current speed, or the current status of her `Dog`'s shots, but you do know what attributes exist for the `Automobile` and `Dog` classes. Similarly, in a GUI operating environment, you expect each component to have specific, consistent attributes, such as a button being clickable or a window being closeable, because each component gains these attributes as a member of the general class of GUI components.

With object-oriented programming:

- You analyze the objects you are working with and the tasks that need to be performed with, and on, those objects.
- You pass messages to objects, requesting the objects to take action.
- The same message works differently (and appropriately) when applied to different objects.
- A module or procedure can work appropriately with different types of data it receives, without the need to write separate modules.
- Objects can share or inherit traits of objects that have already been created, reducing the time it takes to create new objects.
- Encapsulation and information hiding are emphasized.

The real world is full of objects. Consider a door. A door needs to be opened and closed. You open a door with an easy-to-use interface known as a doorknob. Object-oriented programmers would say you are "passing a message" to the door when you "tell" it to open by turning its knob. The same message (turning a knob) has a different result when applied to your radio than when applied to a door. The procedure you use to open something—call it the "open" procedure—works differently on a door to a room than it does on a desk drawer, a bank account, a computer file, or your eyes, but, even though these procedures operate differently using the different objects, you can call all of these procedures "open." In object-oriented programming, procedures are called **methods**.

With object-oriented programming, you focus on the objects that will be manipulated by the program—for example, a customer invoice, a loan application, or a menu from which the user will select an option. You define the characteristics of those objects and the methods each of the objects will use; you also define the information that must be passed to those methods.

You can create multiple methods with the same name, which will act differently and appropriately when used with different types of objects. This concept is **polymorphism**, which literally means "many forms"—a method can have many configurations that each work appropriately based on the context in which they are used. In most object-oriented programming languages, method names are followed by a set of parentheses; this helps you distinguish method names from variable names. For example, you might use a method named `print()` to print a customer invoice, loan application, or envelope. Because you use the same method name, `print()`, to describe the different actions needed to print these diverse objects, you can write statements in object-oriented programming languages that are more like English; you can use the same method name to describe the same type of action, no matter what type of object is being acted upon. Using the method name `print()` is easier than remembering `printInvoice()`, `printLoanApplication()`, and so on. In English, you understand the difference between "running a race," "running a business," and "running a computer program." Object-oriented languages understand verbs in context, just as people do.

As another example of the advantages to using one name for a variety of objects, consider a screen you might design for a user to enter data into an application you are writing. Suppose the screen contains a variety of objects—some forms, buttons, scroll bars, dialog boxes, and so on. Suppose also that you decide to make all the objects blue. Instead of having to memorize the names that these objects use to change color, perhaps `changeFormColor()`, `changeButtonColor()`, and so on, your job would be easier if the creators of all those objects had created a `setColor()` method that works appropriately with each type of object.

Another important concept in object-oriented programming is **inheritance**, which is the process of acquiring the traits of one's predecessors. In the real world, a new door with a stained glass window inherits most of its traits from a standard door. It has the same purpose, it opens and closes in the same way, and it has the same knob and hinges. The door with the stained glass window simply has one additional trait—its window. Even if you have never seen a door with a stained glass window, when you encounter one you know what it is and how to use it because you understand the characteristics of all doors. With object-oriented programming, once you create an object, you can develop new objects that possess all the traits of the original object plus any new traits you desire. If you develop a `customerBill` object, there is no need to develop an `overdueCustomerBill` object from scratch. You can create the new object to contain all the characteristics of the already developed object, and simply add necessary new characteristics. This not only reduces the work involved in creating new objects, but also makes them easier to understand because they possess most of the characteristics of already developed objects.

Real-world objects often employ encapsulation and information hiding. **Encapsulation** is the process of combining all of an object's attributes and methods into a single package. **Information hiding** is the concept that other classes should not alter an object's attributes—only the methods of an object's own class should have that privilege. Outside classes should only be allowed to make a request that an attribute be altered; then it is up to the class methods to determine whether the request is appropriate. When using a door, you usually are unconcerned with the latch or hinge construction features, and you don't have access to the interior workings of the knob or know what color of paint might have been used on the inside of the door panel. You care only about the functionality and the **interface**, the user-friendly boundary between the user and internal mechanisms of the device. Similarly, the detailed workings of objects you create within object-oriented programs can be hidden from outside programs and modules if you want them to be. When the details are hidden, programmers can focus on the functionality and the interface, as people do with real-life objects.

TIP ▫ ▫ ▫ ▫ | Information hiding is also called **data hiding**.

In summary, in order to understand object-oriented programming, you must consider five concepts that are integral components of all object-oriented programming languages:

- classes
- objects
- inheritance
- polymorphism
- encapsulation

DEFINING CLASSES AND CREATING CLASS DIAGRAMS

A class is a category of things; an object is a specific instance of a class. A **class definition** is a set of program statements that tell you the characteristics of the class's objects and the methods that can be applied to its objects.

For example, `Dish` is a class. When you know an object is a `Dish`, you know it can be held in your hand and you can eat from it. The specific object `myBlueDinnnerPlateWithTheChipOnTheEdge` is an instance of the `Dish` class; so is `auntJanesAntiquePunchBowl` and `myCatsFoodBowl`. You can use the phrase **is-a** to test whether an object is an instance of a class. Because you can say, "My plate *is a* `Dish`," you can discern the object-class relationship. On the other hand, you cannot say, "A Dish is my plate," because many dishes are *not* my plate. Each button on the toolbar of a word-processing program is an instance of a `Button` class. In a program used to manage a hotel, `thePentHouse, theBridalSuite, room201`, and `room202` all are instances of `HotelRoom`. Although each room is a different object, as members of the same class they share characteristics—each has a maximum number of occupants, a square footage, and a price.

TIP ▫ ▫ ▫ ▫ | In object-oriented languages such as C++ and Java, most class names are written with the initial letter of each new word in uppercase, as in *Dish* or *HotelRoom*. Specific objects' names usually are written in lowercase or using camel casing.

TIP ☐ ☐ ☐ ☐ | Object-oriented programmers also use the term "is-a" to describe inheritance relationships.

A class can contain three parts:

- Every class has a name.
- Most classes contain data, although this is not required.
- Most classes contain methods, although this is not required.

For example, you can create a class named `Employee`. Each `Employee` object will represent one employee who works for an organization. Data members, or attributes of the `Employee` class, include **fields** such as `idNum`, `lastName`, `hourlyWage`, and `weeklyPay`.

The methods of a class include all actions you want to perform with the class. Appropriate methods for an `Employee` class might include `setFieldValues()`, `calculateWeeklyPay()`, and `printFieldValues()`. The job of `setFieldValues()` is to provide values for an `Employee`'s data fields, the purpose of `calculateWeeklyPay()` is to multiply the `Employee`'s `hourlyWage` by 40 to calculate a weekly salary, and the purpose of `printFieldValues()` is to print the values in the `Employee`'s data fields. With object-oriented languages, you think of the class name, data, and methods as a single encapsulated unit.

Programmers often use a class diagram to illustrate class features. A **class diagram** consists of a rectangle divided into three sections, as shown in Figure 2-1. The top section contains the name of the class, the middle section contains the names and data types of the attributes, and the bottom section contains the methods. This generic class diagram shows two attributes and three methods, but for a given class there might be any number of either, including none. Figure 2-2 shows the class diagram for the `Employee` class.

FIGURE 2-1: GENERIC CLASS DIAGRAM

| Class name |
| Attribute 1: data type |
| Attribute 2: data type |
| Method 1 |
| Method 2 |
| Method 3 |

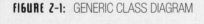 **FIGURE 2-2:** `Employee` CLASS DIAGRAM

| Employee |
| `idNum`: numeric |
| `lastName`: string |
| `hourlyWage`: numeric |
| `weeklyPay`: numeric |
| `setFieldValues()` |
| `calculateWeeklyPay()` |
| `printFieldValues()` |

TIP □ □ □ □ | Later in this chapter you will learn to add access specifiers to your class diagrams.

TIP □ □ □ □ | Some class designers prefer to define any field that never will be used in a computation as a nonnumeric data type. For example, in the **Employee** class diagram in Figure 2-2, you might prefer to define the Employee idNum as a string.

Figures 2-1 and 2-2 both show that a class diagram is intended to be only an overview of class attributes and methods. A class diagram shows *what* data items and methods the class will use, not the details of the methods nor *when* they will be used. It is a design tool that helps you see the big picture in terms of class requirements. Later, when you write the code that actually creates the class, you include method implementation details. For example, Figure 2-3 shows some pseudocode you can use to show the details for the methods contained within the **Employee** class.

FIGURE 2-3: Employee CLASS PARTIAL PSEUDOCODE

```
class Employee
     numeric idNum
     string lastName
     numeric hourlyWage
     numeric weeklyPay
     setFieldValues()
         input idNum
         input lastName
         input hourlyWage
     return
     calculateWeeklyPay()
         weeklyPay = hourlyWage * 40
     return
     printFieldValues()
         print idNum, lastName, hourlyWage, weeklyPay
     return
endClass
```

In Figure 2-3, the **Employee** class attributes or fields are identified with a data type and a field name. In addition to listing the data fields required, Figure 2-3 shows the complete methods for the **Employee** class. The details contained in the three methods, **setFieldValues()**, **calculateWeeklyPay()**, and **printFieldValues()**, will be discussed in great detail in Chapter 3. For now notice that the purpose of two methods is to communicate with the outside world—the **setFieldValues()** method takes values that come in from the outside and assigns them to the Employee's attributes, and the **printFieldValues()** method displays the Employee's attributes on an output device. The purpose of the **calculateWeeklyPay()** module is to multiply the **hourlyWage** by 40.

UNDERSTANDING PUBLIC AND PRIVATE ACCESS

When you buy a product with a warranty, one of the conditions of the warranty is usually that the manufacturer must perform all repair work. For example, if your computer has a warranty and something goes wrong with its operation, you cannot open the system unit yourself, remove and replace parts, and then expect to get your money back for a device that does not work properly. Instead, when something goes wrong with your computer, you must take the device to the manufacturer. The manufacturer guarantees that your machine will work properly only if the manufacturer can control how the internal mechanisms of the machine are modified.

Similarly, in object-oriented design, usually you do not want any outside programs or methods to alter your class's data fields unless you have control over the process. For example, you might design a class that performs a complicated statistical analysis on some data and stores the result. You would not want others to be able to alter your carefully crafted result. As another example, you might design a class from which others can create an innovative and useful GUI screen object. In this case you would not want others altering the dimensions of your artistic design. To prevent outsiders from changing your data fields in ways you do not endorse, you force other programs and methods to use a method that is part of the class, such as `setFieldValues()`, to alter data. (You have already learned that the principle of keeping data private and inaccessible to outside classes is called information or data hiding.) Object-oriented programmers usually specify that their data fields will have **private access**—that is, the data cannot be accessed by any method that is not part of the class. The methods themselves, like `setFieldValues()`, support **public access**—which means that other programs and methods may use the methods that control access to the private data. Figure 2-4 shows a complete `Employee` class to which the **access specifier** (or **access modifier**)—the adjective that defines the type of access that outside classes will have to the attribute or method (`public` or `private`)—has been added to describe each attribute and method. In Figure 2-4, each access specifier is highlighted.

FIGURE 2-4: Employee CLASS USING `private` AND `public` ACCESS SPECIFIERS

```
class Employee
      private numeric idNum
      private string lastName
      private numeric hourlyWage
      private numeric weeklyPay
      public void setFieldValues()
          input idNum
          input lastName
          input hourlyWage
      return
      public void calculateWeeklyPay()
          weeklyPay = hourlyWage * 40
      return
      public void printFieldValues()
          print idNum, lastName, hourlyWage, weeklyPay
      return
endClass
```

TIP ▫ ▫ ▫ ▫   Classes can contain public data and private methods, but it is common for most data to be private and most methods to be public.

TIP ▫ ▫ ▫ ▫   In some object-oriented programming languages, such as C++, you can label a set of data fields or methods as public or private using the access specifier name just once. In other languages, such as Java, you use the specifier public or private with each field or method. For clarity, this book will label each field and method as public or private.

TIP ▫ ▫ ▫ ▫ Many object-oriented languages provide more specific access specifiers than just `public` and `private`. Later in this chapter, you learn about the `protected` access specifier.

Notice that the last line in the `Employee` class in both Figures 2-3 and 2-4 is an `endClass` statement. You learned in Chapter 1 that this book uses the `endClass` statement to clearly mark the end of a class.

Many programmers like to specify in a class diagram whether each data item and method in a class is public or private. Figure 2-5 shows the conventions that are typically used. A minus sign (-) precedes the items that are private; a plus sign (+) precedes those that are public.

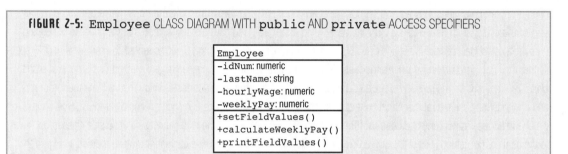

FIGURE 2-5: `Employee` CLASS DIAGRAM WITH `public` AND `private` ACCESS SPECIFIERS

```
Employee
-idNum: numeric
-lastName: string
-hourlyWage: numeric
-weeklyPay: numeric
+setFieldValues()
+calculateWeeklyPay()
+printFieldValues()
```

TIP ▫ ▫ ▫ ▫ When you learn more about inheritance later in this chapter, you will learn about the protected access specifier. You use an octothorpe, also called a pound sign or number sign (#), to indicate protected access.

INSTANTIATING AND USING OBJECTS

When you write an object-oriented program, you create objects that are members of a class. You **instantiate** (or create) a class object (or instance) with a statement that includes the type of object and an identifying name. For example, the following statement creates an `Employee` object named `myAssistant`:

```
Employee myAssistant
```

TIP ▫ ▫ ▫ ▫ In some object-oriented programming languages, to actually create an Employee object, you need to add more to the declaration statement. For example, in Java, you would write:
`Employee myAssistant = new Employee();`
This syntax will be explained in Chapter 3 when you learn about constructor methods.

When you declare `myAssistant` as an `Employee` object, the `myAssistant` object contains all of the data fields or attributes defined in the class, and has access to all the class's methods. You can use any of an `Employee`'s methods—`setFieldValues()`, `calculateWeeklyPay()`, and `printFieldValues()`—with the `myAssistant` object. The usual syntax is to provide an object name, a dot (period), and a method name. For example, you can write a program that contains statements such as the ones shown in the pseudocode in Figure 2-6.

FIGURE 2-6: PROGRAM STATEMENTS THAT USE AN **Employee** OBJECT

```
class EmployeeDemo
   main()
      Employee myAssistant
      myAssistant.setFieldValues()
      myAssistant.calculateWeeklyPay()
      myAssistant.printFieldValues()
   return
endClass
```

TIP ◻ ◻ ◻ ◻ Besides referring to Employee as a class, many programmers would refer to it as a **user-defined type**; a more accurate term is **programmer-defined type**.

The statements **myAssistant.setFieldValues()**, **myAssistant.calculateWeeklyPay()**, and **myAssistant.printFieldValues()** contain method calls. A **method call** is a statement that invokes a procedure, that is, causes the procedure to execute. The methods themselves are part of the **Employee** class, which is why an **Employee** object can use them.

When you write the **EmployeeDemo** application, you do not need to know what statements are written within the **Employee** class methods, although you could make an educated guess based on the methods' names. Before you could execute the application in Figure 2-6, you would have to write appropriate statements within the **Employee** class methods, but if another programmer has already written the methods, then you can use the application in Figure 2-6 without knowing the details contained in the methods. The ability to use methods without knowing the details of their contents is a feature of encapsulation. Programmers like to say the method details are contained in a **black box**—a device you can use without knowing how its contents operate. The real world is full of many black box devices. For example, you can use your television and microwave oven without knowing how they work internally—all you need to understand is the interface. Similarly, with well-written methods that belong to classes you use, you need not understand how they work internally in order to be able to use them; you need only understand what they will do.

A program that uses a class object is a **client** of the class. Many programmers write only client programs, never creating non-client classes themselves, but using only classes that others have created. In the client program segment in Figure 2-6, the focus is on the object—the **Employee** named **myAssistant**—and the methods you can use with that object. This is the essence of object-oriented programming.

TIP ◻ ◻ ◻ ◻ Of course, the program segment in Figure 2-6 is very short. In a more useful real-life program, you might read employee data from a data file before assigning it to the object's fields, and you might create hundreds of objects.

TIP ◻ ◻ ◻ ◻ In older object-oriented programming languages, simple numbers and characters are said to be **primitive data types**; this distinguishes them from objects that are class types. In the newest programming languages, such as C#, every item you name, even one that is a num or char type, really is an object that is a member of a class that contains both data and methods.

TIP ◻ ◻ ◻ ◻ When you instantiate objects, the data fields of each are stored at separate memory locations. However, all members of the same class share one copy of the class methods. You will learn more about this concept in Chapter 3.

UNDERSTANDING INHERITANCE

The concept of class is useful because of its reusability; you can create new classes that are descendents of existing classes. The **descendent classes** (or **child classes**) can inherit all of the attributes of the **original class** (or **parent class**), or the descendent class can override those attributes that are inappropriate. In geometry, a `Cube` is a descendent of a `Square`. A `Cube` has all the attributes of a `Square` plus one more: depth. A `Cube`, however, has a different method of calculating total area (or volume) than a `Square` has; a `Square`'s total area is its length times its width, but to calculate a `Cube`'s volume you must also multiply by its height. In programming, if you have previously created a `Square` class and you need a `Cube` class, it makes sense to inherit existing features from the `Square` class, adding only the new feature (depth) that a `Cube` requires and modifying the method that calculates volume.

TIP ▫ ▫ ▫ ▫ | You can call a parent class a **base class** or **superclass**. You can refer to a child class as a **derived class** or **subclass**.

As another example, to accommodate part-time workers in your personnel programs, you might want to create a child class from the `Employee` class. Part-time workers need an ID, name, and hourly wage, just as regular employees do, but the regular `Employee` pay calculation assumes a 40-hour work week. You might want to create a `PartTimeEmployee` class that inherits all the data fields contained in an `Employee`, but adds a new one—`hoursWorked`. In addition, you want to create a new modified `setFieldValues()` method that includes assigning a value to `hoursWorked`, and a new `calculateWeeklyPay()` method that operates correctly for `PartTimeEmployee` objects. This new method multiplies `hourlyWage` by `hoursWorked` instead of by 40. The `printFieldValues()` module that already exists within the `Employee` class works appropriately for both the `Employee` and the `PartTimeEmployee` classes, so there is no need to include a new version of this module within the `PartTimeEmployee` class; `PartTimeEmployee` objects can simply use their parent's existing method.

TIP ▫ ▫ ▫ ▫ | You can think of a child class as being more specific than a parent class. For example, a `PartTimeEmployee` is a specific type of `Employee`.

TIP ▫ ▫ ▫ ▫ | A child class contains all the data fields and methods of its parent, plus any new ones you define. A parent class does not gain any child class members.

When you create a child class, you can show its relationship to the parent with a class diagram like the one for `PartTimeEmployee` in Figure 2-7. The complete `PartTimeEmployee` class appears in Figure 2-8.

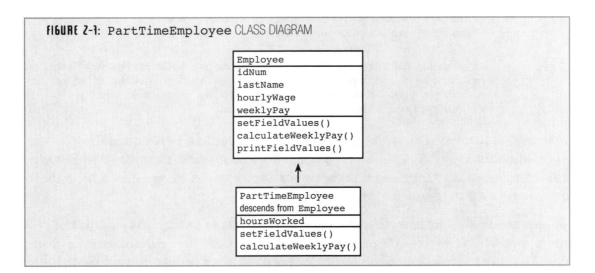

FIGURE 2-7: `PartTimeEmployee` CLASS DIAGRAM

```
Employee
idNum
lastName
hourlyWage
weeklyPay
setFieldValues()
calculateWeeklyPay()
printFieldValues()
```

```
PartTimeEmployee
descends from Employee
hoursWorked
setFieldValues()
calculateWeeklyPay()
```

FIGURE 2-8: THE `PartTimeEmployee` CLASS

```
class PartTimeEmployee descends from Employee
   private numeric hoursWorked
   public void setFieldValues()
      Employee class setFieldValues()
      input hoursWorked
   return
   public void calculateWeeklyPay()
      weeklyPay = hourlyWage * hoursWorked
   return
endClass
```

TIP ▫ ▫ ▫ ▫ The class in Figure 2-8 uses the phrase "descends from" to indicate inheritance. Each programming language uses its own syntax. For example, using Java, you would write "extends", in Visual Basic .NET you would write "inherits", and in C++ and C# you would use a colon between the class name and its parent.

The `PartTimeEmployee` class shown in Figure 2-8 contains five data fields—all the fields that an `Employee` contains plus one new one, `hoursWorked`. The `PartTimeEmployee` class also contains three methods. The methods `setFieldValues()` and `calculateWeeklyPay()` have been rewritten for the `PartTimeEmployee` child class, because they will operate differently when used with a `PartTimeEmployee` than when used with an `Employee`.

For example, `setFieldValues()` will provide not only information that an `Employee` requires, but also will input the number of hours worked, and `calculateWeeklyPay()` will use the variable `hoursWorked` instead of the constant 40 to calculate the weekly pay. The methods in the child class that have the same name as those in the parent class are said to either overload or override the parent class methods.

TIP □ □ □ □ | There is a distinction between overloading and overriding. You will learn a complete definition for these terms and learn more about these concepts in Chapter 3.

TIP □ □ □ □ | Before the `PartTimeEmployee` child class can use the `hoursWorked` field, object-oriented programming languages require one additional modification to the Employee parent class. You will learn about this modification, making the `hoursWorked` field protected, later in this chapter.

Within the `setFieldValues()` method of the `PartTimeEmployee` class, the parent class's `setFieldValues()` is called. Because the parent class method already provides statements that set the values of three of the class fields, the `PartTimeEmployee` class can take advantage of the fact that part of the work has been done. Being able to reuse code is an advantage of inheritance.

The `PartTimeEmployee` class also contains the `printFieldValues()` method, which it inherits unchanged from its parent. You do not see a copy of the `printFieldValues()` method in the `PartTimeEmployee` class in Figure 2-8, because the phrase `descends from Employee` in the first line of the class means that all `Employee` class members automatically are included in the child class unless they have been overridden. When you write an application such as the one shown in Figure 2-9, declaring `Employee` as well as `PartTimeEmployee` objects, different `setFieldValues()` and `calculateWeeklyPay()` methods containing different statements are called for each object, but the same `printFieldValues()` method is called in each case.

FIGURE 2-9: EMPLOYEEDEMO APPLICATION THAT USES `Employee` AND `PartTimeEmployee` OBJECTS

```
class EmployeeDemo
    main()
        Employee myAssistant
        PartTimeEmployee myDriver
        myAssistant.setFieldValues()
        myDriver.setFieldValues()
        myAssistant.calculateWeeklyPay()
        myDriver.calculateWeeklyPay()
        myAssistant.printFieldValues()
        myDriver.printFieldValues()
    return
endClass
```

In the program in Figure 2-9, two objects are declared. The `myAssistant` object is a "plain" `Employee`; the `myDriver` object is a more specific `PartTimeEmployee`. The statement `myDriver.setFieldValues()` calls a different method than `myAssistant.setFieldValues()`; the two methods have the same name, but belong to different classes. The compiler knows which method to call based on the type of object, but the programmer can use one easy-to-remember method name in both cases. The method name `setFieldValues()` can be used with either type of object, and it works appropriately with either type.

In Figure 2-9, the two calls to `calculateWeeklyPay()` work in the same way. Two different methods are called; the compiler knows which version to use because the objects associated with the calls belong to different classes.

The final two statements before the `return` statement in the code in Figure 2-9 call the `printFieldValues()` method with each of the two objects. In these statements, the same method is called each time. Naturally, the `myAssistant` object uses the `printFieldValues()` method contained in the `Employee` class. The `myDriver` object also uses the `printFieldValues()` method from the `Employee` class because of the following reasoning:

- `myDriver` is a `PartTimeEmployee`.
- The `PartTimeEmployee` class does not contain its own version of the `printFieldValues()` method.
- The `PartTimeEmployee` class is a child class of `Employee`.
- The `Employee` class contains a `printFieldValues()` method that the `myDriver` object can use.

A child class will use its parent class methods unless the child class has its own version that either overrides or overloads the parent's version.

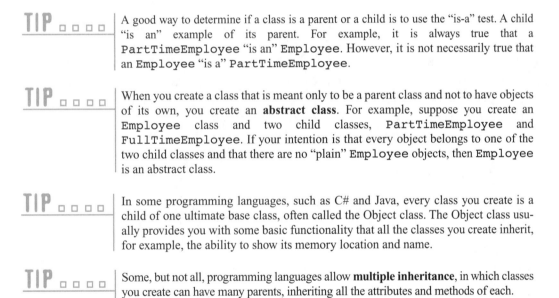

TIP   A good way to determine if a class is a parent or a child is to use the "is-a" test. A child "is an" example of its parent. For example, it is always true that a `PartTimeEmployee` "is an" `Employee`. However, it is not necessarily true that an `Employee` "is a" `PartTimeEmployee`.

TIP   When you create a class that is meant only to be a parent class and not to have objects of its own, you create an **abstract class**. For example, suppose you create an `Employee` class and two child classes, `PartTimeEmployee` and `FullTimeEmployee`. If your intention is that every object belongs to one of the two child classes and that there are no "plain" `Employee` objects, then `Employee` is an abstract class.

TIP   In some programming languages, such as C# and Java, every class you create is a child of one ultimate base class, often called the Object class. The Object class usually provides you with some basic functionality that all the classes you create inherit, for example, the ability to show its memory location and name.

TIP   Some, but not all, programming languages allow **multiple inheritance**, in which classes you create can have many parents, inheriting all the attributes and methods of each.

USING POLYMORPHISM

Object-oriented programs use the feature polymorphism to allow the same request—that is, the same method call—to be carried out differently, depending on the context; this is seldom allowed in non-object-oriented languages. With the `Employee` and `PartTimeEmployee` classes, you need a different `calculateWeeklyPay()` method, depending on the type of object you use. Without polymorphism, you must write a different module with a unique name for each method because two methods with the same name cannot coexist in a program. Just as your blender can produce juice whether you insert a fruit or a vegetable, with polymorphism a `calculateWeeklyPay()` method produces a correct result whether it operates on an `Employee` or a `PartTimeEmployee`. Similarly, you may want a `computeGradePointAverage()` method to operate differently for a Pass-Fail course than it does for a graded one, or you might want a word-processing program to produce different results when you press Delete with one word highlighted in a document than when you press Delete with a file name highlighted.

When you write a polymorphic method in an object-oriented programming language, you must write each version of the method, and that can entail a lot of work. The benefits of polymorphism do not seem obvious while you are writing the methods, but the benefits are realized when you can use the methods in all sorts of applications. When you can use a single, simple, easy-to-understand method name such as `printFieldValues()` with all sorts of objects, such as `Employee`s, `PartTimeEmployee`s, `InventoryItem`s, and `BankTransaction`s, then your objects behave more like their real-world counterparts and your programs are easier to understand.

UNDERSTANDING PROTECTED ACCESS

Making data private is an important object-oriented programming concept. By making data fields private, and allowing access to them only through a class's methods, you protect the ways in which data can be altered.

When a data field within a class is private, no outside class can use it—including a child class. The principle of data hiding would be lost if all you had to do to access a class's private data was to create a child class. However, it can be inconvenient when a child class's methods cannot directly access its own inherited data. Therefore, object-oriented programming languages allow a medium-security access specifier that is more restrictive than public but less restrictive than private. The **protected access** modifier is used when you want no outside classes to be able to use a data field, except classes that are children of the original class. Figure 2-10 shows a rewritten `Employee` class that uses the protected access modifier on its data fields (see highlighting). When this modified class is used as a base class for another class such as `PartTimeEmployee`, the child class's methods will be able to access each of the protected fields originally defined in the parent class.

FIGURE 2-10: Employee CLASS USING protected AND public ACCESS SPECIFIERS

```
class Employee
     protected numeric idNum
     protected string lastName
     protected numeric hourlyWage
     protected numeric weeklyPay
     public void setFieldValues()
        input idNum
        input lastName
        input hourlyWage
     return
     public void calculateWeeklyPay()
        weeklyPay = hourlyWage * 40
     return
     public void printFieldValues()
        print idNum, lastName, hourlyWage, weeklyPay
     return
endClass
```

Although a child class's methods can access data fields originally defined in the parent class, a parent class's methods have no special privileges regarding any of its child's class's data fields. That is, unless the child class's data fields are public, a parent, just like any other unrelated class, cannot access them.

Figure 2-11 contains the class diagram for the version of the `Employee` class shown in Figure 2-10. Notice the octothorpe (#) is used to indicate protected class members.

FIGURE 2-11: `Employee` CLASS DIAGRAM WITH `protected` AND `public` ACCESS SPECIFIERS

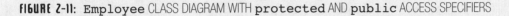

Employee
#idNum: numeric
#lastName: string
#hourlyWage: numeric
#weeklyPay: numeric
+setFieldValues()
+calculateWeeklyPay()
+printFieldValues()

ONE EXAMPLE OF USING PREDEFINED CLASSES: CREATING GUI OBJECTS

When you purchase or download an object-oriented programming language compiler, it comes packaged with myriad predefined, built-in classes. The classes are stored in **libraries**—collections of classes that serve related purposes. Some of the most useful are the classes you can use to create graphical user interface (GUI) objects such as frames, buttons, labels, and text boxes. You place these GUI components within interactive programs so that users can manipulate them using input devices, most frequently a keyboard and a mouse. For example, using a language that supports GUI applications, if you want to place a clickable button on the screen, you instantiate an object that belongs to the already created class named `Button`. The `Button` class is already created and contains private data fields such as `text` and `height` and public methods such as `setText()` and `setHeight()` that allow you to place instructions on your `Button` object and to change its vertical size, respectively.

TIP □ □ □ □ In some languages, such as Java, libraries are also called **packages**.

TIP □ □ □ □ Languages that contain prewritten GUI object classes frequently refer to the class attributes as **properties**.

If no predefined GUI object classes existed, you could create your own. However, there would be several disadvantages to doing this:

- It would be a lot of work. Creating graphical objects requires a lot of code, and at least a modicum of artistic talent.

- It would be repetitious work. Almost all GUI programs require standard components such as buttons and labels. If each programmer created the classes that represent these components from scratch, a lot of work would be unnecessarily repeated.

- The components would look different in various applications. If each programmer created his or her own component classes, then objects like buttons would look and operate slightly differently in different applications. Users like standardization in their components—title bars on windows that are a uniform height, buttons that appear to be pressed when clicked, frames and windows that contain maximize and minimize buttons in predictable locations, and so on. By using standard component classes, programmers are assured that the GUI components in their programs have the same look and feel as those in other programs.

In programming languages that provide preexisting GUI classes, you often are provided with a **visual development environment** in which you can create programs by dragging components such as buttons and labels onto a screen and arranging them visually. Then you write programming statements to control the actions that take place when a user manipulates the controls by clicking them using a mouse, for example. Many programmers never create any classes of their own from which they will instantiate objects, but only write classes that are applications that use built-in GUI component classes. Some languages, particularly Visual Basic, lend themselves very well to this type of programming.

UNDERSTANDING THE ADVANTAGES OF OBJECT-ORIENTED PROGRAMMING

Using the features of object-oriented programming languages provides you with many benefits as you develop your programs. Whether you use classes you have created or use those created by others, when you instantiate objects in programs, you save development time because each object automatically includes appropriate, reliable methods and attributes. When using inheritance you can develop new classes more quickly by extending classes that already exist and work; you need to concentrate only on new features the new class adds. When using preexisting objects, you need to concentrate only on the interface to those objects, not on the internal instructions that make them work. By using polymorphism, you can use reasonable, easy-to-remember names for methods and concentrate on their purpose rather than on memorizing different method names.

CHAPTER SUMMARY

☐ Object-oriented programming is a style of programming that focuses on an application's data and the methods you need to manipulate that data. Objects both in the real world and in object-oriented programming are made up of attributes and methods. In object-oriented terminology, a class is a term that describes a group or collection of objects with common properties. An instance of a class is an existing object of a class. In object-oriented programming, procedures are called methods. Inheritance and polymorphism are important object-oriented programming concepts.

☐ A class definition is a set of program statements that tell you the characteristics of the class's objects and the methods that can be applied to its objects. A class contains three parts: a name, optional data, and optional methods. A class diagram consists of a rectangle divided into three sections containing the name, attributes, and methods.

☐ The principle of keeping data private and inaccessible to outside classes is called data hiding. Object-oriented programmers usually specify that their data fields will have private access—that is, the data cannot be accessed by any method that is not part of the class. The methods themselves support public access—which means that other programs and methods may use the methods that control access to the private data.

☐ When you write an object-oriented program, you create objects that are members of a class. You instantiate (or create) a class object (or instance) with a statement that includes the type of object and an identifying name. A program that uses a class object is a client of the class.

☐ The concept of class is useful because of its reusability; you can create new classes that are descendents of existing classes. The descendent classes (or child classes) can inherit all of the attributes of the original class (or parent class), or the descendent class can override those attributes that are inappropriate. Object-oriented programs use the feature polymorphism to allow the same request—that is, the same method call—to be carried out differently, depending on the context.

☐ Object-oriented programming languages allow a medium-security access specifier that is more restrictive than public but less restrictive than private. The protected access modifier is used when you want no outside classes to be able to use a data field, except classes that are children of the original class.

☐ When you purchase or download an object-oriented programming language compiler, it comes packaged with myriad predefined, built-in classes. The classes are stored in libraries—collections of classes that serve related purposes. Some of the most useful are the classes you can use to create graphical user interface (GUI) objects such as frames, buttons, labels, and text boxes.

☐ Using the features of object-oriented programming languages provides you with many benefits as you develop your programs. Whether you use classes you have created or use those created by others, when you instantiate objects in programs you save development time.

KEY TERMS

Object-oriented programming is a style of programming that focuses on an application's data and the methods you need to manipulate that data.

Attributes are the characteristics that define an object as part of a class.

The **states** of an object are the values of its attributes.

A **class** is a term that describes a group or collection of objects with common properties.

An **instance** of a class is an existing object of a class.

In object-oriented programming, procedures are called **methods**.

Polymorphism is the object-oriented feature that allows you to create multiple methods with the same name, which will act differently and appropriately when used with different types of objects.

Inheritance is the process of acquiring the traits of one's predecessors.

Encapsulation is the process of combining all of an object's attributes and methods into a single package.

Information hiding is the concept that other classes should not alter an object's attributes—outside classes should only be allowed to make a request that an attribute be altered; then it is up to the class methods to determine whether the request is appropriate.

The **interface** is the user-friendly boundary between the user and internal mechanisms of the device.

Information hiding is also called **data hiding**.

A **class definition** is a set of program statements that tell you the characteristics of the class's objects and the methods that can be applied to its objects.

You can use the **is-a** phrase to test whether an object is an instance of a class.

A **field** is a data item within, or attribute of, an object.

A **class diagram** is a tool used to describe a class; it consists of a rectangle divided into three sections.

Object-oriented programmers usually specify that their data fields will have **private access**, which means that the data cannot be accessed by any method that is not part of the class.

Object-oriented programmers usually specify that their methods will have **public access**, which means that other programs and methods may use the methods that control access to the private data.

An **access specifier**, or **access modifier**, is the adjective that defines the type of access that outside classes will have to an attribute or method.

To create a class object is to **instantiate** it.

A **user-defined type** is a class.

A **programmer-defined type** is a class.

A **method call** is a statement that invokes a procedure, that is, causes the procedure to execute.

A **black box** is a device you can use without knowing how its contents operate.

A **client** is a program that uses a class object.

A **primitive data type** is a simple data type, as opposed to a class type.

A **descendent class**, also called a **child class**, **derived class**, or **subclass**, inherits the attributes of another class.

An **original class**, also called a **parent class**, **base class**, or **superclass**, is one that has descendants. In other words, it is a class from which other classes are derived.

An **abstract class** is one that is created only to be a parent class and not to have objects of its own.

Some programming languages support **multiple inheritance**, in which a class can inherit from more than one parent.

The **protected access** modifier is used when you want no outside classes to be able to use a data field, except classes that are children of the original class.

Libraries, or **packages**, are collections of classes that serve related purposes.

Properties are the attributes of prewritten graphical user interface (GUI) classes.

A **visual development environment** is one in which you can create programs by dragging components such as buttons and labels onto a screen and arranging them visually.

REVIEW QUESTIONS

1. **Which of the following is *not* a feature of object-oriented programming?**
   a. You pass messages to objects.
   b. Programming objects mimic real-world objects.
   c. Encapsulation is avoided.
   d. Classes can inherit features of other classes.

2. **With object-oriented programming, the same message _____.**

   a. works the same way with every object
   b. works differently and appropriately when applied to different objects.
   c. can never be used more than once
   d. all of the above

3. **In object-oriented programming, the process of acquiring the traits of one's predecessors is known as _____.**
   a. inheritance
   b. polymorphism
   c. data redundancy
   d. legacy programming

4. **Class is to object as Dog is to _____.**
   a. animal
   b. mammal
   c. poodle
   d. my dog Murphy

5. To programmers, another word for object is _____.

   a. class
   b. instance
   c. structure
   d. item

6. The object-class relationship can be tested using the phrase _____.

   a. can-do
   b. open-close
   c. is-a
   d. can-be

7. Which of the following is least likely to be a feature contained within most classes?

   a. a name
   b. private data
   c. public data
   d. public methods

8. Another term used for class data fields is _____.

   a. attributes
   b. components
   c. points
   d. paths

9. A class diagram consists of a rectangle divided into _____.

   a. two sections: data and methods
   b. three sections: name, data, and methods
   c. four sections: name, data, methods, and purpose
   d. five sections: name, numeric data, text data, methods, and purpose

10. The principle of keeping data private and inaccessible to outside classes is called _____.

   a. information overloading
   b. attribute secrecy
   c. polymorphism
   d. data hiding

11. Object-oriented programmers usually specify that their data fields will have _____ access.

   a. public
   b. private
   c. protected
   d. personal

12. **Creating an object is called _____ the object.**

    a. morphing
    b. declaring
    c. instantiating
    d. formatting

13. **A black box is a device that contains _____.**

    a. nothing
    b. elements you can use, but cannot see
    c. elements you can see, but cannot use
    d. elements you can neither see nor use

14. **One name for a class from which others inherit is a _____ class.**

    a. benefactor
    b. child
    c. descendent
    d. parent

15. **Suppose you have a class named Horse containing such fields as name and age. When you create a child class named RaceHorse, _____.**

    a. every RaceHorse object has an age field
    b. some RaceHorse objects have an age field
    c. no RaceHorse objects have an age field
    d. Horse objects no longer have an age field

16. **Suppose you have a class named Horse containing such fields as name and age. When you create a child class named RaceHorse adding a new field named winnings, _____.**

    a. every RaceHorse object has a winnings field
    b. some RaceHorse objects have a winnings field
    c. every Horse object has a winnings field
    d. every Horse object and every RaceHorse object has a winnings field

17. **The feature of object-oriented programming languages that allows the same method call to be carried out differently, depending on the context, is _____.**

    a. inheritance
    b. ambiguity
    c. polymorphism
    d. overriding

18. **The modifier that allows an intermediate level of access between public and private is _____.**

    a. semiprivate
    b. sheltered
    c. protected
    d. constrained

19. **Collections of classes that serve related purposes are called _____.**
    a. archives
    b. anthologies
    c. compendiums
    d. libraries

20. **Which of the following is *not* a benefit provided by object-oriented programming?**
    a. You save development time because each object automatically includes appropriate, reliable methods and attributes.
    b. When using inheritance, you can develop new classes more quickly by extending classes that already exist and work; you need to concentrate only on new features the new class adds.
    c. When using preexisting objects, you need to concentrate only on the interface to those objects, not on the internal instructions that make them work.
    d. By using method overloading and polymorphism, you can use more precise and unique names for each operation you want to perform using different objects.

EXERCISES

1. **Identify three objects that might belong to each of the following classes:**
   a. `Automobile`
   b. `NovelAuthor`
   c. `CollegeCourse`

2. **Identify three different classes that might contain each of these objects:**
   a. Wolfgang Amadeus Mozart
   b. My pet cat named Socks
   c. Apartment 14 at 101 Main Street

3. **Design a class named `CustomerRecord` that holds a customer number, name, and address. Include methods to set the values for each data field and print the values for each data field. Create the class diagram and write the pseudocode that defines the class.**

4. **Design a class named `House` that holds the street address, price, number of bedrooms, and number of baths in a `House`. Include methods to set the values for each data field, and include a method that displays all the values for a `House`. Create the class diagram and write the pseudocode that defines the class.**

5. **Design a class named `Loan` that holds an account number, name of account holder, amount borrowed, term, and interest rate. Include methods to set values for each data field and a method that prints all the loan information. Create the class diagram and write the pseudocode that defines the class.**

6. **Complete the following tasks:**

   a. Design a class named `Book` that holds a stock number, author, title, price, and number of pages for a book. Include methods to set and print the values for each data field. Create the class diagram and write the pseudocode that defines the class.

   b. Design a class named `TextBook` that is a child class of `Book`. Include a new data field for the grade level of the book. Override the `Book` class methods that set and print the data so that you accommodate the new grade-level field. Create the class diagram and write the pseudocode that defines the class.

7. **Complete the following tasks:**

   a. Design a class named `Player` that holds a player number and name for a sports team participant. Include methods to set the values for each data field and print the values for each data field. Create the class diagram and write the pseudocode that defines the class.

   b. Design two classes named `BaseballPlayer` and `BasketballPlayer` that are child classes of `Player`. Include a new data field in each class for the player's position. Include an additional field in the `BaseballPlayer` class for batting average. Include a new field in the `BasketballPlayer` class for free-throw percentage. Override the `Player` class methods that set and print the data so that you accommodate the new fields. Create the class diagram; then write the pseudocode that defines the class.

CASE PROBLEM

In Chapter 1, you listed objects needed for a business simulation for Cost Is No Object—a car rental service that specializes in lending antique and luxury cars to clients on a short-term basis. Assume you have decided that you will need the following classes: `Employee`, `Customer`, `Automobile`, and `RentalAgreement`. Create a class diagram that could be used to describe data and methods needed for each of these classes.

3

USING METHODS AND PARAMETERS

After studying Chapter 3, you should be able to:

- ☐ Create methods with and without arguments
- ☐ Create instance methods in a class
- ☐ Explore the rationale behind data hiding
- ☐ Organize classes
- ☐ Understand the role of the `this` reference
- ☐ Begin to understand how to use constructors

CREATING METHODS WITH AND WITHOUT ARGUMENTS

A **method** is a program module that contains a series of statements that carry out a task. To execute a method, you **invoke** it or **call** it from another method; the **calling method** invokes the **called method**. Any class can contain an unlimited number of methods, and each method can be called an unlimited number of times. Within a class, the simplest methods you can invoke don't require any data items (called **arguments** or **parameters**) to be sent to them, nor do they send any data back to you (called **returning a value**). Consider the simple `Hello` class application that you saw in Chapter 1 and that appears in Figure 3-1.

FIGURE 3-1: THE `Hello` CLASS

```
class Hello
     main()
         print "Hello"
     return
endClass
```

Suppose you want to add three lines of output to this application to display your company's name and address. You can simply insert three new `print` statements, but instead you might choose to create a separate method to display the three new lines.

There are two major reasons to create a separate method to display the three lines. First, the `main()` method will remain short and easy to follow because `main()` will contain just one statement to call the method, rather than three separate `print` statements to perform the work of the method. What is more important is that a method is easily reusable. After you create the name and address method, you can use it in any application that needs the company's name and address. In other words, you do the work once, and then you can use the method many times.

A method must include the following:

- A declaration (or header or definition)
- A body
- A return statement that marks the end of the method

TIP ▫ ▫ ▫ ▫ | Using a method name to encapsulate a series of statements is an example of the feature that programmers call **abstraction**. When you view abstract art, the artist tries to capture the essence of an object without focusing on the details. Similarly, when programmers employ abstraction , they can use a general method name in a module rather than list all the detailed activities that will be carried out by the method.

TIP ▫ ▫ ▫ ▫ | Methods are sometimes called modules. C++ programmers also use the term "function", Visual Basic programmers use "subroutine", and Object Pascal programmers use "procedure".

TIP ▫ ▫ ▫ ▫ | In most programming languages, if you do not include a return statement at the end of a method, the method will still return. This book follows the convention of explicitly including a return statement with every method.

The **method declaration** is the first line, or **header**, of a method. It contains the following:

- Optional access modifiers
- The return type for the method
- The method name
- An optional list of method arguments (you separate the arguments with commas if there is more than one)

You first learned about access modifiers in Chapter 2. Methods can be public, private, or protected, but public methods are most common. Endowing a method with `public` access means any class can use it.

 In some programming languages, notably Java, any method that can be used without instantiating an object requires the keyword modifier static. The `main( )` method is such a method—a static, class method. Classes can contain instance methods and class methods. Instance methods operate on an object. Static class methods do not need an object instance in order to be used. You will learn more about these concepts later in this chapter.

CREATING METHODS WITH NO ARGUMENTS

You can write the `nameAndAddress( )` method shown in Figure 3-2. According to its declaration, the method is `public` and `static`, meaning any class can use it and no objects need to be created. The `nameAndAddress( )` method returns nothing, so its return type is **void**. The method receives nothing, so its parentheses are empty. Its body consists of three `print` statements.

FIGURE 3-2: THE `nameAndAddress` METHOD

```
public static void nameAndAddress()
     print "Cost is No Object, Inc."
     print "100 South Main Street"
     print "Wild Rose, WI 54984"
return
```

 Some methods contain arguments within their parentheses. The `nameAndAddress( )` method header shown here does not contain any arguments within its parentheses. You will write methods that accept arguments later in this chapter.

You place the entire method within the class that will use it, but not within any other method. Figure 3-3 highlights the two locations where you can place additional methods within the `Hello` class—within the class, but outside of, either before or after, any other methods. Additionally, now that you know about access modifiers, static and nonstatic methods, and return types, `public`, `static`, and `void`, have been added to the `main( )` method header to more closely replicate the code you would write in most object-oriented (OO) programming languages.

FIGURE 3-3: PLACEMENT OF METHODS WITHIN A CLASS

```
public class Hello
  You can place additional methods here, before main()
      public static void main()
                print "Hello"
      return
  You can place additional methods here, after main()
endClass
```

If you want the `main()` method to call the `nameAndAddress()` method, then you simply use the `nameAndAddress()` method's name as a statement within the body of `main()`. Figure 3-4 shows the complete application. In this application, `main()` performs two actions. First, it calls the `nameAndAddress()` method, and then it prints "Hello". The diagram in Figure 3-5 shows that the method call causes program execution to transfer to the `nameAndAddress()` method. At the `return` statement at the end of the `nameAndAddress()` method, control returns to the statement following the method call in the `main()` module.

FIGURE 3-4: Hello CLASS WITH main() CALLING nameAndAddress()

```
public class Hello
    public static void main()
        nameAndAddress()
        print "Hello"
    return
    public static void nameAndAddress()
        print "Cost is No Object, Inc."
        print "100 South Main Street"
        print "Wild Rose, WI 54984"
    return
endClass
```

FIGURE 3-5: DIAGRAM OF CALL TO nameAndAddress() METHOD

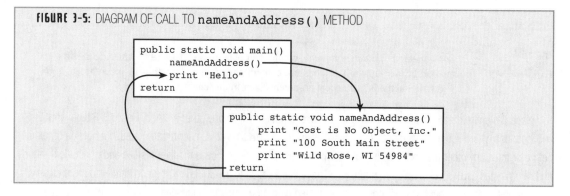

Figure 3-6 shows the output from the execution of the application shown in Figure 3-4. Because the `main()` method calls the `nameAndAddress()` method before it prints "Hello", the name and address appear first in the output.

FIGURE 3-6: OUTPUT OF THE APPLICATION INCLUDING THE `nameAndAddress()` METHOD

```
Cost is No Object, Inc.
100 South Main Street
Wild Rose, WI 54984
Hello
```

The full name of the `nameAndAddress()` method is `Hello.nameAndAddress()`. The full name includes the class name, a dot, and the method name. When you use the `nameAndAddress()` method within its own class, you do not need to use the full name (although you can); the method name alone is enough. However, if you want to use the `nameAndAddress()` method in another class, the compiler will not recognize the method unless you use the full name, writing it as `Hello.nameAndAddress()`. This format notifies the new class that the method is located in the `Hello` class.

TIP ☐ ☐ ☐ ☐ | Think of the class name as the family name. Within your own family, you might refer to an activity as "the family reunion", but outside the family, people need to use a surname as well, as in "the Anderson family reunion". Similarly, within a class, a method name alone is sufficient, but outside the class, you need to use the fully qualified name.

TIP ☐ ☐ ☐ ☐ | Each of two different classes can have their own method named `nameAndAddress()`. Such a method in the second class would be entirely distinct from the identically named method in the first class. Two classes in an application cannot have the same name.

CREATING METHODS THAT REQUIRE A SINGLE ARGUMENT

Some methods require information to be sent in from the outside. If a method could not receive your communications, called arguments, then you would have to write an infinite number of methods to cover every possible situation. As a real-life example, when you make a restaurant reservation, you do not need to employ a different method for every date of the year at every possible time of day. Rather, you can supply the date and time as information to the person who carries out the method. The method, recording the reservation, is then carried out in the same manner, no matter what date and time are involved. In a program, if you design a method to square numeric values, it makes sense to design a `square()` method that you can supply with an argument that represents the value to be squared, rather than having to develop a `square1()` method (that squares the value 1), a `square2()` method (that squares the value 2), and so on. To call a `square()` method, you might write a statement like `square(17)` or `square(86)`.

An important principle of OO programming is the notion of **implementation hiding**, the encapsulation of method details within a class. That is, when you make a request to a method, you don't know the details of how the method is executed. For example, when you make a real-life restaurant reservation, you do not need to know how the reservation is actually recorded at the restaurant—perhaps it is written in a book, marked on a large chalkboard, or entered into a computerized database. The implementation details don't concern you as a client, and if the restaurant changes its methods from one year to the next, the change does not affect your use of the reservation method—you still call and provide your name, a date, and a time. With well-written OO methods, using implementation hiding means that a method that calls another must know the name of the called method, what type of information to send it, and what type of return data to expect, but the program does not need to know how the method works internally. The calling method needs to understand only the **interface** to the called method. In other words, the interface is the only part of a method that the method's client sees or interacts with. Additionally, if you substitute a new, improved method implementation, as long as the interface to the method does not change, you won't need to make any changes in any methods that call the altered method.

When you write the method declaration for a method that can receive an argument, you begin by defining the same elements as with methods that do not accept arguments—optional access modifiers, the return type for the method, and the method name. You must also include the following items within the method declaration parentheses:

- The type of the argument
- A local name for the argument

For example, the declaration for a public method named `predictRaise()` that displays a person's salary plus a 10 percent raise could have the declaration `public static void predictRaise (numeric moneyAmount)`. You can think of the parentheses in a method declaration as a funnel into the method—data arguments listed there are "dropped in" to the method. An argument passed into a method can be any data type including numeric, character, or string; it also can be a class type.

The argument `numeric moneyAmount` within the parentheses indicates that the `predictRaise()` method will receive a value of type `numeric`, and that within the method, the passed value representing a salary will be known as `moneyAmount`. Figure 3-7 shows the relationship between a calling method and the complete `predictRaise()` method.

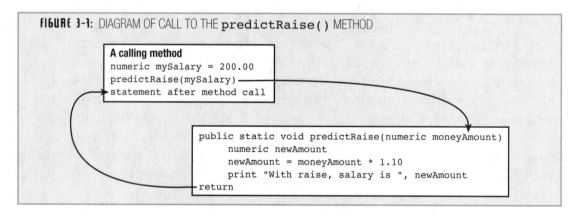

FIGURE 3-7: DIAGRAM OF CALL TO THE `predictRaise()` METHOD

```
A calling method
numeric mySalary = 200.00
predictRaise(mySalary)
statement after method call
```

```
public static void predictRaise(numeric moneyAmount)
      numeric newAmount
      newAmount = moneyAmount * 1.10
      print "With raise, salary is ", newAmount
return
```

The `predictRaise()` method is a `void` method because it does not need to return any value to any other method that uses it—its only function is to receive the `moneyAmount` value, multiply it by 1.10 (resulting in a 10 percent salary increase), and then display the result.

Within another method, you can call the `predictRaise()` method by using either a constant value or a variable as an argument. Thus, both `predictRaise(472.25)` and `predictRaise(mySalary)` invoke the `predictRaise()` method correctly, assuming that `mySalary` is declared as a numeric variable and assigned an appropriate value in the calling method. You can call the `predictRaise()` method any number of times, with a different constant or variable argument each time. Each of these arguments becomes known as `moneyAmount` within the method. The identifier `moneyAmount` represents a variable that holds any numeric value passed into the `predictRaise()` method.

It's interesting to note that if the value used as an argument in the method call to `predictRaise()` is a variable, it might possess the same identifier as `moneyAmount`, or a different one, such as `mySalary`. For example, the code in Figure 3-8 shows three calls to the `predictRaise()` method, and Figure 3-9 shows the output. One call uses a constant, 400.00. The other two use variables—one with the same name as `moneyAmount`, and the other with a different name, `mySalary`. The identifier `moneyAmount` is simply a placeholder while it is being used within the `predictRaise()` method, no matter what name it "goes by" in the calling method. The variable `moneyAmount` is a **local variable** to the `predictRaise()` method; that is, it is known only within the boundaries of the method.

FIGURE 3-8: THE `DemoRaise` CLASS WITH A `main()` METHOD THAT USES THE `predictRaise()` METHOD THREE TIMES

```
class DemoRaise
    public static void main()
        numeric mySalary = 200.00
        numeric moneyAmount = 800.00
        print "Demonstrating some raises"
        predictRaise(400.00)
        predictRaise(mySalary)
        predictRaise(moneyAmount)
    return
    public static void predictRaise(numeric moneyAmount)
        numeric newAmount
        newAmount = moneyAmount * 1.10
        print "With raise, salary is ", newAmount
    return
endClass
```

FIGURE 3-9: OUTPUT OF `DemoRaise` APPLICATION

```
Demonstrating some raises
With raise, salary is 440.00
With raise, salary is 220.00
With raise, salary is 880.00
```

Within the `predictRaise()` method in Figure 3-8, if you later decide to change the way in which the 10 percent raise is calculated—for example, by coding `newAmount = moneyAmount + (moneyAmount * 0.10)`—no method that uses the `predictRaise()` method will ever know the difference. The calling method will pass a value into `predictRaise()` and then a correct calculated result will appear on the screen.

Each time the `predictRaise()` method in Figure 3-8 executes, a `moneyAmount` variable is redeclared—that is, a new memory location large enough to hold a numeric value is set up and named `moneyAmount`. Within the `predictRaise()` method, `moneyAmount` holds whatever value is passed into the method by the `main()` method. When the `predictRaise()` method ends at the `return` statement, the local `moneyAmount` variable ceases to exist. After the raise is calculated in the method, placing a statement such as the following within `predictRaise()` would make no difference.

```
moneyAmount = 100000
```

That is, if you change the value of `moneyAmount` after you have used it in the calculation within `predictRaise()`, it affects nothing else. The memory location that holds `moneyAmount` is released at the end of the method, and if you change its value, it does not affect the calling method. In particular, don't think there would be any change in the variable named moneyAmount in the `main()` method; that variable, even though it has the same name, is a different variable with its own memory address and is totally different from the one in the `predictRaise()` method. When a variable ceases to exist at the end of a method, programmers say the variable "goes out of scope".

CREATING METHODS THAT REQUIRE MULTIPLE ARGUMENTS

A method can require more than one argument. You can pass multiple arguments to a method by listing the arguments within the call to the method and separating them with commas. For example, rather than creating a `predictRaise()` method that adds a 10 percent raise to every person's salary, you might prefer creating a method to which you can pass two values—the salary to be raised, as well as a percentage figure by which to raise it. Figure 3-10 shows a method that uses two such arguments.

FIGURE 3-10: THE `predictRaiseUsingRate()` METHOD THAT ACCEPTS TWO ARGUMENTS

```
public static void predictRaiseUsingRate(numeric money, numeric rate)
     numeric newAmount
     newAmount = money * (1 + rate)
     print "With raise, new salary is ", newAmount
return
```

TIP ▫ ▫ ▫ ▫   Note that a declaration for a method that receives two or more arguments must list the type for each argument separately, even if the arguments have the same type.

In Figure 3-10, two arguments (`numeric money` and `numeric rate`) appear within the parentheses in the method header. A comma separates each argument, and each argument requires its own declared type (in this case, both are numeric) as well as its own identifier. When values are passed to the method in a statement such as `predictRaiseUsingRate (mySalary, promisedRate)`, the first value passed will be referenced as money within the method, and the second value passed will be referenced as `rate`. Therefore, arguments passed to the method must be passed in the correct order. The call `predictRaiseUsingRate (200.00, 0.10)` results in output representing a 10 percent raise based on a $200 salary amount (or $220), but `predictRaiseUsingRate (0.10, 200.00)` results in output representing a 20,000 percent raise based on a salary of 10 cents (or $20.10). Figure 3-11 is a diagram that illustrates this process.

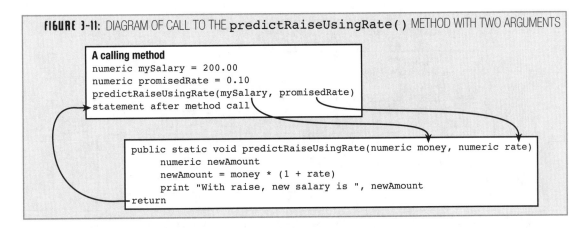

FIGURE 3-11: DIAGRAM OF CALL TO THE `predictRaiseUsingRate()` METHOD WITH TWO ARGUMENTS

```
A calling method
numeric mySalary = 200.00
numeric promisedRate = 0.10
predictRaiseUsingRate(mySalary, promisedRate)
statement after method call
```

```
public static void predictRaiseUsingRate(numeric money, numeric rate)
    numeric newAmount
    newAmount = money * (1 + rate)
    print "With raise, new salary is ", newAmount
return
```

TIP ☐ ☐ ☐ ☐ If two method arguments are the same type—for example, two numeric arguments—passing them to a method in the wrong order results in a logical error; that is, the program will compile and execute, but produce incorrect results. If a method expects arguments of diverse types, then passing arguments in reverse order constitutes a syntax error, and the program will not compile.

You can write a method so that it takes any number of arguments in any order. However, when you call a method, the arguments you send to a method must match in order—both in number and in type—the arguments listed in the method declaration. Thus, a method to compute an automobile salesperson's commission amount might require arguments such as a numeric value of a car sold, a numeric percentage commission rate, and a character code for the vehicle type. The correct method will execute only when three arguments of the correct types are sent in the correct order.

TIP ☐ ☐ ☐ ☐ The arguments in a method call are often referred to as **actual parameters**. The variables in the method declaration that accept the values from the actual parameters are the **formal parameters**.

CREATING METHODS THAT RETURN VALUES

The return type for a method can be any type, which includes numeric, character, and string, as well as class types including class types you create. Of course, a method can also return nothing, in which case the return type is `void`.

A method's return type is known more succinctly as a **method's type**. For example, the declaration for the `nameAndAddress()` method in Figure 3-2 is written `public static void nameAndAddress()`. This method is public and static and it returns no value, so it is type `void`. A method that returns the number of hours an employee has worked might be `public static numeric getHoursWorkedOvertime()`. This method returns a numeric value, so it is type numeric.

The `predictRaise()` method in Figure 3-8 produces output, but does not return any value, so its return type is `void`. If you want to create a method to return the new, calculated salary value rather than display it, the header would be `public numeric static predictRaise(numeric moneyAmount)`. Figure 3-12 shows this method and its relationship to a calling method.

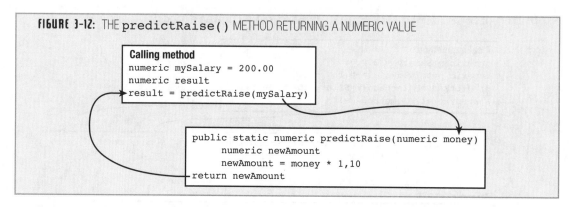

FIGURE 3-12: THE `predictRaise()` METHOD RETURNING A NUMERIC VALUE

```
Calling method
numeric mySalary = 200.00
numeric result
result = predictRaise(mySalary)


                    public static numeric predictRaise(numeric money)
                          numeric newAmount
                          newAmount = money * 1,10
                    return newAmount
```

Notice the return type `numeric` that precedes the method name in the `predictRaise()` method header in Figure 3-12. Also notice the `return` statement that is the last statement within the method. When you place a value after `return` in a `return` statement, a value is sent from the called method back to the calling method. In this case, the value stored in `newAmount` is sent back to any method that calls the `predictRaise()` method. A method's declared return type must match the type of the value used in the return statement; if it does not, the class will not compile.

TIP □ □ □ □ | A method can return, at most, one value. The value can be a simple data type or it can be a class type.

If a method returns a value, then when you call the method, you will usually want to use the returned value, although you are not required to do so. For example, when you invoke the `predictRaise()` method, you might want to assign the returned value (also called the method's value) to a numeric variable named `myNewSalary`, as in `myNewSalary = predictRaise(mySalary)`. The `predictRaise()` method returns a numeric value, so it is appropriate to assign the returned value to a numeric variable.

Alternately, you can choose to use a method's returned value directly, without storing it in any variable. When you use a method's value, you use it the same way you would use any variable of the same type. For example, you can print a return value in a statement such as `print "New salary is ", predictRaise(mySalary)`. In this last statement, the call to the `predictRaise()` method is made from within the `print` statement. Because `predictRaise()` returns a numeric value, you can use the method call `predictRaise()` in the same way that you would use any simple numeric value. As another example, you can perform arithmetic with a method's return value, for example, `spendingMoney = predictRaise(mySalary) - expenses`.

CREATING INSTANCE METHODS IN A CLASS

In Chapter 2, you learned to create classes and endow them with data fields, or attributes, and methods and you learned that the concept of a class is useful because of its reusability. Objects gain their attributes from their classes, and all objects have predictable attributes because they are members of certain classes. For example, if you are invited to a graduation party, you automatically know many things about the object (the party). You assume there will be a starting time, a certain number of guests, some quantity of food, and some kind of gifts. You understand what a party entails because of your previous knowledge of the Party class of which all parties are members. You don't know the number of guests, what food will be served, or what gifts will be received at this particular party, but you understand that because all parties have guests and refreshments, then this one must too. Because you understand the general characteristics of a Party, you anticipate different behaviors than if you plan to attend a Theater Performance object or a Dentist Appointment object.

Class objects also have methods associated with them, and every object that is an instance of a class is assumed to possess the same methods. For example, for all `Party` objects, at some point, you must set the date and time. In a program, you might name these methods `setDate()` and `setTime()`. Party guests need to know the date and time, and might use methods named `getDate()` and `getTime()` to find out the date and time of any `Party` object.

Your graduation party, then, might have the identifier `myGraduationParty`. As a member of the `Party` class, `myGraduationParty`, like all `Party` objects, might have data methods `setDate()` and `setTime()`. When you use them, the `setDate()` and `setTime()` methods require arguments, or information passed to them. For example, statements such as `myGraduationParty.setDate("May 12")` and `myGraduationParty.setTime("6 p.m.")` invoke methods that are available for the `myGraduationParty` object. When you use an object and its methods, think of being able to send a message to the object to direct it to accomplish some task—you can tell the Party object named `myGraduationParty` to set the date and time you request. Even though `yourAnniversaryParty` is also a member of the Party class, and even though it also has `setDate()` and `setTime()` methods, the arguments you send to your `AnniversaryParty` will be different from those you send to `myGraduationParty`. Within any OO program, you are continuously making requests to objects' methods, and often including arguments as part of those requests.

Additionally, some methods used in an application must return a message or value. If one of your party guests uses the `getDate()` method, the guest hopes that the method will respond with the desired information. Similarly, within OO programs, methods are often called upon to return a piece of information to the source of the request. For example, a method within a Payroll class that calculates federal withholding tax might return a tax figure in dollars and cents, and a method within an Inventory class might return true or false, depending on the method's determination of whether an item is at the reorder point.

Figure 3-13 contains a class diagram for an `Employee` class similar to, but shorter than, one you analyzed in Chapter 2. Besides a data field for each Employee's ID number the class contains two methods.

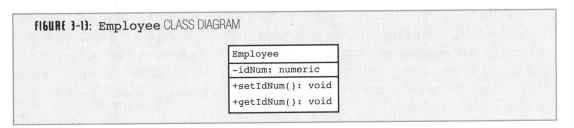

FIGURE 3-13: `Employee` CLASS DIAGRAM

```
Employee
-idNum: numeric
+setIdNum(): void
+getIdNum(): void
```

Figure 3-14 shows the pseudocode for the `Employee` class. This class becomes the model for a new data type named `Employee`; when `Employee` objects eventually are created, each will have its own `idNum` field, and each will have access to two methods—one that provides a value for its `idNum` field, and another that retrieves the value stored there.

FIGURE 3-14: Employee CLASS PSEUDOCODE

```
class Employee
      numeric idNum
      void setIdNum(numeric id)
         idNum = id
      return
      numeric getIdNum()
      return idNum
endClass
```

In Figure 3-14, the method `setIdNum()` is a void method—it returns nothing. It takes one argument—a value for the Employee's ID. The identifier `id` is local to the `setIdNum()` method, and holds a value that will come into the method from the outside. Within the method, the value in `id` is assigned to `idNum`, which is a field within the class. The `setIdNum()` method will assign a value to the `idNum` field for each separate `Employee` object you ever create. Therefore, a method, such as `setIdNum()` is called an **instance method** because it operates correctly yet differently, providing different values for each separate instance of the `Employee` class.

TIP ☐ ☐ ☐ ☐ | Object-oriented programmers also call instance methods nonstatic methods. **Static methods** are those for which no object needs to exist—like the main() method. **Nonstatic methods** are methods that exist to be used with an object created from a class.

In Figure 3-14, the method `getIdNum()` is a numeric method. It returns the value of the ID number back to any calling method. It is only through the `getIdNum()` method that any outside class can ever work with the ID number.

TIP ☐ ☐ ☐ ☐ | In many OO languages, methods that set values within and get values from an object most frequently start with "get" and "set". Using these three-letter prefixes with your method names is not required, but it is conventional.

TIP ☐ ☐ ☐ ☐ | Methods that set values are called **mutator methods**; methods that retrieve values are called **accessor methods**.

Declaring a class does not create any actual objects. A class is just an abstract description of what an object will be like if any objects are ever actually instantiated. Just as you might understand all the characteristics of an item you intend to manufacture long before the first item rolls off the assembly line, you can create a class with fields and methods long before you instantiate any objects which are members of that class. After an object has been instantiated, its methods can be accessed using the object's identifier, a dot, and a method call. For example, Figure 3-15 shows an application that instantiates two `Employee` objects. In this example, the two objects, `clerk` and `driver`, each use the `setIdNum()` and `getIdNum()` methods one time. The DeclareTwoEmployees application can use these methods because they are public; the methods provide the means for "getting at" the private `Employee` data. Figure 3-16 shows the output of the application.

FIGURE 3-15: THE `DeclareTwoEmployees` CLASS

```
public class DeclareTwoEmployees
     public static void main()
          Employee clerk
          Employee driver
          clerk.setIdNum(345)
          driver.setIdNum(567)
          print "The clerk's number is ",    clerk.getIdNum(),
               " and the driver's number is ",   driver.getIdNum()
     return
endClass
```

FIGURE 3-16: OUTPUT OF `DeclareTwoEmployees` APPLICATION

```
The clerk's number is 345 and the driver's number is 567
```

EXPLORING THE RATIONALE BEHIND DATA HIDING

Within the `DeclareTwoEmployees` class, you must use the public methods `setIdNum()` and `getIdNum()` to be able to set and retrieve the value of the `idNum` field for each `Employee` because you cannot access the private `idNum` field directly. For example the following statement would not be allowed:

                    `clerk.idNum = 789`

If you made `idNum` public instead of private, then a direct assignment statement would work, but you would violate an important principle of OO programming—that of data hiding using encapsulation. Data fields should usually be private and a client application should be able to access them only through the public interfaces, that is, through the class's public methods. However, you might reasonably ask, "When I write an application, if I *can't* set an object's data field directly, but I *can* set it using a public method, what's the difference? The field value is set either way!" Actually, the `setIdNum()` method in the `Employee` class in Figure 3-14 *does* accept any numeric value you send into it. However, you could rewrite the `setIdNum()` method to prevent invalid data from being assigned to an object's data fields. For example, perhaps your organization has rules for valid employee ID numbers—they must be no fewer than five digits, or they must start with a 9—or perhaps you calculate a check-digit that is appended to every employee ID number. The statements that enforce these requirements would be part of the `setIdNum()` method.

Similarly, a `get` method might control how a value is retrieved. Perhaps you do not want clients to have access to part of an employee's ID number, or perhaps you always want to add a company code to every ID before it is returned to the client. Even when a field has no data value requirements or restrictions, making data private and providing public `set` and `get` methods establishes a framework that make such modifications easier in the future.

TIP ☐ ☐ ☐ ☐ | Checking a value for validity requires decision making. You will begin to learn about making decisions in Chapter 5.

TIP ☐ ☐ ☐ ☐ | A check-digit is a number appended to a field, typically an ID number or account number. The check-digit ensures the number is valid. For example, an organization might use five-digit employee ID numbers in which the fifth digit is calculated by dividing the first four by 7 and taking the remainder. As an example, if the first four digits of your ID number are 7235, then the fifth digit is 4, the remainder when you divide the first four digits by 7. So the five-digit ID becomes 72354. Later, if you make a mistake, and enter your ID into a company application as 82354, the application would divide the first four digits, 8235, by 7. The remainder is not 4, and the ID would be found invalid.

TIP ☐ ☐ ☐ ☐ | You will not necessarily write set and get methods for every field in a class; there are some fields that clients will not be allowed to alter. Some fields will simply be assigned values, and some field values might be calculated from the values of others.

ORGANIZING CLASSES

Most classes you create will have more than one data field and more than two methods. For example, in addition to requiring an employee number, an Employee needs a last name, a first name, and a salary, as well as methods to set and get those fields. Figure 3-17 shows how you could code the data fields for `Employee`.

FIGURE 3-17: AN `Employee` CLASS WITH SEVERAL DATA FIELDS

```
public class Employee
    private numeric idNum
    private string lastName
    private string firstName
    private numeric salary
```

Although there is no requirement to do so, most programmers place data fields in some logical order at the beginning of a class. For example, `idNum` is most likely used as a unique identifier for each employee (what database users often call a **primary key**), so it makes sense to list the employee number first in the class. An employee's last name and first name "go together," so it makes sense to store these two `Employee` components adjacently. Despite these common-sense rules, you have a lot of flexibility in how you position your data fields within any class.

TIP ☐ ☐ ☐ ☐ | A unique identifier is one that should have no duplicates within an application. For example, an organization might have many employees with the last name Johnson or a salary of $400.00, but there will be only one employee with employee number 128.

You can place a class's data fields and methods in any order within a class. For example, you could place all the methods first, followed by all the data fields, or you could organize the class so that several data fields are followed by methods that use them, then several more data fields are followed by the methods that use them. This book will follow the convention of placing all data fields first so that you can see their names and data types before reading the methods that use them.

Even if the only methods created for the `Employee` class include one `set` method and one `get` method for each instance variable, eight methods are required. Consider an Employee record for most organizations and you will realize that many more fields are often required (such as address, phone number, hire date, number of dependents, and so on), as well as many more methods. Finding your way through the list can become a formidable task. For ease in locating class methods, many programmers store them in alphabetical order. Other programmers arrange values in pairs of `get` and `set` methods, an order that also results in functional groupings. Figure 3-18 shows how the complete class definition for an Employee might appear.

FIGURE 3-18: Employee CLASS WITH SEVERAL DATA FIELDS AND CORRESPONDING METHODS

```
public class Employee
     private numeric idNum
     private string lastName
     private string firstName
     private numeric salary

     public numeric getIdNum()
     return idNum

     public void setIdNum(numeric emp)
          idNum = emp
     return

     public string getLastName()
     return lastName

     public void setLastName(string name)
          lastName = name
     return

     public string getFirstName()
     return firstName

     public void setFirstName(string name)
          firstName = name
     return

     public numeric getSalary()
     return salary

     public void setSalary(numeric sal)
          salary = sal
     return
endClass
```

UNDERSTANDING THE ROLE OF THE this REFERENCE

After you create a class such as the **Employee** class in Figure 3-18, any number of **Employee** objects might eventually be instantiated from it. Each **Employee** will have its own **idNum**, **lastName**, and other values, and enough computer memory must be set aside to hold all the attributes needed for each individual **Employee**. Each **Employee** object also will have access to each method within the class, but because each **Employee** uses the same set of methods, it would be a waste of memory resources to store a separate copy of each method for each **Employee**. Luckily, in OO languages, just one copy of each method in a class is stored, and all instantiated objects can use that copy.

When you use an instance method with an object, you use the object name, a dot, and the method name—for example, `clerk.getIdNum()`. When you execute the `clerk.getIdNum()` method, you are running the general, shared `Employee` class `getIdNum()` method; the `clerk` object has access to the method because it is a member of the `Employee` class. However, within the `getIdNum()` method, when you access the `idNum` *field*, you access the `clerk`'s private, individual copy of the field. Because many `Employee` objects might exist, but just one copy of the method exists no matter how many `Employees` there are, when you call `clerk.getIdNum()`, the compiler must determine *whose* copy of the `idNum` value should be returned by the single `getIdNum()` method.

The compiler accesses the correct object's field because you implicitly pass the memory address of the `clerk` to the `getIdNum()` method. Depending on the language you use to write your programs, an object's memory address is called a **reference** or is said to be held in a **pointer variable**. Therefore, the memory address of an object that is passed to any object's instance method is called the **`this` reference** or the **`this` pointer**. The word `this` is a reserved word in most OO languages, and the syntax you employ to use it is a little different in each language. However, you can write pseudocode like that shown in Figure 3-19 to explicitly use the `this` reference. The two `getIdNum()` methods shown in Figure 3-19 perform identically. The first method simply uses the `this` reference without you being aware of it; the second method uses the `this` reference explicitly. You can interpret its meaning as returning the ID number of "this current instance of the class" that is being used to call `this`.

FIGURE 3-19: TWO VERSIONS OF THE `getIdNum()` METHOD, WITH AND WITHOUT AN EXPLICIT `this` REFERENCE

```
public numeric getIdNum()
return idNum

public numeric getIdNum()
return this.idNum
```

Usually you neither want nor need to refer to the `this` reference within the methods you write, but the `this` reference is always there, working behind the scenes, so that the data field for the correct object can be accessed.

 TIP As a example of an occasion when you might use the `this` reference explicitly, consider the following `setIdNum()` method and compare it to the version in the Employee class in Figure 3-18.

```
public void setIdNum(numeric idNum)
      this.idNum = idNum
return
```

In this version, the programmer has chosen to use the variable name `idNum` as the argument to the method as well as the instance field within the class. To differentiate the two, you explicitly use the `this` reference with the copy of `idNum` that is a member of the class.

AN INTRODUCTION TO USING CONSTRUCTORS

When you create a class, such as `Employee`, and instantiate an object with a statement such as `Employee chauffeur`, you are actually calling a method named `Employee()` that is provided by default by the compiler of the object-oriented language in which you are working. A constructor method, or more simply, a **constructor**, is a method that establishes an object. A **default constructor** is one that requires no arguments; in OO languages, a default constructor is created automatically by the compiler for every class you write.

When the prewritten, default constructor for the `Employee` class is called (the constructor is the method named `Employee()`), it establishes one `Employee` object with the identifier provided. Depending on the programming language, a default constructor might provide initial values for the object's data fields. If you do not want an object's fields to hold these default values, or if you want to perform additional tasks when you create an instance of a class, then you can write your own constructor. Any constructor method you write must have the same name as the class it constructs, and constructor methods cannot have a return type. Normally, you declare constructors to be public so that other classes can instantiate objects that belong to the class.

For example, if you want every `Employee` object to have a starting salary of $300.00 per week, then you could write the constructor for the `Employee` class that appears in Figure 3-20. Any `Employee` object instantiated will have a `salary` field value equal to 300.00, and the other `Employee` data fields will contain the default values.

FIGURE 3-20: The `Employee` class constructor

```
public Employee()
     salary = 300.00
return
```

You can write any statement in a constructor you like; it is just a method. Although you usually have no reason to do so, you could print a message from within a constructor or perform any other task. You can place the constructor anywhere inside the class, outside of any other method. Typically, a constructor will be placed with the other methods. Often, programmers list the constructor first, because it is the first method used when an object is created.

For example, consider the `Employee` class shown in Figure 3-21. Its constructor method assigns 999 to the `idNum` of each potentially instantiated `Employee` object. Any time an `Employee` object is created using a statement such as `Employee partTimeWorker`, even if no other data-assigning methods are ever used, you are ensured that the `partTimeWorker Employee`, like all `Employee` objects, will have an initial `idNum` of 999.

FIGURE 3-21: `Employee` class with constructor that initializes `idNum` field

```
public class Employee
     private numeric idNum
     Employee()
          idNum = 999
     return
endClass
```

TIP ▢ ▢ ▢ ▢ You can use a `setIdNum( )` method to assign values to individual `Employee` objects after construction, but a constructor method assigns the values at the time of creation.

Alternately, you might choose to create `Employee` objects with initial `idNum` values that differ for each `Employee`. To accomplish this when the object is instantiated, you can pass an employee number to the constructor; in other words, you can write constructors that receive arguments. Figure 3-22 shows an `Employee` class containing a constructor that receives an argument. With this constructor, an argument is passed using a statement, such as `Employee partTimeWorker(881)`. When the constructor executes, the numeric value within the method call is passed to `Employee()` as the argument num, which is assigned to the `idNum` within the constructor method.

FIGURE 3-22: `Employee` CLASS WITH CONSTRUCTOR THAT ACCEPTS A VALUE

```
public class Employee
    private numeric idNum
    public Employee(numeric num)
         idNum = num
    return
endClass
```

When you create an `Employee` class with a constructor such as the one shown in Figure 3-22, then every `Employee` object you create must be created using a numeric argument. In other words, with this new version of the class, the declaration statement `Employee partTimeWorker` no longer works. Once you write a constructor for a class, you no longer receive the automatically written default constructor. If a class's only constructor requires an argument, then you must provide an argument for every object of that class that you create.

TIP ▢ ▢ ▢ ▢ A class can contain multiple constructors. You will learn how to overload constructors in Chapter 11.

CHAPTER SUMMARY

☐ A method is a program module that contains a series of statements that carry out a task. To execute a method, you invoke it or call it from another method; the calling method invokes the called method. Any class can contain an unlimited number of methods, and each method can be called an unlimited number of times. Within a class, the simplest methods you can invoke don't require any data items (called arguments or parameters) to be sent to them, nor do they send any data back to you (called returning a value).

☐ An important principle of object-oriented (OO) programming is the notion of implementation hiding, the encapsulation of method details within a class. That is, when you make a request to a method, you don't know the details of how the method is executed. A calling method needs to understand only the interface to the called method. When you write the method declaration for a method that can receive an argument, you begin by defining the same elements as with methods that do not accept arguments—optional access modifiers, the return type for the method, and the method name. Additionally, you must include the following items within the method declaration parentheses: the type of the argument and a local name for the argument.

☐ You can pass multiple arguments to a method by listing the arguments within the call to the method and separating them with commas. When you call a method, the arguments you send to a method must match in order—both in number and in type—the arguments listed in the method declaration.

☐ The return type for a method can be any type, which includes numeric, character, and string, as well as class types including class types you create. Of course, a method can also return nothing, in which case the return type is **void**. A method's return type is known more succinctly as a method's type.

☐ Class objects have methods associated with them, and every object that is an instance of a class is assumed to possess the same methods.

☐ If you made class attributes public instead of private, then you violate an important principle of OO programming—that of data hiding using encapsulation. Data fields should usually be private and a client application should be able to access them only through the public interfaces, that is, through the class's public methods.

☐ Although there is no requirement to do so, most programmers place data fields in some logical order at the beginning of a class. For ease in locating class methods, many programmers store them in alphabetical order. Other programmers arrange values in pairs of "get" and "set" methods, an order that also results in functional groupings.

☐ When you use an instance method, the compiler accesses the correct object's field because you implicitly pass the memory address of the object to the method. Depending on the language you use to write your programs, an object's memory address is called a reference or is said to be held in a pointer variable. Therefore, the memory address of an object that is passed to any object's instance method is called the **this** reference or the **this** pointer.

❑ A constructor method, or more simply, a constructor, is a special method that establishes an object. A default constructor is one that is created automatically by the compiler.

KEY TERMS

A **method** is a program module that contains a series of statements that carry out a task.

When you **invoke** or **call** a method, you execute it.

The **calling method** invokes the **called method**.

Arguments or **parameters** are the data items sent to methods.

Returning a value sends a data value from a called method back to the calling method.

Abstraction is the programming feature that allows you to use a method name to encapsulate a series of statements.

The **method declaration** is the first line, or **header**.

The data type **void** means a method returns nothing.

Implementation hiding is a principle of object-oriented (OO) programming that describes the encapsulation of method details within a class.

The **interface** to a method includes the method's return type, name, and arguments. It is the part that a client sees and uses.

A **local variable** is known only within the boundaries of a method.

The arguments in a method call are often referred to as **actual parameters**.

The variables in the method declaration that accept the values from the actual parameters are the **formal parameters**.

A method's return type is known more succinctly as a **method's type**.

An **instance method** operates correctly for each separate instance of a class.

Static methods are those for which no object needs to exist.

Nonstatic methods are methods that exist to be used with an object created from a class.

Methods that set values are called **mutator methods**.

Methods that retrieve values are called **accessor methods**.

A **primary key** is a value that makes an object unique from all others; database designers frequently use this term.

A **reference** is an object's memory address.

A **pointer variable** holds a memory address.

The `this` **reference** or the `this` **pointer** is an object's memory address implicitly passed to an instance method.

A **constructor** is a method that establishes an object.

A **default constructor** is one that requires no arguments; the compiler automatically creates a default constructor when you create a class.

REVIEW QUESTIONS

1. **A(n) _____ is a program module that contains a series of statements that carry out a task.**

    a. object
    b. field
    c. attribute
    d. method

2. **Arguments are method _____.**

    a. return types
    b. parameters
    c. instructions
    d. names

3. **A method must include the all of following except _____.**

    a. a declaration (or header or definition)
    b. a body
    c. a return statement
    d. the name of the class of which it is a member

4. **A method that returns nothing _____.**

    a. is illegal
    b. has no return type
    c. must also take no arguments
    d. none of the above

5. **A method header can contain all of the following except _____.**

    a. access modifiers
    b. the method body
    c. the return type for the method
    d. a list of arguments

6. **You can place a method _____.**

    a. within a class
    b. within another method
    c. either of these
    d. none of these

7. **The encapsulation of method details within a class is known as _____.**

    a. overloading data
    b. implementation hiding
    c. orienting methods
    d. containing parameters

8. If a method requires an argument, the method header must include _____ .

    a. the type of the argument

    b. the type of and a value for the argument

    c. the type of and local name for the argument

    d. the type of, value of, and local name for the argument

9. When you use a variable name in a method call, it _____ the same name as the variable in the method header.

    a. can have

    b. cannot have

    c. must have

    d. must not have

10. Assume you have written a method with the header `void myMethod(numeric a, string b)`. Which of the following is a correct method call?

    a. `myMethod(12)`

    b. `myMethod(12, "Hello")`

    c. `myMethod("Goodbye")`

    d. It is impossible to tell.

11. Assume you have written a method with the header `numeric myMethod(string name, character code)`. The method's type is _____ .

    a. numeric

    b. string

    c. character

    d. void

12. Assume you have written a method with the header `string myMethod(numeric score, character grade)`. Also assume you have declared a numeric variable named `test`. Which of the following is a correct method call?

    a. `myMethod()`

    b. `myMethod(test)`

    c. `myMethod(test, test)`

    d. `myMethod(test,'A')`

13. If a method returns a value, then when you call the method, you _____ the returned value.

    a. must use

    b. must not use

    c. usually will want to use

    d. usually will not want to use

14. A `void` method _____ .

    a. returns nothing

    b. accepts no arguments

    c. has an empty body

    d. all of the above

15. A(n) _____ method operates correctly yet differently, providing different values for each separate object in a class.

    a. static
    b. variable
    c. instance
    d. case

16. In object-oriented programming, a client application should be able to access an object's attributes only through _____.

    a. polymorphism
    b. static methods
    c. public interfaces
    d. private inheritance

17. Within a class you create, you can place methods _____.

    a. in the order in which they are typically used
    b. in alphabetical order
    c. in numeric order by the number of arguments each requires
    d. any of these

18. An object's memory address is called a(n) _____.

    a. locator
    b. thesaurus
    c. orientation
    d. reference

19. The `this` reference is _____ passed to an instance method.

    a. explicitly
    b. implicitly
    c. never
    d. partially

20. A method that establishes an object is a(n) _____.

    a. instantiator
    b. constructor
    c. assembler
    d. complier

EXERCISES

1. Name any device you use every day. Discuss how implementation hiding is demonstrated in the way this device works. Is it a benefit or a drawback to you that implementation hiding exists for methods associated with this object?

2. **Complete the following tasks:**

   a. Create an application class named `Numbers` whose `main()` method holds two integer variables. Assign values to the variables. Pass both variables to methods named `sum()` and `difference()`. Create the methods `sum()` and `difference()`; they compute the sum of and difference between the values of two arguments, respectively. Each method should perform the appropriate computation and display the results.

   b. Add a method named `product()` to the `Numbers` class. The `product()` method should compute the multiplication product of two integers, but not display the answer. Instead, it should return the answer to the calling method, which displays the answer.

3. **Create an application class named `Monogram`. Its `main()` method holds three character variables that hold your first, middle, and last initials, respectively. Create a method to which you pass the three initials and which displays the initials twice—once in the order first, middle, last, and a second time in traditional monogram style (first, last, middle).**

4. **Create an application class named `Exponent`. Its `main()` method holds an integer value, and in turn passes the value to a method that squares the number and to a method that cubes the number. The `main()` method prints the results. Create the two methods that respectively square and cube an integer that is passed to them, returning the calculated value.**

5. **Create an application class named `Cube` that displays the result of cubing a number. Pass a number to a method that cubes a number and returns the result. The result is displayed from within the `main()` method.**

6. **Create an application class that contains a method that computes the final price for a sales transaction. The `main()` method contains variables that hold the price of an item, the salesperson's commission expressed as a percentage, and the customer discount, expressed as a percentage. Create a `calculation()` method that determines the final price and returns the value to the calling method. The `calculation()` method requires three arguments: product price, salesperson commission rate, and customer discount rate. A product's final price is the original price plus the commission amount minus the discount amount; the customer discount is taken as a percentage of the total price after the salesperson commission has been added to the original price.**

7. **Write a program that calculates and displays the amount of money you would have if you invested $1,000 at 5 percent interest for one year. Create a separate method to do the calculation and return the result to be displayed.**

8. **Complete the following tasks:**

   a. Create a class named `Pizza`. Data fields include a string for toppings (such as pepperoni), and numeric values for diameter in inches (such as 12), and price (such as 13.99). Include methods to get and set values for each of these fields.

   b. Create a class named `TestPizza` that instantiates one `Pizza` object and demonstrates the use of the `Pizza` set and get methods.

9. **Complete the following tasks:**

   a. Create a class named `Student`. A `Student` has fields for an ID number, number of credit hours earned, and number of points earned. (For example, many schools compute grade point averages based on a scale of 4, so a three-credit-hour class in which a student earns an A is worth 12 points.) Include methods to assign values to all fields. A `Student` also has a field for grade point average. Include a method to compute the grade point average field by dividing points by credit hours earned. Write methods to display the values in each `Student` field.

   b. Write a class named `ShowStudent` that instantiates a `Student` object from the class you created. Compute the `Student` grade point average, and then display all the values associated with the `Student`.

   c. Create a constructor method for the `Student` class you created. The constructor should initialize each `Student`'s ID number to 9999 and his or her grade point average to 4.0.

10. **Complete the following tasks:**

    a. Create a class named `Circle` with fields named radius, area, and diameter. Include a constructor that sets the radius to 1. Also include methods named `setRadius()`, `getRadius()`, `computeDiameter()`, which computes a circle's diameter, and `computeArea()`, which computes a circle's area. (The diameter of a circle is twice its radius, and the area is 3.14 multiplied by the square of the radius.)

    b. Create a class named `TestCircle` whose `main()` method declares three `Circle` objects. Using the `setRadius()` method, assign one `Circle` a small radius value and assign another a larger radius value. Do not assign a value to the radius of the third circle; instead, retain the value assigned at construction. Call `computeDiameter()` and `computeArea()` for each circle and display the results.

11. **Complete the following tasks:**

    a. Create a class named `Checkup` with fields that hold a patient number, two blood pressure figures (systolic and diastolic), and two cholesterol figures (LDL and HDL). Include methods to get and set each of the fields. Include a method named `computeRatio()` that divides LDL cholesterol by HDL cholesterol and displays the result. Include an additional method named `explainRatio()` that explains that HDL is known as "good cholesterol" and that a ratio of 3.5 or lower is considered optimum.

    b. Create a class named `TestCheckup` whose `main()` method declares four `Checkup` objects. Provide values for each field for each patient. Then display the values. Blood pressure numbers are usually displayed with a slash between the systolic and diastolic values. (Typical numbers are values such as 110/78 or 130/90.) With the cholesterol figures, display the explanation of the cholesterol ratio calculation. (Typical cholesterol numbers are values such as 100 and 40 or 180 and 70.)

CASE PROBLEM

In Chapter 2, you designed classes needed for a business simulation for Cost Is No Object—a car rental service that specializes in lending antique and luxury cars to clients on a short-term basis. You created class diagrams for Employee, Customer, Automobile, and RentalAgreement classes. Revise those classes, if necessary, so each contains at least three attributes. Write pseudocode for each of these classes, including implementing **get** and **set** methods for each field.

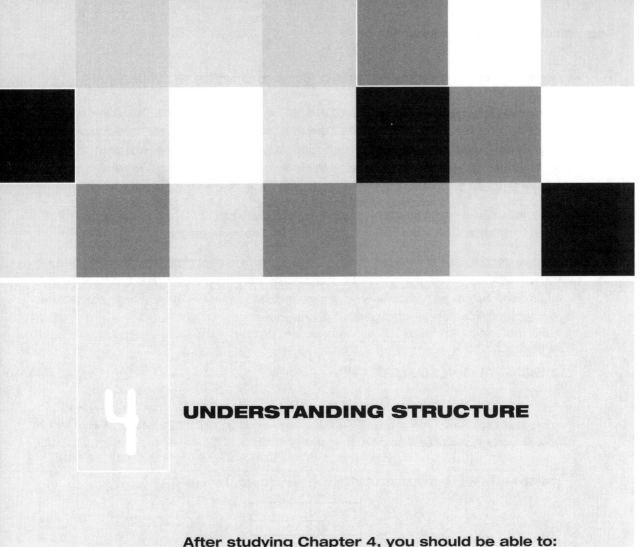

4

UNDERSTANDING STRUCTURE

After studying Chapter 4, you should be able to:

- ☐ Describe the role of structure in object-oriented methods
- ☐ Draw flowcharts
- ☐ Understand unstructured spaghetti code
- ☐ Understand the three basic structures of sequence, selection, and loop
- ☐ Build structured methods
- ☐ Use a priming read
- ☐ Understand the need for structure
- ☐ Recognize structure
- ☐ Describe two special structures—case and do until

THE ROLE OF STRUCTURE IN OBJECT-ORIENTED METHODS

When you write object-oriented programs, you create classes that you use to instantiate objects. These classes almost always contain private data as well as public methods. The nonstatic, instance methods you write for these classes include public get methods that retrieve the data stored in private fields, and set methods that assign values to the private class data fields. Classes often contain additional instance methods that accomplish tasks such as performing arithmetic computations with the values stored in the data fields or formatting output so it can be displayed in a useful way.

When you write object-oriented applications, you also sometimes create `static` methods—methods for which no object exists, but methods that might manipulate objects instantiated from prewritten classes.

Whether you are writing static or nonstatic methods, correct programming practice requires that your methods be **structured methods**—methods that follow a specific set of rules for their logical design, including containing a single entry and exit point. Methods can always be written in a nonstructured way, and they can still execute; however, in this chapter, you learn how and why to create methods that are structured.

DRAWING FLOWCHARTS

Methods within professional computer programs usually get far more complicated than the `main()` module from the `DeclareTwoEmployees` class in Chapter 3. The `Employee` class diagram and the `main()` method from the `DeclareTwoEmployees` class are shown in Figure 4-1.

FIGURE 4-1: THE `main()` MODULE FROM THE `DeclareTwoEmployees` CLASS

```
Employee
-idNum: numeric
+setIdNum(): void
+getIdNum(): void
```

```
public static void main()
     Employee clerk
     Employee driver
     clerk.setIdNum(345)
     driver.setIdNum(567)
     print "The clerk's number is ", clerk.getIdNum(),
           " and the driver's number is ", driver.getIdNum()
return
```

As an alternative to using the pseudocode in Figure 4-1 to plan the `main()` method for the `DeclareTwoEmployees` class, some programmers prefer to use a more graphical approach; many of these programmers use a flowchart. Figure 4-2 shows the flowchart for the `main()` method of the `DeclareTwoEmployees` class.

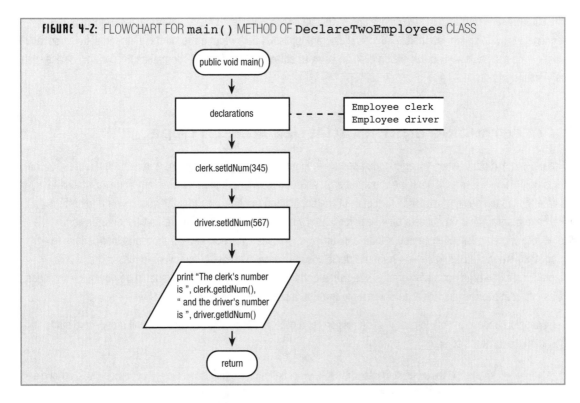

FIGURE 4-2: FLOWCHART FOR `main()` METHOD OF `DeclareTwoEmployees` CLASS

Figure 4-2 illustrates typical flowchart features. The method header and return statements each appear in a **lozenge**—a racetrack-shaped symbol that marks the beginning or end of a method. The task of the `main()` method is to provide declarations for the objects the method needs. In this case, two Employee objects are declared. The actual declarations appear in an **annotation symbol**—a three-sided box attached to the flowchart by a dashed line. The annotation symbol is used when you want to provide details for a step, though the details take a lot of room, not easily fitting within a flowchart symbol. In this case, only two objects are declared, so a programmer might choose to place the two Employee declarations within the main line of the flowchart. The flowchart examples in this book will list all declarations in an annotation box because some examples contain many declarations, and by placing the declarations in a consistent place, they will be easier for you to locate in a diagram.

The two processing statements of the `main()` method in Figure 4-2 appear in rectangles. **Processing statements** work with and alter objects. Typical processing statements include calls to get and set methods and arithmetic statements.

TIP ☐ ☐ ☐ ☐ | Recall that get and set methods are those that typically are included as public methods within classes to retrieve and provide values for private data fields.

TIP ☐ ☐ ☐ ☐ | In Figure 4-2, some programmers would prefer to place a horizontal stripe across the top of the processing steps that include the calls to `setIdNum()` and `getIdNum()`. This convention shows that the methods are predefined processes.

The output statement that prints the clerk's and driver's information in Figure 4-2 appears in a parallelogram. By convention, those who create flowcharts use a parallelogram to display both **input statements** (that read data in from an input device such as a keyboard or file on disk) and **output statements** (that send information to an output device such as a monitor or printer).

UNDERSTANDING UNSTRUCTURED SPAGHETTI CODE

The `main()` module whose pseudocode appears in Figure 4-1 and whose flowchart appears in Figure 4-2 contains only a few statements. Imagine the number of instructions in the computer program that NASA uses to calculate the launch angle of a space shuttle, or in the application the IRS uses to audit your income tax return. Even the program that produces a paycheck for you in your job contains many more instructions. Designing the logic for such an application can be a time-consuming task. When you add several thousand instructions to a program, perhaps including several hundred decisions, it is easy to create a complicated mess. The popular name for snarled program statements is **spaghetti code**. The reason for the name should be obvious—the code is as confusing to read as following one noodle through a plate of spaghetti.

For example, suppose you are in charge of admissions at a college, and you've decided to admit prospective students based on the following criteria:

- You will admit students who score 90 or better on the admissions test your college gives, as long as they are in the upper 75 percent of their high-school graduating class. (These are smart students who score well on the admissions test. Maybe they didn't do so well in high school because it was a tough school, or maybe they have matured.)

- You will admit students who score at least 80 on the admissions test if they are in the upper 50 percent of their high-school graduating class. (These students score fairly well on the test, and do fairly well in school.)

- You will admit students who score as low as 70 on your test if they are in the top 25 percent of their class. (Maybe these students don't take tests well, but obviously they are achievers.) Figure 4-3 summarizes the admission requirements.

FIGURE 4-3: ADMISSION REQUIREMENTS

Test score	High-school rank (%)
90–100	25–100
80–89	50–100
70–79	75–100

The flowchart for the module that determines admission status could look like the one in Figure 4-4. The method name used in the flowchart is `determineAdmission()`. As Figure 4-4 shows, flowchart decisions are represented using a diamond. Because every computer decision ultimately can be reduced to a two-possibility yes-or-no decision, each decision in a flowchart has one flowline leading into the question, and two flowlines leading out—one path representing the route to take when the answer to the question is "Yes" and the other path representing the route to take when the answer to the question is "No".

FIGURE 4-4: SPAGHETTI CODE EXAMPLE

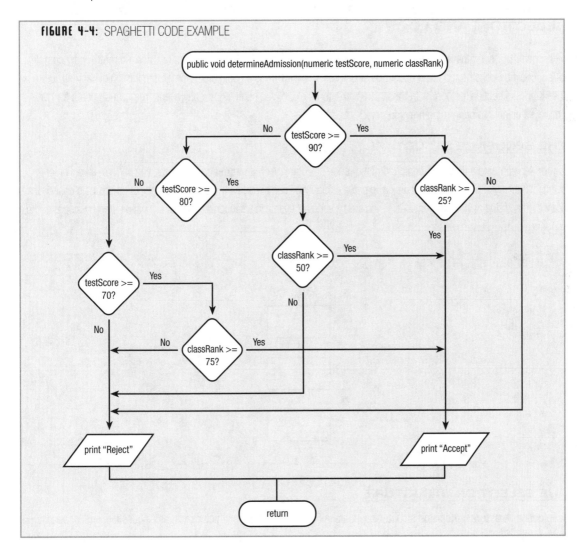

The kind of flowchart represented in Figure 4-4 is an example of spaghetti code. Many computer programs (especially older ones) bear a striking resemblance to the flowchart in Figure 4-4. The lines cross each other, and it is difficult to follow a path of logic. Such programs might "work"—that is, they might produce correct results—but they are very difficult to read and maintain, and their logic is difficult to follow.

UNDERSTANDING THE THREE BASIC STRUCTURES OF SEQUENCE, SELECTION, AND LOOP

In the mid-1960s, mathematicians proved that any program or method within a program or class, no matter how complicated, could be constructed using only three structures. A **structure** is a basic unit of programming logic; each structure is a sequence, selection, or loop. With these three structures alone, you can diagram any event, from printing data for two Employee objects to performing brain surgery.

THE SEQUENCE STRUCTURE

Figure 4-5 contains a flowchart depicting a sequence structure. With a **sequence structure**, you perform an action or event, and then you perform the next action, in order. A sequence can contain any number of events, but there is no chance to branch off and skip any of the events. Once you start a series of events in a sequence, you must continue step-by-step until the sequence ends.

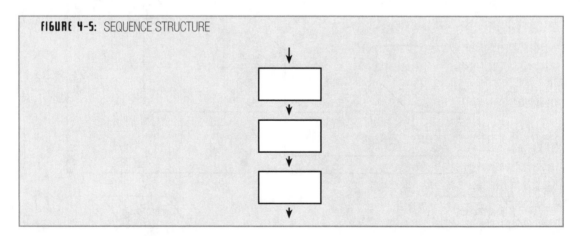

FIGURE 4-5: SEQUENCE STRUCTURE

THE SELECTION STRUCTURE

A **selection structure** or **decision structure** appears in Figure 4-6. With this structure, you ask a question, and, depending on the answer, you take one of two courses of action. Then, no matter which path you follow, you continue with the next event.

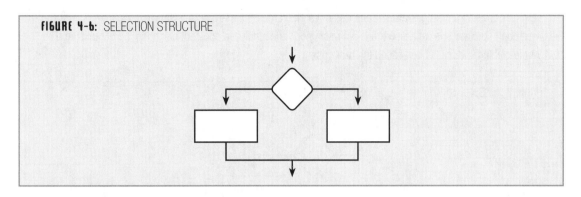

FIGURE 4-6: SELECTION STRUCTURE

Some people call the selection structure an **if-then-else** because it fits the statement

```
if someCondition is true then
    do oneProcess
else
    do the otherProcess
```

For example, while cooking you may decide

```
if we have brownSugar then
    use brownSugar
else
    use whiteSugar
```

Similarly, a payroll application might include a statement such as

```
if hoursWorked is more than 40 then
    calculate overtimePay
else
    calculate regularPay
```

The previous examples can also be called **dual-alternative ifs** because they contain two alternatives—the action taken when the tested condition is true, and the action taken when it is false. Note that it is perfectly correct for one branch of the selection to be a "do nothing" branch. For example:

```
if it is raining then
    take anUmbrella
```

or

```
if employee belongs to dentalPlan then
    deduct $40 from employessGrossPay
```

The previous examples are **single-alternative ifs**, and a diagram of their structure is shown in Figure 4-7. In these cases you don't take any special action if it is not raining or if the employee does not belong to the dental plan. The case where nothing is done is often called the **null case**.

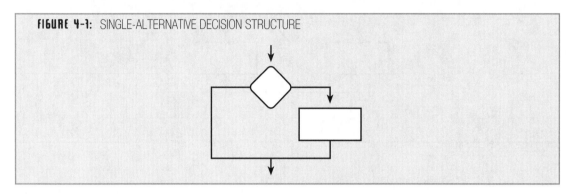

FIGURE 4-7: SINGLE-ALTERNATIVE DECISION STRUCTURE

THE LOOP STRUCTURE

Besides sequence and selection structures, you can use a third structure, a loop, as shown in Figure 4-8. In a **loop structure**, you ask a question; if the answer requires an action, you perform the action and ask the original question again. If the answer requires that the action be taken again, you take the action and then ask the original question again. This continues until the answer to the question is such that the action is no longer required; then you exit the structure. You may hear programmers refer to looping as **repetition** or **iteration**.

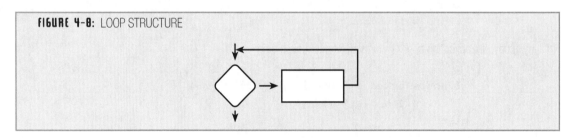

FIGURE 4-8: LOOP STRUCTURE

Some programmers call the loop structure a **while loop** or a **while-do loop** because it fits the statement

```
while testCondition continues to be true,
    do someProcess
```

You encounter examples of looping every day, as in

```
while you continue to beHungry
    take anotherBiteOfFood
```

or

```
while unreadPages remain in the readingAssignment
    read another unreadPage
```

In a business application, you might write

```
while quantityInInventory remains low
    continue to orderItems
```

or

```
while there are more retailPrices to be discounted
    compute a discount
```

BUILDING STRUCTURED METHODS

All logic problems can be solved using only these three structures: sequence, selection, and looping. Every method you ever write can be built from just these three structures, possibly combined in an infinite number of ways. For example, you can have a sequence of steps followed by a selection, or a loop followed by a sequence. Attaching structures end-to-end is called **stacking structures**. For example, Figure 4-9 shows a structured flowchart achieved by stacking structures, and pseudocode that might follow that flowchart logic.

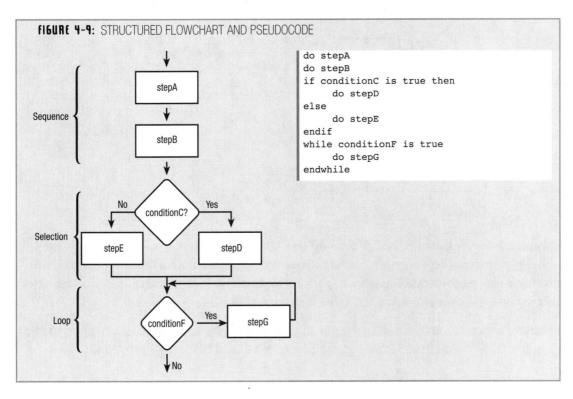

FIGURE 4-9: STRUCTURED FLOWCHART AND PSEUDOCODE

```
do stepA
do stepB
if conditionC is true then
     do stepD
else
     do stepE
endif
while conditionF is true
     do stepG
endwhile
```

The pseudocode in Figure 4-9 shows two end-structure statements—`endif` and `endwhile`. You can use an `endif` statement to clearly show where the actions that depend on a decision end. The instruction that follows `if` occurs when its tested condition is true, the instruction that follows `else` occurs when the tested condition is false, and the instruction that follows the `endif` occurs in either case—it is not dependent on the `if` statement at all. In other words, statements beyond the `endif` statement are "outside" the decision structure. Similarly, you use an `endwhile` statement to show where a loop structure ends. In Figure 4-9, while `conditionF` continues to be true, `stepG` continues to execute. If any statements followed the `endwhile` statement, they would be outside of, and not a part of, the loop.

Besides stacking structures, you can replace any individual steps in a structured flowchart diagram or pseudocode segment with additional structures. In other words, any sequence, selection, or loop can contain other sequences, selections, or loops. For example, you can have a sequence of three steps on one side of a selection, as shown in Figure 4-10. Placing a structure within another structure is called **nesting** the structures.

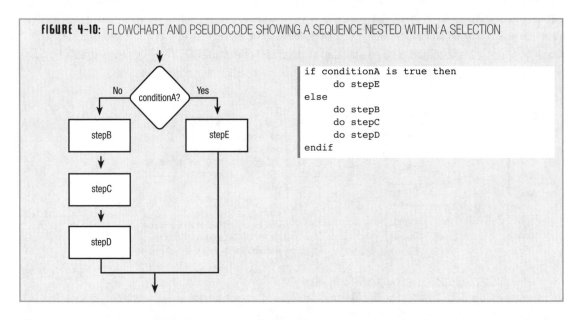

FIGURE 4-10: FLOWCHART AND PSEUDOCODE SHOWING A SEQUENCE NESTED WITHIN A SELECTION

```
if conditionA is true then
     do stepE
else
     do stepB
     do stepC
     do stepD
endif
```

When you write the pseudocode for the logic shown in Figure 4-10, the convention is to indent all statements that depend on one branch of the decision, as shown in the pseudocode. The indentation and the `endif` statement both show that all three statements (`do stepB`, `stepC`, and `stepD`) must execute if `conditionA` is not true. The three statements constitute a **block**, or group of statements that execute as a single unit.

In place of one of the steps in the sequence in Figure 4-10, you can insert a selection. In Figure 4-11, the process named `stepC` has been replaced with a selection structure that begins with a test of the condition named `conditionF`.

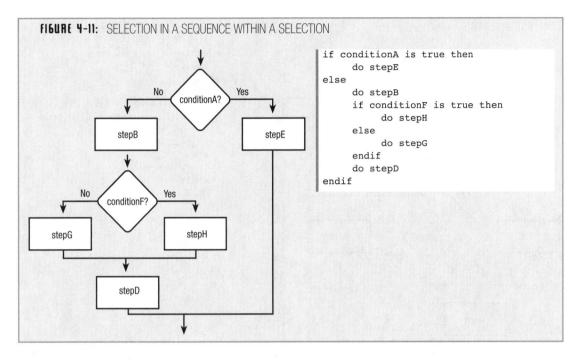

FIGURE 4-11: SELECTION IN A SEQUENCE WITHIN A SELECTION

```
if conditionA is true then
     do stepE
else
     do stepB
     if conditionF is true then
          do stepH
     else
          do stepG
     endif
     do stepD
endif
```

In the pseudocode shown in Figure 4-11, notice that `do stepB`, `if conditionF is true then`, `else`, and `do stepD` all align vertically with each other. This shows that they are all "on the same level." If you look at the same problem flowcharted in Figure 4-11, you see that you could draw a vertical line through the symbols containing `stepB`, `conditionF`, and `stepD`. The flowchart and the pseudocode represent exactly the same logic. The `stepH` and `stepG` processes, on the other hand, are one level "down"; they are dependent on the answer to the `conditionF` question. Therefore, the `do stepH` and `do stepG` statements are indented one additional level in the pseudocode.

Also notice that the pseudocode in Figure 4-11 has two `endif` statements. Each is aligned to correspond to an `if`. An `endif` always partners with the most recent `if` that does not already have an `endif` partner, and an `endif` should always align vertically with its `if` partner.

In place of `do stepH` on one side of the new selection in Figure 4-11, you can insert a loop. This loop, based on `conditionI`, appears inside the selection that is within the sequence that constitutes the "no" side of the original `conditionA` selection. In the pseudocode in Figure 4-12, notice that the `while` aligns with the `endwhile`, and that the entire `while` structure is indented within the true half of the `if` structure that begins with the decision based on `conditionF`. The indentation used in the pseudocode reflects the logic you can see laid out graphically in the flowchart.

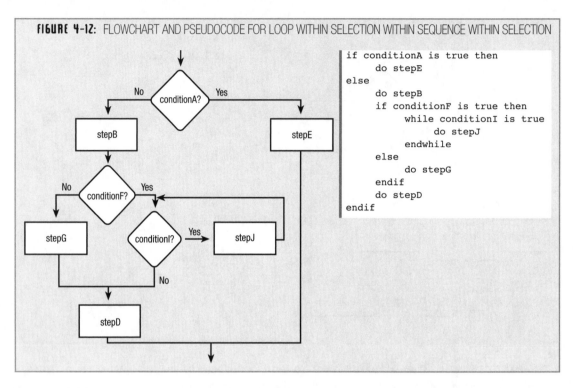

FIGURE 4-12: FLOWCHART AND PSEUDOCODE FOR LOOP WITHIN SELECTION WITHIN SEQUENCE WITHIN SELECTION

```
if conditionA is true then
    do stepE
else
    do stepB
    if conditionF is true then
        while conditionI is true
            do stepJ
        endwhile
    else
        do stepG
    endif
    do stepD
endif
```

The combinations are endless, but each of a structured method's segments is a sequence, a selection, or a loop. The three structures are shown together in Figure 4-13. Notice that each structure has one entry and one exit point. One structure can attach to another only at one of these entry or exit points.

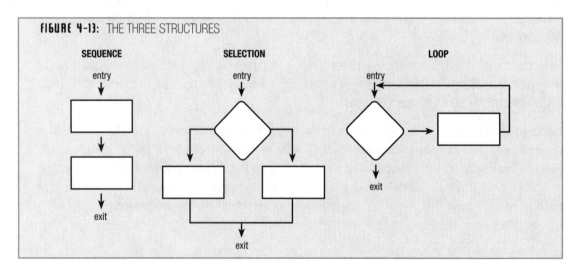

FIGURE 4-13: THE THREE STRUCTURES

 Try to imagine physically picking up any of the three structures using the "handles" marked entry and exit. These are the spots at which you could connect a structure to any of the others. Similarly, any complete structure, from its entry point to its exit point, can be inserted within the process symbol of any other structure.

In summary, a structured method has the following characteristics:

- A structured method includes only combinations of the three structures: sequence, selection, and loop.
- Structures can be stacked or connected to one another only at their entrance or exit points.
- Any structure can be nested within another structure.

 A structured method is never required to contain examples of all three structures; a structured method might contain only one or two of them. For example, many simple methods contain only a sequence of several events that execute from start to finish without any needed selections or loops.

 All programming languages contain a while statement to control loops. Most also contain a for statement you can use as a shorthand. You will learn about the for statement in Chapter 6.

USING A PRIMING READ

For a method to be structured and also work the way you want it to, sometimes you need to add extra steps. The priming read is one kind of added step. A **priming read** or **priming input** is the first read or data input statement that occurs before and outside of the loop that performs the rest of the input statements. If a method accepts user input or reads data records from an input file, you accept the first data item or record in a statement that is separate from all the other input statements. You must do this to keep each method structured.

Suppose you write a method that accepts a number input by a user, doubles the number, and displays the result. You want the method to continue to accept numbers and double them while the user continues to enter nonzero values. You might design the method to look like Figure 4-14.

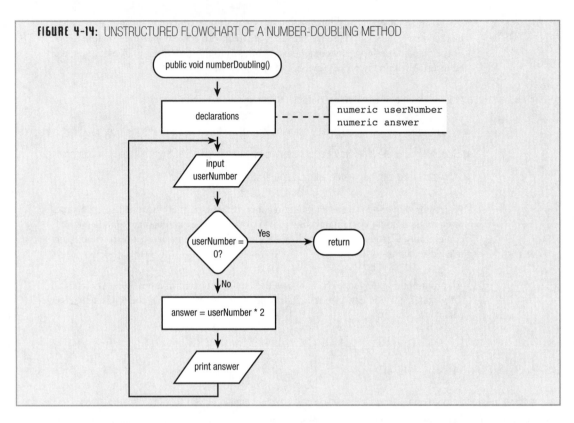

FIGURE 4-14: UNSTRUCTURED FLOWCHART OF A NUMBER-DOUBLING METHOD

At first, it might be hard to tell whether the flowchart in Figure 4-14 is structured. The flowchart in Figure 4-14 does not look exactly like any of the three allowed structures shown in Figure 4-13. However, because you may stack and nest structures while retaining overall structure, it might be difficult to determine at first glance whether a flowchart as a whole is structured. It's easiest to analyze the flowchart in Figure 4-14 one step at a time. The beginning of the flowchart looks like Figure 4-15.

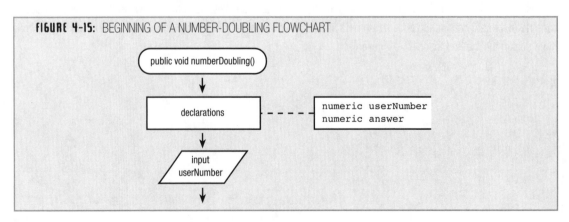

FIGURE 4-15: BEGINNING OF A NUMBER-DOUBLING FLOWCHART

Is the portion of the flowchart shown in Figure 4-15 structured? Yes, it's a sequence. Adding the next step, the flowchart looks like Figure 4-16.

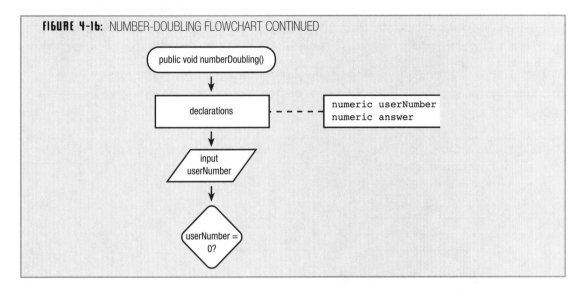

FIGURE 4-16: NUMBER-DOUBLING FLOWCHART CONTINUED

In Figure 4-16, the sequence is finished; either a selection or a loop is starting. You might not know which one, but you do know the sequence is not continuing, because sequences can't contain questions. With a sequence, each step must follow without any opportunity to branch off. Therefore, which type of structure starts with the question in Figure 4-16? Is it a selection or a loop?

With a selection structure, the logic goes in one of two directions after the question, and then the flow comes back together; the question is not asked a second time. However, in a loop, if the answer to the question results in the loop being entered and the loop statements executing, then the logic returns to the question that started the loop; when the body of a loop executes, the question that controls the loop is always asked again.

In the doubling problem in the original Figure 4-14, if the number the user enters is not 0, some math is done, an answer is printed, a new number is obtained, and the `userNumber = 0?` question is asked again. In other words, while the answer to the question about the user's input value continues to be *no*, eventually the logic will return to the same question. (Another way to phrase this is that while it continues to be true that 0 has not yet been entered, the logic keeps returning to the same question.) Therefore, the doubling problem contains a structure beginning with the `userNumber` question that is more like the beginning of a loop than it is like a selection.

The doubling problem *does* contain a loop, but it's not a structured loop. In a structured loop, the rules are:

1. You ask a question.
2. If the answer indicates you should perform one or more tasks, you do so.
3. If you perform the tasks, then you must go right back to repeat the question.

The flowchart in Figure 4-14 asks a question; if the answer is *no* (that is, while it is true that 0 has not been entered), the method performs two tasks: it does the arithmetic and it prints the results. Doing two things is acceptable because two steps constitute a sequence, and it is fine to nest a structure within another structure. However, when the sequence ends, the logic doesn't flow right back to the question. Instead, it goes *above* the question to get another number. For the loop in Figure 4-14 to be a structured loop, the logic must return to the loop-starting question when the sequence ends.

The flowchart in Figure 4-17 shows the flow of logic returning to the question immediately after the sequence. Figure 4-17 shows a structured flowchart segment, but the flowchart has one major flaw—it doesn't do the job of continuously doubling numbers.

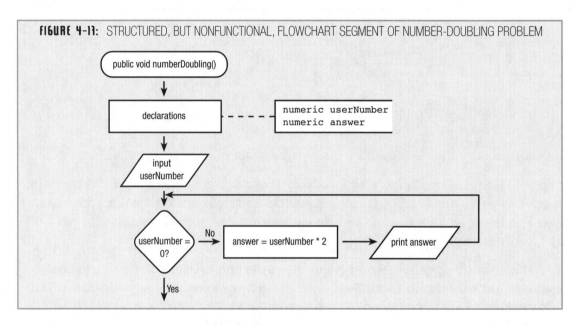

FIGURE 4-17: STRUCTURED, BUT NONFUNCTIONAL, FLOWCHART SEGMENT OF NUMBER-DOUBLING PROBLEM

Follow the flowchart in Figure 4-17 through a typical execution. Suppose when the method starts, the user enters a 9 for the value of **userNumber**. That's not 0, so the number doubles, and 18 prints out as the value of **answer**. Then the question **userNumber = 0?** is asked again. It can't be 0 because a new value for **userNumber** can't be entered. The logic never returns to the **input userNumber** step, so the value of **userNumber** never changes. Therefore, 9 doubles again and the answer 18 prints again. It's still not 0, so the same steps are repeated. This goes on *forever*, with the answer 18 printing repeatedly. The method logic shown in Figure 4-17 is structured, but it doesn't work; the logic in Figure 4-18 works, but it isn't structured!

TIP □ □ □ □ | The loop in Figure 4-18 is not structured because in a structured loop, after the steps that execute within the loop, the flow of logic must return directly to the loop-controlling question. In Figure 4-18, the logic does not return to the loop-controlling question; instead, it goes "too high" outside the loop to repeat the **input userNumber** step.

How can the number-doubling problem be both structured and work? Often, for a method to be structured, you must add something extra. In this case, it's an extra **input userNumber** step. Consider the solution in Figure 4-19; it's structured, *and* it does what it's supposed to do. The logic illustrated in Figure 4-19 contains a sequence and a loop. The loop contains another sequence.

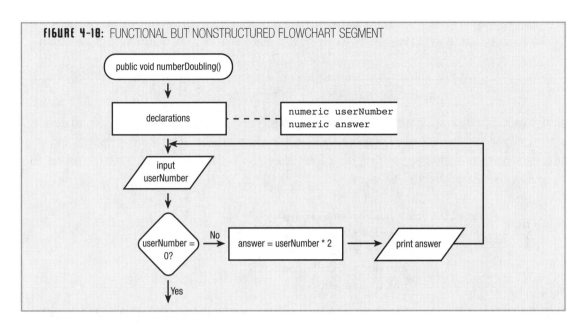

FIGURE 4-18: FUNCTIONAL BUT NONSTRUCTURED FLOWCHART SEGMENT

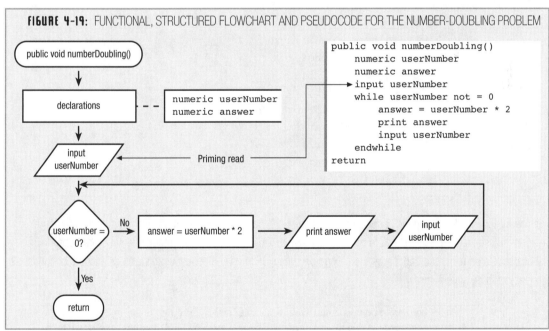

FIGURE 4-19: FUNCTIONAL, STRUCTURED FLOWCHART AND PSEUDOCODE FOR THE NUMBER-DOUBLING PROBLEM

```
public void numberDoubling()
    numeric userNumber
    numeric answer
    input userNumber
    while userNumber not = 0
        answer = userNumber * 2
        print answer
        input userNumber
    endwhile
return
```

The additional `input userNumber` step shown in Figure 4-19 is typical in structured methods. The first of the two input steps is the priming input, or priming read. The term *priming* comes from the fact that the read is first, or *primary* (what gets the process going, as in "priming the pump"). The purpose of the priming read step is to control the upcoming loop that begins with the `userNumber = 0?` question. The last element within the structured loop gets the next, and all subsequent, input values. This is also typical in structured loops—the last step executed within the loop alters the condition tested in the question that begins the loop, which in this case is the question that asks whether the user had input a 0.

As an additional way to determine whether a flowchart segment is structured, you can try to write pseudocode for it. Examine the unstructured flowchart in Figure 4-14 again. To write pseudocode for it, you would begin with the following:

```
public void numberDoubling()
        input userNumber
```

When you encounter the question in the flowchart that tests the user's input, comparing it to 0, you know that either a selection or looping structure should begin. Because you return to a location higher in the flowchart when the answer to the question is *no* (that is, while the user continues to enter values other than 0), you know that a loop is beginning. So you continue to write the pseudocode as follows:

```
public void numberDoubling()
      input userNumber
      while userNumber not = 0
             answer = userNumber * 2
             print answer
```

Continuing, the step after `print answer` is `input userNumber`. This ends the while loop that began with the question. So the pseudocode becomes:

```
public void numberDoubling()
        numeric userNumber
        numeric answer
        input userNumber
        while userNumber not = 0
             answer = userNumber * 2
             print answer
             input userNumber
        endwhile
    return
```

This pseudocode is identical to the pseudocode in Figure 4-19, and now matches the flowchart in the same figure. Creating the pseudocode requires you to repeat the `input userNumber` statement. The structured pseudocode makes use of a priming read and forces the logic to become structured—a sequence followed by a loop that contains a sequence of three statements.

TIP □ □ □ □ | Years ago, programmers could avoid using structure by inserting a "go to" statement into their pseudocode. A "go to" statement would say something like "after print answer, go to the first input number box", and would be the equivalent of drawing an arrow starting after "print answer" and pointing directly to the first "input number" box in the flowchart. Because "go to" statements cause spaghetti code, they are not allowed in structured programming.

Figure 4-20 shows another way you might attempt to draw the logic for the number-doubling method. At first glance, the figure might seem to show an acceptable solution to the problem—it is structured, containing a single loop with a sequence of three steps within it, and it appears to eliminate the need for the priming input statement. When the method starts, the question `userNumber = 0?` is asked. The answer is *no*, because the `userNumber` is set to 1 before the question is asked, so the method gets an input number, doubles, and prints it. Then, if it is still not 0, the method gets another number, doubles it, and prints it. The method continues until the user enters a 0, but the method does not stop after the input statement—instead it calculates and prints one last time. This last output is extraneous—the 0 value should not be doubled and printed. As a general rule, an input loop-ending question should always come immediately after an input statement. Therefore, the best solution to the number-doubling problem remains the one shown in Figure 4-19—the solution containing the priming input statement.

FIGURE 4-20: STRUCTURED BUT INCORRECT SOLUTION TO THE NUMBER-DOUBLING PROBLEM

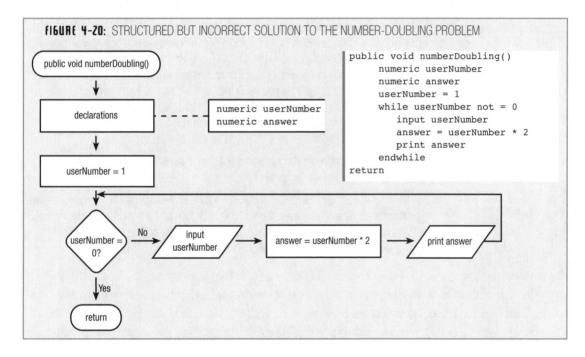

```
public void numberDoubling()
    numeric userNumber
    numeric answer
    userNumber = 1
    while userNumber not = 0
        input userNumber
        answer = userNumber * 2
        print answer
    endwhile
return
```

TIP □ □ □ □   A few languages do not always require the priming read. For example, when you write applications in Visual Basic that read data from a file, the language can "look ahead" to determine if the end of the file will be reached on the next input record. However, most programming languages cannot predict the end of file until an actual read operation is performed, and they require a priming read to properly handle file data. You will learn more about looping to handle data from an input file in Chapter 6.

UNDERSTANDING THE REASONS FOR STRUCTURE

At this point you may very well be saying, "I liked the original doubling method just fine. I could follow it. Also, the first method had one less step in it, so it was less work. Who cares if a method is structured?"

Until you have some programming experience, it is difficult to appreciate the reasons for using only the three structures—sequence, selection, and loop. However, staying with these three structures is better for the following reasons:

- *Clarity*—The doubling method is a small method. As methods get bigger, they get more confusing if they're not structured.

- *Professionalism*—All other programmers (and programming teachers you might encounter) expect your methods to be structured. It's the way things are done professionally.

- *Efficiency*—Most recent computer languages are structured languages with syntax that lets you deal efficiently with sequence, selection, and looping. Older languages such as assembly languages, Common Business-Oriented Language (COBOL), and Report Program Generator (RPG) were developed before the principles of structured programming were discovered. However, even programs that use those older languages can be written in a structured form, and many older languages, such as COBOL, have been updated to accommodate structured techniques. Structured methods are expected in professional programming environments today. Newer languages such as C#, C++, and Java enforce structure by their syntax.

- *Maintenance*—You, as well as other programmers, will find it easier to modify and maintain structured methods as changes are required in the future.

- *Modularity*—Structured methods can be easily broken into routines that can be assigned to any number of programmers. The routines are then pieced back together like modular furniture at each routine's single entry or exit point. Additionally, often a module can be used in multiple methods, saving development time in the new project.

Most programs that you purchase are huge, consisting of thousands or millions of statements. If you've worked with a word-processing program or spreadsheet, think of the number of menu options and keystroke combinations available to the user. Such programs are not the work of one programmer. Using object-oriented and structured techniques, the work can more easily be divided among many programmers. The objects created can communicate with each other, the code in their structured modules can be understood and revised more easily, and a large application can be developed much more quickly. Money is often a motivating factor—the more quickly you write a program and make it available for use, the sooner it begins making money for the developer.

Consider the college admissions module from the beginning of the chapter. It has been rewritten in structured form in Figure 4-21, and is easier to follow now. Figure 4-21 also shows structured pseudocode for the same problem.

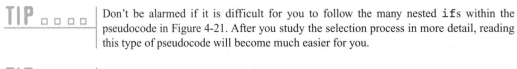

TIP   Don't be alarmed if it is difficult for you to follow the many nested **ifs** within the pseudocode in Figure 4-21. After you study the selection process in more detail, reading this type of pseudocode will become much easier for you.

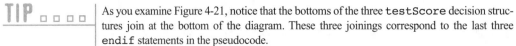

TIP   As you examine Figure 4-21, notice that the bottoms of the three **testScore** decision structures join at the bottom of the diagram. These three joinings correspond to the last three **endif** statements in the pseudocode.

FIGURE 4-21: FLOWCHART AND PSEUDOCODE OF STRUCTURED COLLEGE ADMISSION METHOD

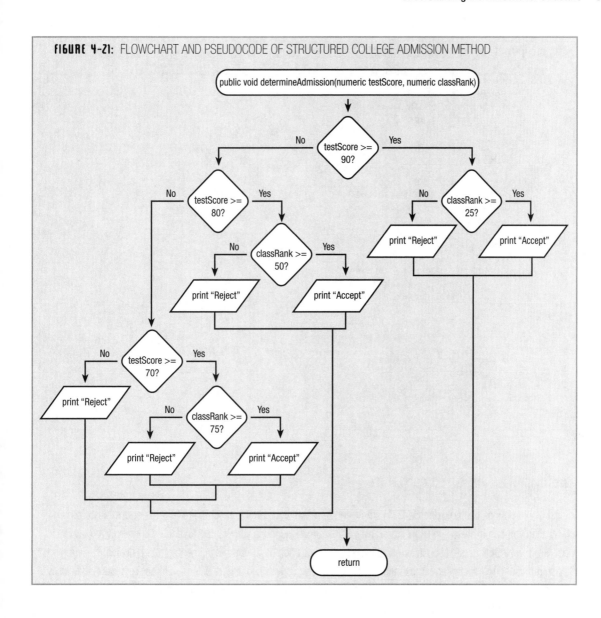

FIGURE 4-21: FLOWCHART AND PSEUDOCODE OF STRUCTURED COLLEGE ADMISSION METHOD (CONTINUED)

```
determineAdmission(numeric testScore, numeric classRank)
    if testScore >= 90 then
          if classRank >= 25 then
              print "Accept"
          else
              print "Reject"
          endif
    else
          if testScore >= 80 then
              if classRank >= 50 then
                  print "Accept"
              else
                  print "Reject"
              endif
          else
              if testScore >= 70 then
                  if classRank >= 75 then
                      print "Accept"
                  else
                      print "Reject"
                  endif
              else
                  print "Reject"
              endif
          endif
    endif
return
```

RECOGNIZING STRUCTURE

Any set of instructions can be expressed in a structured format. If you can teach someone how to perform any ordinary activity, then you can express it in a structured way. For example, suppose you wanted to teach a child how to play Rock, Paper, Scissors. In this game, two players simultaneously show each other one hand, in one of three positions—clenched in a fist, representing a rock; flat, representing a piece of paper; or with two fingers extended in a V, representing scissors. The goal is to guess which hand your opponent might show, so that you can show the hand that beats it. The rules are that a flat hand beats a fist (because a piece of paper can cover a rock), a fist beats a hand with two extended fingers (because a rock can smash a pair of scissors), and a hand with two extended fingers beats a flat hand (because scissors can cut paper). Figure 4-22 shows the pseudocode for the game.

FIGURE 4-22: PSEUDOCODE FOR THE ROCK, PAPER, SCISSORS GAME

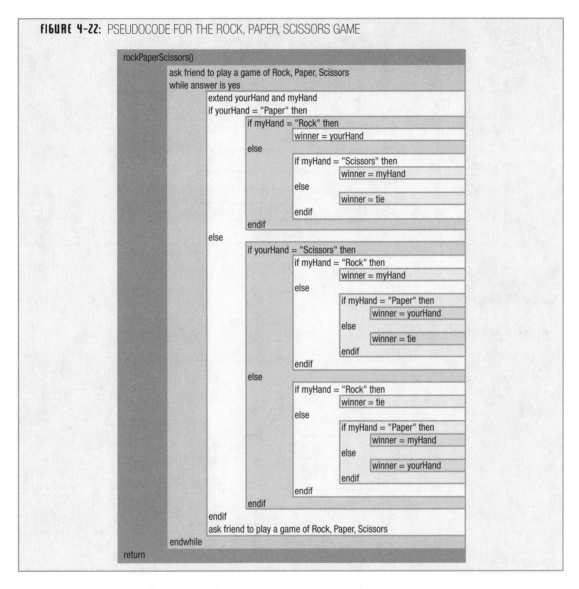

Figure 4-22 shows a fairly complicated set of statements. Its purpose is not to teach you how to play a game (although you could learn how to play by following the logic), but rather to convince you that any task to which you can apply rules can be expressed logically using only combinations of sequence, selection, and looping. In this example, a game continues while a friend agrees to play, and within that loop, several decisions must be made in order to determine the winner.

When you are just learning about structured program design, it is difficult to detect whether a flowchart of a method's logic is structured or not. For example, is the flowchart segment in Figure 4-23 structured?

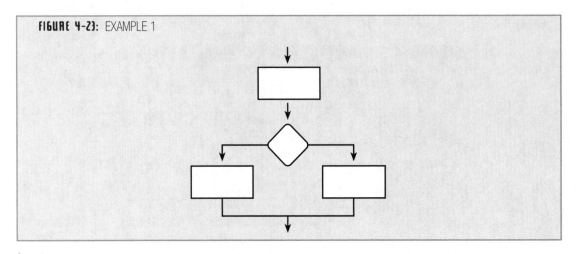

FIGURE 4-23: EXAMPLE 1

Yes, it is. It has a sequence and a selection structure.

Is the flowchart segment in Figure 4-24 structured?

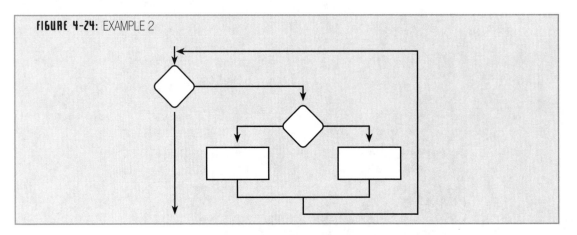

FIGURE 4-24: EXAMPLE 2

Yes, it is. It has a loop, and within the loop is a selection.

Is the flowchart segment in Figure 4-25 structured? (The symbols are lettered so you can better follow the discussion.)

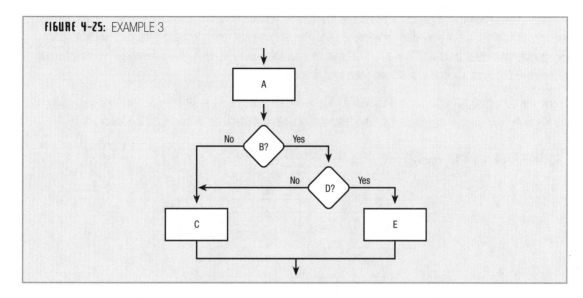

FIGURE 4-25: EXAMPLE 3

No, it isn't; it is not constructed from the three basic structures. One way to straighten out a flowchart segment that isn't structured is to use what you can call the "spaghetti bowl" method; that is, picture the flowchart as a bowl of spaghetti that you must untangle. Imagine you can grab one piece of pasta at the top of the bowl, and start pulling. As you "pull" each symbol out of the tangled mess, you can untangle the separate paths until the entire segment is structured. For example, with the diagram in Figure 4-25, if you start pulling at the top, you encounter a procedure box, labeled A (see Figure 4-26).

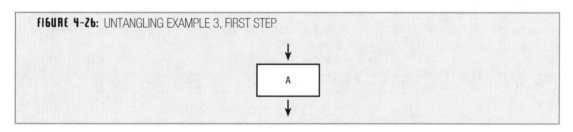

FIGURE 4-26: UNTANGLING EXAMPLE 3, FIRST STEP

A single process like A is part of an acceptable structure—it constitutes at least the beginning of a sequence structure. Imagine that you continue pulling symbols from the tangled segment. The next item in the flowchart is a question that tests a condition labeled B, as you can see in Figure 4-27.

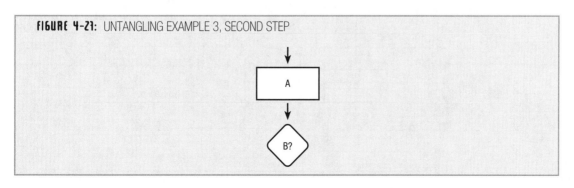

FIGURE 4-27: UNTANGLING EXAMPLE 3, SECOND STEP

At this point, you know the sequence that started with A has ended. Sequences never have decisions in them, so the sequence is finished; either a selection or a loop is beginning. A loop must return to the question at some later point. You can see from the original logic in Figure 4-27 that whether the answer to B is yes or no, the logic never returns to B. Therefore, B begins a selection structure, not a loop structure.

To continue detangling the logic, you pull up on the flowline that emerges from the left side (the "No" side) of Question B. You encounter C, as shown in Figure 4-28. When you continue beyond C, you reach the end of the flowchart.

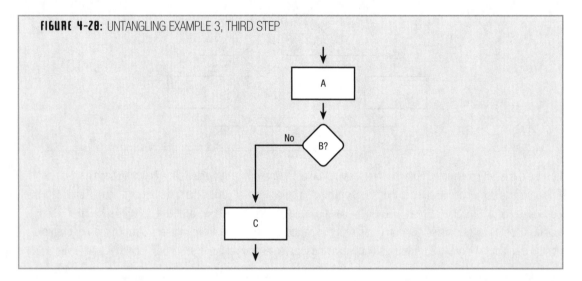

FIGURE 4-28: UNTANGLING EXAMPLE 3, THIRD STEP

Now you can turn your attention to the "Yes" side (the right side) of the condition tested in B. When you pull up on the right side, you encounter Question D (see Figure 4-29).

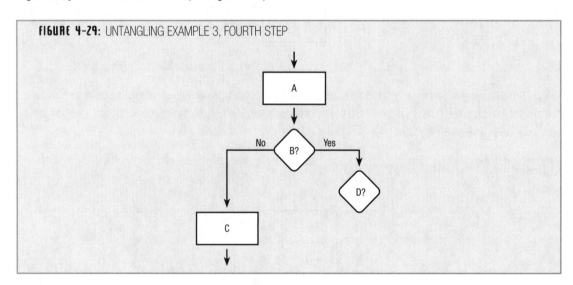

FIGURE 4-29: UNTANGLING EXAMPLE 3, FOURTH STEP

Follow the line on the left side of Question D. If the line is attached somewhere else, as it is (to Step C) in Figure 4-25, just untangle it by repeating the step that is tangled. (In this example you repeat Step C to untangle it from the other usage of C.) Continue pulling on the flowline that emerges from Step C, and you reach the end of the program segment, as shown in Figure 4-30.

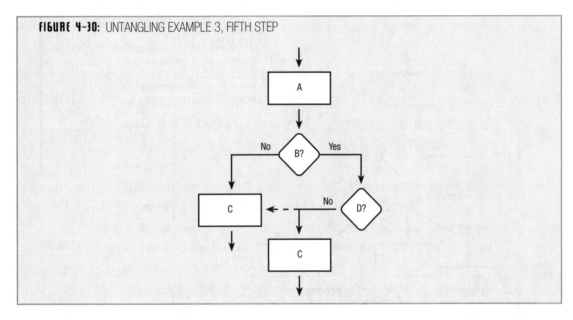

FIGURE 4-30: UNTANGLING EXAMPLE 3, FIFTH STEP

Now pull on the right side of Question D. Process E pops up, as shown in Figure 4-31; then you reach the end.

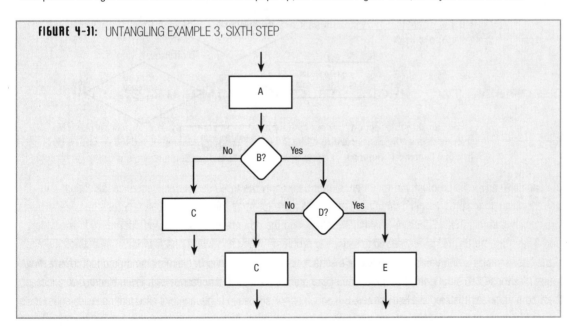

FIGURE 4-31: UNTANGLING EXAMPLE 3, SIXTH STEP

At this point, the untangled flowchart has three loose ends. The loose ends of Question D can be brought together to form a selection structure, then the loose ends of Question B can be brought together to form another selection structure. The result is the flowchart shown in Figure 4-32. The entire flowchart segment is structured—it has a sequence (A) followed by a selection inside a selection.

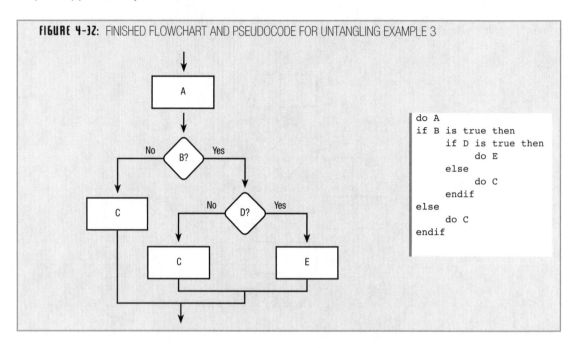

FIGURE 4-32: FINISHED FLOWCHART AND PSEUDOCODE FOR UNTANGLING EXAMPLE 3

```
do A
if B is true then
        if D is true then
                do E
        else
                do C
        endif
else
        do C
endif
```

TIP □ □ □ □ If you would like to try structuring a very difficult example of an unstructured application, see Appendix A.

DESCRIBING TWO SPECIAL STRUCTURES—CASE AND DO UNTIL

TIP □ □ □ □ You can skip this section for now without any loss in continuity. Your instructor may prefer to discuss the case structure with Chapter 5 (Making Decisions), and the do until loop with Chapter 6 (Looping).

You can solve any logic problem you might encounter using only the three structures: sequence, selection, and loop. However, many programming languages allow two more forms of the three basic structures: the case structure, which is an alternative decision-making structure, and the do until loop, which is an alternative to the while loop. These structures are never *needed* to solve any problem—you can always use a series of selections instead of the case structure, and you can always use a sequence plus a while loop in place of the do until loop. However, sometimes these two additional structures—the case and the do until—are convenient. Programmers consider them both to be acceptable, legal structures.

THE CASE STRUCTURE

You can use the **case structure** when there are several distinct possible values for a single variable you are testing, and each value requires a different course of action. Suppose you administer a school where tuition is $75, $50, $30, or $10 per credit hour, depending on whether a student is a freshman, sophomore, junior, or senior. The structured flowchart in Figure 4-33 shows a series of decisions that assigns the correct tuition to a student.

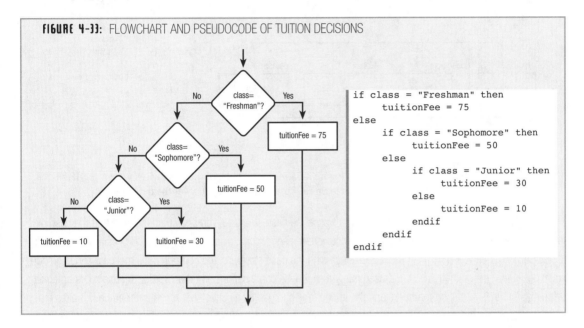

FIGURE 4-33: FLOWCHART AND PSEUDOCODE OF TUITION DECISIONS

```
if class = "Freshman" then
      tuitionFee = 75
else
      if class = "Sophomore" then
            tuitionFee = 50
      else
            if class = "Junior" then
                  tuitionFee = 30
            else
                  tuitionFee = 10
            endif
      endif
endif
```

The logic shown in Figure 4-33 is absolutely correct and completely structured. The `class="Junior"` selection structure is contained within the `class="Sophomore"` structure, which is contained within the `class="Freshman"` structure. Note that there is no need to ask if a student is a senior, because if a student is not a freshman, sophomore, or junior, it is assumed that the student is a senior.

Even though the program segments in Figure 4-33 are correct and structured, many programming languages permit using a case structure, as shown in Figure 4-34. When using the case structure, you test a variable against a series of values, taking appropriate action based on the variable's value. To many, such structures seem easier to read, and the case structure is allowed because the same results *could* be achieved with a series of structured selections (thus making the method structured). That is, if the first example is structured and the second one reflects the first one point by point, then the second one must be structured also.

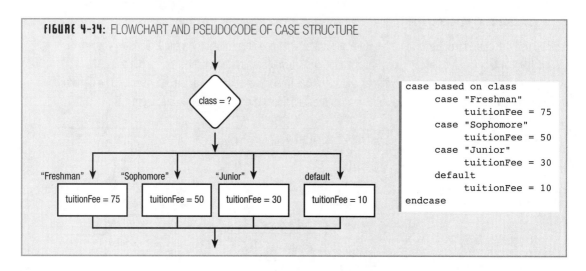

FIGURE 4-34: FLOWCHART AND PSEUDOCODE OF CASE STRUCTURE

```
case based on class
     case "Freshman"
          tuitionFee = 75
     case "Sophomore"
          tuitionFee = 50
     case "Junior"
          tuitionFee = 30
     default
          tuitionFee = 10
endcase
```

TIP □ □ □ □ | The term "default" used in Figure 4-34 means "if none of the other cases were true." Each programming language you learn may use a different syntax for the default case.

Even though a programming language permits you to use the case structure, you should understand that the case structure is just a convenience that might make a flowchart, pseudocode, or actual program code easier to understand at first glance. When you write a series of decisions using the case structure, the computer still makes a series of individual decisions, just as though you had used many if-then-else combinations. In other words, you might prefer looking at the diagram in Figure 4-34 to understand the tuition fees charged by a school, but a computer actually makes the decisions, as shown in Figure 4-33—one at a time. When you write your own programs, it is always acceptable to express a complicated decision-making process as a series of individual selections.

TIP □ □ □ □ | You usually use the case structure only when a series of decisions is based on different values stored in a single variable. If multiple variables are tested, then most programmers use a series of decisions.

THE DO UNTIL LOOP

Recall that a structured loop (often called a while loop) looks like Figure 4-35. A special case loop called a do until loop looks like Figure 4-36.

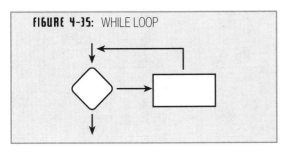

FIGURE 4-35: WHILE LOOP

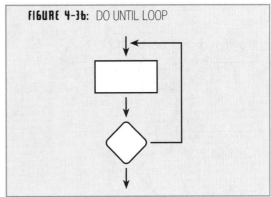

FIGURE 4-36: DO UNTIL LOOP

An important difference exists between these two structures. In a while loop, you ask a question and, depending on the answer, you might or might not enter the loop to execute the loop's procedure. Conversely, in a **do until loop** you ensure that the procedure executes at least once; then, depending on the answer to the controlling question, the loop may or may not execute additional times.

TIP ▫ ▫ ▫ ▫ | In a while loop, the question that controls a loop comes at the beginning, or "top," of the loop body. A while loop is also called a pre-test loop, because the test is made at the beginning. In a do until loop, the question that controls the loop comes at the end, or "bottom," of the loop body. For this reason, a do until loop is called a post-test loop.

You encounter examples of do until looping every day. For example:

```
do
      pay bills
until all bills are paid
```

and

```
do
      wash dishes
until all dishes are washed
```

In these examples, the activity (paying bills or washing dishes) must occur at least one time. You ask the question that determines whether you continue only after the activity has been executed at least one time.

You can duplicate the same series of events generated by any do until loop by creating a sequence followed by a while loop. For example:

```
pay bills
while there are more bills to pay
      pay bills
endwhile
```

Consider the flowcharts and pseudocode in Figures 4-37 and 4-38.

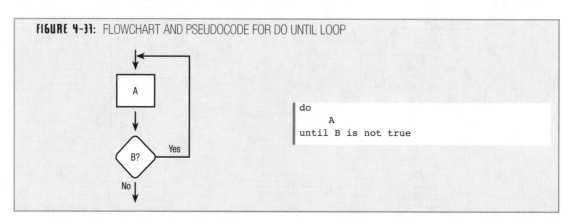

FIGURE 4-37: FLOWCHART AND PSEUDOCODE FOR DO UNTIL LOOP

```
do
    A
until B is not true
```

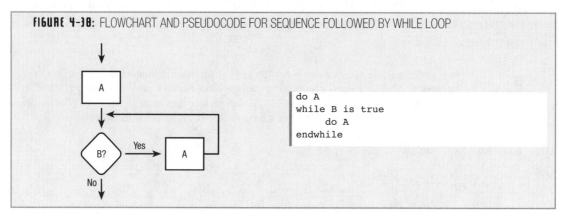

FIGURE 4-38: FLOWCHART AND PSEUDOCODE FOR SEQUENCE FOLLOWED BY WHILE LOOP

```
do A
while B is true
    do A
endwhile
```

In Figure 4-37, A is done, then B is asked. If B is yes, then A is done and B is asked again. In Figure 4-38, A is done, then B is asked. If B is yes, then A is done and B is asked again. In other words, both flowcharts and pseudocode segments do exactly the same thing.

Because programmers understand that a do until loop can be expressed with a sequence followed by a while loop, most languages allow the do until loop. Again, you are never required to use a do until loop; you can always accomplish the same events with a sequence followed by a while loop.

Figure 4-39 shows an unstructured loop. It is neither a while loop (that begins with a decision and, after an action, returns to the decision), nor a do until loop (that begins with an action and ends with a decision that might repeat the action). Instead, it begins like a do until loop, with a process followed by a decision, but one branch of the decision does not repeat the initial process; instead, it performs an additional new action before repeating the initial process. If you need to use the logic shown in Figure 4-39—performing a task, asking a question, and perhaps performing an additional task before looping back to the first process—then the way to make the logic structured is to repeat the initial process within the loop, at the end of the loop. Figure 4-40 shows the same logic as Figure 4-39, but now it is structured logic, with a sequence of two actions occurring within the loop. Does this diagram look familiar to you? It uses the same technique of repeating a needed step that you saw earlier in this chapter, when you learned the rationale for the priming read.

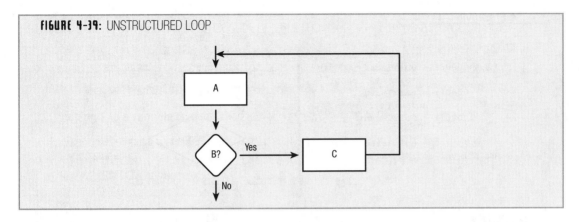

FIGURE 4-39: UNSTRUCTURED LOOP

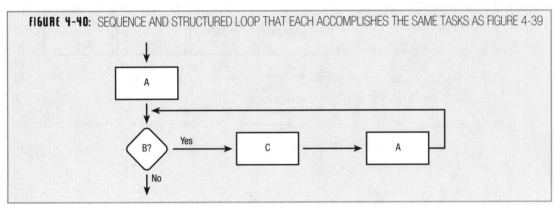

FIGURE 4-40: SEQUENCE AND STRUCTURED LOOP THAT EACH ACCOMPLISHES THE SAME TASKS AS FIGURE 4-39

TIP ▫ ▫ ▫ ▫

It is difficult for beginning programmers to distinguish between while and do until loops. You can think of a while loop as one that continues to execute while a condition remains true—for example, `while not end of file is true, process records`, or `while hungry is true, eat food`. On the other hand, a do until loop continues until some condition becomes false—for example, `address envelopes until there are no more envelopes`. When you use a do until loop, at least one performance of the action always occurs.

CHAPTER SUMMARY

- ☐ In a flowchart, the method header and return statements each appear in a lozenge. Declarations appear in an annotation symbol—a three-sided box attached to the flowchart by a dashed line. Processing statements appear in rectangles, while input and output statements appear in parallelograms.

- ☐ The popular name for snarled program statements is spaghetti code.

- ☐ Clearer programs can be constructed using only three basic structures: sequence, selection, and loop. These three structures can be combined in an infinite number of ways by stacking and nesting them. Each structure has one entry and one exit point; one structure can attach to another only at one of these entry or exit points.

- ☐ A priming read or priming input is the first read or data input statement prior to beginning a structured loop. The last step within the loop gets the next, and all subsequent, input values.

- ☐ You use structured techniques to promote clarity, professionalism, efficiency, and modularity.

- ☐ One way to straighten a flowchart segment that isn't structured is to imagine the flowchart as a bowl of spaghetti that you must untangle.

- ☐ You can use a case structure when there are several distinct possible values for a variable you are testing. When you write a series of decisions using the case structure, the computer still makes a series of individual decisions.

- ☐ In a while loop, you ask a question and, depending on the answer, you might never enter the loop to execute the loop's procedure. In a do until loop, you ensure that the procedure executes at least once. You can duplicate the same series of events generated by any do until loop by creating a sequence followed by a while loop.

KEY TERMS

Structured methods are those that follow a specific set of rules for their logical design, including containing a single entry and exit point.

A **lozenge** is a racetrack-shaped symbol that marks the beginning or end of a method in a flowchart.

An **annotation symbol** is a three-sided box attached to a flowchart by a dashed line. It is used when you want to provide details for a step, though the details take a lot of room, not easily fitting within a flowchart symbol.

Processing statements work with and alter objects. In a flowchart, they appear in a rectangle.

Input statements read data in from an input device such as a keyboard or file on disk. By convention, those who create flowcharts use a parallelogram to display input statements.

Output statements send information to an output device such as a monitor or printer. By convention, those who create flowcharts use a parallelogram to display output statements.

Spaghetti code is snarled, unstructured program logic.

A **structure** is a basic unit of programming logic; each structure is a sequence, selection, or loop.

With a **sequence structure**, you perform an action or event, and then you perform the next action, in order. A sequence can contain any number of events, but there is no chance to branch off and skip any of the events.

With a **selection** or **decision structure**, you ask a question, and, depending on the answer, you take one of two courses of action. Then, no matter which path you follow, you continue with the next event.

An **if-then-else** is another name for a selection structure.

Dual-alternative ifs define one action to be taken when the tested condition is true, and another action to be taken when it is false.

Single-alternative ifs take action on just one branch of the decision.

The **null case** is the branch of a decision in which no action is taken.

With a **loop structure**, you ask a question; if the answer requires an action, you perform the action and ask the original question again.

Repetition and **iteration** are alternate names for a loop structure.

A **while loop** or a **while-do loop** is a loop in which a process continues while some condition continues to be true.

Attaching structures end-to-end is called **stacking structures**.

Placing a structure within another structure is called **nesting** the structures.

A **block** is a group of statements that execute as a single unit.

A **priming read** or **priming input** is the first read or data input statement that occurs before and outside of the loop that performs the rest of the input statements.

You can use the **case structure** when there are several distinct possible values for a single variable you are testing, and each requires a different course of action.

In a **do until loop** you ensure that a procedure executes at least once; then, depending on the answer to the controlling question, the loop may or may not execute additional times.

REVIEW QUESTIONS

1. **Snarled program logic is called _____ code.**

   a. snake

   b. spaghetti

   c. string

   d. gnarly

2. **A sequence structure can contain _____.**

   a. only one event

   b. exactly three events

   c. no more than three events

   d. any number of events

3. **Which of the following is *not* another term for a selection structure?**

   a. decision structure

   b. if-then-else structure

   c. loop structure

   d. dual-alternative if structure

4. **The structure in which you ask a question, and, depending on the answer, take some action, then ask the question again can be called all of the following except _____.**

   a. if-then-else

   b. loop

   c. repetition

   d. iteration

5. **Placing a structure within another structure is called _____ the structures.**

   a. stacking

   b. nesting

   c. building

   d. untangling

6. **Attaching structures end-to-end is called _____.**

   a. stacking

   b. nesting

   c. building

   d. untangling

7. **The statement** `if age >= 65 then seniorDiscount = "yes"` **is an example of a _____.**

   a. single-alternative if

   b. loop

   c. dual-alternative if

   d. sequence

8. **The statement** `while temperature remains below 60, leave the furnace on` **is an example of a _____.**

   a. single-alternative if

   b. loop

   c. dual-alternative if

   d. sequence

9. **The statement** `if age < 13 then movieTicket = 4.00 else movieTicket = 8.50` **is an example of a _____.**

   a. single-alternative if

   b. loop

   c. dual-alternative if

   d. sequence

10. **Which of the following attributes do all three basic structures share?**

    a. Their flowcharts all contain exactly three processing symbols.

    b. They all contain a decision.

    c. They all begin with a process.

    d. They all have one entry and one exit point.

11. **The first input statement in an application or method that occurs outside of and before the loop that performs the rest of the input _____.**

    a. is called a priming input

    b. must be included in its own method

    c. is the only part of a program allowed to be unstructured

    d. executes hundreds or even thousands of times in most business programs

12. **A group of statements that execute as a unit is a _____.**

    a. cohort

    b. family

    c. sequence

    d. block

13. **Which of the following is acceptable in a structured program?**

    a. placing a sequence within the true half of a dual-alternative decision

    b. placing a decision within a loop

    c. placing a loop within one of the steps in a sequence

    d. all of the above

14. **Which of the following is *not* a reason for enforcing structure rules in computer programs?**

    a. Structured programs are clearer to understand than unstructured ones.

    b. Other professional programmers will expect programs to be structured.

    c. Structured programs can be broken into modules easily.

    d. Structured programs usually are shorter than unstructured ones.

15. **Which of the following is *not* a benefit of modularizing programs?**

    a. Modular programs are easier to read and understand than nonmodular ones.

    b. Modular components are reusable in other programs.

    c. If you use modules you can ignore the rules of structure.

    d. Multiple programmers can work on different modules at the same time.

16. **Which of the following is true of structured logic?**

    a. Any task can be described using the three structures.

    b. You can use structured logic with newer programming languages like Java and C#, but not with older ones.

    c. Structured programs require that you break the code into easy-to-handle modules or they will not compile.

    d. all of the above

17.   The structure that you can use when you must make a decision with several possible outcomes, depending on the value of a single variable, is the _____.

    a. multiple-alternative if structure

    b. case structure

    c. while structure

    d. do until structure

18.   Which type of loop ensures that an action will take place at least one time?

    a. a do until loop

    b. a while loop

    c. a do over loop

    d. any structured loop

19.   A do until loop can always be converted to _____.

    a. a while-do followed by a sequence

    b. a sequence followed by a while-do

    c. a case structure

    d. a selection followed by a while-do

20.   Which of the following is never required by any program?

    a. a while loop

    b. a do until

    c. a selection

    d. a sequence

EXERCISES

1.   Match the term with the following structure diagram. (Because the structures go by more than one name, there are more terms than diagrams.)

    1. sequence   5. decision

    2. selection   6. if-then-else

    3. loop   7. iteration

    4. while-do

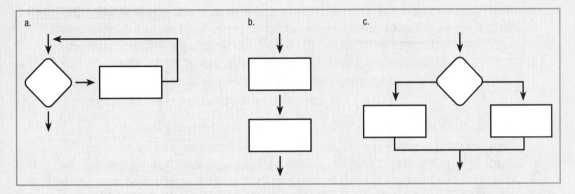

2. **Match the term with the pseudocode segment. (Because the structures go by more than one name, there are more terms than pseudocode segments.)**

1. sequence   4. decision

2. selection   5. if-then-else

3. loop   6. iteration

```
a.   while userNumber not = 0
         print theAnswer
     endwhile
b.   if inventoryQuantity  >  0 then
         do fillOrderProcess
     else
         do backOrderNotification
     endif
c.   do localTaxCalculation
     do stateTaxCalculation
     do federalTaxCalculation
```

3. **Is each of the following segments structured, or unstructured? If unstructured, redraw it so that it does the same thing but is structured.**

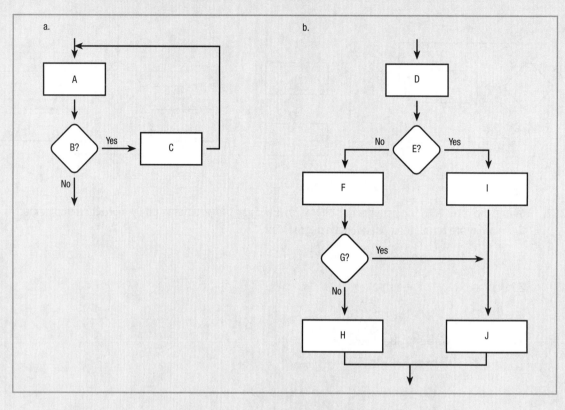

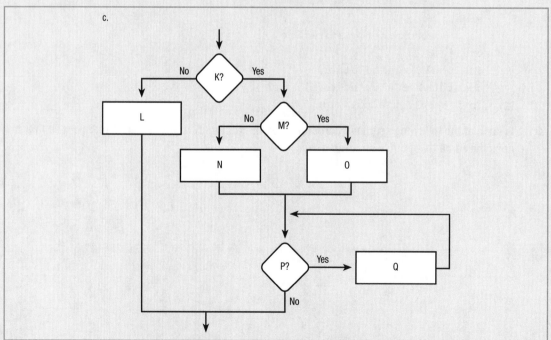

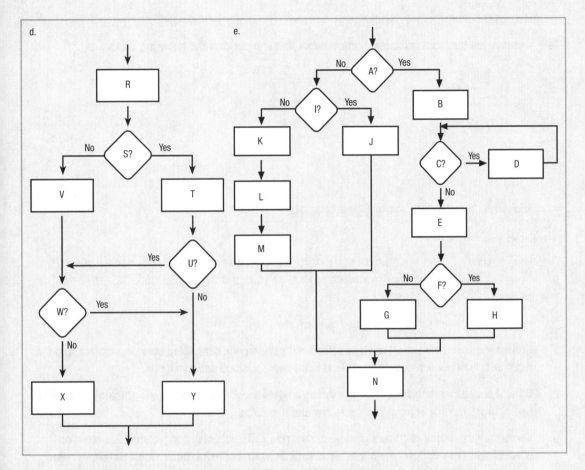

d.

e.

4. Write pseudocode for each example (a through e) in Exercise 3.

5. Assume you have created a mechanical arm that can hold a pen. The arm can perform the following tasks:

☐ Lower the pen to a piece of paper.

☐ Raise the pen from the paper.

☐ Move the pen one inch along a straight line (if the pen is lowered, this action draws a one-inch line from left to right; if the pen is raised, this action just repositions the pen one inch to the right).

☐ Turn 90 degrees to the right.

☐ Draw a circle that is one inch in diameter.

Draw a structured flowchart or write pseudocode that would describe the logic that would cause the arm to draw the following:

a. a one-inch square
b. a two-inch by one-inch rectangle
c. a string of three beads

Have a fellow student act as the mechanical arm and carry out your instructions.

6. **Assume you have created a mechanical robot that can perform the following tasks:**

   ☐ Stand up.

   ☐ Sit down.

   ☐ Turn left 90 degrees.

   ☐ Turn right 90 degrees.

   ☐ Take a step.

   Additionally, the robot can determine the answer to one test condition:

   ☐ Am I touching something?

   Place two chairs 20 feet apart, directly facing each other. Draw a structured flowchart or write pseudocode that would describe the logic that would allow the robot to start from a sitting position in one chair, cross the room, and end up sitting in the other chair.

   Have a fellow student act as the robot and carry out your instructions.

7. **Draw a structured flowchart or write structured pseudocode describing your preparation to go to work or school in the morning. Include at least two decisions and two loops.**

8. **Draw a structured flowchart or write structured pseudocode describing your preparation to go to bed at night. Include at least two decisions and two loops.**

9. **Choose a very simple children's game and describe its logic, using a structured flowchart or pseudocode. For example, you might try to explain Musical Chairs; Duck, Duck, Goose; the card game War; or the elimination game Eenie, Meenie, Minie, Moe.**

10. **Draw a structured flowchart or write structured pseudocode describing how your paycheck is calculated. Include at least two decisions.**

11. **Draw a structured flowchart or write structured pseudocode describing the steps a retail store employee should follow to process a customer purchase. Include at least two decisions.**

CASE PROBLEM

In Chapter 3, you continued to develop classes needed for Cost is No Object—a car rental service that specializes in lending antique and luxury cars to clients on a short-term basis. You created pseudocode for `Employee`, `Customer`, `Automobile`, and `RentalAgreement` classes including attributes and methods to get and set those attributes. Draw a structured flowchart or write structured pseudocode describing the process you envision a clerk would execute in order to rent an `Automobile` to a `Customer`. Include at least three decisions and two loops in your logic including, but not limited to, checking the renter's driving record and credit worthiness, explaining the rental agreement, and so on.

5

MAKING DECISIONS

After studying Chapter 5, you should be able to:

- [ ] Evaluate Boolean expressions to make comparisons
- [ ] Use the relational comparison operators
- [ ] Make decisions with objects
- [ ] Understand AND logic
- [ ] Understand OR logic
- [ ] Use selections within ranges
- [ ] Understand common errors using range checks
- [ ] Understand precedence when combining AND and OR selections
- [ ] Understand the case structure
- [ ] Use a decision table

EVALUATING BOOLEAN EXPRESSIONS TO MAKE COMPARISONS

The reason people frequently think computers are smart lies in the computer program's ability to make decisions. A medical diagnosis program that can decide if your symptoms fit various disease profiles seems quite intelligent, as does a program that can offer you different potential vacation routes based on your destination.

The selection structure (sometimes called a decision structure) involved in such programs is not new to you—it's one of the basic structures of structured programming you learned about in Chapter 4. See Figures 5-1 and 5-2.

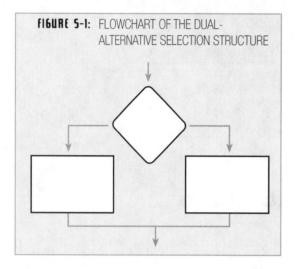

FIGURE 5-1: FLOWCHART OF THE DUAL-ALTERNATIVE SELECTION STRUCTURE

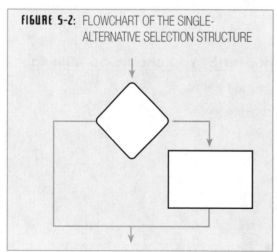

FIGURE 5-2: FLOWCHART OF THE SINGLE-ALTERNATIVE SELECTION STRUCTURE

You can refer to the structure in Figure 5-1 as a **dual-alternative**, or **binary**, selection because there is an action associated with each of two possible outcomes: depending on the answer to the question represented by the diamond, the logical flow proceeds either to the left branch of the structure or to the right. The choices are mutually exclusive; that is, the logic can flow only to one of the two alternatives, never to both. This selection structure is also called an **if-then-else** structure because it fits the statement:

```
if the answer to the question is yes, then
    do something
else
    do somethingElse
endif
```

The flowchart segment in Figure 5-2 represents a **single-alternative**, or **unary**, selection where action is required for only one outcome of the question. You call this form of the if-then-else structure an **if-then**, because no alternative or "else" action is necessary.

TIP ▯ ▯ ▯ ▯ | You can call a single-alternative decision (or selection) a *single-sided decision*. Similarly, a dual-alternative decision is a *double-sided decision* (or selection).

For example, Figure 5-3 shows the flowchart and pseudocode for a typical if-then-else decision in a business program. Many organizations pay employees time and a half (one and one-half times their usual hourly rate) for hours in excess of 40 per week. The logic segments in the figure show this decision.

FIGURE 5-3: FLOWCHART AND PSEUDOCODE FOR OVERTIME PAY DECISION

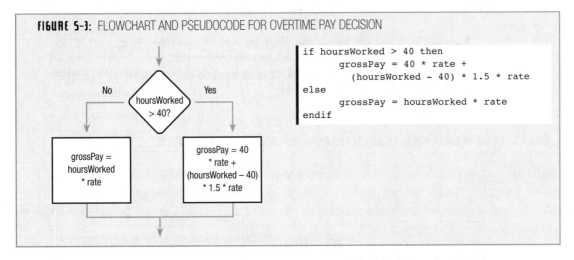

```
if hoursWorked > 40 then
        grossPay = 40 * rate +
            (hoursWorked - 40) * 1.5 * rate
else
        grossPay = hoursWorked * rate
endif
```

In the example in Figure 5-3, the longer calculation that adds a time-and-a-half factor to an employee's gross pay executes only when the expression `hoursWorked > 40` is true. The long calculation exists in the **if clause** of the decision—the part of the decision that holds the action or actions that execute when the tested condition in the decision is true. The shorter calculation, which produces `grossPay` by multiplying `hoursWorked` by `rate`, constitutes the **else clause** of the decision—the part that executes only when the tested condition in the decision is false.

The typical if-then decision in Figure 5-4 shows the employee's paycheck being reduced if the employee participates in the dental plan. No action is taken if the employee is not a dental plan participant.

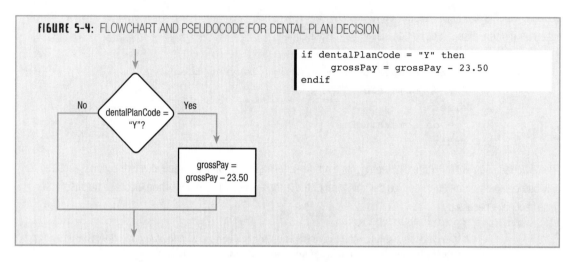

FIGURE 5-4: FLOWCHART AND PSEUDOCODE FOR DENTAL PLAN DECISION

```
if dentalPlanCode = "Y" then
     grossPay = grossPay - 23.50
endif
```

The expressions `hoursWorked > 40` and `dentalPlanCode = "Y"` that appear in Figures 5-3 and 5-4 are Boolean expressions. A **Boolean expression** is one that represents only one of two states, usually expressed as true or false. Every decision you make in a computer program involves evaluating a Boolean expression. True/false evaluation is "natural" from a computer's standpoint, because computer circuitry consists of two-state, on-off switches, often represented by 1 or 0. Every computer decision yields a true-or-false, yes-or-no, 1-or-0 result.

TIP ◻ ◻ ◻ ◻ | George Boole was a mathematician who lived from 1815 to 1864. He approached logic more simply than his predecessors did, by expressing logical selections with common algebraic symbols. He is considered the founder of mathematical logic, and Boolean (true/false) expressions are named for him.

USING THE RELATIONAL COMPARISON OPERATORS

Usually, you can compare only values that are of the same type; that is, you can compare numeric values to other numeric values, and character values to other characters. You can ask every programming question by using one of only three types of comparison operators in a Boolean expression. For any two values that are the same type, you can decide whether:

- The two values are equal.
- The first value is greater than the second value.
- The first value is less than the second value.

TIP ◻ ◻ ◻ ◻ | Usually, character variables are not considered to be equal unless they are identical, including the spacing and whether they appear in upper or lowercase. For example, "black pen" is *not* equal to "blackpen", "BLACK PEN", or "Black Pen".

TIP □ □ □ □ | Some programming languages allow you to compare a character to a number. If this is the case, then a single character's numeric code value is used in the comparison. For example, most microcomputers use the American Standard Code for Information Interchange (ASCII) coding system or the Unicode system. In both these coding schemes, an uppercase "A" is represented numerically as a 65, an uppercase "B" is a 66, and so on.

In any Boolean expression, the two values compared can be either variables or constants. For example, the expression `currentTotal = 100?` compares a variable, `currentTotal`, to a numeric constant, 100. Depending on the `currentTotal` value, the expression is true or false. In the expression `currentTotal = previousTotal?`, both values are variables, and the result is also true or false depending on the values stored in each of the two variables. Although it's legal to do so, you would never use expressions in which you compare two constants, for example `20 = 20?` or `30 = 40?`. Such expressions are considered **trivial** because each will always evaluate to the same result: true for `20 = 20?` and false for `30 = 40?`.

Each programming language supports its own set of **relational comparison operators**, or comparison symbols, that express these Boolean tests. For example, many languages such as Visual Basic and Pascal use the equal sign (=) to express testing for equivalency, so `balanceDue = 0?` compares `balanceDue` to zero. COBOL programmers can use the equal sign, but they also can spell out the expression, as in `balanceDue equal to 0?`. Report Program Generator (RPG) programmers use the two-letter operator `EQ` in place of a symbol. C#, C++, and Java programmers use two equal signs to test for equivalency, so they write `balanceDue == 0?` to compare the two values. Although each programming language supports its own syntax for comparing values' equivalency, all languages provide for the same logical concept of equivalency.

 TIP □ □ □ □ | The reason some languages use two equal signs for comparisons is to avoid confusion with assignment statements such as `balanceDue = 0`. In C++ or Java, this statement only assigns the value 0 to `balanceDue`; it does not compare `balanceDue` to zero.

 TIP □ □ □ □ | Whenever you use a comparison operator, you must provide a value on each side of the operator. Comparison operators are sometimes called *binary operators* because of this requirement.

Most languages allow you to use the algebraic signs for greater than (>) and less than (<) to make the corresponding comparisons. In addition to the three basic comparisons of equal to, greater than, and less than, most programming languages provide three others. For any two values that are the same type, you can decide whether:

- The first is greater than or equal to the second.
- The first is less than or equal to the second.
- The two are not equal.

Most programming languages allow you to express "greater than or equal to" by typing a greater-than sign immediately followed by an equal sign (>=). When you are drawing a flowchart or writing pseudocode, you might prefer a greater-than sign with a line under it (≥) because mathematicians use that symbol to mean "greater than or equal to." However, when you write a program, you type >= as two separate characters, because no single key on the keyboard expresses this concept and no programming language has been designed to understand it. Similarly, "less than or equal to" is written with two symbols, < immediately followed by =.

TIP ☐ ☐ ☐ ☐ | The operators >= and <= are always treated as a single unit; no spaces separate the two parts of the operator. Also, the equal sign always appears second. No programming language allows => or =< as a comparison operator.

Any relational situation can be expressed using just three types of comparisons: equal, greater than, and less than. You never need the three additional comparisons (greater than or equal, less than or equal, or not equal), but using them often makes decisions more convenient. For example, assume you need to issue a 10 percent discount to any customer whose age is 65 or greater, and charge full price to other customers. You can use the greater-than or equal-to symbol to write the logic as follows:

```
if customerAge >= 65 then
        discount = 0.10
else
        discount = 0
endif
```

As an alternative, if you want to use only the three basic comparisons (=, >, and <), you can express the same logic by writing:

```
if customerAge < 65 then
        discount = 0
else
        discount = 0.10
endif
```

In any decision for which a >= b is true, then a < b is false. Conversely, if a >= b is false, then a < b is true. By rephrasing the question and swapping the actions taken based on the outcome, you can make the same decision in multiple ways. The clearest route is often to ask a question so the positive or true outcome results in the unusual action. When your company policy is to "provide a discount for those who are 65 and older," the phrase "greater than or equal to" comes to mind, so it is the most natural to use. Conversely, if your policy is to "provide no discount for those under 65," then it is more natural to use the "less than" syntax. Either way, the same people receive a discount.

Comparing two amounts to decide if they are *not* equal to each other is the most confusing of all the comparisons. Using "not equal to" in decisions involves thinking in double negatives, which makes you prone to include logical errors in your programs. For example, consider the flowchart segment in Figure 5-5.

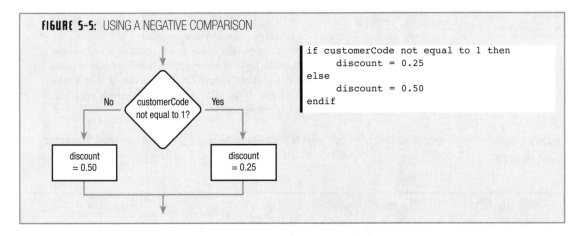

FIGURE 5-5: USING A NEGATIVE COMPARISON

```
if customerCode not equal to 1 then
      discount = 0.25
else
      discount = 0.50
endif
```

In Figure 5-5, if the value of `customerCode` *is* equal to 1, the logical flow follows the false branch of the selection. If `customerCode not equal to 1` is true, the `discount` is 0.25; if `customerCode not equal to 1` is not true, it means the `customerCode` *is* 1, and the `discount` is 0.50. Even using the phrase "`customerCode not equal to 1 is not true`" is awkward.

Figure 5-6 shows the same decision, this time asked in the positive. Making the decision `if customerCode is 1 then discount = 0.50` is clearer than trying to determine what `customerCode` is *not*.

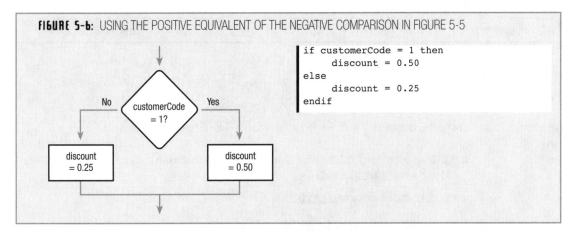

FIGURE 5-6: USING THE POSITIVE EQUIVALENT OF THE NEGATIVE COMPARISON IN FIGURE 5-5

```
if customerCode = 1 then
      discount = 0.50
else
      discount = 0.25
endif
```

Besides being awkward to use, the "not equal to" comparison operator is the one most likely to be different in the various programming languages you may use. Visual Basic and Pascal use a less-than sign followed immediately by a greater-than sign (<>); C#, C++, C, and Java use an exclamation point followed by an equal sign (!=). In a flowchart or in pseudocode, you can use the symbol that mathematicians use to mean "not equal," an equal sign with a slash through it (≠). When you program, you will not be able to use this symbol, because no single key on the keyboard produces it.

Although NOT comparisons can be awkward to use, there are times when your meaning is clearest if you use one. Frequently, this occurs when you take action only when some condition is false. An example would be: if customerZipCode is not equal to localZipCode then add deliveryCharge to total. The main logic of many applications that accept input data includes a negative comparison that controls a loop. The pseudocode of such a program would be similar to: while not the end of the input data, perform mainLoop(). You learn more about controlling loops in Chapter 6.

Table 5-1 summarizes the six comparison operators and contrasts trivial (both true and false) examples with typical examples of their use.

TABLE 5-1: RELATIONAL COMPARISONS

Comparison	Trivial True Example	Trivial False Example	Typical Example
Equal to	7 = 7?	7 = 4?	amtOrdered = 12?
Greater than	12 > 3?	4 > 9?	hoursWorked > 40?
Less than	1 < 8?	13 < 10?	hourlyWage < 5.65?
Greater than or equal to	5 >= 5?	3 >= 9?	customerAge >= 65?
Less than or equal to	4 <= 4?	8 <= 2?	daysOverdue <= 60?
Not equal to	16 <> 3?	18 <> 18?	customerBalance <> 0?

MAKING DECISIONS WITH OBJECTS

When you write object-oriented programs, you make decisions in two slightly different situations:

- You make decisions about primitive data types, perhaps within the instance methods of classes and perhaps within static methods.
- You make decisions about class objects.

In both of these cases, the logic of decision making is the same.

Recall from Chapter 2 that in older object-oriented (OO) languages, simple numbers and characters are said to be primitive data types. In some languages, every item you name really is an object that is a member of a class; however, numeric and character types that can be used directly still act like primitive types.

MAKING DECISIONS ABOUT PRIMITIVE DATA TYPES

For example, consider the `Employee` class in Figure 5-7, which is similar to one you saw in Chapter 3. This class contains just one data field named `idNum`, and a pair of methods for setting and retrieving the field's value. The `getIdNum()` method simply returns an object's private `idNum` value to a method that wants it. The `setIdNum()` method is more complicated—it makes a decision about the method's argument. When the method receives a value for the `idNum` field, it is assigned to the field only if it is not more than 999; otherwise, the value is forced to be 999. In other words, the `setIdNum()` method ensures that the `idNum` will not be 1,000 or higher. Besides making a useful decision that ensures that all employees' IDs will be valid, this example illustrates a major purpose of information hiding—the public `setIdNum()` method that other classes can use protects its private data field by controlling the value of outside values that can be assigned to it.

FIGURE 5-1: AN `Employee` CLASS WITH A METHOD CONTAINING A SELECTION

```
public class Employee
     private numeric idNum

     public numeric getIdNum()
     return idNum

     public void setIdNum(numeric emp)
         if emp <= 999 then
            idNum = emp
         else
             idNum = 999
         endif
     return
endClass
```

TIP □ □ □ □   The Employee class in Figure 5-7 is much smaller than an Employee class would be in a typical business application. Organizations would want to store many more data fields for each employee, for example, first and last names, pay rate, and hire date. Each of these fields would most likely also need get and set methods to support it. The class examples in this chapter are kept brief so you can concentrate on the decision-making logic used, not the composition of a full-blown class.

Within a method in an application, you also might make decisions about primitive-typed variables, such as simple numbers, that are not fields in an object. For example, you might write an application in which you ask the user to input a number representing a menu selection, then based on that value you might take different actions, such as creating different types of objects. Such decisions would look identical to those within class instance methods.

MAKING DECISIONS ABOUT OBJECTS

The syntax used to make decisions about class objects is sometimes a little more complex than making decisions about primitive data types. The complexity arises not because the decision-making process itself is any more difficult, but because the data about which you want to make comparisons is usually hidden.

For example, consider the application in Figure 5-8. The `CompareEmployees` class is an application that contains just one method—a `main()` method. After declaring two `Employee` objects, it tests whether the `anAccountant` object is greater than the `aProgrammer` object. The application will produce results, but the results are meaningless. When you declare an object such as `anAccountant` and `aProgrammer`, each object name is a **reference**, or memory address. When you compare the two references, you are determining whether one is located at a numerically higher memory address than the other—a value that is useless to you. The `Employee` class in Figure 5-7 contains a single data field—idNum, so you might assume that the two Employees' ID numbers would be compared, but they are not. To compare the ID numbers, you would write an application like the one in Figure 5-9.

FIGURE 5-8: THE `CompareEmployees` CLASS WITH A MEANINGLESS COMPARISON

```
class CompareEmployees
   public static void main()
        Employee anAccountant
        Employee aProgrammer
        if anAccountant > aProgrammer then
            print "Accountant is greater"
        else
            print "Accountant is not greater"
        endif
   return
endClass
```

FIGURE 5-9: THE `CompareEmployees` CLASS WITH A USEFUL COMPARISON

```
class CompareEmployees
   public static void main()
        Employee anAccountant
        Employee aProgrammer
        if anAccountant.getIdNum() > aProgrammer.getIdNum() then
            print "Accountant is greater"
        else
            print "Accountant is not greater"
   return
endClass
```

In the `main()` method of the `CompareEmployees` class in Figure 5-9, the `getIdNum()` instance method for each Employee is called. Each call to the method returns an appropriate integer for the object; these are the integers that can be legitimately compared. If the `Employee` class was more comprehensive, you could make similar comparisons about salaries, length of time on the job, department numbers, or any other fields for which you had methods that provide public access.

TIP □ □ □ □ In C++ you can overload operators. When you do so, you write a special-purpose method that indicates what comparison will be made by each of the operators you choose. For example, you can write a method named `operator>()` that defines what the > operator means for two objects.

TIP □ □ □ □ In Figure 5-9, you could accomplish the same results by assigning one or both of the returned values of the instance methods before comparing them. For example, a statement like `numeric firstId = anAccountant.getIdNum()` stores a number in `firstId`, which can then be compared to another value.

UNDERSTANDING AND LOGIC

Often you need more than one selection structure to determine whether an action should take place. For example, suppose you have salespeople for whom you calculate bonus payments based on sales performance factors, and that you have created a `Salesperson` class as shown in Figure 5-10. The class contains data fields for an ID number, number of items sold, dollar value of goods sold, and a bonus. The class contains methods to set the ID number and sales data, but the bonus is not set from an application—instead, the bonus is determined from the number of items sold and their value.

FIGURE 5-10: THE `Salesperson` CLASS IN WHICH A $50 BONUS IS ASSIGNED WHEN TWO CRITERIA ARE MET

```
class Salesperson
    private numeric idNum
    private numeric itemsSold
    private numeric valueSold
    private numeric bonus

    public void setIdNum(numeric num)
        idNum = num
    return

    public void setSalesRecord(numeric numSold, numeric valSold)
        bonus = 0
        itemsSold = numSold
        valueSold = valSold
        if itemsSold > 3 then
            if valueSold >= 1000 then
                bonus = 50
            endif
        endif
    return
endClass
```

TIP ▢▢▢▢ | Notice in Figure 5-10 that there is no need to return the bonus value that is assigned. That's because the `setSalesRecord()` method and the `bonus` variable are both parts of the `Salesperson` class. Every class method has access to its own private data members. The public `setSalesRecord()` method is the means through which outside methods can alter the private data.

TIP ▢▢▢▢ | In Figure 5-10, `bonus` is set to 0 before any decisions are made. If this did not happen, and the `itemsSold` or `valueSold` fields were too low, the method would end without bonus being assigned any value. As a class data field, many OO languages would have initialized the `bonus` field to 0 anyhow, but your intentions are clearer if you make the assignment explicit within the method.

In the highlighted portion of the `Salesperson` class in Figure 5-10, you can see that a Salesperson object receives a $50 bonus only if the salesperson sells more than three items that total at least $1,000 in value. This type of situation is known as an **AND decision** because the Salesperson's data must pass two tests—a minimum number of items sold *and* a minimum value—before the salesperson receives the bonus. A compound, or AND, decision requires a **nested decision**, or a **nested if**—that is, a decision "inside of" another decision. The flowchart of the decision's logic looks like Figure 5-11.

TIP ▫ ▫ ▫ ▫ You first learned about nesting structures in Chapter 4. You can always stack and nest any of the basic structures.

TIP ▫ ▫ ▫ ▫ A series of nested if statements can also be called a **cascading if statement**.

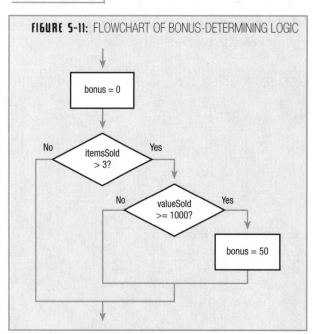

FIGURE 5-11: FLOWCHART OF BONUS-DETERMINING LOGIC

In the `if` statement code shown in Figures 5-10 and 5-11, the expression `itemsSold > 3` is evaluated first. If this expression is `true`, then, and only then, the second Boolean expression (`valueSold >= 1000`) is evaluated. If that expression is also `true`, then the bonus assignment executes and the nested `if` structure ends.

When you use nested `if` statements, you must pay careful attention to the placement of any `else` clauses and the `endif` statements in your pseudocode. For example, suppose you want to distribute bonuses on a revised schedule, as shown in Figure 5-12. Now, if the salesperson does not sell at least three items, you want to give a $10 bonus; if the salesperson sells at least three items, then the bonus is either $25 if the value of the items is under $1,000, or $50 if the value is $1,000 or more. Figure 5-13 shows the pseudocode that assigns the bonuses. The highlighted statements that begin with the forward slash characters have been inserted into the code to explain the relationship of the `else` and `endif` statements to their `if` partners—they are not part of the code; they are just comments.

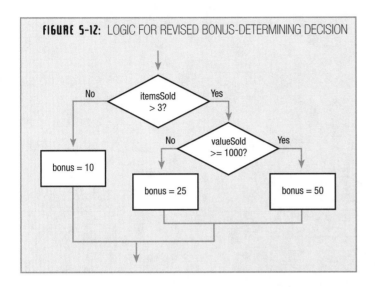

FIGURE 5-12: LOGIC FOR REVISED BONUS-DETERMINING DECISION

FIGURE 5-13: CODE FOR BONUS-DETERMINING DECISION USING NESTED `if` STATEMENTS

```
if itemsSold > 3 then
     if valueSold >= 1000 then
          bonus = 50
     else  // This else goes with the second if
          bonus = 25
     endif // This endif goes with the second if
else // This else goes with the first if
     bonus = 10
endif // This endif goes with the first if
```

As Figure 5-13 shows, when one `if` statement follows another, the first else clause encountered is paired with the last `if` encountered. The complete nested `if-else` structure fits entirely within the `if` portion of the outer `if-else` statement. No matter how many levels of `if-else` statements are needed to produce a solution, the `else` statements always are associated with their ifs on a "first in—last out" basis.

NESTING AND DECISIONS FOR EFFICIENCY

When you nest decisions because the resulting action requires that two conditions be true, you must decide which of the two decisions to make first. Logically, either selection in an AND decision can come first. However, when there are two selections, you often can improve your program's performance by making an appropriate choice as to which selection to make first.

For example, Figure 5-14 shows the nested decision structure in the method that assigns a $50 bonus to salespeople who sell more than three items valued at $1,000 or more. Figure 5-15 also shows logic that assigns $50 bonuses to the same salespeople.

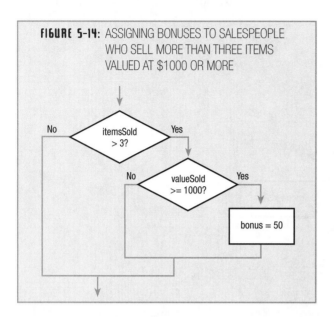

FIGURE 5-14: ASSIGNING BONUSES TO SALESPEOPLE WHO SELL MORE THAN THREE ITEMS VALUED AT $1000 OR MORE

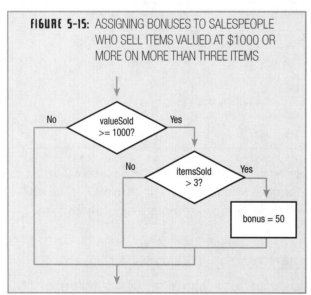

FIGURE 5-15: ASSIGNING BONUSES TO SALESPEOPLE WHO SELL ITEMS VALUED AT $1000 OR MORE ON MORE THAN THREE ITEMS

Examine the decision statements in Figures 5-14 and 5-15. If you want to assign a $50 bonus to salespeople who sell three or more items with a total value of at least $1,000, you can ask about the items sold first, eliminate those salespeople who do not qualify, and ask about the value of the items sold only for those salespeople who "pass" the number of items test. Or you could ask about the value of the items first, eliminate those who do not qualify, and ask about the number of items only for those salespeople who "pass" the value test. Either way, only those salespeople who pass both tests receive the $50 bonus.

Does it make a difference which question is asked first? As far as the result goes, no, it does not. Either way, the same salespeople receive the bonus—those who qualify on the basis of both criteria. As far as program efficiency goes, however, it *might* make a difference which question is asked first.

Assume you know that out of 1,000 salespeople in your company, about 90 percent, or 900, sell more than three items in a pay period. Assume you also know that because the items are low-priced, out of 1,000 salespeople only about half, or 500, sell items valued at $1,000 or more.

If you use the logic contained in Figure 5-14 in your `Salesperson` class, and you execute an application containing 1,000 Salesperson objects, the first question, `itemsSold > 3?`, will execute 1,000 times. For approximately 90 percent of the Salesperson objects, or 900 of them, the answer is `true`, so 100 Salespersons are eliminated from the bonus assignment, and 900 proceed to the next question about the value of the items sold. Only about half of the Salespeople sell at least $1,000 worth of merchandise, so 450 out of the 900 will receive the bonus.

Using the alternate logic in Figure 5-15, the first question `valueSold >= 1000?` will also be asked 1,000 times—once for each Salesperson. Because only about half of the company's salespeople sell at this higher dollar level, only 500 will "pass" this test and proceed to the number of items sold question. Then about 90 percent of the 500, or 450 salespeople, will pass this test and receive the bonus.

Whether you use the logic in Figure 5-14 or 5-15, the same 450 employees who surpass both sales criteria receive the bonus. The difference lies in the fact that when you use the logic in Figure 5-14, the program must ask 1,900 questions to assign the correct bonuses—the first question tests all 1,000 Salesperson objects, and 900 continue to the second question. If you use the logic in Figure 5-15 to determine bonuses, the program asks only 1,500 questions—all 1,000 records are tested with the first question, but only 500 proceed to the second question. By asking about the dollar value of the goods first, you "save" 400 decisions.

The 400-question difference between the first set of decisions and the second set really doesn't take much time on most computers. But it will take *some* time, and if there are hundreds of thousands of salespeople instead of only 1000, or if many such decisions have to be made within a program, performance time can be significantly improved by asking questions in the proper order.

In many AND decisions, you have no idea which of two events is more likely to occur; in that case, you can legitimately ask either question first. In addition, even though you know the probability of each of two conditions, the two events might not be mutually exclusive; that is, one might depend on the other. For example, salespeople who sell more items are also likely to have achieved a higher value with those items. Depending on the relationship between these phenomena, the order in which to ask the questions might matter less or not matter at all. However, if you do know the probabilities of the conditions, or can make a reasonable guess, the general rule is: *In an AND decision, first ask the question that is less likely to be true.* This eliminates as many instances of the second decision as possible, which speeds up processing time.

COMBINING DECISIONS IN AN AND SELECTION

Most programming languages allow you to ask two or more questions in a single comparison by using a **logical AND operator**. For example, if you want to provide a bonus for salespeople who sell more than three items and at least $1,000 in value, you can use nested `if`s, or you can include both decisions in a single statement by writing `itemsSold > 3 AND valueSold >= 1000?`. When you use one or more AND operators to combine two or more Boolean expressions, each Boolean expression must be true in order for the entire expression to be evaluated as true. For example, if you ask, "Are you at least 18, and are you a registered voter, and did you vote in the last election?", the answer to all three parts of the question must be "yes" before the response can be a single, summarizing "yes". If any part of the question is false, then the entire question is false.

If the programming language you use allows an AND operator, you still must realize that the question you place first is the question that will be asked first, and cases that are eliminated based on the first question will not proceed to the second question. The computer can ask only one question at a time; even when your pseudocode looks like Figure 5-16, the computer will execute the logic shown in Figure 5-17.

FIGURE 5-16: PSEUDOCODE OF AN AND DECISION USING AN AND OPERATOR

```
if itemsSold > 3 AND valueSold >= 1000 then
        bonus = 50
endif
```

FIGURE 5-17: COMPUTER LOGIC OF PSEUDOCODE IN FIGURE 5-16

```
if itemsSold > 3 then
    if valueSold >= 1000 then
        bonus = 50
    endif
endif
```

TIP □ □ □ □   The AND operator in Java, C++, and C# consists of two ampersands, with no spaces between them (&&). These languages also provide a different operator represented by a single ampersand (&), which operates on bits. This discussion is only about the logical AND used between two conditional tests.

TIP □ □ □ □   Using an AND operator in a decision that involves multiple conditions does not eliminate your responsibility for determining which of the conditions to test first. Even when you use an AND operator, the computer makes decisions one at a time, and makes them in the order you ask them. If the first question in an AND expression evaluates to false, then the entire expression is false, and the second question will not even be tested.

TIP □ □ □ □   You never are required to use the AND operator because using nested `if` statements can always achieve the same result, but using the AND operator often makes your code more concise, less error-prone, and easier to understand.

AVOIDING COMMON ERRORS IN AN AND SELECTION

When you must satisfy two or more criteria to initiate an event in a program, you must make sure that the second decision is made entirely within the first decision. For example, if a program's objective is to assign a $50 bonus to salespeople who sell more than three items valued at least $1,000, then the program segment shown in Figure 5-18 contains three different types of logic errors.

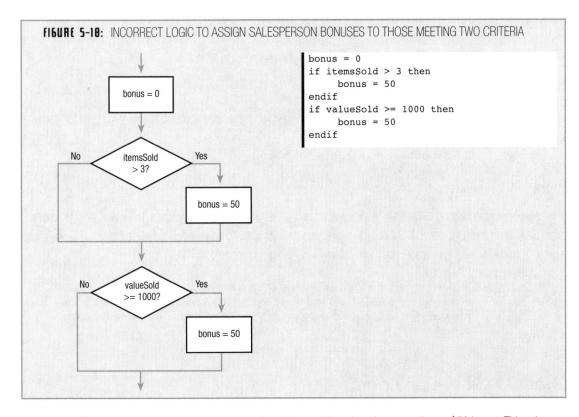

FIGURE 5-18: INCORRECT LOGIC TO ASSIGN SALESPERSON BONUSES TO THOSE MEETING TWO CRITERIA

```
bonus = 0
if itemsSold > 3 then
    bonus = 50
endif
if valueSold >= 1000 then
    bonus = 50
endif
```

The logic in Figure 5-18 shows that a salesperson who sells more than three items receives a $50 bonus. This salesperson should not receive the bonus—the dollar value might not be high enough, and it has not yet been tested. In addition, a salesperson who has not sold the minimum number of items is not eliminated from the second question as the salesperson should be. Instead, all salespeople endure the dollar value question, and some are assigned the bonus even though they might not have passed the number of items sold criterion. Additionally, any salesperson who passes both tests has a bonus assigned twice. This does not result in an error, because the second $50 assignment replaces the first one, but processing time is wasted. For many reasons, the logic shown in Figure 5-18 is *not* correct for this problem.

Beginning programmers often make another type of error when they must make two comparisons on the same field while using a logical AND operator. For example, suppose you want to assign a $75 bonus to those who have sold between 5 and 10 items inclusive. When you make this type of decision, you are basing it on a **range of values**—every value between low and high limits. For example, you want to select salespeople whose `itemsSold value` is greater than or equal to 5 AND whose `itemsSold` value is less than or equal to 10; therefore, you need to make two comparisons on the same field. Without the logical AND operator, the comparison is:

```
if itemsSold >= 5 then
    if itemsSold <=10 then
        bonus = 75
    endif
endif
```

The correct way to make this comparison with the AND operator is as follows:

```
if itemsSold >= 5 AND itemsSold <=10 then
     bonus = 75
endif
```

You substitute the AND operator for the phrase `then if`. However, some programmers might try to make the comparison as follows:

```
if itemsSold >= 5 AND <=10 then
     bonus = 75
endif
```

In most programming languages, the phrase `itemsSold >= 5 AND <=10` is incorrect. The logical AND is usually a binary operator that requires a complete Boolean expression on each side. The expression to the right of the AND, `<= 10`, is not a complete Boolean expression; you must indicate *what* is being compared to 10.

TIP □ □ □ □ | In some programming languages, such as COBOL and RPG, you can write the equivalent of itemsSold >= 5 AND <=10? and the `itemsSold` variable is implied for both comparisons. Still, it is clearer, and therefore preferable, to use the two full Boolean expressions.

UNDERSTANDING OR LOGIC

Sometimes you want to take action when one *or* the other of two conditions is true. This is called an **OR decision** because either one condition must be met *or* some other condition must be met, in order for an event to take place. If someone asks you, "Are you free Friday or Saturday?" only one of the two conditions has to be true in order for the answer to the whole question to be "yes"; only if the answers to both halves of the question are false is the value of the entire expression false.

For example, suppose you want to assign a $300 bonus to salespeople when they have achieved one of two goals—selling at least five items, or selling at least $2000 worth of merchandise. The `Salesperson` class in Figure 5-19 includes a `setSalesRecord()` method that accomplishes this.

FIGURE 5-19: THE `Salesperson` CLASS IN WHICH BONUS IS ASSIGNED WHEN EITHER OF TWO CRITERIA IS MET

```
class Salesperson
     private numeric idNum
     private numeric itemsSold
     private numeric valueSold
     private numeric bonus

     public void setIdNum(numeric num)
          idNum = num
     return

     public void setSalesRecord(numeric numSold, numeric valSold)
        bonus = 0
        itemsSold = numSold
        valueSold = valSold
        if itemsSold >= 5 then
             bonus = 300
        else
             if valueSold >= 2000 then
                  bonus = 300
             endif
        endif
     return
endClass
```

In Figure 5-19, as each salesperson's data is set, you ask the question `itemsSold >= 5?`, and if the result is true, you assign the $300 bonus; because selling five items is enough to qualify for the bonus, there is no need for further questioning. If the salesperson has not sold at least five items, only then do you need to ask if `valueSold >= 2000?`. If the employee did not sell five or more items, but did sell a high dollar value nonetheless, you want this salesperson to receive the bonus.

WRITING OR DECISIONS FOR EFFICIENCY

As with an AND selection, when you use an OR selection, you can choose to ask either question first. For example, you can assign a bonus to salespeople who meet one or the other of two criteria using the logic in either Figure 5-20 or Figure 5-21.

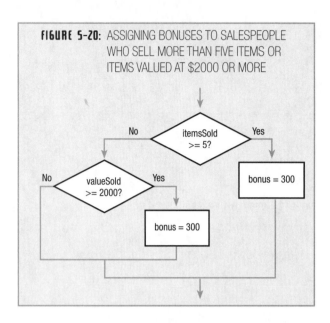

FIGURE 5-20: ASSIGNING BONUSES TO SALESPEOPLE WHO SELL MORE THAN FIVE ITEMS OR ITEMS VALUED AT $2000 OR MORE

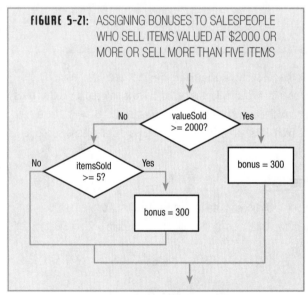

FIGURE 5-21: ASSIGNING BONUSES TO SALESPEOPLE WHO SELL ITEMS VALUED AT $2000 OR MORE OR SELL MORE THAN FIVE ITEMS

You might have guessed that one of these selections is superior to the other if you have some background information about the relative likelihood of each condition you are testing. For example, assume you know that out of 1,000 employees in your company, about 70 percent, or 700, sell more than five items during a given period of time, and that only 40 percent, or 400, sell $2000 worth of goods or more.

When you use the logic shown in Figure 5-20 to assign bonuses, you first ask about the number of items sold. For 700 salespeople the answer is true; and you assign the bonus. Only about 300 records continue to the next question regarding the dollar amount sold, where about 40 percent of the 300, or 120, fulfill the bonus requirement. In the end, you have made 1,300 decisions to be able to correctly assign bonuses to 820 employees (700 plus 120).

If you use the OR logic in Figure 5-21, you ask about the dollar value sold first—1,000 times, once each for 1,000 salespeople. The result is true for 40 percent, or 400 employees, who receive a bonus. For 600 salespeople, you ask whether `itemsSold` is at least 5. For 70 percent of the 600, the result is `true`, so bonuses are assigned to 420 additional people. In all, 820 salespeople (400 plus 420) receive a bonus after executing 1,600 decisions—300 more than when using the logic in Figure 5-20.

The general rule is: *In an OR decision, first ask the question that is more likely to be true.* In the salesperson bonus example, a salesperson qualifies for a bonus as soon as the person's data passes one test. Asking the question that is more likely true first eliminates as many repetitions as possible of the second decision, and the time it takes to process all the salespeople is decreased. As with the AND situation, you might not always know which question is more likely to be true, but when you can make a reasonable guess, it is more efficient to eliminate as many extra decisions as possible.

COMBINING DECISIONS IN AN OR SELECTION

When you need to take action when either one or the other of two conditions is met, you can use two separate, nested selection structures, as in the previous examples. However, most programming languages allow you to ask two or more questions in a single comparison by using a **logical OR operator**—for example, `valueSold >= 2000 OR itemsSold >= 5`. When you use the logical OR operator, only one of the listed conditions must be met for the resulting action to take place. If the programming language you use allows this construct, you still must realize that the question you place first is the question that will be asked first, and cases that pass the test of the first question will not proceed to the second question. The computer can ask only one question at a time; even when you write code as shown in Figure 5-22, the computer will execute the logic shown in Figure 5-23.

FIGURE 5-22: PSEUDOCODE OF AN OR DECISION USING AN OR OPERATOR

```
if valueSold >= 2000 OR itemsSold >= 5 then
     bonus = 300
endif
```

FIGURE 5-23: COMPUTER LOGIC OF PSEUDOCODE IN FIGURE 5-22

```
if valueSold >= 2000 then
     bonus = 300
else
     if itemsSold >= 5 then
          bonus = 300
     endif
endif
```

TIP ◻ ◻ ◻ ◻ C#, C++, C, and Java use the symbol || to represent the logical OR. These languages also contain a separate bitwise OR operator represented by a single pipe (|).

TIP ☐ ☐ ☐ ☐ | As with the AND operator, most programming languages require a complete Boolean expression on each side of the OR.

AVOIDING COMMON ERRORS IN AN OR SELECTION

You might have noticed that the assignment statement `bonus = 300` appears twice in the decision-making processes shown in Figures 5-22 and 5-23. When creating a flowchart, the temptation is to draw the logic to look like Figure 5-24. Logically, you can argue that the flowchart in Figure 5-24 is correct because the correct salespeople receive bonuses. However, this flowchart is not allowed because it is not structured.

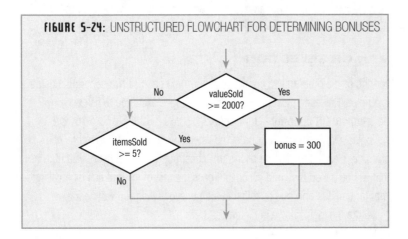

FIGURE 5-24: UNSTRUCTURED FLOWCHART FOR DETERMINING BONUSES

TIP ☐ ☐ ☐ ☐ | If you do not see that Figure 5-24 is unstructured, go back and review Chapter 4.

An additional source of error that is specific to the OR selection stems from a problem with language and the way people use it more casually than computers do. When a sales manager wants to assign bonuses to salespeople who have sold five or more items or who have achieved $2,000 in sales, she is likely to say, "Give a bonus to anyone who has sold at least three items and to anyone who has achieved $2,000 in sales." The request contains the word "and," and bonuses should be given to those who have sold a high number of items and those who have sales dollars. However, the bonuses you want to assign are for salespeople who have surpassed one goal OR the other OR both. The logical situation requires an OR decision. Instead of saying "Give a bonus to anyone who has sold at least three items and to anyone who has achieved $2,000 in sales," it would be clearer if the manager said, "Give a bonus to anyone who has sold at least three items or has achieved $2,000 in sales." In other words, it would be more correct to put the question-joining "or" conjunction between the sales goals achieved by each person than between the people, but bosses and other human beings often do not speak like computers. As a programmer, you have the job of clarifying what really is being requested, and determining that often a request for A *and* B means a request for A *or* B.

The way we casually use English can cause another type of error when you require a decision based on a value falling between two values. For example, a movie theater manager might say, "Provide a discount to patrons who are under 13 years old and those who are over 64 years old; otherwise, charge the full price." Because the manager has used the word "and" in the request, you might be tempted to create the decision shown in Figure 5-25; however, this logic will not provide a discounted price for any movie patron. You must remember that every time the decision in Figure 5-25 is made, it is made for a single movie patron. If the age field for that object contains an age lower than 13, then it cannot possibly contain an age over 64. Similarly, if it contains an age over 64, then there is no way it can contain an age under that. Therefore, there is no value that could be stored in the age field of a movie patron record for which both parts of the AND question could be true—and the price will never be set to the `discountPrice` for any record. Figure 5-26 shows the correct logic.

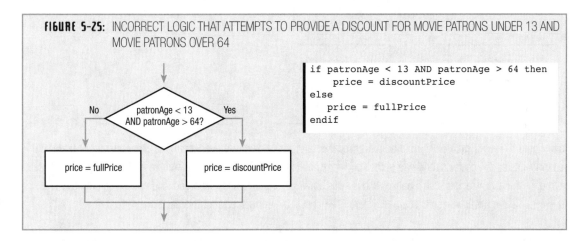

FIGURE 5-25: INCORRECT LOGIC THAT ATTEMPTS TO PROVIDE A DISCOUNT FOR MOVIE PATRONS UNDER 13 AND MOVIE PATRONS OVER 64

```
if patronAge < 13 AND patronAge > 64 then
    price = discountPrice
else
    price = fullPrice
endif
```

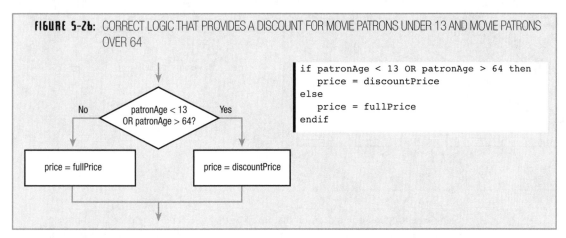

FIGURE 5-26: CORRECT LOGIC THAT PROVIDES A DISCOUNT FOR MOVIE PATRONS UNDER 13 AND MOVIE PATRONS OVER 64

```
if patronAge < 13 OR patronAge > 64 then
    price = discountPrice
else
    price = fullPrice
endif
```

A similar error can occur in your logic if the theater manager says something like, "Don't give a discount—that is, charge full price—if a patron is over 12 or under 65." Because the word "or" appears in the request, you might plan your logic like that shown in Figure 5-27.

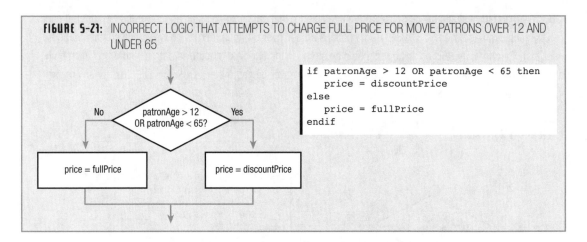

FIGURE 5-27: INCORRECT LOGIC THAT ATTEMPTS TO CHARGE FULL PRICE FOR MOVIE PATRONS OVER 12 AND UNDER 65

As in Figure 5-25, in Figure 5-27, no patron ever receives a discount, because every patron is either over 12 or under 65. Remember, in an OR decision, only one of the conditions needs to be true in order for the entire expression to be evaluated as true. So, for example, because a patron who is 10 is under 65, the full price is charged, and because a patron who is 70 is over 12, the full price also is charged. Figure 5-28 shows the correct logic for this decision.

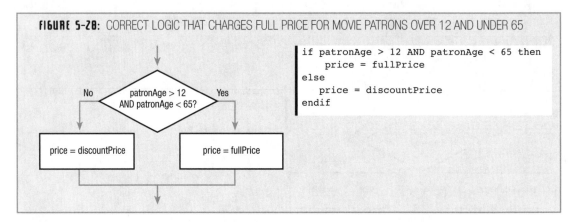

FIGURE 5-28: CORRECT LOGIC THAT CHARGES FULL PRICE FOR MOVIE PATRONS OVER 12 AND UNDER 65

TIP □ □ □ □ Using an OR operator in a decision that involves multiple conditions does not eliminate your responsibility for determining which of the conditions to test first. Even when you use an OR operator, the computer makes decisions one at a time, and makes them in the order you ask them. If the first question in an OR expression evaluates to true, then the entire expression is true, and the second question will not even be tested.

TIP □ □ □ □ Besides AND and OR, most languages support a NOT operator. You use the **logical NOT operator** to reverse the meaning of a Boolean expression. For example, the statement `if NOT (age < 21) print "OK"` prints "OK" when age is greater than or equal to 21. The NOT operator is unary instead of binary—that is, you do not use it between two expressions, but you use it in front of a single expression. In C++, Java, and C#, the exclamation point is the symbol used for the NOT operator.

USING SELECTIONS WITHIN RANGES

You often need to make selections based on a variable falling within a range of values. For example, suppose a company president wants to meet with every department next week to discuss an impending merger, and wants to print a series of memos to employees notifying them of their department's meeting day and time. Figure 5-29 shows the meeting schedule, which has been arranged by the employees' department numbers, so that each meeting group is a manageable size. Figure 5-30 shows a typical memo—the highlighted portions of the memo will change for each employee. Figure 5-31 shows the `Employee` class in which Employee data is stored.

FIGURE 5-29: PROPOSED MEETING SCHEDULE

Meeting Day and Time	Departments
Monday at 9 a.m.	1 through 4
Monday at 1 p.m.	5 through 9
Tuesday at 1 p.m.	10 through 17
Wednesday at 9 a.m.	18 through 20

FIGURE 5-30: TYPICAL MEETING MEMO

```
To: Allison Darnell
From: Walter Braxton
Re: Pending merger

Your department will meet with me on Monday at 9 a.m. in the Blue
Conference Room where we will address questions about the upcoming
merger.
```

FIGURE 5-31: THE `Employee` CLASS

```
public class Employee
     private numeric idNum
     private string lastName
     private string firstName
     private numeric department

     public numeric getIdNum()
     return idNum

     public string getLastName()
     return lastName

     public numeric getFirstName()
     return firstName

     public numeric getDepartment()
     return department
endClass
```

When you write the program that reads each employee's record, you could make 20 decisions before printing each employee's memo, such as `department = 1?`, `department = 2?`, and so on. However, it is more convenient to find the supervisor by using a range check.

When you use a **range check**, you compare a variable to a series of values between limits. To perform a range check, make comparisons using either the lowest or highest value in each range of values you are using. For example, to find each employee's meeting day and time as listed in Figure 5-29, either use the values 1, 5, 10, and 18, which represent the low ends of each meeting's department range, or use the values 4, 9, 17, and 20, which represent the high ends.

Figure 5-32 shows the flowchart and pseudocode that represent the logic for the module that chooses a meeting time by using the high-end department number range values. The `printMemo()` is a `public, static` method that can be used in an application. It returns nothing, so its return type is `void`. The method receives an `Employee` object as an argument. During the execution of the application that uses this method, the method might be called hundreds of times, once for each employee in the organization. You extract the private `department` number from the `Employee` object using the public `getDepartment()` instance method. Then, you test whether the `department` value is less than or equal to the high end of the lowest range group. If the comparison evaluates as true, you know the meeting time, and can store it in the module's local `meetingTime string` variable; if not, you continue checking. When the comparisons are done, you use the `Employee` class `getFirstName()` and `getLastName()` modules to complete the first memo line (inserting a space between them), then you print the rest of the memo, including the meeting time you determined based on the `department` number.

FIGURE 5-32: THE `printMemo()` MODULE USING HIGH-END VALUES FOR A RANGE CHECK

```
public static void printMemo(Employee anEmployee)
   string meetingTime
   numeric department
   department = anEmployee.getDepartment()
   if department <= 4 then
      meetingTime = "Monday at 9 a.m."
   else
      if department <= 9 then
         meetingTime = "Monday at 1 p.m."
      else
         if department <= 17 then
            meetingTime = "Tuesday at 1 p.m."
         else
            meetingTime = "Wednesday at 9 a.m."
         endif
      endif
   endif
   print "To: ", anEmployee.getFirstName(), " ",
         anEmployee.getLastName()
   print "From: Walter Braxton"
   print "Re: Pending merger"
   print "Your department will meet with me on",
         meetingTime, " in the Blue"
   print "Conference Room where we will address
         questions about the upcoming"
   print "merger."
return
```

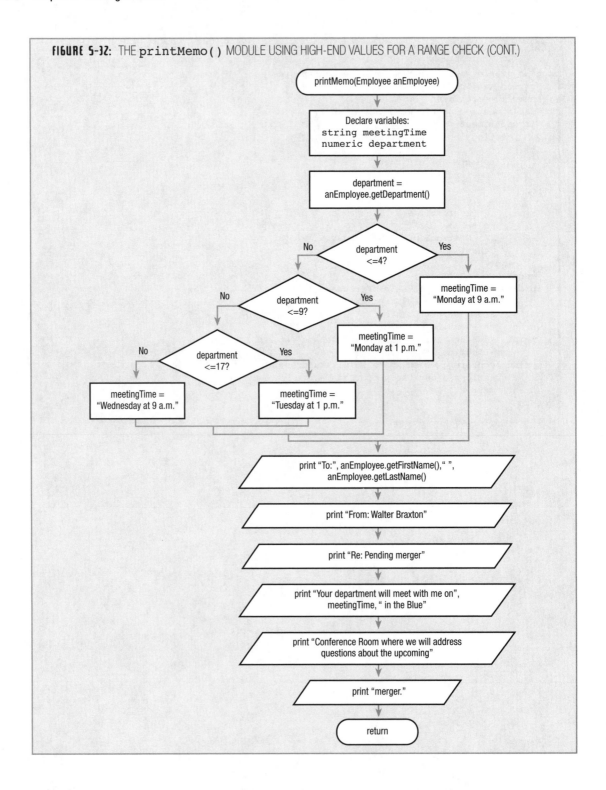

FIGURE 5-32: THE `printMemo()` MODULE USING HIGH-END VALUES FOR A RANGE CHECK (CONT.)

TIP ☐ ☐ ☐ ☐ In the pseudocode in Figure 5-32, notice how each if, else, and endif group aligns vertically.

TIP ☐ ☐ ☐ ☐ This book assumes one print statement prints one line of output. In most programming languages you can print many lines with a single statement; you also can use several statements to print one line. The exact process varies among languages.

For example, consider four `Employee` objects containing four different values for the `department` field, and compare how they would be handled by the set of decisions in Figure 5-32.

- First, assume that the value of `department` for an Employee record is 2. Using the logic in Figure 5-32, the value of the Boolean expression `department <= 4` is true, the `meetingTime` is set to "Monday at 9 a.m.", and the `if` structure ends. In this case, the second decision, `department <= 9`, is never made, because the `else` half of the `department <= 4` never executes.

- Next, assume that for `Employee`, the value of `department` is 7. Then, `department <= 4` evaluates as false, so the `else` clause of the decision executes. There, `department <= 9` is evaluated, and found to be `true`, so the `meetingTime` becomes "Monday at 1 p.m.".

- Next, assume an `Employee` object contains 17 in the `department` field. The expression `department <= 4` evaluates as false, so the `else` clause of the decision executes. There, `department <= 9` also evaluates to `false,` so its `else` clause executes. The expression `department <= 17` is true, so the `meetingTime` becomes "Tuesday at 1 p.m.".

- Finally, assume that the value of `department` is 19. In this case, the first decision, `department <= 4`, is false, so the `else` clause executes. Then, the second decision, `department <= 9`, also evaluates as `false`, so the `else` clause of the second decision executes. The expression `department <= 17` is false so the `else` clause of this decision executes, and the `meetingTime` becomes "Wednesday at 9 a.m.". In this example, the 9 a.m. Wednesday meeting represents a default value, because if none of the decision expressions is true, the last meeting time is selected by default. A **default value** is the value assigned after a series of selections all are false.

TIP ☐ ☐ ☐ ☐ Using the logic in Figure 5-32, the 9 a.m. Wednesday meeting time is set even if the `department` is a high invalid value like 21, 22, or even 300. The example is intended to be simple, using only three decisions. However, in a business application, you might consider amending the logic so an additional, fourth decision is made that compares `department` to 20. Then, you could assign the Wednesday meeting time when the department is less than or equal to 20, and issue an error message if the department is not. You might also want to insert a similar decision at the beginning of the method to make sure the `department` is not less than 1.

The flowchart and pseudocode for choosing a meeting time using the reverse of this method, by comparing the employee department to the low end of the range values that represent each meeting, appear in Figure 5-33. Using the technique shown in Figure 5-33, you compare `department` to the low end (18) of the highest range (18 to 20) first; if the `Employee`'s `department` falls in the range, the meeting day and time are known; otherwise, you check the next lower group. In this example, "Monday at 9 a.m." becomes the default value. That is, if the department number is not greater than or equal to 18, and it is also not greater than or equal to 10, and it also is not greater than or equal to 5, then by default, the meeting is on Monday morning.

FIGURE 5-33: THE `printMemo()` MODULE USING LOW-END VALUES FOR A RANGE CHECK

```
public static void printMemo(Employee anEmployee)
   string meetingTime
   numeric department
   department = anEmployee.getDepartment()
   if department >= 18 then
       meetingTime = "Wednesday at 9 a.m."
   else
      if department >= 10 then
         meetingTime = "Tuesday at 1 p.m."
      else
         if department >= 5 then
              meetingTime = "Monday at 1 p.m."
         else
              meetingTime = "Monday at 9 a.m."
         endif
      endif
   endif
   print "To: ", anEmployee.getFirstName(), " ",
        anEmployee.getLastName()
   print "From: Walter Braxton"
   print "Re: Pending merger"
   print "Your department will meet with me on",
        meetingTime, " in the Blue"
   print "Conference Room where we will address
        questions about the upcoming"
   print "merger."

return
```

FIGURE 5-33: THE `printMemo()` MODULE USING LOW-END VALUES FOR A RANGE CHECK (CONT.)

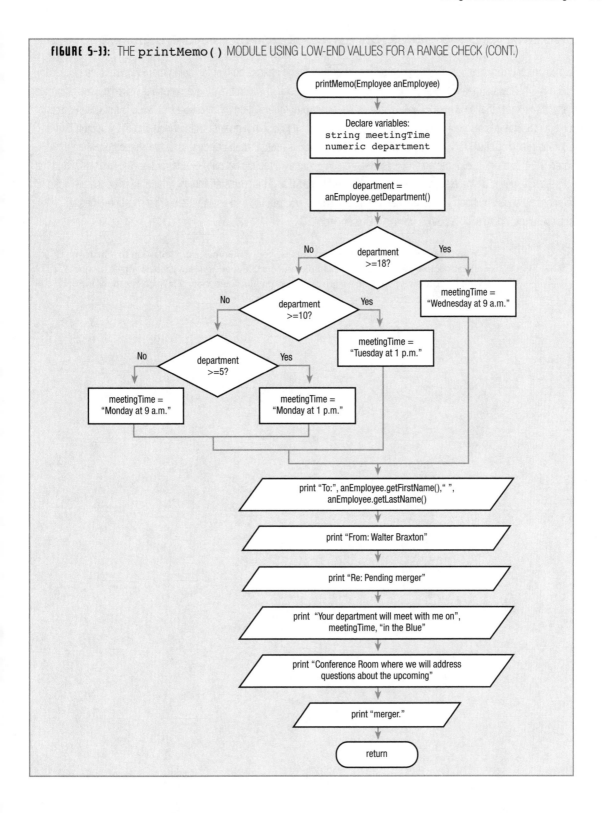

UNDERSTANDING COMMON ERRORS USING RANGE CHECKS

Two common errors that occur when programmers perform range checks both entail doing more work than is necessary. Figure 5-34 shows a method segment that contains a range check in which the programmer has asked one question too many. If you know that all `department` values are positive numbers, then if the `department` is not greater than or equal to 18, and it is also not greater than or equal to 10, and it is also not greater than or equal to 5, by default it must be greater than or equal to 1. Asking whether `department` is greater than or equal to 1 (the shaded question in Figure 5-34) is a waste of time; no employee record can ever travel the logical path on the far left. You might say that the path that can never be traveled is a **dead** or **unreachable path**, and that the statements written there constitute dead or unreachable code. Although a program containing such logic will execute and assign the correct meeting times to employees, providing such a path is always a logical error.

 **TIP** ☐ ☐ ☐ ☐ | When you ask questions of human beings, you sometimes ask a question to which you already know the answer. For example, in court, a good trial lawyer seldom asks a question if the answer will be a surprise. With computer logic, however, such questions are an inefficient waste of time.

FIGURE 5-34: INEFFICIENT RANGE SELECTION INCLUDING UNREACHABLE PATH

```
if department >= 18 then
    meetingTime = "Wednesday at 9 a.m."
else
   if department >= 10 then
      meetingTime = "Tuesday at 1 p.m."
   else
      if department >= 5 then
          meetingTime = "Monday at 1 p.m."
      else
          if department >= 1 then
              meetingTime = "Monday at 9 a.m."
          else
          endif
      endif
   endif
endif
```

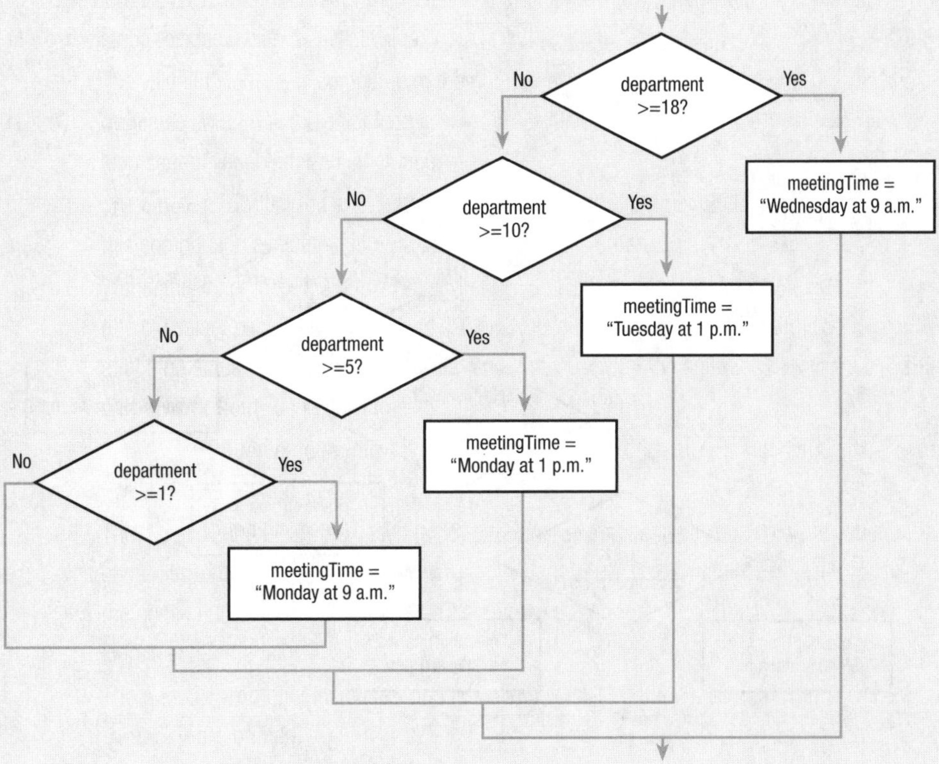

Another error that programmers make when writing the logic to perform a range check also involves asking unnecessary questions. You should never ask a question if there is only one possible answer or outcome. Figure 5-35 shows an inefficient range selection that asks two unneeded questions. In the figure, if **department** is greater than or equal to 18, "Wednesday at 9 a.m." is the scheduled meeting. If the **department** is not greater than or equal to 18, then it must be less than 18, so the next question (highlighted in the figure) does not have to check for less than 18. The computer logic will never execute the second decision unless the `department` is already less than 18—that is, unless it follows the false branch of the first selection. If you use the logic in Figure 5-35, you are wasting computer time asking a question that has previously been answered. Similarly, if the `department` is not greater than or equal to 18 and it is also not greater than or equal to 10, then it must be less than 10. Therefore, there is no reason to compare `department` to 10 in the last decision.

FIGURE 5-35: INEFFICIENT RANGE SELECTION INCLUDING UNNECESSARY QUESTION

```
if department >= 18 then
    meetingTime = "Wednesday at 9 a.m."
else
    if department < 18 AND department >= 10 then
        meetingTime = "Tuesday at 1 p.m."
    else
        if department < 10 AND department >= 5 then
            meetingTime = "Monday at 1 p.m."
        else
            meetingTime = "Monday at 9 a.m."

        endif
    endif
endif
```

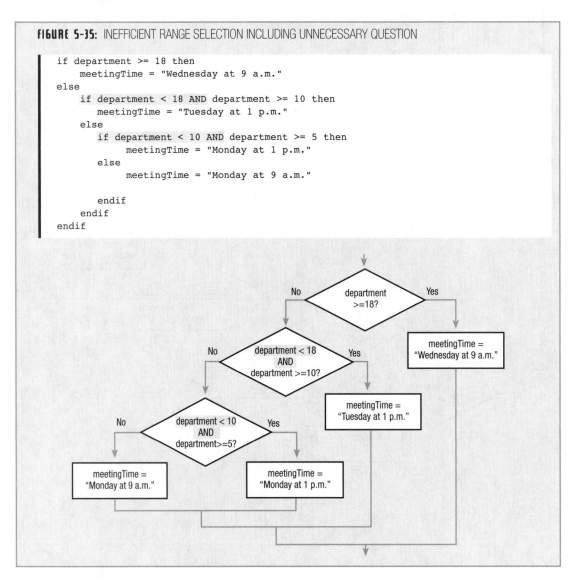

TIP ▫ ▫ ▫ ▫ Beginning programmers sometimes justify their use of unnecessary questions as "just making really sure." Such caution is unnecessary when writing computer logic.

UNDERSTANDING PRECEDENCE WHEN COMBINING AND AND OR SELECTIONS

Most programming languages allow you to combine as many AND and OR operators in an expression as you need. For example, assume you need to achieve a score of at least 75 on each of three tests in order to pass a course. When multiple conditions must be true before performing an action, you can use an expression like the following:

```
if score1 >= 75 AND score2 >= 75 AND score3 >= 75 then
    classGrade = "Pass"
else
    classGrade = "Fail"
endif
```

On the other hand, if you need to pass only one test in order to pass the course, then the logic is as follows:

```
if score1 >= 75 OR score2 >= 75 OR score3 >= 75 then
    classGrade = "Pass"
else
    classGrade = "Fail"
endif
```

The logic becomes more complicated when you combine AND and OR operators within the same statement. When you combine AND and OR operators, the AND operators take **precedence**, meaning their Boolean values are evaluated first.

For example, consider a program that determines whether a movie theater patron can purchase a discounted ticket. Assume discounts are allowed for children (age 12 and under) and senior citizens (age 65 and older) who attend "G"-rated movies. The following code looks reasonable, but produces incorrect results, because the AND operator evaluates before the OR.

```
if age <= 12 OR age >= 65 AND rating = "G" then
    print "Discount applies"
```

For example, assume a movie patron is 10 years old and the movie rating is "R". The patron should not receive a discount (or be allowed to see the movie!). However, within the `if` statement previously discussed, the part of the expression containing the AND, `age >= 65 AND rating = "G"`, evaluates first. For a 10 year old and an "R" rated movie, the question is false (on both counts), so the entire if statement becomes the equivalent of the following:

```
if age <= 12 OR aFalseExpression
```

Because the patron is 10, `age <= 12` is true, so the original `if` statement becomes the equivalent of:

```
if aTrueExpression OR aFalseExpression
```

which evaluates as true. Therefore, the statement "Discount applies" prints when it should not.

Many programming languages allow you to use parentheses to correct the logic and force the expression `age <= 12 OR age >= 65` to evaluate first, as shown in the following pseudocode.

```
if (age <= 12 OR age >= 65) AND rating = "G" then
    print "Discount applies"
```

With the added parentheses, if the patron's age is 12 or under OR 65 or over, the expression is evaluated as:

```
if aTrueExpression AND rating = "G"
```

When the age value qualifies a patron for a discount, then the rating value must also be acceptable before the discount applies. This was the original intention of the statement.

You always can avoid the confusion of mixing AND and OR decisions by nesting `if` statements instead of using ANDs and ORs. With the flowchart and pseudocode shown in Figure 5-36, it is clear which movie patrons receive the discount. In the flowchart in the figure, you can see that the OR is nested entirely within the Yes branch of the `rating = "G"?` selection. Similarly, by examining the pseudocode in Figure 5-36, you can see by the alignment that if the rating is not "G", the logic proceeds directly to the last `endif` statement, bypassing any checking of the age at all.

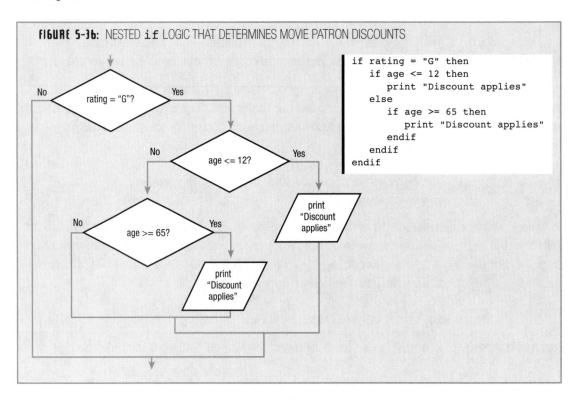

FIGURE 5-36: NESTED `if` LOGIC THAT DETERMINES MOVIE PATRON DISCOUNTS

```
if rating = "G" then
    if age <= 12 then
        print "Discount applies"
    else
        if age >= 65 then
            print "Discount applies"
        endif
    endif
endif
```

TIP ▫ ▫ ▫ ▫ | In every programming language, multiplication has precedence over addition in an arithmetic statement. That is, the value of 2 + 3 * 4 is 14 because the multiplication occurs before the addition. Similarly, in every programming language, AND has precedence over OR. That's because computer circuitry treats the AND operator as multiplication and the OR operator as addition. In every programming language, 1 represents true and 0 represents false. So, for example, aTrueExpression AND aTrueExpression results in true, because 1 * 1 is 1, and aTrueExpression AND aFalseExpression is false, because 1 * 0 is 0. Similarly, aFalseExpression OR aFalseExpression AND aTrueExpression evaluates to aFalseExpression because 0 + 0 * 1 is 0, while aFalseExpression AND aFalseExpression OR aTrueExpression evaluates to aTrueExpression result because 0 * 0 + 1 evaluates to 1.

UNDERSTANDING THE CASE STRUCTURE

When you have a series of decisions based on the value stored in the same variable, most languages allow you to use a case structure. You first learned about the case structure in Chapter 4. There you learned that you can solve any programming problem using only the three basic structures—sequence, selection, and loop. You are never required to use a case structure—you can always substitute a series of selections. The **case structure** simply provides a convenient alternative to using a series of decisions when you must make choices based on the value stored in a single variable.

TIP ▫ ▫ ▫ ▫ | The syntax used to implement the case structure varies among languages. For example, Visual Basic uses `select case`, and C++ and Java use `switch`.

For example, suppose you work for a real estate developer who is selling houses that have one of three different floor plans. The logic segment of a program that determines the base price of the house might look like the logic shown in Figure 5-37.

FIGURE 5-37: FLOWCHART AND PSEUDOCODE DETERMINING HOUSE PRICE USING **if** STATEMENTS

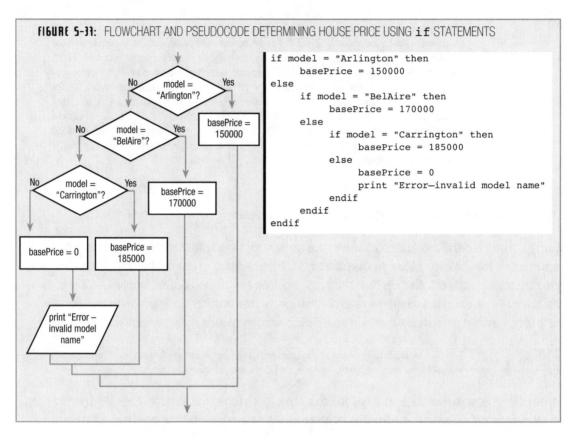

```
if model = "Arlington" then
     basePrice = 150000
else
     if model = "BelAire" then
          basePrice = 170000
     else
          if model = "Carrington" then
               basePrice = 185000
          else
               basePrice = 0
               print "Error—invalid model name"
          endif
     endif
endif
```

The logic shown in Figure 5-37 is completely structured. However, rewriting the logic using a case structure, as shown in Figure 5-38, might make it easier to understand. When using the case structure, you test a variable against a series of values, taking appropriate action based on the variable's value.

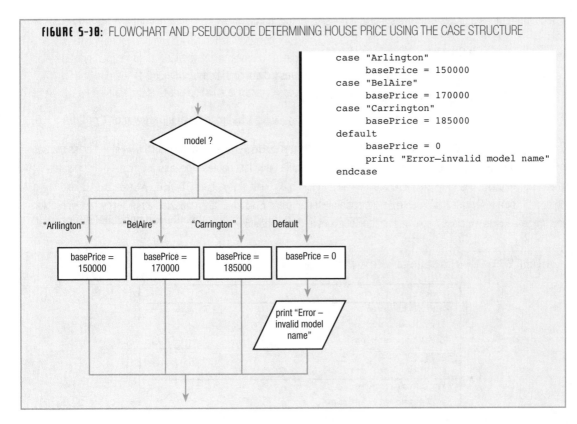

FIGURE 5-38: FLOWCHART AND PSEUDOCODE DETERMINING HOUSE PRICE USING THE CASE STRUCTURE

```
case "Arlington"
      basePrice = 150000
case "BelAire"
      basePrice = 170000
case "Carrington"
      basePrice = 185000
default
      basePrice = 0
      print "Error—invalid model name"
endcase
```

In Figure 5-38, the `model` variable is compared in turn with "Arlington", "BelAire", and "Carrington", and an appropriate `basePrice` value is set. The default case is the case that executes in the event no other cases execute. The logic shown in Figure 5-37 is identical to that shown in Figure 5-38; your choice of method to set the housing model prices is entirely a matter of preference.

TIP ☐ ☐ ☐ ☐ When you look at a nested `if-else` structure containing an outer and inner selection, if the inner nested `if` is within the `if` portion of the outer `if`, the program segment is a candidate for AND logic. On the other hand, if the inner `if` is within the `else` portion of the outer `if`, the program segment might be a candidate for the case structure.

TIP ☐ ☐ ☐ ☐ Some languages require a `break` statement at the end of each case selection segment. In those languages, once a case is true, all the following cases execute until a `break` statement is encountered. When you study a specific programming language, you will learn how to use `break` statements if they are required in that language.

USING DECISION TABLES

Some applications require multiple decisions to produce useful results. Managing all the possible outcomes of multiple decisions can be a difficult task, so programmers sometimes use a tool called a decision table to help organize the possible decision outcome combinations.

A **decision table** is a problem-analysis tool that consists of four parts:

- Conditions
- Possible combinations of Boolean values for the conditions
- Possible actions based on the outcomes
- The specific action that corresponds to each Boolean value of each condition

For example, suppose a college collects input data to create a `Student` class like the one shown in the class diagram in Figure 5-39. Each student's record includes an ID number, first and last names, age, and a variable that indicates whether the student has requested a residence hall that enforces quiet study hours. The `quietRequest` field holds either a "Y" or an "N" for each `Student` indicating whether the `Student` has requested a residence hall with quiet hours. The `Student` class also contains the usual get and set methods.

FIGURE 5-39: THE `Student` CLASS DIAGRAM

```
Student
-idNum: numeric
-firstName: string
-lastName: string
-age: numeric
-quietRequest: string
+getIdNum(): numeric
+getLastName(): string
+getFirstName(): string
+getAge(): numeric
+getQuietRequest: string
+setIdNum(numeric num): void
+setFirstName(string name): void
+setLastName(string name): void
+setAge(numeric age): void
+setQuietRequest(string request): void
```

Assume the residence hall director makes residence hall assignments based on the following rules:

- Students who are under 21 years old and request a residence hall with quiet study hours are assigned to Addams Hall.
- Students who are under 21 years old and who do not request a residence hall with quiet study hours are assigned to Grant Hall.

- Students who are 21 years old or older and request a residence hall with quiet study hours are assigned to Lincoln Hall.

- Students who are 21 years old and over who do not request a residence hall with quiet study hours are also assigned to Lincoln Hall, because that is the only residence hall for students over 21 years old.

You want to write an application that contains a method that accepts a `Student` argument and assigns the `Student` to the appropriate residence hall. Before you draw the flowchart or write the pseudocode, you can create a decision table to help you manage the decisions. You can begin to create a decision table by listing all the possible conditions that affect the outcome. They are:

- Student's `age is` under 21, or not

- Student's `quietRequest` is "Y", or not

Next, you determine all the possible Boolean value combinations that exist for the conditions. In this case, there are four possible combinations, as shown in Table 5-2.

TABLE 5-2: CONDITIONS AND POSSIBLE VALUES FOR RESIDENCE HALL DETERMINATION

Condition	Outcome			
age < 21	T	T	F	F
quietRequest = "Y"	T	F	T	F

Next, add rows to the decision table to list the possible outcome actions. A `Student` might be assigned to Addams, Grant, or Lincoln Hall. There are no other possibilities, so three possible action or outcome rows are added to the decision table. Table 5-3 shows the expanded table including the possible outcomes.

TABLE 5-3: CONDITIONS, POSSIBLE VALUES, AND POSSIBLE ACTIONS FOR RESIDENCE HALL DETERMINATION

Condition	Outcome			
age < 21	T	T	F	F
quietRequest = "Y"	T	F	T	F
assignedHall = "Addams"				
assignedHall = "Grant"				
assignedHall = "Lincoln"				

To complete the decision table, you choose one outcome for each possible combination of conditions. As shown in Table 5-4, you place an "X" (or any other symbol you prefer) in the Addams Hall row when a student's age is less than 21 and the `Student` has requested quiet study hours. You place an "X" in the Grant Hall row when the `Student` is under 21 and has not requested study hours. Finally, you place an "X" in the Lincoln Hall row whenever a `Student` is not under 21 years old. In this case, the request for quiet study hours is irrelevant because all `Students` who are 21 and older are assigned to Lincoln Hall.

TABLE 5-4: COMPLETED DECISION TABLE FOR RESIDENCE HALL SELECTION

Condition	Outcome			
`age < 21`	T	T	F	F
`quietRequest = "Y"`	T	F	T	F
`assignedHall = "Addams"`	X			
`assignedHall = "Grant"`		X		
`assignedHall = "Lincoln"`			X	X

In Table 5-4, the decision table is complete. There are four possible outcomes, and there is one "X" for each. Now, you can begin to design the logic that achieves the correct results. You can begin to write pseudocode for the decision-making process by writing a selection statement for the first condition as follows:

```
if age < 21 then
```

Whether this expression is `true` or `false`, you do not know the final residence hall assignment—in the decision table, when the expression is true, two columns are affected, and results are marked with an "X" in two different rows. Therefore, you need to insert another question, and the code becomes:

```
if age < 21 then
    if quietRequest = "Y" then
        assignedHall = "Addams"
```

At this point, you have written pseudocode that describes the first column of the decision table. The second column of the table describes the situation when the first decision is `true`, but the second decision is `false`. To include the information in the second column, the code becomes:

```
if age < 21 then
    if quietRequest = "Y" then
        assignedHall = "Addams"
    else
        assignedHall = "Grant"
    endif
```

If the `Student`'s `age` field value is not less that 21, then a second set of decisions applies as follows:

```
if age < 21 then
     if quietRequest = "Y" then
        assignedHall = "Addams"
     else
        assignedHall = "Grant"
     endif
else
     if quietRequest = "Y" then
        assignedHall = "Lincoln"
     else
        assignedHall = "Lincoln"
     endif
endif
```

Now, the code matches the decision table exactly. However, you might notice if the `Student`'s age is not under 21, then the `quietRequest` really does not matter—the `Student` is assigned to Lincoln Hall no matter what the `Student`'s study request was. Whenever both the `true` and `false` outcomes of a Boolean selection result in the same action, there is no need to make the selection. Figure 5-40 shows a completed `assignHall()` method that contains the abbreviated residence hall selection code. The method accepts a `Student` argument, declares a local variable named `assignedHall`, then starts the selection process using public get methods to access the private `age` and `quietRequest` fields from the `Student` class. After the decision-making process ends, the `Student`'s name and residence hall assignment are printed.

FIGURE 5-40: FLOWCHART AND PSEUDOCODE FOR THE `assignHall()` METHOD

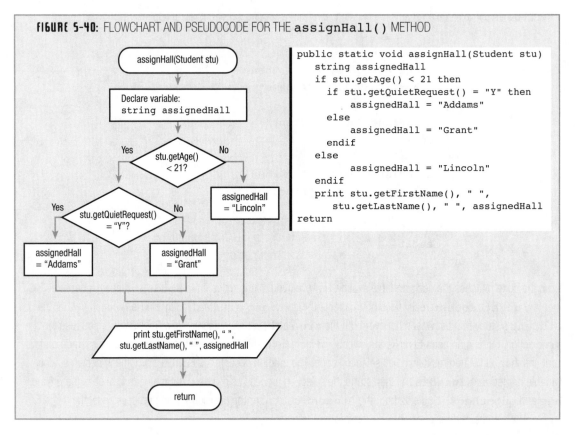

```
public static void assignHall(Student stu)
    string assignedHall
    if stu.getAge() < 21 then
        if stu.getQuietRequest() = "Y" then
            assignedHall = "Addams"
        else
            assignedHall = "Grant"
        endif
    else
        assignedHall = "Lincoln"
    endif
    print stu.getFirstName(), " ",
        stu.getLastName(), " ", assignedHall
return
```

Perhaps you could have created the final decision-making `assignHall()` method without creating the decision table first. If so, you need not use the decision table. Decision tables are more useful to the programmer when the decision-making process becomes more complicated. Additionally, they frequently serve as a useful graphic tool when you want to explain the decision-making process of a program to a user who is not familiar with flowcharting symbols or the format of pseudocode statements.

CHAPTER SUMMARY

☐ Every decision you make in a computer program involves evaluating a Boolean expression. You can use dual-alternative, or binary, selections or if-then-else structures to choose between two possible outcomes. You also can use single-alternative, or unary, selections or if-then structures when there is only one outcome for the question where action is required.

☐ For any two values that are the same type, you can use relational comparison operators to decide whether the two values are equal, the first value is greater than the second value, or the first value is less than the second value. The two values used in a Boolean expression can be either variables or constants.

☐ An AND decision occurs when two conditions must be true in order for a resulting action to take place. An AND decision requires a nested decision or a nested if.

☐ In an AND decision, first ask the question that is less likely to be true. This eliminates as many records as possible from the number that have to go through the second decision, which speeds up processing time.

☐ Most programming languages allow you to ask two or more questions in a single comparison by using a logical AND operator.

☐ When you must satisfy two or more criteria to initiate an event in a program, you must make sure that the second decision is made entirely within the first decision, and that you use a complete Boolean expression on both sides of the AND.

☐ An OR decision occurs when you want to take action when one or the other of two conditions is true.

☐ Errors occur in OR decisions when programmers do not maintain structure. An additional source of errors that are particular to the OR selection stems from people using the word AND to express OR requirements.

☐ In an OR decision, first ask the question that is more likely to be true.

☐ Most programming languages allow you to ask two or more questions in a single comparison by using a logical OR operator.

☐ To perform a range check, make comparisons with either the lowest or highest value in each range of values you are using.

☐ Common errors that occur when programmers perform range checks include asking unnecessary and previously answered questions.

☐ The case structure provides a convenient alternative to using a series of decisions when you must make choices based on the value stored in a single variable.

☐ A decision table is a problem-analysis tool that lists conditions and combinations of outcomes when those conditions are tested. It helps you identify the conditions under which each possible outcome occurs.

KEY TERMS

A **dual-alternative**, or **binary**, selection offers two actions, each associated with one of two possible outcomes. It is also called an **if-then-else** structure.

In a **single-alternative**, or **unary**, selection, action is required for only one outcome of the question. You call this form of the selection structure an **if-then**, because no "else" action is necessary.

An **if clause** of a decision holds the action that results when a Boolean expression in a decision is true.

The **else clause** of a decision holds the action or actions that execute only when the Boolean expression in the decision is false.

A **Boolean expression** is one that represents only one of two states, usually expressed as true or false.

A **trivial** Boolean expression is one that always evaluates to the same result.

Relational comparison operators are the symbols that express Boolean comparisons. Examples include =, >, <, >=, <=, and <>.

When you declare an object, each object name is a **reference**, or memory address.

With an **AND decision**, two conditions must both be true for an action to take place. An AND decision requires a **nested decision**, or a **nested if**—that is, a decision "inside of" another decision. A series of nested if statements can also be called a **cascading if statement**.

A **logical AND operator** is a symbol that you use to combine decisions so that two (or more) conditions must be true for an action to occur.

A **range of values** encompasses every value between a high and low limit.

An **OR decision** contains two (or more) decisions; if at least one condition is met, the resulting action takes place.

A **logical OR operator** is a symbol that you use to combine decisions when any one condition can be true for an action to occur.

The **logical NOT operator** is a symbol that reverses the meaning of a Boolean expression.

When you use a **range check**, you compare a variable to a series of values between limits.

A **default value** is one that is assigned after all test conditions are found to be false.

A **dead** or **unreachable path** is a logical path that can never be traveled.

When an operator has **precedence**, it is evaluated before others.

The **case structure** provides a convenient alternative to using a series of decisions when you must make choices based on the value stored in a single variable.

A **decision table** is a problem-analysis tool that lists conditions, combinations of outcomes when those conditions are tested, and possible actions based on the outcomes.

REVIEW QUESTIONS

1. The selection statement `if quantity > 100 then discountRate = 0.20` **is an example of a** _____ .

   a. single-alternative selection
   b. dual-alternative selection
   c. binary selection
   d. all of these

2. The selection statement `if dayOfWeek = "S" then price = 5.00 else price = 6.00` **is an example of a** _____ .

   a. unary selection
   b. single-alternative selection
   c. binary selection
   d. all of the above

3. **All selection statements must have** _____ .

   a. an `if` clause
   b. an `else` clause
   c. both of these
   d. none of these

4. **An expression like** `amount < 10` **is a** _____ **expression.**

   a. Gregorian
   b. Boolean
   c. unary
   d. binary

5. **Usually, you compare only variables that have the same** _____ .

   a. value
   b. size
   c. name
   d. type

6. **Symbols like > and < are known as** _____ **operators.**

   a. arithmetic
   b. relational comparison
   c. sequential
   d. scripting accuracy

7. **If you could use only three relational comparison operators, you could get by with** _____ .

   a. greater than, less than, and greater than or equal to
   b. less than, less than or equal to, and not equal to
   c. equal to, less than, and greater than
   d. equal to, not equal to, and less than

8. **If a > b is false, then which of the following is always true?**

   a. $a < b$

   b. $a <= b$

   c. $a = b$

   d. $a >= b$

9. **Usually, the most difficult comparison operator to work with is _____.**

   a. equal to

   b. greater than

   c. less than

   d. not equal to

10. **Which of the lettered choices is equivalent to the following decision?**

    ```
    if x > 10 then
        if y > 10 then
            print "X"
        endif
    endif
    ```

    a. `if x > 10 AND y > 10 then print "X"`

    b. `if x > 10 OR y > 10 then print "X"`

    c. `if x > 10 AND x > y then print "X"`

    d. `if y > x then print "X"`

11. **The Midwest Sales region of Acme Computer Company consists of five states—Illinois, Indiana, Iowa, Missouri, and Wisconsin. Suppose you have input records containing Acme customer data, including state of residence. To most efficiently select and display all customers who live in the Midwest Sales region, you would use _____.**

    a. five completely separate unnested `if` statements

    b. nested `if` statements using AND logic

    c. nested `if` statements using OR logic

    d. Not enough information is given.

12. **The Midwest Sales region of Acme Computer Company consists of five states—Illinois, Indiana, Iowa, Missouri, and Wisconsin. About 50 percent of the regional customers reside in Illinois, 20 percent in Indiana, and 10 percent in each of the other three states. Suppose you have input records containing Acme customer data, including state of residence. To most efficiently select and display all customers who live in the Midwest Sales region, you would ask first about residency in _____.**

    a. Illinois

    b. Indiana

    c. Wisconsin

    d. either Iowa, Missouri, or Wisconsin—it does not matter which one is first

13. The Boffo Balloon Company makes helium balloons. Large balloons cost $13.00 a dozen, medium-sized balloons cost $11.00 a dozen, and small balloons cost $8.60 a dozen. About 60 percent of the company's sales are the smallest balloons, 30 percent are the medium, and large balloons constitute only 10 percent of sales. Customer order records include customer information, quantity ordered, and size. When you write a program to determine price based on size, for the most efficient decision, you should ask first whether the size is _____ .

   a. large
   b. medium
   c. small
   d. It does not matter.

14. The Boffo Balloon Company makes helium balloons in three sizes, 12 colors, and with a choice of 40 imprinted sayings. As a promotion, the company is offering a 25-percent discount on orders of large, red "Happy Valentine's Day" balloons. To most efficiently select the orders to which a discount applies, you would use _____ .

   a. three completely separate unnested `if` statements
   b. nested `if` statements using AND logic
   c. nested `if` statements using OR logic
   d. Not enough information is given.

15. Radio station FM 99 keeps a record of every song played on the air in a week. Each record contains the day, hour, and minute the song started, and the title and artist of the song. The station manager wants a list of every title played during the important 8 a.m. commute hour on the two busiest traffic days, Monday and Friday. Which logic would select the correct titles?

```
a. if day = "Monday" OR day = "Friday" OR hour = 8 then
        print title
   endif

b. if day = Monday" then
        if hour = 8 then
           print title
        else
           if day = "Friday" then
               print title
           endif
        endif
     endif
   endif

c. if hour = 8 AND day = "Monday" OR day = "Friday" then
        print title
   endif
```

```
d. if hour = 8 then
        if day = "Monday" OR day = "Friday" then
            print title
        endif
    endif
endif
```

16. **In the following pseudocode, what percentage raise will an employee in Department 5 receive?**

```
if department < 3 then
    raise = 25
else
    if department < 5 then
        raise = 50
    else
        raise = 75
    endif
endif
```

   a. 25
   b. 50
   c. 75
   d. impossible to tell

17. **In the following pseudocode, what percentage raise will an employee in Department 8 receive?**

```
if department < 5 then
    raise = 100
else
    if department < 14 then
        raise = 250
    else
        if department < 9
            raise = 375
        endif
    endif
endif
```

   a. 100
   b. 250
   c. 375
   d. impossible to tell

18. In the following pseudocode, what percentage raise will an employee in Department 10 receive?

```
if department < 2 then
   raise = 1000
else
   if department < 6 then
     raise = 2500
   else
       if department < 10
          raise = 3000
       endif
   endif
endif
```

a. 1,000
b. 2,500
c. 3,000
d. impossible to tell

19. When you use a range check, you compare a variable to the _____ value in the range.

a. lowest
b. middle
c. highest
d. lowest or highest

20. Which of the following can be used as an alternative to a series of `if` statements based on the same variable?

a. a sequence structure
b. a loop structure
c. an action structure
d. a case structure

EXERCISES

1. Assume the following variables contain the values shown:

numberRed = 100   numberBlue = 200   numberGreen = 300

wordRed = "Wagon"   wordBlue = "Sky"   wordGreen = "Grass"

For each of the following Boolean expressions, decide whether the statement is true, false, or illegal.

a. numberRed = numberBlue?
b. numberBlue > numberGreen?
c. numberGreen < numberRed?
d. numberBlue = wordBlue?
e. numberGreen = "Green"?
f. wordRed = "Red"?

    g. wordBlue = "Blue"?

    h. numberRed <= numberGreen?

    i.   numberBlue >= 200?

    j.   numberGreen >= numberRed + numberBlue?

2.   **Chocolate Delights Candy Company manufactures several types of candy. Design the following:**

    a. A `Candy` class containing fields for the candy name (for example, "chocolate covered blueberries"), price per pound, and number of pounds sold in the average month. Include get and set methods for each field.

    b. A method that can be used in an application. The method receives a `Candy` object argument and displays the item's data fields only if it is a best-selling item. Best-selling items are those that sell more than 2,000 pounds per month.

    c. A method that receives a `Candy` object and produces a list of high-priced, best-selling items. Best-selling items are those that sell more than 2,000 pounds per month. High-priced items are those that sell for $10 per pound or more.

3.   **Pastoral College is a small college in the Midwest. Design the following:**

    a. A `Student` class that contains an ID number, first and last names, major field of study, grade point average, and a field that contains an asterisk if the student is on academic probation. Include get and set methods for the first five fields. The set method for the grade point average places the asterisk in the academic probation field when the `Student`'s grade point average is below 2.0.

    b. The Dean of Students needs a list of those students on academic probation. Design a method that receives a `Student` object and can be used in an application to display those students.

    c. The Literary Honor Society needs a list of English majors who have a grade point average of 3.5 or higher. Design a method that receives a `Student` object and can be used in an application to display those students.

4.   **The Summerville Telephone Company charges 10 cents per minute for all calls outside the customer's area code that last over 20 minutes. All other calls are 13 cents per minute. Design the following:**

    a. A `PhoneCall` class that holds data about one phone call. Fields for each call include customer area code (three digits), customer phone number (seven digits), called area code (three digits), called number (seven digits), and call time in minutes (four digits). Each of these fields has a get and set method that can be used with it. The class also contains a field that holds the charge for the call and a method that calculates the charge.

    b. A method that can be used by an application. The method receives a `PhoneCall` object as an argument and displays all the details about calls that cost over $10.

    c. A method that can be used by an application. The method receives two arguments—a `PhoneCall` object and a three-digit area code. The method displays any `PhoneCall` to the specified area code.

    d. A method that can be used by an application. The method receives two arguments—a PhoneCall object and a three-digit area code. The method displays any PhoneCall to or from the specified area code.

5. **Equinox Nursery maintains records about all the plants it has in stock. Design the following:**

   a. A `Plant` class that contains fields for the name of a plant, its price, and fields that indicate the plant's light and soil requirements. Include get and set methods for each field. The light field should contain either "sunny", "partial sun", or "shady". The soil field should contain either "clay" or "sandy".

   b. Only 20 percent of the nursery stock does well in shade, and 50 percent does well in sandy soil. Design a method that accepts a `Plant` argument and displays the Plant details for any `Plant` that would be appropriate in a shady, sandy yard.

6. **The Drive-Rite Insurance Company provides automobile insurance policies for drivers. Design the following:**

   a. Create a `PolicyHolder` class that contains a policy number, customer last name, customer first name, age, premium due month, day and year, and the number of accidents in which the driver has been involved in the last three years. Include get and set methods for each field. If a policy number is not between 1000 and 9999 inclusive, then set the policy number to 0. If the month is not between 1 and 12 inclusive, or the day is not correct for the month (that is, between 1 and 31 for January, 1 and 29 for February, and so on, then set the month, day and year all to 0.

   b. Create a method that receives a `PolicyHolder` argument and displays the data for any PolicyHolder over 35 years old.

   c. Create a method that receives a `PolicyHolder` argument and displays the data for any `PolicyHolder` who is at least 21 years old.

   d. Create a method that receives a `PolicyHolder` argument and displays the data for any `PolicyHolder` no more than 30 years old.

   e. Create a method that receives a `PolicyHolder` argument and displays the data for any `PolicyHolder` whose premium is due no later than March 15 any year.

   f. Create a method that receives a `PolicyHolder` argument and displays the data for any `PolicyHolder` whose premium is due up to and including January 1, 2007.

   g. Create a method that receives a `PolicyHolder` argument and displays the data for any `PolicyHolder` whose premium is due by April 27, 2009.

   h. Create a method that receives a `PolicyHolder` argument and displays the data for any `PolicyHolder` who has had fewer than 11 accidents.

   i. Create a method that receives a `PolicyHolder` argument and displays the data for any `PolicyHolder` who has had no more than five accidents.

   j. Create a method that receives a `PolicyHolder` argument and displays the data for any `PolicyHolder` who has had no accidents.

7. **The Barking Lot is a dog day care center. Design the following:**

   a. A `Dog` class that holds fields for ID number of owner, and the name, breed, age and weight of the dog. Include get and set methods for each field.

   b. An `Owner` class that holds ID number of owner, and owner's name, address, and phone number. Include get and set methods for each field.

   c. A method that accepts two objects—a `Dog` and an `Owner`. If the `Dog` and `Owner` IDs do not match, display an error message. Otherwise, display a bill containing the `Owner` and `Dog` data and the weekly day care fee which is $55 for dogs under 15 pounds, $75 for dogs at least 15 pounds but no more than 30 pounds, $105 for dogs over 30 pounds but no more than 80 pounds, and $125 for dogs over 80 pounds.

8. **Rick Hammer is a carpenter who wants an application to compute the price of any desk a customer orders, based on the following: desk length and width in inches, type of wood, and number of drawers. The price is computed as follows:**

   - The charge for all desks is a minimum $200.

   - If the surface (length * width) is over 750 square inches, add $50.

   - If the wood is "mahogany" add $150; for "oak" add $125. No charge is added for "pine."

   - For every drawer in the desk, there is an additional $30 charge.

   Design the following:

   a. An `Order` class including the order number, customer name, and all the fields mentioned above. Include get and set methods for each field.
   b. An application that accepts an `Order` and displays all the relevant information and the price.

9. **Black Dot Printing is attempting to organize carpools to save energy. Each input record contains an employee's name and town of residence. Ten percent of the company's employees live in Wonder Lake. Thirty percent of the employees live in Woodstock. Because these towns are both north of the company, the company wants a list of employees who live in either town, so it can recommend that these employees drive to work together. Design the following:**

   a. An `Employee` class containing relevant fields and methods.
   b. A method that accepts an `Employee` object and prints the `Employee`'s name and address when the Employee is a candidate for the carpool.

10. **Diana Lee is a supervisor in a manufacturing company wants to know which employees have increased their production this year over last year, so that she can issue them certificates of commendation and bonuses. Design the following:**

    a. A `ProductionWorker` class containing first and last names, this year's number of units produced, and last year's number of units produced. Include appropriate get and set methods.
    b. A method that accepts a `ProductionWorker` object and displays the employees whose production is increased over last year's production.
    c. A method that displays a `ProductionWorker`'s name and a bonus amount. The bonuses will be distributed as follows:

    If this year's production is:

    - 1,000 units or fewer, the bonus is $25

    - 1,001 to 3,000 units, the bonus is $50

    - 3,001 to 6,000 units, the bonus is $100

    - 6,001 units and up, the bonus is $200

d. Modify Exercise 10c to reflect the following new facts, and have the method execute as efficiently as possible:

■ Only employees whose production this year is higher than it was last year will receive bonuses. This is true for approximately 30 percent of the employees.

■ Sixty percent of employees produce over 6,000 units per year; 20 percent produce 3,001 to 6,000; 15 percent produce 1,001 to 3,000 units; and only 5 percent produce fewer than 1,001.

11. **The Richmond Riding Club wants to assign the title of Master or Novice to each of its members. A member earns the title of Master by accomplishing two or more of the following:**

■ Participating in at least eight horse shows

■ Winning a first or second place ribbon in at least two horse shows, no matter how many shows the member has participated in

■ Winning a first, second, third, or fourth place ribbon in at least four horse shows, no matter how many shows the member has participated in

Design the following:

a. A `Rider` class that contains a last name, first name, number of shows in which the Rider has participated, and number of first, second, third and fourth place ribbons the Rider has received. Also include a field that holds the "Master" or "Novice" status label. Include two set methods—one that receives both the first and last names of the `Rider` and the other that receives the numbers of shows and each category of ribbons. If the sum of the first, second, thirds and fourth place ribbons exceeds the number of shows, then set all the ribbon fields to 0 and display an error message. The method that sets the shows and ribbons fields also determines the "Master" or "Novice" status of the `Rider`. Also include a get method for each field.
b. A method that accepts a Rider object and displays only "Master" `Rider`s.

12. **The Dorian Gray Portrait Studio charges its customers for portrait sittings based on the number of subjects posing for the portrait. The fee schedule is as follows:**

Subjects in Portrait	Base Price
1	$100
2	$130
3	$150
4	$165
5	$175
6	$180
7 or more	$185

Portrait sittings on Saturday or Sunday cost an extra 20 percent more than the base price.

Design the following:

a. A `PortraitSitting` class that includes private fields to hold the last name of the family sitting for the portrait, the number of subjects in the portrait, the schedule day of the week, the scheduled time of day, and the fee. Provide public set methods that accept arguments for all of the fields except for the fee; the fee is calculated by a public `calculateFee()` method that contains a case structure that determines the base fee and a decision structure that determines whether a weekend premium is charged. Also include a get method for each field.

b. A method that can be used by an application. The method accepts a `PortraitSitting` object as an argument. The method prompts the user for a day and displays the `PortraitSitting` details if the sitting is scheduled for that day.

CASE PROJECT

In earlier chapters you developed classes needed for Cost Is No Object—a car rental service that specializes in lending antique and luxury cars to clients on a short-term basis. You created pseudocode for **Employee**, **Customer**, **Automobile**, and **RentalAgreement** classes including attributes and methods to get and set those attributes.

The **RentalAgreement** class contains all the attributes and methods associated with one rental contract. Modify your **RentalAgreement** class to contain fields to hold the following:

- Contract number

- Customer ID number

- Automobile vehicle identification number

- Starting date for the rental agreement stored as three separate fields—month, day, and year

- Length, in days, for the rental agreement

- Expected ending date for the rental agreement stored as three separate fields—month, day, and year

- Indicator of whether the customer has elected to buy the optional insurance policy

Include a get method for each field that returns the field's value.

Include set methods as follows. Each assigns a value to one or more of the class fields, or displays an error message as follows:

- `void setContractNumber(numeric number)`—If the contract number is not between 10000 and 99999 inclusive, issue an error message.

- `void setCustomerIDNumber(numeric number)`—If the customer ID number is not between 100 and 999 inclusive, issue an error message.

- `void setVehicleIdentificationNumber(numeric number)`—If the vehicle identification number is not between 100 and 999 inclusive, issue an error message.

- `void setStartingDate(numeric month, numeric day, numeric year)`—If the starting date for the rental agreement is prior to today's date, issue an error message. Otherwise, make sure the month is between 1 and 12, inclusive. If the month is 1, 3, 5, 7, 8, 10, or 12, the day must be between 1 and 31, inclusive. If the month is 2, the day must be between 1 and 28, inclusive. (You do not need to check for leap years.). If the month is 4, 6, 9, or 11, the day must be between 1 and 30, inclusive. Assign values to the class starting date month, day, and year fields only if all three are valid; if any of the field values are not valid, assign 0 to all three and display an error message.

- `void setAgreementLength(int days)`—If the length of the agreement is not between 1 and 30 days inclusive, issue an error message. Otherwise, calculate the ending month, day, and year based on the starting date and length of the agreement.

- `void setInsuranceIndicator(string insuranceIndicator)`—The insurance indicator must be "Y" or "N" (for "Yes" or "No"); otherwise, display an error message.

LOOPING

After studying Chapter 6, you should be able to:

- [ ] Understand the advantages of looping
- [ ] Control loops with variables, counters, and sentinel values
- [ ] Avoid common loop mistakes
- [ ] Use a **for** loop
- [ ] Use a **do until** loop
- [ ] Recognize the characteristics shared by all loops
- [ ] Nest loops
- [ ] Use a loop to accumulate totals

UNDERSTANDING THE ADVANTAGES OF LOOPING

While making decisions is what makes computers seem intelligent, it's looping that makes computer programming both efficient and worthwhile. When you use a loop within a computer program, you can write one set of instructions that operates on multiple, separate sets of data. Consider the following set of tasks required for each employee in a typical payroll program:

- Determine regular pay.
- Determine overtime pay, if any.
- Determine federal withholding tax based on gross wages and number of dependents.
- Determine state withholding tax based on gross wages, number of dependents, and state of residence.
- Determine insurance deduction based on insurance code.
- Determine Social Security deduction based on gross pay.
- Subtract federal tax, state tax, Social Security, and insurance from gross pay.

In reality, this list is too short—companies deduct stock option plans, charitable contributions, union dues, and other items from checks in addition to the items mentioned in this list. Also, they might pay bonuses and commissions and provide sick days and vacation days that must be taken into account and handled appropriately. As you can see, payroll programs are complicated.

The advantage of having a computer perform payroll calculations is that all of the deduction instructions need to be written *only once* and can be repeated over and over again for each paycheck, using a **loop**, the structure that repeats actions while some condition continues.

CONTROLLING LOOPS WITH VARIABLES, COUNTERS, AND SENTINEL VALUES

Recall the loop, or while structure, that you learned about in Chapter 4. See Figure 6-1. The loop is a structure in which you ask a question, and if the answer is true, you perform a task or set of tasks, and immediately ask the same question again. As long as the answer continues to be true, the cycle repeats.

FIGURE 6-1: THE while LOOP

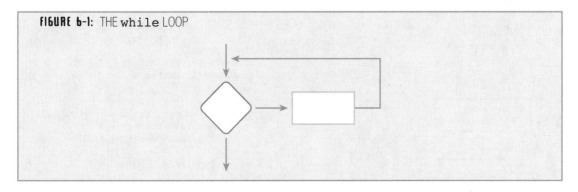

To determine whether and how many times a loop repeats, you can use loop control variables, counters, or sentinel values. Each technique is discussed in the following sections.

USING A WHILE LOOP WITH A LOOP CONTROL VARIABLE

Almost every business application contains a **main loop**, or a basic set of instructions that is repeated for every record. The main loop is a typical loop—within it, you write one set of instructions that executes repeatedly while records continue to be read from an input file, for example, producing a paycheck for each employee. When an application processes data records, most of its tasks are located in a main loop; these tasks repeat over and over for many records (sometimes hundreds, thousands, or millions). For example, consider the `Employee` class shown in Figure 6-2 and the application that uses it in Figure 6-3.

FIGURE 6-2: AN Employee CLASS

```
public class Employee
     private numeric idNum
     private numeric hourlyRate

     public numeric getIdNum()
     return idNum

     public numeric getHourlyRate()
     return hourlyRate

     public void setIdNum(numeric emp)
          idNum = emp
     return

     public void setHourlyRate(numeric rate)
          hourlyRate = rate
     return
endClass
```

TIP ▢ ▢ ▢ ▢ | Just as in an `Employee` class example you saw in Chapter 5, this class is also much smaller than the class that would be used by a company to store Employee data. The example classes are small so you can more easily follow the logic.

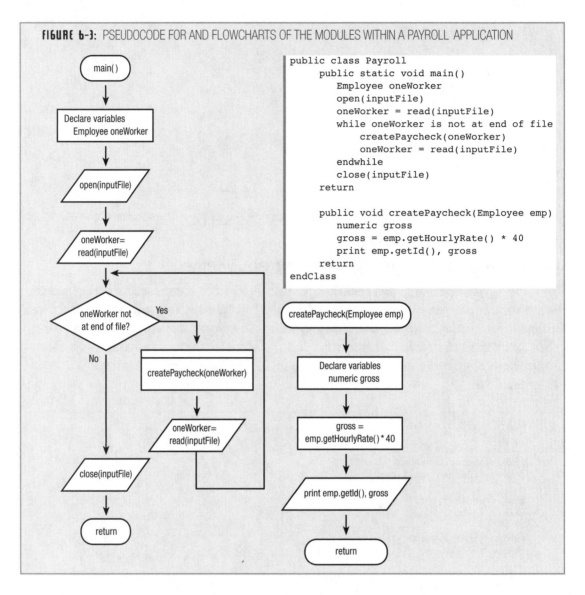

FIGURE 6-3: PSEUDOCODE FOR AND FLOWCHARTS OF THE MODULES WITHIN A PAYROLL APPLICATION

```
public class Payroll
    public static void main()
        Employee oneWorker
        open(inputFile)
        oneWorker = read(inputFile)
        while oneWorker is not at end of file
            createPaycheck(oneWorker)
            oneWorker = read(inputFile)
        endwhile
        close(inputFile)
    return

    public void createPaycheck(Employee emp)
        numeric gross
        gross = emp.getHourlyRate() * 40
        print emp.getId(), gross
    return
endClass
```

TIP ▫ ▫ ▫ ▫ | The stripe across the top of the process symbol that calls `createPaycheck()` in Figure 6-3 shows that the statement is a method call. Using the stripe is a common way to indicate a processing step in a flowchart.

In the application in Figure 6-3, an `Employee` object named `oneWorker` is declared. Then an input file is opened. **Opening a file** instructs the computer to find a stored file and prepare it for reading data into an application. The exact syntax of this statement differs among programming languages, but it often is a built-in method call and always involves both providing a path to and naming the file to be opened. In the pseudocode, the statement `oneWorker = read(inputFile)` means to access the input file using a language's `read()` method, retrieve the number of bytes that is the same size as the `oneWorker Employee` object, and store those bytes in the memory allocated for `oneWorker`. In other words, both the ID number and hourly rate from the first record stored on disk will be placed into the appropriate fields within the `Employee` object declared in the application.

 When you open a file in an application, you might also want to include a decision that would display an error message in the event the requested file is not found. That step is eliminated in this example to keep the example simple.

In Figure 6-3, the `while` loop begins with the `while oneWorker is not at end of file` statement in the application. This syntax will differ among programming languages, but the file manipulation functions in every language provide a way for applications to determine whether all of the input records in the file have been accessed. When the first input record is read, if the file is empty, the end of file condition is met immediately, and the statements within the loop never execute. However, assuming a record exists, the loop is entered, the `oneWorker` object is passed to the `createPaycheck()` method, and a second data record is read from the input file. The loop continues to execute while there are more records. When there are no more records, a built-in method to close the file is called. **Closing a file** makes it no longer available for reading.

 As a form of shorthand, many languages provide a constant value that represents the end of file value; frequently the name of this constant is EOF. In subsequent file-reading examples, this text will use a shorthand statement such as `while oneWorker not EOF` to check for the EOF condition.

 In the application in Figure 6-3, the `createPaycheck()` module accepts a copy of the current `Employee` object and stores it in the local variable named `emp`. Then, it simply multiplies the employee's pay rate by 40 and prints the ID number and gross pay. A real payroll application might use a variable number of hours worked instead of 40, calculate many deductions, and print additional employee information such as a name.

 In most programming languages, if you do not close the file from which you read records, nothing bad will happen. However, explicitly closing a file clearly shows your intentions. In some languages, the file will automatically close when it goes out of scope—that is, when the method or block of statements in which it was declared ends.

The flowchart and pseudocode segments in Figure 6-3 show three steps that must occur in every loop:

1. You must provide a starting value that will control the loop. In this case, the starting value is provided by the first `oneWorker = read(inputFile)` statement. Either the `oneWorker` object contains valid Employee data, or it contains the language's symbols for the EOF condition.

2. You must make a comparison using the value that controls whether the loop continues or stops. In this case, you compare what is returned from a read method to an EOF value.

3. Within the loop, you must alter the value that controls the loop. In this case, you read from the input file again, changing the values in the `oneWorker` object, and perhaps providing it with the EOF value.

TIP □ □ □ □ | The first read statement in the application in Figure 6-3 is a priming input statement. You learned about the priming input statement in Chapter 4.

On each pass through the loop, the value in the `oneWorker` variable determines whether the loop will continue. Therefore variables like `oneWorker` are known as **loop control variables**. Any variable that determines whether a loop will continue is a loop control variable.

In addition to this main loop, loops also appear within modules. They are used any time you need to perform a task several times and don't want to write identical or similar instructions over and over. Suppose for example, as part of a much larger application, you want to display a warning message on the computer screen when the user has made a potentially dangerous menu selection (say, "Delete all files"). To get the user's attention, you want to display the message four times. You can write this module as shown in Figure 6-4, but using a loop, as shown in Figure 6-5, is much more efficient.

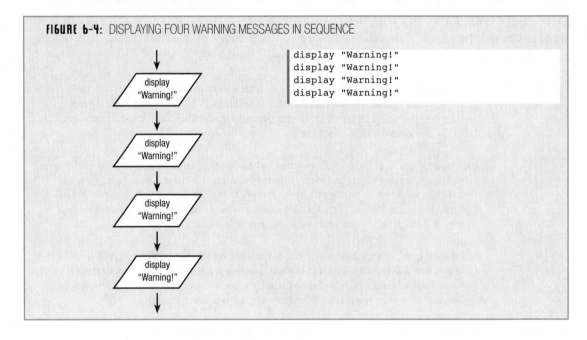

FIGURE 6-4: DISPLAYING FOUR WARNING MESSAGES IN SEQUENCE

```
display "Warning!"
display "Warning!"
display "Warning!"
display "Warning!"
```

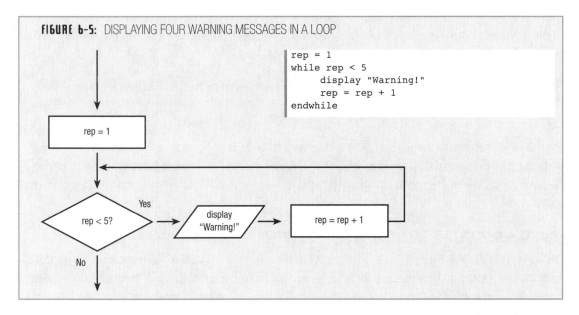

FIGURE 6-5: DISPLAYING FOUR WARNING MESSAGES IN A LOOP

```
rep = 1
while rep < 5
     display "Warning!"
     rep = rep + 1
endwhile
```

As with the flowchart and pseudocode segments in Figure 6-3, those in Figure 6-5 show the three steps that must occur in every loop:

1. You must initialize the loop control variable. The variable in this case is named **rep**, and it is initialized to 1.
2. You must compare the variable to some value that controls whether the loop continues or stops. In this case, you compare **rep** to the value 5.
3. Within the loop, you must alter the variable that controls the loop. In this case, you alter **rep** by adding 1 to it.

On each pass through the loop, the value in the **rep** variable determines whether the loop will continue.

TIP □ □ □ □ | A value like 5 that stops loop execution is sometimes called a **sentinel value** (also known as a limit, or ending value).

The loops in Figure 6-3 and 6-5 are very similar, but they do illustrate one major difference between loops. When the Payroll application in Figure 6-3 executes, it might execute any number of times. In other words, if you execute the application with different payroll data files, each might contain a different number of data records, and the application will process all of them. Looking at the code in the Payroll application, you cannot tell how many times the loop will execute the next time the application is used. A loop for which you cannot predict the number of repetitions is sometimes called an **indefinite**, or **indeterminate**, **loop**.

On the other hand, the loop in Figure 6-5 executes exactly four times. The **rep** value is set to 1, increased by 1 on every pass through the loop, and stops when **rep** reaches 5. A loop for which you do know the number of repetitions that will take place is a **definite loop**.

The decision that controls every loop is always based on a Boolean comparison. You can use any of the six comparison operators that you learned about in Chapter 5 to control a loop—equal to, greater than, less than, greater than or equal to, less than or equal to, and not equal to.

TIP ▫ ▫ ▫ ▫ | Just as with a selection, the Boolean comparison that controls a while loop must compare same-type values: numeric values are compared to other numeric values, and character values to other character values.

The statements that execute within a loop are known as the **loop body**. The body of a loop might contain any number of statements, including method calls, decisions, and other loops. Once your logic enters the body of a structured loop, the entire loop body must execute. Your program can leave a structured loop only at the comparison that tests the loop control variable.

USING A COUNTER TO CONTROL LOOPING

The looping logic shown in Figure 6-5 uses a counter. A **counter** is any numeric variable you use to count the number of times an event has occurred. In Figure 6-5 the variable `rep` is a counter; it is initialized to 1, then increases by 1 each time though the loop. The same results could be achieved by starting the loop control variable value at 0 and continuing the loop while the value is less than 4, as shown in Figure 6-6.

FIGURE 6-6: DISPLAYING FOUR WARNING MESSAGES IN A LOOP, STARTING THE COUNTER AT 0

```
rep = 0
while rep < 4
     display "Warning!"
     rep = rep + 1
endwhile
```

TIP ▫ ▫ ▫ ▫ | Many programmers prefer starting their loops with a variable containing a 0 value for two reasons. First, in many computer applications, numbering starts with 0 because of the 0-and-1 nature of computer circuitry. Second, when you learn about arrays in Chapter 7, you will discover that array manipulation naturally lends itself to 0-based loops.

Similarly, you could achieve the same results by starting `rep` at 17 and continuing while it is less than 21, or starting `rep` at 108 and continuing while it is less than 112. These approaches would be awkward, however—most loops will start with a loop control variable receiving a 0 or 1 starting value.

Adding 1 (or any other constant) to a variable is called **incrementing** the variable. Incrementing a counter variable is a common necessary loop task.

TIP ▫ ▫ ▫ ▫ | Because you so frequently need to increment a variable, many programming languages contain a shortcut operator for incrementing. For example, in C++, Java, and C#, you can replace the statement `rep = rep + 1` with `++rep` or `rep++`. You pronounce these statements, "plus plus rep" and "rep plus plus". Both statements increase the value of rep by 1. There is a difference in how these statements operate; you learn the difference when you study a programming language that uses them.

USING CONSTANT AND VARIABLE SENTINEL VALUES

Suppose you own a factory and have decided to place a label on every product you manufacture. The label contains the words "Made for you personally by" followed by the first name of one of your employees. Assume that for one week's production, you need 100 personalized labels for each employee.

Assume you already have a `Personnel` class created, and that a data file contains Personnel records that can be used for input to this application. This class and file might have more information than you'll need for this application, but the important feature of the class is that it contains each employee's name. The class diagram for the `Personnel` class appears in Figure 6-7. You can see from the diagram that the `Personnel` class contains five private fields; each of the fields has two public methods associated with it—one to set the field value and one to retrieve it.

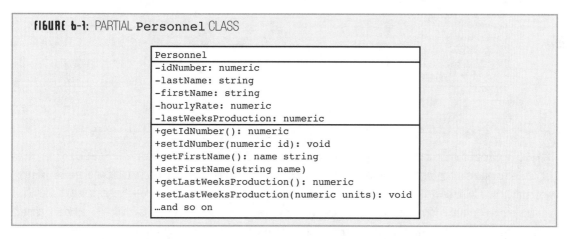

FIGURE 6-7: PARTIAL `Personnel` CLASS

```
Personnel
-idNumber: numeric
-lastName: string
-firstName: string
-hourlyRate: numeric
-lastWeeksProduction: numeric
+getIdNumber(): numeric
+setIdNumber(numeric id): void
+getFirstName(): name string
+setFirstName(string name)
+getLastWeeksProduction(): numeric
+setLastWeeksProduction(numeric units): void
…and so on
```

Figure 6-8 shows the application that creates 100 labels for each employee. In the `main()` method, a `Personnel` object is created, the input file is opened, and the first worker is read into memory from the data file. While records continue to be found, each `Personnel` object is passed to the `createLabels()` method. The `createLabels()` method accepts a copy of the passed `Personnel` object, and locally names it `per`. Within the method, a loop that executes 100 times uses the `Personnel` class `getFirstName()` instance method to retrieve the first name and print it on the label. After `createLabels()` returns, the next record is read from the input file.

FIGURE 6-8: A LABEL-MAKING APPLICATION

```
public class Create100Labels
    public void main()
        Personnel aWorker
        open(inputFile)
        aWorker = read(inputFile)
        while aWorker not EOF
            createLabels(aWorker)
            aWorker = read(inputFile)
        endwhile
    return

    public void createLabels(Personnel per)
        numeric num
        num = 0
        while num < 100
            print "Made for you personally by ",
                per.getFirstName()
            num = num + 1
        endwhile
    return
endClass
```

The `main()` method in Figure 6-8 contains the loop that reads records from a data file. The `createLabels()` method also contains a loop. Although the loop in the `main()` method is indefinite—that is, any number of `Personnel` objects might eventually be retrieved—the loop in the `createLabels()` method is definite—that is, it uses a counter that varies from 0 to 100 in increments of 1. While the counter, named `num`, continues to be less than 100, a label is printed and the number is increased. When 100 labels have printed, control returns to the `main()` method, where the next record is retrieved from the input file. The 100 is a fixed, or constant, sentinel value—it is the value that will be used for every employee, no matter how many exist.

TIP □ □ □ □ Setting the `label counter num` to 0 within the `createLabels()` method is important. Although some languages initialize a newly declared variable to 0 for you, some do not, and either way, your intentions are clearer if you explicitly assign 0 to num.

TIP □ □ □ □ You could make the `createLabels()` method in Figure 6-8 more efficient by retrieving the first name from the **per** object once, before the loop begins. That way, you would avoid 99 method calls, each of which takes time. In other words, the method could be written as follows:

```
public void createLabels(Personnel per)
        string name = per.getFirstName()
        numeric num
        num = 0
        while num < 100
            print "Made for you personally by ",
                name
            num = num + 1
        endwhile
    return
```

Sometimes you don't want to be forced to repeat every pass through a loop the same number of times. For example, instead of printing 100 labels for each employee, you might want to vary the number of labels based on how many items a worker actually produces. That way, high-achieving workers won't run out of labels, and less productive workers won't have too many. Instead of printing the same, constant number of labels for every employee, a more sophisticated program prints a different number of labels for each employee, depending on that employee's previous week's production. For example, you might decide to print enough labels to cover 110 percent of each employee's production rate from the previous week; this ensures that the employee will have enough labels for the week, even if his or her production level improves.

For example, assume that the number of units an employee produced in the previous week is stored in an input file in the field named `lastWeeksProduction` in the **Personnel** class in Figure 6-7. To write an application that produces an appropriate number of labels for each employee, you can make some minor modifications to the original label-making method. For example, Figure 6-9 shows a modified `createLabels()` method that uses each employee's previous week production figure to calculate the number of labels needed. The changes from the method in Figure 6-8 are highlighted. The number of labels printed is equivalent to 1.10 times the previous week's production—that is, last week's production, plus 10 percent more. The Boolean expression used in the `while` statement in the method compares the counter variable to `labelsToPrint`, instead of to a fixed value.

FIGURE 6-9: A LABEL-MAKING METHOD THAT USES A VARIABLE SENTINEL

```
public void createLabels(Personnel per)
     numeric labelsToPrint
     numeric num
     num = 0
     labelsToPrint = per.getLastWeeksProduction() * 1.10
     while num < labelsToPrint
          print "Made for you personally by ",
               per.getFirstName()
          num = num + 1
     endwhile
return
```

TIP ▫ ▫ ▫ ▫   The statement `labelsToPrint = per.getLastWeeksProduction() * 1.10` calculates `labelsToPrint` as 110 percent of the production volume from the previous week. Alternately, you could perform the calculation as `labelsToPrint = per.getLastWeeksProduction() + 0.10 * per.getLastWeeksProduction()`. The mathematical result is the same, but this later version requires two calls to the method that returns the production value, and so takes slightly longer to execute.

LOOPING BY DECREMENTING

Rather than increasing a loop control variable until it passes some sentinel value, sometimes it is more convenient to reduce a loop control variable on every cycle through a loop. For example, again assume you want to print enough labels for every worker to cover 110 percent of the previous week's production. As an alternative to setting a `num` variable to 0 and increasing it after each label prints, you initially can set `labelsToPrint` equal to the number of labels to print (`per.getLastWeeksProduction() * 1.10`), and subsequently reduce the `labelsToPrint` value every time a label prints. You continue printing labels and reducing the `labelsToPrint` until you have counted down to zero. Decreasing a variable by 1 (or any other constant value) is called **decrementing** the variable.

For example, when you write the method in Figure 6-10, you produce enough labels to equal 110 percent of the last week's production units. The changes from Figure 6-9 are highlighted.

FIGURE 6-10: A LABEL-MAKING METHOD THAT DECREMENTS A VARIABLE SENTINEL

```
public void createLabels(Personnel per)
    numeric labelsToPrint
    labelsToPrint = per.getLastWeeksProduction() * 1.10
    while labelsToPrint > 0
        print "Made for you personally by ",
            per.getFirstName()
        labelsToPrint = labelsToPrint - 1
    endwhile
return
```

When you decrement, you can avoid declaring a special variable such as `num`, which was used in the example in Figure 6-9. The `labelsToPrint` variable starts with a value that represents the labels to print, and works its way down to zero.

TIP □ □ □ □ | Because you so frequently need to decrement a variable, many programming languages contain a shortcut operator for decrementing. For example, in C++, Java, and C#, you can replace the statement labelsToPrint = labelsToPrint −1 with --labelsToPrint or labelsToPrint--. You pronounce these statements, "minus minus labelsToPrint" and "labelsToPrint minus minus". Both statements decrease the value of labelsToPrint by 1. There is a difference in how these statements operate; you learn the difference when you study a programming language that uses them.

AVOIDING COMMON LOOP MISTAKES

The mistakes programmers make most often with loops are:

- Neglecting to initialize the loop control variable
- Neglecting to alter the loop control variable
- Using the wrong comparison with the loop control variable
- Including statements inside the loop that belong outside the loop

NEGLECTING TO INITIALIZE THE LOOP CONTROL VARIABLE

It is always a mistake to fail to initialize a loop's control variable. For example, assume you remove the statement `num = 0` from the `createLabels()` method illustrated in Figure 6-8. The result is the method in Figure 6-11. Notice that although `num` is declared as a numeric variable in the highlighted line, it never receives a starting value. When `num` is compared to `labelsToPrint` at the start of the `while` loop, it is impossible to predict whether the result is true or false; you can't predict whether any labels will print. Because in most programming languages, uninitialized values contain unknown, unpredictable garbage, comparing such a variable to another value is meaningless.

FIGURE 6-11: A METHOD THAT FAILS TO INITIALIZE ITS LOOP CONTROL VARIABLE AND PRODUCES UNPREDICTABLE RESULTS

```
public void createLabels(Personnel per)
    numeric labelsToPrint
    numeric num
    labelsToPrint = per.getLastWeeksProduction() * 1.10
    while num < labelsToPrint
        print "Made for you personally by ",
            per.getFirstName()
        num = num + 1
    endwhile
return
```

NEGLECTING TO ALTER THE LOOP CONTROL VARIABLE

A different sort of error will occur if you remove the statement that adds 1 to the label-counting `num` variable in the method in Figure 6-9. This error will result in the following code shown in Figure 6-12.

FIGURE 6-12: A LABEL-MAKING METHOD INCLUDING AN INFINITE LOOP

```
public void createLabels(Personnel per)
    numeric labelsToPrint
    numeric num
    num = 0
    labelsToPrint = per.getLastWeeksProduction() * 1.10
    while num < labelsToPrint
        print "Made for you personally by ",
            per.getFirstName()
    endwhile
return
```

Following this logic, when `num` is set to 0 and `labelsToPrint` is, for example, 110, then `num` will be less than `labelsToPrint` forever. The loop body consists only of the print statement; nothing in the loop changes either `num` or `labelsToPrint`, so when `num` is less than `labelsToPrint` once, then `num` is less than `labelsToPrint` forever. Labels containing "Made for you personally by" and the same worker's name will continue to print. A loop that never stops executing is an **infinite loop**. It is always incorrect to create a loop that cannot terminate.

USING THE WRONG COMPARISON WITH THE LOOP CONTROL VARIABLE

Programmers must be careful to use the correct comparison in the statement that controls a loop. Although there is only a one-keystroke difference between the following two code segments, one performs the loop 10 times and the other performs the loop 11 times.

```
counter = 0
while counter < 10
      perform someMethod()
      counter = counter + 1
endwhile
```

and

```
counter = 0
while counter <= 10
      perform someMethod()
      counter = counter + 1
endwhile
```

The seriousness of the error of using <= or >= when only < or > is needed depends on the actions performed within the loop. For example, if such an error occurred in a loan company application, each customer might be charged a month's additional interest; if the error occurred in an airline's application, it might overbook a flight; and if it occurred in a pharmacy's drug-dispensing application, each patient might receive one extra (and possibly harmful and expensive) unit of medication.

INCLUDING STATEMENTS INSIDE THE LOOP THAT BELONG OUTSIDE THE LOOP

When you run a computer application that uses the loop in Figure 6-9, hundreds or thousands of employee records might pass through the `createLabels()` method. If there are 100 employee records, `num` is set to 0 exactly 100 times; it must be reset to 0 once for each employee, in order to count each employee's labels correctly. Similarly, `labelsToPrint` is reset (to 1.10 times the current `per.getLastWeeksProduction()` value) once for each employee.

If the average employee produces 100 items during a week, then the loop within the `createLabels()` method, the one controlled by the statement `while num < labelsToPrint`, executes 11,000 times—110 times each for 100 employees. This number of repetitions is necessary to print the correct number of labels.

A repetition that is *not* necessary would be to execute 11,000 separate multiplication statements to recalculate the value to compare to `labelsToPrint`. See Figure 6-13.

FIGURE 6-13: INEFFICIENT PSEUDOCODE FOR `createLabels()` METHOD

```
public void createLabels(Personnel per)
    numeric num
    num = 0
    while num < per.getLastWeeksProduction() * 1.10
        print "Made for you personally by ",
            per.getFirstName()
        num = num + 1
    endwhile
return
```

Although the logic shown in Figure 6-13 produces the correct number of labels for every employee, the statement `while num < per.getLastWeeksProduction() * 1.10` executes an average of 110 times for each employee. That means the arithmetic operation that is part of the question—multiplying the value of last week's production by 1.10—occurs 110 separate times for each employee. Performing the same calculation that results in the same mathematical answer 110 times in a row is inefficient. Instead, it is superior to perform the multiplication just once for each employee and use the result 110 times, as shown in the original version of the program in Figure 6-9. In the pseudocode in Figure 6-9, you still must recalculate `labelsToPrint` once for each record, but not once for each label, so you have improved efficiency.

The methods illustrated in Figures 6-9 and 6-13 do the same thing—print enough labels for every employee to cover 110 percent of production. However, one does it more efficiently. As you become more proficient at programming, you will recognize many opportunities to perform the same tasks in alternate, more elegant, and more efficient ways.

USING A FOR LOOP

The label-making application discussed in this chapter contains two loops. As Figure 6-8 shows, the `main()` method performs the `createLabels()` module while there are still more employees, and the `createLabels()` module prints labels while there are still labels to print for a specific employee. Entry to the loop in the `main()` logic is controlled by the EOF decision and is an indefinite loop. The label-producing loop in the `createLabels()` module, however, is a definite loop, the kind of loop in which you definitely know the repetition factor. Every high-level computer programming language contains a `while` statement that you can use to code any loop, including indefinite loops (like one that reads an unknown number of records from a file) and definite loops (like one that prints exactly 100 labels).

In addition to the `while` statement, most computer languages also support a `for` statement. You can use the **for statement**, or **for loop**, with definite loops—those that will loop a specific number of times—frequently when you know exactly how many times the loop will repeat. The `for` statement provides you with three actions in one compact statement. The `for` statement uses a loop control variable that it automatically:

- Initializes
- Evaluates
- Increments

The `for` statement usually takes the form:

```
for initialValue to finalValue
     do something
endfor
```

For example, to print 100 labels you can write:

```
for num = 0 to 99
   print "Made for you personally by ",
              aWorker.getFirstName()
endfor
```

This `for` statement accomplishes several tasks at once in a compact form:

- The `for` statement initializes the `num` variable to 0.

- The `for` statement checks `num` against the limit value 99 and makes sure that the `num` is less than or equal to that value.

- If the evaluation is true, the `for` statement body that prints the label executes.

- After the `for` statement body executes, the value of the `num` variable increases by 1, and the comparison to the limit value is made again.

TIP □ □ □ □ | As an alternative to using the loop `for num = 0 to 99`, you can use `for num = 1 to 100`. To achieve the same results, you can use any combination of values, as long as there are 100 whole number values between (and including) the two limits.

You are never required to use a `for` statement; the label loop executes correctly using a `while` statement with `num` as a loop control variable. However, when a loop is based on a loop control variable progressing from a known starting value to a known ending value in equal increments, the `for` loop presents you with a convenient shorthand.

TIP □ □ □ □ | The programmer doesn't need to know the starting or the ending value for the loop control variable; only the application must know those values. For example, you don't know the value of a specific worker's `lastWeeksProduction`, but when you tell the application to read a record, access the `getLastWeeksProduction()` method, and store the result in `labelsToPrint`, the application knows. To use the variable that holds the number of labels to print, you can write a `for` loop that begins `for num = 1 to labelsToPrint`.

TIP □ □ □ □ | In most programming languages, you can provide a `for` loop with a step value other than 1. A step value is a number you use to increase a loop control variable on each pass through a loop. In most programming languages, the default loop step value is 1. You specify a step value when you want each pass through the loop to change the loop control variable by a value other than 1.

USING A DO UNTIL LOOP

When you use either a `while` (also called a `while-do`) or a `for` loop, the body of the loop may never execute. For example, in the `main()` method of the original label-making application, it's possible that the loop never executes. If the input file used in the application contains no records, the result of the EOF decision is true, and the `createLabels()` module is never called.

Similarly, when you produce labels based on a worker's previous production, as in Figure 6-10 or Figure 6-11, it's possible that a 0 is stored for a worker's `lastWeeksProduction`—for example, in the case of a new employee or an employee who was on vacation during the previous week. In such a case, the value of `labelsToPrint` would be 0, and the label-producing body of the loop would never execute. With a `while` loop, you evaluate the loop control variable prior to executing the loop body, and the evaluation might indicate that you can't enter the loop.

When you want to ensure that a loop's body executes at least one time, you can use a `do until` loop. In a `do until` loop, the loop control variable is evaluated after the loop body executes instead of before. Therefore, the body always executes at least one time.

 You first learned about the do until loop in Chapter 4. Review Chapter 4 to reinforce your understanding of the differences between a while loop and a do until loop.

 Because the question that controls a while loop is asked before you enter the loop body, programmers say a while loop has a pretest. Because the question that controls a do until loop occurs after the loop body executes, programmers say the do until loop contains a posttest.

 Some languages support a do-until loop in which the loop body executes continuously until the condition tested at the bottom of the loop is true. Others support a do-while loop in which the loop body executes continuously while the posttest condition is true; that is, until it is false.

For example, suppose you want to produce one label for each employee to wear as identification, before you produce enough labels to cover 110 percent of last week's production. You can write the `do until` loop that appears in Figure 6-14.

FIGURE 6-14: USING A `do until` LOOP TO PRINT ONE IDENTIFICATION LABEL, THEN PRINT ENOUGH TO COVER PRODUCTION REQUIREMENTS

```
public void createLabels(Personnel per)
     numeric labelsToPrint
     numeric num
     num = 0
     labelsToPrint = per.getLastWeeksProduction() * 1.10
     do
          print "Made for you personally by ",
               per.getFirstName()
          num = num + 1
     until num > labelsToPrint
return
```

In Figure 6-14, the num variable is set to 0 and `labelsToPrint` is calculated. Suppose `labelsToPrint` is computed to be 0. The do loop will be entered, a label will print, 1 will be added to the num, and then and only then will num be compared to `labelsToPrint`. Because num is now 1 and `labelsToPrint` is only 0, the loop is exited, having printed a single identification label and no product labels.

As a different example using the logic in Figure 6-14, suppose that for a worker `labelsToPrint` is calculated to be 1. In this case, the loop is entered, a label prints, and 1 is added to num. Now, the value of num is not yet greater than the value of `labelsToPrint`, so the loop repeats, a second label prints, and num is incremented again. This time num (with a value of 2) exceeds `labelsToPrint` (with a value of 1), so the loop ends. This employee gets an identification label as well as one product label.

Of course, you could achieve the same results by printing one label, then entering a `while` loop, as in Figure 6-15. In this example, one label prints before num is compared to `labelsToPrint`. No matter what the value of `labelsToPrint` is, even 0, one identification label is produced.

FIGURE 6-15: USING A `while` LOOP TO PRINT ONE IDENTIFICATION LABEL, THEN PRINT ENOUGH TO COVER PRODUCTION REQUIREMENTS

```
public void createLabels(Personnel per)
    numeric labelsToPrint
    numeric num
    num = 0
    labelsToPrint = per.getLastWeeksProduction() * 1.10
    print "Made for you personally by ",
            aWorker.getFirstName()
    while num < labelsToPrint
        print "Made for you personally by ",
                per.getFirstName()
        num = num + 1
    endwhile
return
```

TIP □ □ □ □   The logic in Figure 6-15, in which you print one label, then test a value to determine whether you will print more, takes the same form as the main( ) file-reading logic in Figure 6-8. When you read records from a file, you read one record (the priming read) and then test for EOF before continuing. In effect, the first label printed in Figure 6-15 is a "priming label."

The results of the methods shown in Figures 6-14 and 6-15 are the same. Using either, every employee will receive an identification label and enough labels to cover production. Each module works correctly, and neither is logically superior to the other. There is almost always more than one way to solve the same programming problem. As you learned in Chapter 4, a `do until` loop can always be replaced by pairing a sequence and a `while` loop. Which method you choose depends on your (or your instructor's or supervisor's) preferences.

There are several additional ways to approach the logic shown in the applications in Figures 6-14 and 6-15. For example, after calculating `labelsToPrint`, you could immediately add 1 to the value. Then you could use the logic in Figure 6-14, as long as you change the loop-ending question to `num >= labelsToPrint` (instead of only `>`). Alternately, using the logic in Figure 6-15, after adding 1 to `labelsToPrint`, you could remove the lone first label-printing instruction; that way one identification label would always be printed, even if the last production figure was 0.

RECOGNIZING THE CHARACTERISTICS SHARED BY ALL LOOPS

You can see from Figure 6-15 that you are never required to use a `do until` loop. The same results always can be achieved by performing the loop body steps once before entering a `while` loop. If you follow the logic of either loop shown in Figure 6-14 or 6-15, you discover that when an employee has a `lastWeeksProduction` value of 3, then exactly four labels print. Likewise, when an employee has a `lastWeeksProduction` value of 0, then in both cases exactly one label prints. You can accomplish the same results with either type of loop; the `do until` loop is simply a convenience when you need a loop to execute at least one time.

TIP In some languages, the `do until` loop is called a `repeat until` loop.

TIP If you can express the logic you want to perform by saying "while a is true, keep doing b," you probably want to use a `while` loop. If what you want to accomplish seems to fit the statement "do a until b is true," you can probably use a `do until` loop.

As you examine Figures 6-14 and 6-15, notice that with the `do until` loop, the loop-controlling question is placed at the *end* of the sequence of the steps that repeat. With the `while` loop, the loop-controlling question is placed at the *beginning* of the steps that repeat. All structured loops share these characteristics:

- The loop-controlling question provides either entry to or exit from the repeating structure.
- The loop-controlling question provides the *only* entry to or exit from the repeating structure.

You should also notice the difference between *unstructured* loops and the structured `do until` and `while` loops. Figure 6-16 diagrams the outline of two unstructured loops. In each case, the decision labeled X breaks out of the loop prematurely. The loop control variable (labeled `LC`) does not provide the only entry to or exit from either loop.

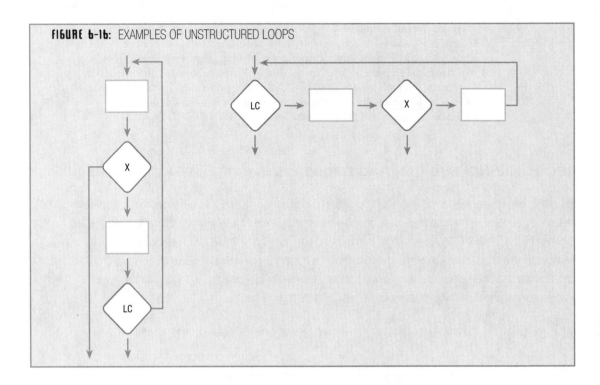

FIGURE 6-16: EXAMPLES OF UNSTRUCTURED LOOPS

NESTING LOOPS

Program logic gets more complicated when you must use loops within loops, or **nesting loops**. When one loop appears inside another, the loop that contains the other loop is called the **outer loop**, and the loop that is contained is called the **inner loop**. You need to create nesting (or nested) loops when the values of two (or more) variables repeat to produce every combination of values.

For example, suppose you work for a company that pays staff members twice per month. The company has decided on an incentive plan to provide each staff member with a one-fourth of one percent raise for each pay period during the coming year, and it wants a report like that shown in Figure 6-17. A list will be printed for each staff member showing the exact paycheck amounts for each of the next 24 pay periods—two per month for 12 months.

SAMPLE PROJECTED PAYROLL REPORT FOR ONE STAFF MEMBER

Projected Payroll for
Roberto Martinez

Month	Check	Amount
1	1	501.25
1	2	502.50
2	1	503.76
2	2	505.02
3	1	506.28

Assume you have a `StaffMember` class as described in Figure 6-18 and that a record containing each staff member's data has been stored in a file on a disk. To produce the Projected Payroll report, you need to maintain two separate counters to control two separate loops. One counter will keep track of the month (1 through 12), and another will keep track of the pay period within the month (1 through 2). When nesting loops, you must maintain individual loop control variables—one for each loop—and alter each at the appropriate time.

FIGURE 6-18: A `StaffMember` CLASS

```
public class StaffMember
     private numeric idNum
     private string name
     private numeric weeklyPay

     public numeric getIdNum()
     return idNum

     public string getName()
     return name

     public numeric getWeeklyPay()
     return weeklyPay

     public void setIdNum(numeric emp)
          idNum = emp
     return

     public void setName(string nm)
          name = nm
     return

     public void setWeeklyPay(numeric pay)
          weeklyPay = pay
     return
endClass
```

Figure 6-19 shows the application that could produce the report for each staff member. In the `main()` method, a `StaffMember` object is declared and the input file is opened. Then a loop continues to execute while the file does not reach its end. This loop performs two major tasks—passing the `StaffMember` that was input from the file to the `createReport()` method, and after returning from that task, reading the next `StaffMember` object from the input file.

FIGURE 6-19: `ProjectedPayrollReport` APPLICATION

```
public class ProjectedPayrollReport
    public void main()
        StaffMember staff
        open(inputFile)
        staff = read(inputFile)
        while staff not EOF
            createReport(staff)
            staff  = read(inputFile)
        endwhile
        close(inputFile)
    return

    public void createReport(StaffMember staff)
        numeric month
        numeric check
        numeric pay
        numeric rate = .0025
        numeric monthsInYear = 12
        numeric checksInMonth = 2
        numeric salary = staff.getWeeklyPay()
        print "Projected Payroll for"
        print staff.getName()
        print "Month  Check  Amount"
        month = 1
        while month <= monthsInYear
            check = 1
            while check <= checksInMonth
                pay = salary + salary * rate
                print month, check, salary
                check = check + 1
            endwhile
            month = month + 1
        endwhile
    return
endClass
```

The `createReport()` method in the `ProjectedPayrollReport` application contains nesting loops. The method receives a `StaffMember` and declares the variables that will be used to control the loops—`month`, which keeps track of the month that is currently printing, and `check`, which keeps track of which check within the month is currently printing.

In the `createReport()` method, three additional declarations hold the number of months in a year (12), the number of checks in a month (2), and the rate of increase (0.0025). Declaring these variables is not required; the program could just use the numeric constants 12, 2, and 0.0025, but providing those values with names serves two purposes.

First, the program becomes more **self-documenting**—that is, it describes itself to the reader because the choice of variable names is clear. When other programmers read a program and encounter a number like 2, they might wonder about the meaning. Instead, if the value is named `checksInMonth`, the meaning of the value is much clearer. Second, after the program is in production, the company might choose to change one of the values, for example, by going to an 11-month year, producing more or fewer paychecks in a month, or changing the raise rate. In those cases, the person who modifies the program would not have to search for appropriate spots to make those changes, but would simply redefine the values assigned to the appropriate variables at the beginning of the method.

When the `createReport()` method accepts a `StaffMember` argument, it is processed as follows:

1. The `StaffMember`'s `salary` is extracted from the staff object using the `getWeeklyPay()` instance method. The `salary` variable will be used to hold the calculated bi-monthly increases.

2. The first heading prints, "Projected Payroll for", followed by the staff member's name and the column headings.

3. The `month` variable is set to 1; `month` is the loop control variable for the outer loop, and this step provides it with its initial value.

4. The value of `month` is compared to the number of months in a year, and because the comparison evaluates as `true`, the outer loop is entered. Within this loop, the `check` variable is used as a loop control variable for an inner loop.

5. The `check` is initialized to 1, and then compared to the number of checks in a month. Because this comparison evaluates as `true`, the inner loop is entered.

6. Within this inner loop, the employee's weekly `salary` is increased by one-quarter of one percent (the old salary plus 0.0025 of the old salary). Notice that this newly calculated `salary` does not affect the actual `StaffMember` data record stored by the organization. The variable `salary` is only a **work field**—one used to hold a temporary calculation.

7. The `month` number (currently 1), `check` number (also currently 1), and newly calculated `salary` are printed.

8. The `check` number is increased (to 2), and inner loop reaches its end. This causes the logical control to return to the top of the inner loop, where the `while` condition is tested again. Because the check number (2) is still less than or equal to the number of checks in a month (2), the inner loop is entered again.

9. The `salary` amount increases, and the `month` (still 1), the `check` number (2), and the new `salary` are printed.

10. Then the `check` number becomes 3. Now, when the loop condition is tested for the third time, the `check` number is no longer less than or equal to the number of checks in a month, so the inner loop ends.

11. As the last step in the outer loop, the `month` becomes 2.

12. After the `month` increases to 2, control returns to the entry point of the outer loop.

13. The `while` condition is tested, and because 2 is not greater than the number of months in a year (12), the outer loop is entered for a second time.

14. The `check` variable that counts checks printed for a month is reset to 1 so that it will correctly count two checks for this month.

15. Because the newly reset `check` value is not more than the number of checks in a month, the `salary` is increased, and the amount prints for `month` 2, `check` 1.

16. The value of `check` increases to 2 and another `salary` value is calculated and printed for `month` 2, `check` 2 before the inner loop ends and the `month` is increased to 3. The inner loop is evaluated again. The `month` is 3, so the evaluation result is `false`.

17. Then `month` 3, `check` 1 is calculated and printed, followed by `month` 3, `check` 2.

18. The loop with the `createReport()` method continues printing two check amounts for each of the 12 months before the outer loop is finished, when the `month` counter variable eventually exceeds 12. Only then does the `createReport()` method end, returning control to the `main()` method, where the next `StaffMember`'s record is read into memory from the input file. If a new record exists, control returns to the `createReport()` method for the new staff member, for whom headings are printed, and the `month` is set to 1 to start the set of 24 calculations for this employee. If no more records need to be processed, then the input file closes and the application ends.

There is no limit to the number of loop-nesting levels a program can contain. For instance, suppose that in the projected payroll example, the company wanted to provide a slight raise each hour or each day of each pay period in each month for each of several years. Values might vary for the hour, day, check, month, and year; each would control a nested loop. No matter how many levels deep the nesting goes, each loop must still have a loop control variable that is initialized, tested, and altered.

USING A LOOP TO ACCUMULATE TOTALS

Business reports often include totals. The supervisor requesting a list of employees who participate in the company dental plan is often as much interested in *how many* such employees there are as in *who* they are. When you receive your telephone bill at the end of the month, you are usually more interested in the total than in the charges for the individual calls. Some business reports list no individual detail records, just totals. Such reports are called **summary reports**.

For example, a real estate broker might maintain a file of company real estate listings based on the `Property` class. The `Property` class diagram, shown in Figure 6-20, shows that each `Property` contains a street address value of a property for sale.

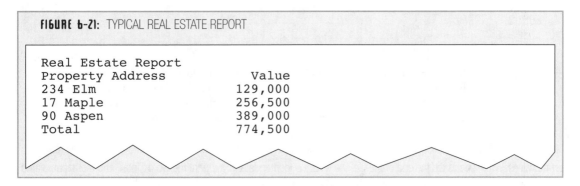

FIGURE 6-20: Property CLASS DIAGRAM

```
Property
-address: string
-value: numeric
+getAddress(): string
+getValue(): numeric
+setAddress(string address): void
+setValue(numeric value): void
```

Assume the broker wants a listing of all the properties for sale; she also wants a total value for all the company's list-ings. A typical report might look like Figure 6-21.

FIGURE 6-21: TYPICAL REAL ESTATE REPORT

```
Real Estate Report
Property Address          Value
234 Elm                 129,000
17 Maple                256,500
90 Aspen                389,000
Total                   774,500
```

In order to calculate the total value of all properties, when you read a real estate listing record, besides printing it you must add its value to an accumulator. An **accumulator** is a variable that you use to gather or accumulate values. An accumulator is very similar to a counter. The difference lies in the value that you add to the variable; usually you add just one to a counter, whereas you add some other value to an accumulator. If the real estate broker wants to know how many listings the company holds, you count them. When she wants to know total real estate value, you accumulate it.

In order to accumulate total real estate prices, you declare a numeric variable at the beginning of the application, as shown in Figure 6-22. You must initialize the accumulator, `accumValue`, to 0. As you read each real estate `Property` record, you print it and add its value to the accumulator `accumValue`, as shown in the highlighted statement. Then you can read the next record.

TIP □ □ □ □ Some programming languages assign 0 to a variable you fail to initialize explicitly. Some programming languages issue an error message if you don't initialize a variable you use for accumulating; others let you accumulate, but the results are worthless because you start with garbage. The safest and clearest course of action is to assign the value 0 to accumulators before using them.

FIGURE 6-22: THE REAL ESTATE PROGRAM

```
public class RealEstateValue
    public void main()
        Property house
        numeric accumValue = 0
        open(inputFile)
        house = read(inputFile)
        while house not EOF
            print house.getAddress(), house.getValue()
            accumValue = accumValue + house.getValue()
            house  = read(inputFile)
        endwhile
        print "Total", accumValue
        close(inputFile)
    return
endClass
```

TIP ▫ ▫ ▫ ▫ | In the application in Figure 6-22, two calls are made to the `getValue()` method. Program performance could be improved by declaring a variable to hold the house object's value, calling `getValue()` one time and storing the value there, and then using the variable in both the output and addition statements within the loop.

After the RealEstateValue application reaches the end of the file, the accumulator will hold the grand total of all the real estate values. When you reach the end of the file, the `while` loop ends and you print the word "Total" and the accumulated value, `accumValue`. After printing the total, you can close the input file.

New programmers often want to reset the `accumValue` to zero after printing it. Although you *can* take this step without harming the execution of the program, it does not serve any useful purpose. You cannot set `accumValue` to zero in anticipation of having it ready for the next program, or even for the next time you execute this program. Variables exist only for the life of the application, and even if a future application happens to contain a variable named `accumValue`, the variable will not necessarily occupy the same memory location as this one. Even if you run the same application a second time, the variables might occupy physical memory locations different from those they occupied during the first run. At the beginning of any method, it is the programmer's responsibility to initialize all variables that must start with a specific value. There is no benefit to changing a variable's value when it will never be used again during the current execution.

TIP ▫ ▫ ▫ ▫ | It is especially important to avoid changing the value of a variable unnecessarily when the change occurs within a loop. One extra, unnecessary statement in a loop that executes hundreds of thousands of times can significantly slow a program's performance speed.

CHAPTER SUMMARY

- ☐ When you use a loop within a computer program, you can write one set of instructions that operates on multiple, separate sets of data.

- ☐ Three steps must occur in every loop: You must initialize a loop control variable, compare the variable to some value that controls whether the loop continues or stops, and alter the variable that controls the loop.

- ☐ A counter is a numeric variable you use to count the number of times an event has occurred. You can count occurrences by incrementing a variable.

- ☐ You can use a variable sentinel value to control a loop.

- ☐ Sometimes it is convenient to reduce, or decrement, a loop control variable on every cycle through a loop.

- ☐ The two mistakes programmers make most often with loops are neglecting to initialize the loop control variable, and neglecting to alter the loop control variable. Additionally, when a calculation can be performed once before entering a loop, it is inefficient to place the calculation within the loop. It is incorrect to attempt to initialize a variable by using data values that have not been read into memory yet.

- ☐ Most computer languages support a `for` statement or `for` loop that you can use with definite loops when you know how many times a loop will repeat. The `for` statement uses a loop control variable that it automatically initializes, evaluates, and increments.

- ☐ When you want to ensure that a loop's body executes at least one time, you can use a `do until` loop, in which the loop control variable is evaluated after the loop body executes.

- ☐ All structured loops share these characteristics: The loop-controlling question provides either entry to or exit from the repeating structure, and the loop-controlling question provides the *only* entry to or exit from the repeating structure.

- ☐ When you must use loops within loops, you use nesting loops. When nesting loops, you must maintain two individual loop control variables and alter each at the appropriate time.

- ☐ Business reports often include totals. Summary reports list no detail records—only totals. An accumulator is a variable that you use to gather or accumulate values.

KEY TERMS

A **loop** is a structure that repeats actions while some condition continues.

A **main loop** is a basic set of instructions that is repeated for every record.

Opening a file instructs the computer to find a stored file and prepare it for reading data into an application.

Closing a file makes it no longer available for reading.

A **loop control variable** is a variable that determines whether a loop will continue.

A **sentinel value** is a limit, or ending, value.

An **indeterminate**, or **indefinite**, **loop** is one for which you cannot predetermine the number of executions.

A loop for which you definitely know the repetition factor is a **definite loop**.

A **loop body** is the set of statements that executes within a loop.

A **counter** is any numeric variable you use to count the number of times an event has occurred.

Incrementing a variable is adding a constant value to it, frequently 1.

Decrementing a variable is decreasing it by a constant value, frequently 1.

An **infinite loop** is a loop that never stops executing.

A **for statement**, or **for loop**, can be used to code definite loops. It contains a loop control variable that it automatically initializes, evaluates, and increments.

Nesting loops are loops within loops.

When one loop appears inside another, the loop that contains the other loop is called the **outer loop**, and the loop that is contained is called the **inner loop**.

A **self-documenting** program is one in which the choice of variable names is clear so that the program code describes the program's purpose to the reader.

A **work field** is a variable used to hold a temporary calculation.

A **summary report** lists only totals, without individual detail records.

An **accumulator** is a variable that you use to gather or accumulate values.

REVIEW QUESTIONS

1. The structure that allows you to write one set of instructions that operates on multiple, separate sets of data is the _____.
    a. sequence
    b. selection
    c. loop
    d. case

2. Which of the following is not a step that must occur in every loop?
    a. Initialize a loop control variable.
    b. Compare the loop control value to a sentinel.
    c. Set the loop control value equal to a sentinel.
    d. Alter the loop control variable.

3. The statements executed within a loop are known collectively as the _____.
    a. sentinels
    b. loop controls
    c. sequences
    d. loop body

4. **A counter keeps track of** _____.

    a. the number of times an event has occurred
    b. the number of machine cycles required by a segment of a program
    c. the number of loop structures within a program
    d. a total that prints at the end of a summary report

5. **Adding 1 to a variable is also called** _____.

    a. digesting
    b. incrementing
    c. decrementing
    d. resetting

6. **In the following pseudocode, what is printed?**

    ```
    a = 1
    b = 2
    c = 5
    while a < c
         a = a + 1
         b = b + c
    endwhile
    print a, b, c
    ```

    a. 1 2 5
    b. 5 22 5
    c. 5 6 5
    d. 6 22 9

7. **In the following pseudocode, what is printed?**

    ```
    d = 4
    e = 6
    f = 7
    while d > f
         d = d + 1
         e = e - 1
    endwhile
    print d, e, f
    ```

    a. 7 3 7
    b. 8 2 8
    c. 4 6 7
    d. 5 5 7

8. **When you decrement a variable, you _____.**

   a. set it to 0
   b. reduce it by one-tenth
   c. subtract 1 from it
   d. remove it from a program

9. **In the following pseudocode, what is printed?**

   ```
   g = 4
   h = 6
   while g < h
         g = g + 1
   endwhile
   print g, h
   ```

   a. nothing
   b. 4 6
   c. 5 6
   d. 6 6

10. **Most programmers use a `for` loop _____.**

    a. for every loop they write
    b. when they know the exact number of times a loop will repeat
    c. when they do not know the exact number of times a loop will repeat
    d. when a loop will not repeat

11. **Unlike a `while` loop, you use a `do until` loop when _____.**

    a. you can predict the exact number of loop repetitions
    b. the loop body might never execute
    c. the loop body must execute exactly one time
    d. the loop body must execute at least one time

12. **Which of the following is a characteristic shared by `while` loops and `do until` loops?**

    a. Both have one entry and one exit.
    b. Both have a body that executes at least once.
    c. Both compare a loop control variable at the top of the loop.
    d. all of the above

13. **A comparison with a loop control variable provides _____.**

    a. the only entry to a while loop
    b. the only exit from a do until loop
    c. both of the above
    d. none of the above

14. **When two loops are nested, the loop that is contained by the other is the _____ loop.**

   a. inner
   b. outer
   c. unstructured
   d. captive

15. **In the following pseudocode, how many times is "Hello" printed?**

```
j = 2
k = 5
m = 6
n = 9
while j < k
     while m < n
          print "Hello"
          m = m + 1
     endwhile
     j = j + 1
endwhile
```

   a. zero
   b. three
   c. six
   d. nine

16. **In the following pseudocode, how many times is "Hello" printed?**

```
j = 2
k = 5
n = 9
     while j < k
          m = 6
          while m < n
               print "Hello"
               m = m + 1
          endwhile
          j = j + 1
     endwhile
```

   a. zero
   b. three
   c. six
   d. nine

17. In the following pseudocode, how many times is "Hello" printed?

```
p = 2
q = 4
while p < q
        print "Hello"
        r = 1
        while r < q
                print "Hello"
                r = r + 1
        endwhile
        p = p + 1
endwhile
```

   a. zero
   b. four
   c. six
   d. eight

18. A report that lists no details about individual records, but totals only, is a(n) _____ report.

   a. accumulator
   b. final
   c. summary
   d. detailless

19. Typically, the value added to a counter variable is _____.

   a. 0
   b. 1
   c. 10
   d. 100

20. Typically, the value added to an accumulator variable is _____.

   a. zero
   b. one
   c. smaller than a value added to a counter variable
   d. larger than a value added to a counter variable

EXERCISES

1. Design the logic for a module that would print every number from 1 through 10.

2. Design the logic for a module that would print every number from 1 through 10 along with its square and cube.

3. The No Interest Credit Company provides zero-interest loans to customers. (They make a profit by selling advertising space in their monthly statements and selling their customer lists.) Design the following:

    a. A `Customer` class that contains an account number, customer name, and balance due. The class also contains get and set methods for each field.

    b. An application that reads `Customer` account records from a file and sends them, one at a time, to a method that prints a payoff schedule for each customer. For each customer, print the account number and name; then print the customer's projected balance each month for the next 10 months. Assume that there is no finance charge on this account, that the customer makes no new purchases, and that the customer pays off the balance with equal monthly payments, which are 10 percent of the original bill.

4. The Some Interest Credit Company provides loans to customers, at 1.5 percent interest per month. Design the following:

    a. A `Customer` class that contains an account number, customer name, and balance due. The class also contains get and set methods for each field.

    b. An application that reads `Customer` account records from a file and sends them, one at a time, to a method that prints a payoff schedule for each customer. For each customer, print the account number and name; then print the customer's projected balance each month for the next 10 months. Assume that when the balance reaches $10 or less, the customer can pay off the account. At the beginning of every month, 1.5 percent interest is added to the balance, and then the customer makes a payment equal to 5 percent of the current balance. Assume the customer makes no new purchases.

5. The Howell Bank provides savings accounts that compound interest on a yearly basis. In other words, if you deposit $100 for two years at 4 percent interest, at the end of 1 year you will have $104. At the end of 2 years, you will have the $104 plus 4 percent of that, or $108.16. Design the following:

    a. An `Account` class that contains fields for an account number, the owner's first and last names, and a balance. Also provide get and set methods for each field.

    b. An application that reads in Account records from an input file and sends them to a method that prints the projected running total balance for each year for the next 20 years.

6. Henry Clay Community College wants to print name tags for each student and teacher to wear at the first meeting of each class this semester. The tags look like the following:

> Hello!
>
> My name is _____
>
> Class: XXXXXX Section: 999

The name tag border is preprinted, but you must design the program to print all the text you see on the sticker. Design the following:

a. A `CourseSection` class that includes fields for the class code (for example, CIS111), the three-digit section number (for example, 101), the teacher's last name (for example, "Zaplatynsky"), the number of students enrolled in the section (for example, 25), and the room in which the class meets (for example, "A213"). Design get and set methods for each field. One `CourseSection` record for each section offered by the college has been stored in a file.

b. An application that prints as many name tags as a section needs to provide one for each enrolled student, plus one for the teacher. Each name tag leaves a blank for the student's (or teacher's) name—the individual student names are not part of the `CourseSection` class.

7. The Vernon Hills Mail-Order Company often sends multiple packages per order. For each customer order, print enough mailing labels to use on each of the separate boxes that will be mailed. The mailing labels contain the customer's complete name and address, along with a box number in the form "Box 9 of 9". For example, an order that requires three boxes produces three labels: "Box 1 of 3", "Box 2 of 3", and "Box 3 of 3". Design the following:

a. An `Order` class that contains fields that hold a customer's title (for example "Mrs."), a first name, last name, street address, city, state, ZIP code, and number of boxes in the order. Include get and set methods for each field.

b. An application that reads Order objects from an input file and produces enough mailing labels for each order.

8. Secondhand Rose Resale Shop is having a seven-day sale during which the price of any unsold item drops 10 percent each day. The inventory file includes an item number, description, and original price on day one. For example, an item that costs $10.00 on the first day costs 10 percent less, or $9.00, on the second day. On the third day, the same item is 10 percent less than $9.00, or $8.10. Design the following:

a. An `Inventory` class that contains the necessary fields and get and set methods.

b. An application that reads `Inventory` records and produces a report that shows the price of every item on each day, one through seven.

9. The state of Florida maintains a census file in which each record contains the name of a county, the current population, and a number representing the rate at which population is increasing per year. The governor wants a report listing each county and the number of years it will take for the population of the county to double, assuming the present rate of growth remains constant. Design the following:

a. A `County` class containing the necessary fields and get and set methods.

b. An application that reads `County` records from an input file and prints the County's name and the number of years it will take for the population to double.

10. The Human Resources Department of Apex Manufacturing Company wants a report that shows its employees the benefits of saving for retirement. Produce a report that shows 12 predicted retirement account values for each employee—the values if the employee saves 5, 10, or 15 percent of his or her annual salary for 10, 20, 30, or 40 years. Design the following:

    a. An `Employee` class containing the name of an employee and the employee's current annual salary. Include get and set methods for the fields.

    b. An application that reads `Employee` records from an input file and prints a report for each `Employee`. Assume that savings grow at a rate of 8 percent per year.

11. Mr. Furly owns 20 apartment buildings. Each building contains 15 units that he rents for $800 per month each. Design the application that would print 12 payment coupons for each of the 15 apartments in each of the 20 buildings. Each coupon should contain the building number (1 through 20), the apartment number (1 through 15), the month (1 through 12), and the amount of rent due.

12. Mr. Furly owns 20 apartment buildings. Each building contains 15 units that he rents. The usual monthly rent for apartments numbered 1 through 9 in each building is $700; the monthly rent is $850 for apartments numbered 10 through 15. The usual rent is due every month except July and December; in those months Mr. Furly gives his renters a 50 percent credit, so they owe only half the usual amount. Design the application that would print 12 payment coupons for each of the 15 apartments in each of the 20 buildings. Each coupon should contain the building number (1 through 20), the apartment number (1 through 15), the month (1 through 12), and the amount of rent due.

CASE PROJECT

In earlier chapters you developed classes needed for Cost Is No Object—a car rental service that specializes in lending antique and luxury cars to clients on a short-term basis. You created pseudocode for Employee, Customer, Automobile, and RentalAgreement classes including attributes and methods to get and set those attributes.

The Employee class contains all the attributes and methods associated with one employee customer. Modify your Employee class to contain fields to hold the following:

    ☐ An employee ID number

    ☐ A first name

    ☐ A last name

    ☐ A street address

    ☐ A ZIP code

    ☐ A job description code

    ☐ An hourly pay rate

    ☐ An insurance plan code

Include a simple get and set method for each field.

Create an application that continues to prompt the user for Employee data and writes the data to a file; the application continues until the user enters 0 for an ID number to indicate the desire to quit. While the ID number is not zero, prompt the user for a value for each Employee field and assign it to an Employee object. Any time the user enters an invalid field value, continue to reprompt the user for the same data. Only when a data item is valid, assign it to the appropriate field. Invalid field values are:

- ☐ An employee ID number that is greater than 999

- ☐ A ZIP code that is greater than 99999

- ☐ A job description code that is not between 10 and 19 inclusive

- ☐ An hourly pay rate that is not between $6.00 and $25.00 inclusive

- ☐ An insurance plan code that is not 1 or 2

When all the needed data has been entered correctly for an Employee, write the Employee record to a data file and prompt the user for the next ID number.

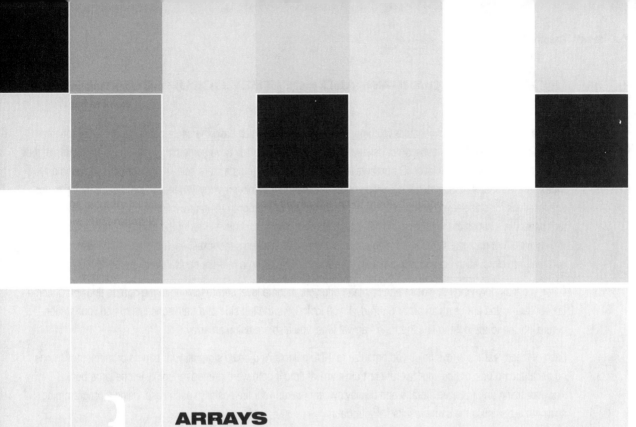

ARRAYS

7

After studying Chapter 7, you should be able to:

☐ Understand arrays and how they occupy computer memory

☐ Manipulate an array to replace nested decisions

☐ Declare and initialize an array

☐ Understand the difference between initialized and uninitialized arrays

☐ Load array values from a file

☐ Search an array for an exact match

☐ Use a constant to store an array size

☐ Search an array for a range match

UNDERSTANDING ARRAYS AND HOW THEY OCCUPY COMPUTER MEMORY

An **array** is a series or list of variables in computer memory, all of which have the same name but are differentiated with special numbers called subscripts. Usually, all the values in an array have something in common; for example, they might represent a list of employee ID numbers or a list of prices for items a store sells. A **subscript**, also called an **index**, is a number that indicates the position of a particular item within an array. Whenever you require multiple storage locations for objects, you are using a real-life counterpart of a programming array. For example, if you store important papers in a series of file folders and label each folder with a consecutive letter of the alphabet, then you are using the equivalent of an array. If you store mementos in a series of stacked shoeboxes, each labeled with a year, or if you sort mail into slots, each labeled with a name, then you are also using a real-life equivalent of a programming array.

When you look down the left side of a tax table to find your income level before looking to the right to find your income tax obligation, you are using an array. Similarly, if you look down the left side of a train schedule to find your station before looking to the right to find the train's arrival time, you also are using an array.

Each of these real-life arrays helps you organize real-life objects. You *could* store all your papers or mementos in one huge cardboard box, or find your tax rate or train's arrival time if both were printed randomly in one large book. However, using an organized storage and display system makes your life easier in each case. Using a programming array will accomplish the same results for your data.

TIP ▫ ▫ ▫ ▫ | Some programmers refer to an array as a *table* or a *matrix*.

HOW ARRAYS OCCUPY COMPUTER MEMORY

When you declare an array, you declare a programming structure that contains multiple variables. Each variable within an array has the same name and the same data type; each separate array variable is one **element** of the array. Each array element occupies an area in memory next to, or contiguous to, the others, as shown in Figure 7-1. You can indicate the number of elements an array will hold—the **size of the array**—when you declare the array along with your other variables.

All array elements have the same group name, but each individual element also has a unique subscript indicating how far away it is from the first element. Therefore, any array's subscripts are always a sequence of integers such as 0 through 4 or 0 through 9.

TIP ▫ ▫ ▫ ▫ | An error commonly made by beginning programmers is to forget that array subscripts start with 0. If you assume an array's first subscript is 1, you will always be "off by one" in your array manipulation.

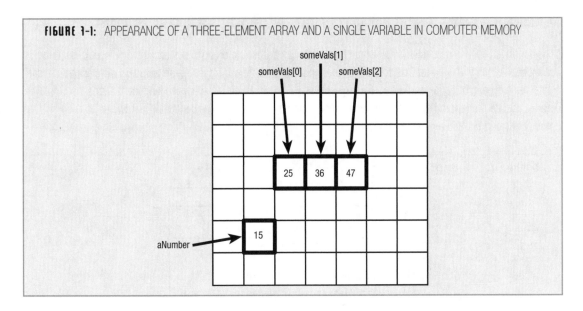

FIGURE 1-1: APPEARANCE OF A THREE-ELEMENT ARRAY AND A SINGLE VARIABLE IN COMPUTER MEMORY

Depending on the syntax rules of the programming language you use, you place the subscript within parentheses or square brackets following the group name; when writing pseudocode or drawing a flowchart, you can use either form of notation. This text will use square brackets to hold array element subscripts so that you don't mistake array names for method names, and because most object-oriented programming (OOP) languages such as C++, Java, and C# use the bracket notation. For example, Figure 7-1 shows how a single variable and an array are stored in computer memory. The single variable named **aNumber** holds the value 15. The array named **someVals** contains three elements, so the elements are **someVals[0]**, **someVals[1]**, and **someVals[2]**. The value stored in **someVals[0]** is 25; **someVals[1]** holds 36, and **someVals[2]** holds 47. The element **someVals[0]** is zero numbers away from the beginning of the array—in other words, it is located at the same memory address as the array. The element **someVals[1]** is one number away from the beginning of the array and **someVals[2]** is two numbers away.

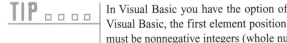

TIP ▫ ▫ ▫ ▫ In Visual Basic you have the option of using 1 as an array's first subscript, but even in Visual Basic, the first element position is 0 by default. In all languages, subscript values must be nonnegative integers (whole numbers) and sequential.

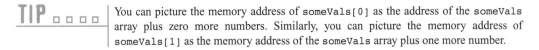

TIP ▫ ▫ ▫ ▫ You can picture the memory address of **someVals[0]** as the address of the **someVals** array plus zero more numbers. Similarly, you can picture the memory address of **someVals[1]** as the memory address of the **someVals** array plus one more number.

You are never required to use arrays within your programs, but learning to use arrays correctly can make many programming tasks far more efficient and professional. When you understand how to use arrays, you will be able to provide elegant solutions to problems that otherwise would require tedious programming steps.

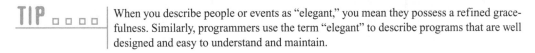

TIP ▫ ▫ ▫ ▫ When you describe people or events as "elegant," you mean they possess a refined gracefulness. Similarly, programmers use the term "elegant" to describe programs that are well designed and easy to understand and maintain.

MANIPULATING AN ARRAY TO REPLACE NESTED DECISIONS

Consider an application requested by a Human Resources Department to produce statistics on employee's claimed dependents. When you write an OOP to produce the report, you create two classes—an **Employee** class that encapsulates employee information and a **CountDependents** class, which is the application that analyzes the Employee data to produce the report. Figure 7-2 shows an abbreviated **Employee** class containing just two fields—an Employee ID number and a number of dependents claimed by the **Employee**.

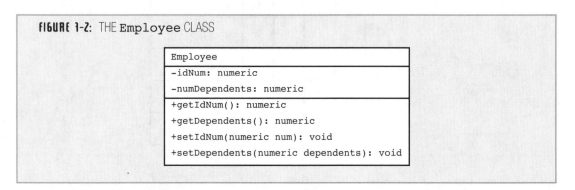

FIGURE 7-2: THE **Employee** CLASS

Employee
-idNum: numeric
-numDependents: numeric
+getIdNum(): numeric
+getDependents(): numeric
+setIdNum(numeric num): void
+setDependents(numeric dependents): void

Assume you have already written an application that stores **Employee** records in a file, and now you want to produce a report that lists the number of **Employee**s who have claimed 0, 1, 2, 3, 4, or 5 dependents. (Assume you know that no employees have more than five dependents.) For example, Figure 7-3 shows a typical report.

FIGURE 7-3: THE DEPENDENTS REPORT

```
        Dependents Report

     Dependents   Count
         0          34
         1          62
         2          71
         3          42
         4          28
         5           7
```

Without using an array, you could write the application that produces the six counts (for each number of dependents, 0 through 5) by using a series of decisions. Figure 7-4 shows the pseudocode for the application and a flowchart for the method that counts dependents.

FIGURE 1-4: PSEUDOCODE FOR **CountDependents** CLASS AND FLOWCHART FOR METHOD THAT COUNTS DEPENDENTS

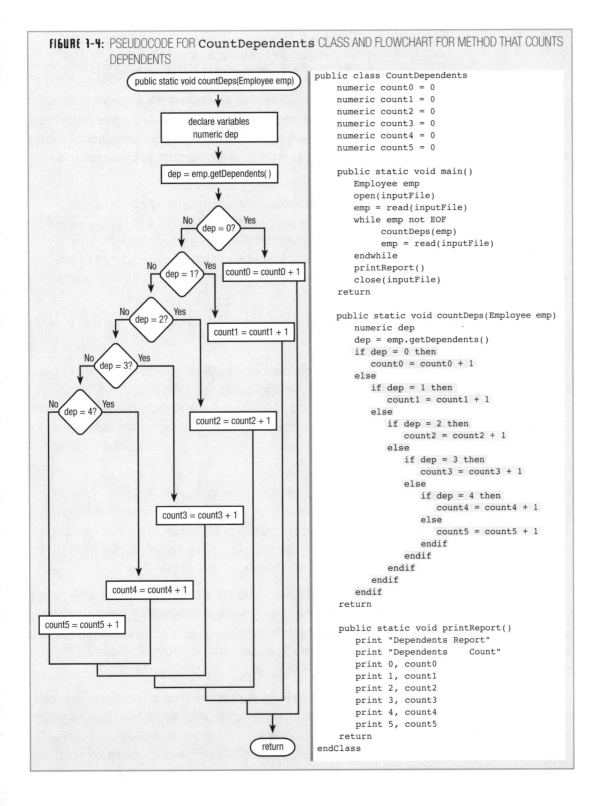

```
public class CountDependents
    numeric count0 = 0
    numeric count1 = 0
    numeric count2 = 0
    numeric count3 = 0
    numeric count4 = 0
    numeric count5 = 0

    public static void main()
        Employee emp
        open(inputFile)
        emp = read(inputFile)
        while emp not EOF
            countDeps(emp)
            emp = read(inputFile)
        endwhile
        printReport()
        close(inputFile)
    return

    public static void countDeps(Employee emp)
        numeric dep
        dep = emp.getDependents()
        if dep = 0 then
            count0 = count0 + 1
        else
            if dep = 1 then
                count1 = count1 + 1
            else
                if dep = 2 then
                    count2 = count2 + 1
                else
                    if dep = 3 then
                        count3 = count3 + 1
                    else
                        if dep = 4 then
                            count4 = count4 + 1
                        else
                            count5 = count5 + 1
                        endif
                    endif
                endif
            endif
        endif
    return

    public static void printReport()
        print "Dependents Report"
        print "Dependents     Count"
        print 0, count0
        print 1, count1
        print 2, count2
        print 3, count3
        print 4, count4
        print 5, count5
    return
endClass
```

TIP □ □ □ □ | The application shown in Figure 7-4 accomplishes its purpose, but is cumbersome. Follow its logic here so that you understand how the application works. Later in this chapter, you will see how to write the same program much more efficiently using an array.

In the `CountDependents` application in Figure 7-4, you declare six separate counter variables and initialize each to 0. In the `main()` method, you declare an `Employee` object that holds one `Employee` at a time as you read each record in from the input file. You pass the `Employee` to the `countDeps()` method, and then read the next `Employee`, continuing until all records have been read. The `main()` method then calls the `printReport()` method, closes the file, and ends.

The `countDeps()` method contains the decision-making process. As each `Employee` is passed to the `countDeps()` method, you use the public `getDependents()` method to access the private `numDependents` field for the current object, and you store its value in a local variable named `dep`. Then, in the highlighted lines, you ask a series of questions. If the Employee has 0 dependents, you add 1 to `count0`, if the `Employee` has one dependent, you add 1 to `count1`, and so on. After adding 1 to the appropriate counter, you return to the `main()` method to read the next `Employee` record.

When the entire file has been read and counted, the `main()` method calls `printReport()`, which prints two heading lines and then prints the six counted values.

The dependent-counting application in Figure 7-4 works just fine, and there is absolutely nothing wrong with it logically, but even with only six categories of dependents, the decision-making process is unwieldy. What if the number of dependents might be any value from 0 to 10, or 0 to 20? With either of these scenarios, the basic logic of the program would remain the same; however, you would need to declare many additional accumulator variables and you would need many additional decisions within the `countDeps()` method and many additional output statements in the `printReport()` method.

Using an array provides an alternate approach to this programming problem, which greatly reduces the number of statements you need. When you declare an array, you provide a group name for a number of associated variables in memory. For example, the six dependent count accumulators can be redefined as a single array named `count`. The individual elements become `count[0]`, `count[1]`, `count[2]`, `count[3]`, `count[4]`, and `count[5]`, as shown in the revised decision-making process in the `countDeps()` method in Figure 7-5.

The highlighted statements in Figure 7-5 show that when the `dep` value is 0, 1 is added to `count[0]`, when the `dep` value is 1, 1 is added to `count[1]`, and so on. When the `dep value` is 5, 1 is added to `count[5]`. In other words, 1 is added to one of the elements of the `count` array instead of to a single variable named `count0`, `count1`, `count2`, `count3`, `count4`, or `count5`. Is this version a big improvement over the original in Figure 7-4? Of course, it isn't. You still have not taken advantage of the benefits of using the array in this application.

The true benefit of using an array lies in your ability to use a variable as a subscript to the array, instead of using a constant such as 1 or 5. Notice in the `countDeps()` method in Figure 7-5 that within each decision, the value you are comparing to `dep` and the constant you are using as a subscript in the resulting "Yes" process are always identical. That is, when `dep` is 0, the subscript used to add 1 to the `count` array is 0; when `dep` is 1, the subscript used for the `count` array is 1, and so on. Therefore, you can just use `dep` as a subscript to the array. You can rewrite the decision-making process as shown in Figure 7-6.

FIGURE 7-5: REVISED `countDeps()` METHOD DECISION-MAKING PROCESS THAT USES AN ARRAY TO ACCUMULATE DEPENDENT COUNTS

```
public static void countDeps(Employee emp)
   numeric dep
   dep = emp.getDependents()
   if dep = 0 then
      count[0] = count[0] + 1
   else
      if dep = 1 then
         count[1] = count[1] + 1
      else
         if dep = 2 then
            count[2] = count[2] + 1
         else
            if dep = 3 then
               count[3] = count[3] + 1
            else
               if dep = 4 then
                  count[4] = count[4] + 1
               else
                  count[5] = count[5] + 1
               endif
            endif
         endif
      endif
   endif
return
```

FIGURE 7-6: MODIFIED `countDeps()` METHOD USING VARIABLE **dep** AS A SUBSCRIPT TO THE COUNT ARRAY

```
public static void countDeps(Employee emp)
   numeric dep
   dep = emp.getDependents()
   if dep = 0 then
      count[dep] = count[dep] + 1
   else
      if dep = 1 then
         count[dep] = count[dep] + 1
      else
         if dep = 2 then
            count[dep] = count[dep] + 1
         else
            if dep = 3 then
               count[dep] = count[dep] + 1
            else
               if dep = 4 then
                  count[dep] = count[dep] + 1
               else
                  count[dep] = count[dep] + 1
               endif
            endif
         endif
      endif
   endif
return
```

Of course, the code segment in Figure 7-6 looks no more efficient than the one in Figure 7-5. However, notice that in Figure 7-6 the highlighted statements are all the same—in other words, the process that occurs after each decision is exactly the same process. In each case, no matter what the value of **dep** is, you always add 1 to **count[dep]**. If you are always going to take the same action no matter what the answer to a question is, why ask the question? Instead, you can write the decision-making process as shown in Figure 7-7.

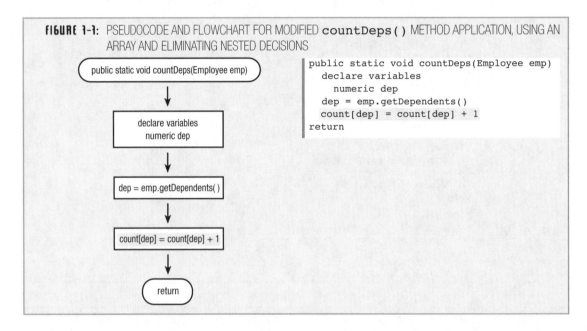

FIGURE 7-7: PSEUDOCODE AND FLOWCHART FOR MODIFIED **countDeps()** METHOD APPLICATION, USING AN ARRAY AND ELIMINATING NESTED DECISIONS

```
public static void countDeps(Employee emp)
    declare variables
        numeric dep
    dep = emp.getDependents()
    count[dep] = count[dep] + 1
return
```

The single highlighted statement in the **countDeps()** method in Figure 7-7 eliminates the *entire* decision-making process that was the original highlighted section in Figure 7-4! When **dep** is 2, 1 is added to **count[2]**; when **dep** is 4, 1 is added to **count[4]**, and so on. *Now* you have a big improvement to the original process. What's more, this process does not change whether there are 20, 30, or any other number of possible categories. To use more than five accumulators, you would declare additional **count** elements in the array, but the categorizing logic would remain the same as it is in Figure 7-7.

The report-writing portion of the application originally shown in Figure 7-4 also can be improved. Instead of six separate print statements to display the values stored in the six **count** fields, you can use a variable to control a printing loop, as shown in Figure 7-8. In Figure 7-8, the local loop control variable declared within the **printReport()** method is named **dep**. After printing the report headers, you can set **dep** to 0, then print **dep** and **count[dep]**. Then, add 1 to **dep** and use the same set of instructions again. You can use **dep** as a loop control variable to print the six individual **count** values. The improved application appears in Figure 7-8.

FIGURE 7-8: COUNTDEPENDENTS APPLICATION THAT USES AN ARRAY

```
public class CountDependents
    numeric count[0] = 0
    numeric count[1] = 0
    numeric count[2] = 0
    numeric count[3] = 0
    numeric count[4] = 0
    numeric count[5] = 0

    public static void main()
       Employee emp
       open(inputFile)
       emp = read(inputFile)
       while emp not EOF
            countDeps(emp)
            emp = read(inputFile)
       endwhile
       printReport()
       close(inputFile)
    return

    public static void countDeps(Employee emp)
       numeric dep
       dep = emp.getDependents()
       count[dep] = count[dep] + 1
    return

    public static void printReport()
       numeric dep
       print "Dependents Report"
       print "Dependents     Count"
       dep = 0
       while dep < 6
          print dep, count[dep]
          dep = dep + 1
       endwhile
    return
endClass
```

When printing the final count values in the `CountDependents` class in Figure 7-8, naming the loop control variable `dep` makes sense because it represents a number of dependents. However, this variable could be named `department`, `sub`, `x`, or any other legal identifier and used as a subscript to the array as long as it is:

- Numeric with no decimal places
- Initialized to 0
- Incremented by 1 each time the logic passes through the loop

In other words, nothing is linking the name `dep` to the `count` array per se; when you cycle through the array to print in the `printReport()` method, you are welcome to use a different variable name than you use when accumulating counts in the `countDeps()` method.

The dependent-counting application *worked* when it contained a long series of decisions and print statements, but the application is easier to write when you employ arrays. Additionally, the application is more efficient, easier for other programmers to understand, and easier to maintain. Arrays are never mandatory, but often they can drastically cut down on your programming time and make your logic easier to understand.

ARRAY DECLARATION AND INITIALIZATION

In the completed dependent-counting application in Figure 7-8, the six `count` array elements were declared and initialized to 0s at the start of the class. The `count` values are declared there, outside of any method, so that both the `countDeps()` and `printReport()` methods can use them. They need to be initialized to 0 so they can be added to during the course of the program. In Figure 7-8, the initialization is provided using six separate statements:

```
numeric count[0] = 0
numeric count[1] = 0
numeric count[2] = 0
numeric count[3] = 0
numeric count[4] = 0
numeric count[5] = 0
```

Separately declaring and initializing each `count` element is acceptable only if there are a small number of `count`s. If the dependent-counting application were updated to keep track of employees with up to 20 dependents, you would have to initialize 20 separate fields; it would be tedious to write 20 separate declaration statements.

Programming languages do not require the programmer to name each `count` element `count[0]`, `count[1]`, and so on. Instead, you can make a declaration such as one of those in Table 7-1.

TABLE 7-1: DECLARING A 20-ELEMENT ARRAY NAMED **count** IN SEVERAL COMMON LANGUAGES

Programming Language	Declaration of a 20-element Array
Visual Basic	`Dim Count[1 to 20] As Integer`
C#, C++	`int count[20]`
Java	`int[] count = new int[20]`

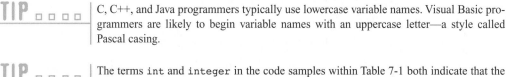

TIP ▢ ▢ ▢ ▢ C, C++, and Java programmers typically use lowercase variable names. Visual Basic programmers are likely to begin variable names with an uppercase letter—a style called Pascal casing.

TIP ▢ ▢ ▢ ▢ The terms `int` and `integer` in the code samples within Table 7-1 both indicate that the `count` array will hold whole-number values. These terms are more specific than the `numeric` identifier this book uses to declare all numeric variables.

All the declarations in Table 7-1 have two things in common: They name the `count` array and indicate that there will be 20 separate numeric elements. For flowcharting or pseudocode purposes, a statement such as `numeric count[20]` indicates the same thing.

Declaring a numeric array does not necessarily set its individual elements to zero (although it does in some programming languages, such as Visual Basic and Java). Most programming languages allow the equivalent of `num count[20] = 0`; you should use a statement like this when you want to initialize an array in your flowcharts or pseudocode.

When you want to initialize all the elements in an array to different values, you can always make individual assignments, as in the following:

```
numeric count[0] = 5
numeric count[1] = 12
numeric count[2] = 24
```

As an alternative to defining `count[0]`, `count[1]`, and so on separately, most programming languages allow a more concise version that takes the general form:

```
numeric count[3] = 5, 12, 24
```

When you use this form of array initialization, the first value you list is assigned to the first array element, and the subsequent values are assigned in order. Most programming languages allow you to assign fewer values than there are array elements declared, but none allows you to assign more values.

Alternately, to start all array elements with the same initial value, you can use an initialization loop. An **initialization loop** is a loop structure that provides initial values for every element in any array. To create an initialization loop, you must use a numeric field as a subscript. For example, if you declare a field named `sub`, and initialize `sub` to 0, then you can use a loop like the one shown in Figure 7-9 to set all the array elements to zero.

FIGURE 7-9: A LOOP THAT INITIALIZES 20 ARRAY ELEMENTS TO 0

```
numeric count[20]
numeric sub = 0
while sub < 20
    count[sub] = 0
    sub = sub + 1
endwhile
```

TIP ☐ ☐ ☐ ☐ In the loop in Figure 7-9, notice that the subscript varies from 0 through 19, never becoming equal to 20. If you accessed the array with a subscript value 20, an error would occur. You will learn more about errors caused by using too-high subscripts in Chapter 8.

TIP ☐ ☐ ☐ ☐ Providing array values is also called **populating the array**.

Explicitly initializing all variables is a good programming practice; assuming anything about uninitialized variable values is a dangerous practice. Array elements are no exception to this rule.

INITIALIZED AND UNINITIALIZED ARRAYS

The array that you used to accumulate dependent counts in the `CountDependents` application is an uninitialized array because the values that you want to use—the final dependent counts—are created during an actual run, or execution, of the application. In other words, if there are going to be 200 employees with 0 dependents, you don't know that fact at the beginning of the program. Instead, that value is accumulated during the execution of the application and not known until the end.

TIP □ □ □ □ In many object-oriented programming languages, all array values are initialized—for example, numeric values in an array often are all initialized to 0. For discussion purposes, this book refers to an array that is not explicitly initialized as being uninitialized.

Some arrays are not populated, or filled with useable values, during the run of an application, but instead, they receive their final values when you write the program code. For example, let's say you own an apartment building with apartments in the basement as well as three other floors, and you have records for all your tenants stored in a class similar to the `Tenant` class in Figure 7-10. Along with other data, each `Tenant` object holds the tenant's name and a floor number—0 for the basement, or 1, 2, or 3.

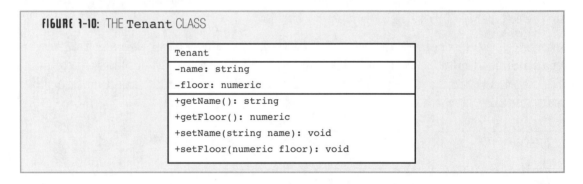

FIGURE 7-10: THE `Tenant` CLASS

Tenant
-name: string
-floor: numeric
+getName(): string
+getFloor(): numeric
+setName(string name): void
+setFloor(numeric floor): void

Every month you print a rent bill for each tenant. Your rent charges are based on the floor of the building, as shown in Figure 7-11.

To create an application that prints each tenant's name and rent due, you could use a series of decisions concerning the floor number. However, it is more efficient to use an array to hold the four rent figures. The array is initialized with values that are **hard-coded** into the array; that is, they are explicitly assigned to the array elements.

TIP □ □ □ □ Remember that another name for an array is a *table*. If you can use paper and pencil to list items like tenants' rent values in a table format, then using an array is an appropriate programming option.

FIGURE 7-11: RENTS BY FLOOR

FIGURE 7-11: RENTS BY FLOOR

Floor	Rent in $
0 (basement)	350
1	400
2	600
3 (penthouse)	1000

The PrintRentBills application is shown in Figure 7-12. When you declare variables at the start of the application, you create an array for the four rent figures and initialize each to the correct rent as described in Figure 7-11.

FIGURE 7-12: PSEUDOCODE FOR PRINTRENTBILLS APPLICATION

```
public class PrintRentBills
    numeric rent[4] = 350, 400, 600, 1000
    public static void main()
       Tenant ten
       open(inputFile)
       ten = read(inputFile)
       while ten not EOF
            printBill(ten)
            ten  = read(inputFile)
       endwhile
       close(inputFile)
    return

    public static void printBill(Tenant ten)
       numeric floor
       floor = ten.getFloor()
       print "Dear ", ten.getName(), ","
       print "Your rent is due: ", rent[floor]
    return
endClass
```

TIP ▫ ▫ ▫ ▫   In an application like PrintRentBills, the array values could also be defined as constant, or unchangeable values.

In the PrintRentBills application in Figure 7-12, after you open the input file, you read a first record into memory. While the end-of-file (EOF) condition is not met, you pass the **Tenant** to the **printBill()** method. There, you print five separate items spread over two lines:

- The string "Dear"
- The Tenant's name, retrieved from the **Tenant** object with **ten.getName()**
- A string containing a comma to follow the name
- A string containing "Your rent is due:"
- The rent amount, retrieved from the array with **rent[floor]**

Instead of making a series of selections such as `if ten.getFloor() = 0 then print rent[0]` and `if ten.getFloor() = 1 then print rent[1]`, you take advantage of the `rent` array by using the Tenant's `floor` as a subscript to access the correct `rent` array element. When deciding what variable to use as a subscript with an array, ask yourself, "Of all the values available in the array, what does the correct selection depend on?" When printing a `rent` value, the rent you use depends on the floor on which the tenant lives, so the correct action is `print rent[floor]`.

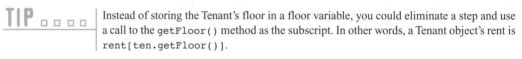 Instead of storing the Tenant's floor in a floor variable, you could eliminate a step and use a call to the `getFloor()` method as the subscript. In other words, a Tenant object's rent is `rent[ten.getFloor()]`.

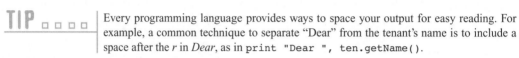 Every programming language provides ways to space your output for easy reading. For example, a common technique to separate "Dear" from the tenant's name is to include a space after the *r* in *Dear*, as in `print "Dear ", ten.getName()`.

Without a `rent` array, the PrintRentBills application would have to contain three decisions and four different resulting actions. With the `rent` array, there are no decisions. Each tenant's rent is simply based on the `rent` element that corresponds to the tenant's floor number; in other words, the floor number indicates the positional value of the corresponding rent. Arrays can really lighten the work load required to write a program.

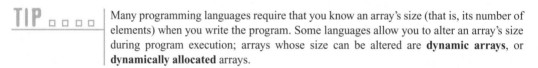 Many programming languages require that you know an array's size (that is, its number of elements) when you write the program. Some languages allow you to alter an array's size during program execution; arrays whose size can be altered are **dynamic arrays**, or **dynamically allocated** arrays.

LOADING AN ARRAY FROM A FILE

Writing the rent program from the last section requires you to set values for four `rent` array elements before you can assign any `Tenant` the correct rent. If you write the rent program for a skyscraper, you may have to initialize 100 array elements. Additionally, building managers sometimes change rent amounts; when they do, you must alter the array element values within the application (and recompile it) to reflect the new rent charges. If the rent values change frequently, it is inconvenient to have hard-coded values in your application. Instead, you can write your application so that it loads the array rent amounts from a file. The array of rents that gets its values from a file is an example of an array that gets its values during the execution of the program.

Apartment building management can update a file that contains all the rent amounts as frequently as needed. Suppose you periodically receive a file named RentFile.txt that is created by the building management and always contains the current rent values. The file contains Rent objects, as defined by the class diagram in Figure 7-13. You can write the rent program so that it accepts all records from the input file at the beginning of the application. After this file has been exhausted, the application can read Tenant records from another file one by one and determine each Tenant's bill. Figure 7-14 shows how this is accomplished.

FIGURE 7-13: THE Rent CLASS

```
Rent
-floor: numeric
-rentAmount: numeric
+getFloor(): numeric
+getRent(): numeric
+setFloor(numeric floor): void
+setRent(numeric amount): void
```

FIGURE 7-14: THE PRINTRENTBILLS2 APPLICATION

```
public class PrintRentBills2
    numeric rent[4]
    public static void main()
        Tenant ten
        Rent rentRec
        open(inputRentFile)
        rentRec = read(inputRentFile)
        while rentRec not EOF
            rent[rentRec.getFloor] = rentRec.getRent()
            rentRec = read(inputRentFile)
        endwhile
        close(inputRentFile)
        open(inputFile)
        ten = read(inputFile)
        while ten not EOF
            printBill(ten)
            ten = read(inputFile)
        endwhile
        close(inputFile)
    return

    public static void printBill(Tenant ten)
        numeric floor
        floor = ten.getFloor()
        print "Dear ", ten.getName(), ","
        print "Your rent is due: ", rent[floor]
    return
endClass
```

In the highlighted portion of the `main()` method in Figure 7-14, you read a `rentRec` record from the input file. Within your application, the file is named `inputRentRec`, to distinguish it from the different file that contains the `Tenant`'s records. Each `Rent` object stored in the input file contains a floor and the rent that is charged on that floor. When you read in the first `rentRec` record, you store it in the correct element of the `rent` array based on the floor. After the rent file is exhausted, you can close it and begin to read the file containing the `Tenant` records, and then the application proceeds as usual.

TIP ▫ ▫ ▫ ▫ Instead of closing the rent file as soon as you have read in the rents, you could wait, and close all files at the same time at the end of the application.

In most languages, the RentFile.txt file name would be associated with the `inputRentRec` identifier in the open statement. That step is eliminated from this pseudocode for simplicity.

When you use this method—reading the rents from an input file instead of hard-coding them into the class—clerical employees can update the rent values in the rent file as needed. Your application takes care of loading the rents into the array from the most recent copy of the RentFile.txt, ensuring that each rent is always accurate and up-to-date. Using this technique, you avoid the necessity of changing code within the program with each rent update.

Another way to organize the RentFile.txt file would be to include just one field in the `Rent` object—rent—and make sure the records were always stored in sequential order based on the floor. Then, the first rent value read in would represent the rent for the basement, the second rent would represent the first floor, and so on.

SEARCHING AN ARRAY FOR AN EXACT MATCH

In both the dependent-counting application and the rent-determining application that you've seen in this chapter, the fields that the arrays depend on conveniently hold small whole numbers. The number of dependents allowed in the first application was 0 through 5, and the number of a tenant's floor in the building in the second application was 0 through 3. Unfortunately, real life doesn't always happen in small integers. Sometimes you don't have a variable that conveniently holds an array position; sometimes you have to search through an array to find a value you need.

Consider a mail-order business in which orders come in with a customer name, address, item number ordered, and quantity ordered. The `CustomerOrder` class is described in Figure 7-15.

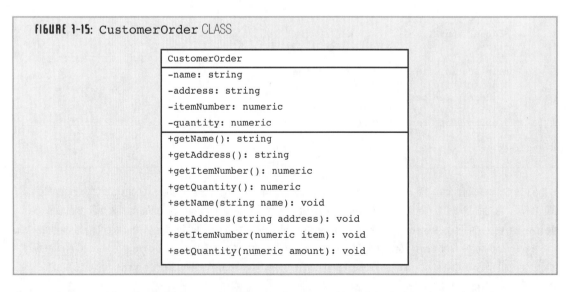

FIGURE 7-15: `CustomerOrder` CLASS

CustomerOrder
-name: string
-address: string
-itemNumber: numeric
-quantity: numeric
+getName(): string
+getAddress(): string
+getItemNumber(): numeric
+getQuantity(): numeric
+setName(string name): void
+setAddress(string address): void
+setItemNumber(numeric item): void
+setQuantity(numeric amount): void

Assume the item numbers from which a `Customer` can choose are three-digit numbers, but perhaps they are not consecutive 001 through 999. Instead, over the years, items have been deleted and new items have been added to the inventory. For example, there might no longer be an item with number 105 or 129. Sometimes there might be a hundred-number gap or more between items.

For example, let's say that this season you are down to offering the six items shown in Figure 7-16.

FIGURE 7-16: AVAILABLE ITEMS IN MAIL-ORDER COMPANY

Item Number	Item Price in $
106	0.59
108	0.99
307	4.50
405	15.99
457	17.50
688	35.00

When a customer orders an item, you want to determine whether the customer has ordered a valid item number. You could use a series of six decisions to determine whether the ordered item is valid by comparing, in turn, each customer order's item number to each of the six allowed values. However, a superior approach is to create an array that holds the list of valid item numbers. Then you can search through the array for an exact match to the ordered item. If you search through the entire array without finding a match for the item the customer ordered, you can print an error message, for example: "No such item."

Suppose you create an array named `validItem` that contains six elements, and that you set each to a valid item number. If a customer orders item 307, a clerical worker can tell whether it is valid by looking down the list and verifying that 307 is a member of the list. In a similar fashion, you can use a loop to test each `validItem` against the ordered item number.

The technique for verifying that an item number exists involves setting a subscript to 0 and setting a flag variable to indicate that you have not yet determined whether the customer's order is valid. A **flag** is a variable that you set to indicate whether some event has occurred; frequently it holds a true or false value. For example, you can set a string variable named `foundIt` to "N", indicating "No". (See the first highlighted statement in Figure 7-17.) Then you compare the customer's ordered item number to the first item in the array. If the customer-ordered item matches the first item in the array, you can set the flag variable to "Y", or any other value that is not "N". (See the second highlighted statement in Figure 7-17.) If the items do not match, you increase the subscript and continue to look down the list of numbers stored in the array. If you check all six valid item numbers and the customer item matches none of them, then the flag variable `foundIt` still holds the value "N". If the flag variable is "N" after you have looked through the entire list, you can issue an error message indicating that no match was ever found. Figure 7-17 shows a method that accepts a `CustomerOrder` object and accomplishes the item verification.

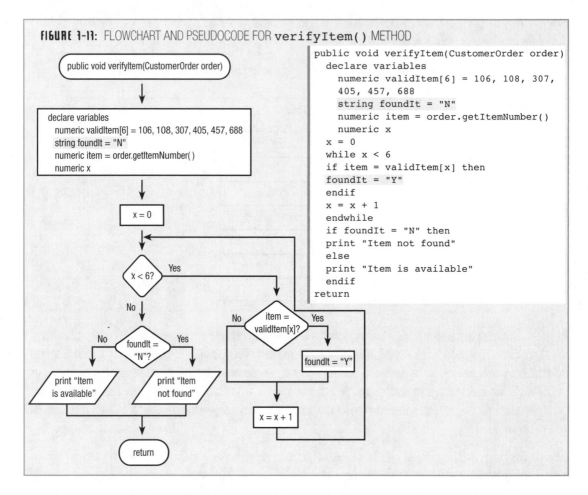

FIGURE 7-17: FLOWCHART AND PSEUDOCODE FOR `verifyItem()` METHOD

```
public void verifyItem(CustomerOrder order)
   declare variables
      numeric validItem[6] = 106, 108, 307,
      405, 457, 688
      string foundIt = "N"
      numeric item = order.getItemNumber()
      numeric x
   x = 0
   while x < 6
   if item = validItem[x] then
   foundIt = "Y"
   endif
   x = x + 1
   endwhile
   if foundIt = "N" then
   print "Item not found"
   else
   print "Item is available"
   endif
   return
```

TIP ▢ ▢ ▢ ▢ Instead of the string `foundIt` variable in the method in Figure 7-17, you might prefer to use a numeric variable that you set to 1 or 0. Most programming languages also support a Boolean data type that you can use for foundIt; when you declare a variable to be Boolean, you can set its value to true or false.

USING PARALLEL ARRAYS

In a mail-order company, when you read in a customer's order, you usually want to accomplish more than simply to verify that the item exists. For example, you might want to determine the price of the ordered item, multiply that price by quantity ordered, and print a bill. Using the prices listed in Figure 7-16, you *could* write a program in which you read in a customer order record and then use the order's item number as a subscript to pull a price from an array. To use this method, you would need an array with at least 688 elements. If a customer orders item 405, item is determined with `item = order.getItemNumber()`, and the price is found at `validItemPrice[item]`, which is `validItem[405]`, or the 405th element of the array. Such an array would need 688 elements (because the highest item number is 688), but because you sell only six items, you would waste 682 of the reserved memory positions. Instead of reserving a large quantity of memory that remains unused, you can set up this program to use two much smaller arrays.

Consider the `findPrice()` method in Figure 7-18. Two arrays are set up—one contains six elements named `validItem`; all six elements are valid item numbers. The other array, highlighted in the figure, also has six elements. The array is named `validItemPrice`; all six elements are prices. Each price in this `validItemPrice` array is conveniently and purposely in the same position as the corresponding item number in the other `validItem` array. Two corresponding arrays such as these are **parallel arrays** because each element in one array is associated with the element in the same relative position in the other array.

FIGURE 7-18: THE `findPrice()` METHOD

```
public void findPrice(CustomerOrder order)
        numeric validItem[6] = 106, 108, 307, 405, 457, 688
        numeric validItemPrice[6] = 0.59, 0.99, 4.50,
            15.99, 17.50, 35.00
        string foundIt = "N"
        numeric item = order.getItemNumber()
        numeric x
        numeric price
        x = 0
        while x < 6
           if item = validItem[x] then
                price = validItemPrice[x]
                foundIt = "Y"
           endif
           x = x + 1
        endwhile
        if foundIt = "N" then
            print "Item not found"
        else
            print "Item is available for $", price
            print "Total bill is $",
                price * order.getQuantity()
        endif
    return
```

As the `findPrice()` module in Figure 7-18 receives each `CustomerOrder`, you look through each of the `validItem` values separately by varying the subscript `x` from 0 to the number of items available. When a match for the `CustomerOrder`'s item number is found, you pull the corresponding parallel price out of the list of `validItemPrice` values and store it in the `price` variable. (See highlighted statements in Figure 7-18.)

TIP ▫ ▫ ▫ ▫ | Some programmers object to using a cryptic variable name such as x because it is not descriptive. These programmers would prefer a name like priceIndex. Others approve of short names like x when the variable is used only in a limited area of a program, as it is used here, to step through an array. There are many style issues like this on which programmers disagree. As a programmer, it is your responsibility to find out what conventions are used among your peers in your organization.

Once you find a match for the ordered item number in the `validItem` array, you know that the price of that item is in the same position in the other array, `validItemPrice`. When `validItem[x]` is the correct item, `validItemPrice[x]` must be the correct price. You can then print the price, and multiply it by the quantity ordered to produce a total, as shown in the last highlighted statements in Figure 7-18.

Suppose that a customer orders item 457. Walk through the logic yourself to see if you come up with the correct price, $17.50.

IMPROVING SEARCH EFFICIENCY USING AN EARLY EXIT

The mail-order program is still a little inefficient. The problem is that if lots of customers order item 106 or 108, their price is found on the first or second pass through the loop. The application continues searching through the item array, however, until **x** reaches the value 6. One way to stop the search when the item has been found and **foundIt** is set to "Y", is to force (that is, explicitly assign) **x** to 6 immediately. Then, when the program loops back to check whether **x** is still less than 6, the loop will be exited and the program won't bother checking any of the higher item numbers. Leaving a loop as soon as a match is found is called an **early exit**; it improves the program's efficiency. The larger the array, the more beneficial it becomes to exit the searching loop as soon as you find what you're looking for.

> **TIP** □ □ □ □ | Instead of forcing x to 6, you could change the comparison that controls the while loop to continue while x < 6 AND foundIt = "N". If you use this approach, as soon as an item is found and foundIt becomes "Y", the loop exits.

Figure 7-19 shows the improved version of the **findPrice()** method. Notice the highlighted improvement. You search the **validItem** array, element by element. If an item number is not matched in a given location, the subscript is increased and the next location is checked. As soon as an item number is located in the array, you store the price, turn on the flag, and force the subscript to a high number (6) so the program will not check the item number array any further.

FIGURE 7-19: THE `findPrice()` METHOD CONTAINING A MORE EFFICIENT SEARCH

```
public void findPrice(CustomerOrder order)
  declare variables
    numeric validItem[6] = 106, 108, 307, 405, 457, 688
    numeric validItemPrice[6] = 0.59, 0.99, 4.50,
      15.99, 17.50, 35.00
    string foundIt = "N"
    numeric item = order.getItemNumber()
    numeric x
    numeric price
  x = 0
  while x < 6
    if item = validItem[x] then
        price = validItemPrice[x]
        foundIt = "Y"
        x = 6
    endif
    x = x + 1
  endwhile
  if foundIt = "N" then
    print "Item not found"
  else
    print "Item is available for $", price
    print "Total bill is $",
        price * order.getQuantity()
  endif
return
```

TIP ▫ ▫ ▫ ▫ | In the `findPrice()` method in Figure 7-19, x could be set to any value 5 or over. At the end of the loop 1 is added to x; at long as the result is 6 or more, the loop will not continue.

TIP ▫ ▫ ▫ ▫ | Notice that the `findPrice()` method is most efficient when the most frequently ordered items are stored at the beginning of the array. When you use this technique, only the seldom-ordered items require many cycles through the searching loop before finding a match.

USING A CONSTANT TO STORE AN ARRAY SIZE

You can make programs that contain arrays more flexible by declaring a variable or named constant to hold the size of the array. Then, whenever you need to refer to the size of the array within the program—for example, when you loop through the array during a search operation—you can use the variable name instead of a hard-coded value like 6. If the program must be altered later to accommodate more or fewer array elements, you need to make only one change—you change the value of the array-size variable where it is declared. For example, Figure 7-20 shows the `findPrice()` module including a constant named NUM_PRODUCTS that holds the array size. The word `constant` before the declaration in the first highlighted line shows that value of the named memory location is fixed when it is declared and cannot be changed later during the execution of the method. Although not required, it is a programming convention to use uppercase letters in constant identifiers, and to use underscores to separate words for readability. The named constant, NUM_PRODUCTS, is used in each of the highlighted statements in the `findPrice()` method. If the mail order company expands to offer additional products, or reduces the inventory to offer fewer, only one change will be necessary in the method—you would modify the value of NUM_PRODUCTS and recompile the class in which it resides.

TIP ▫ ▫ ▫ ▫ | You first learned about named constants in Chapter 1. A named constant is declared like a variable, but its value cannot change during program execution. Instead of constant, Java uses the keyword final to identify constants, and C++ and C# use the keyword const.

Besides making your code easier to modify, using a named constant makes the code easier to understand. In general, you should avoid using a number in a program without explanation. Such numbers are called **magic numbers** because they do not naturally reveal their purpose the way a symbolic name would; using them is a bad programming practice. Many programmers suggest that you never use hard-coded numbers in your programs—neither with arrays nor anywhere else.

TIP ▫ ▫ ▫ ▫ | In some programming languages, arrays automatically acquire a field that holds their size. For example, in Java, if you declare a 10-element array named array, then you can use a field named array.length in place of the number 10.

FIGURE 7-20: THE `findPrice()` METHOD CONTAINING A CONSTANT TO HOLD THE ARRAY SIZE

```
public void findPrice(CustomerOrder order)
  declare variables
     constant numeric NUM_PRODUCTS = 6
     numeric validItem[NUM_PRODUCTS] = 106, 108, 307,
         405, 457, 688
     numeric validItemPrice[NUM_PRODUCTS] = 0.59,
         0.99, 4.50, 15.99, 17.50, 35.00
     string foundIt = "N"
     numeric item = order.getItemNumber()
     numeric x
     numeric price
  x = 0
  while x < NUM_PRODUCTS
    if item = validItem[x] then
         price = validItemPrice[x]
         foundIt = "Y"
         x = NUM_PRODUCTS
    endif
    x = x + 1
  endwhile
  if foundIt = "N" then
    print "Item not found"
  else
    print "Item is available for $", price
    print "Total bill is $",
         price * order.getQuantity()
  endif
return
```

SEARCHING AN ARRAY FOR A RANGE MATCH

Customer order item numbers need to match available item numbers exactly in order to determine the correct price of an item. Sometimes, however, programmers want to work with ranges of values in arrays. A **range of values** is any series of values, for example 1 through 5, or 20 through 30.

Recall the `CustomerOrder` class description from earlier in this chapter, shown again in Figure 7-21.

Suppose the company decides to offer quantity discounts, as shown in Figure 7-22.

You want to be able to read in a `CustomerOrder` from an input file and determine a discount percentage based on the value in the `quantity` field. For example, if a customer has ordered 20 items, you want to be able to print "Your discount is 15 percent". One ill-advised approach might be to set up an array with as many elements as any customer might ever order, and store the appropriate discount for each possible number, as shown in Figure 7-23.

FIGURE 7-21: `CustomerOrder` CLASS DIAGRAM

```
CustomerOrder
-name: string
-address: string
-itemNumber: numeric
-quantity: numeric
+getName(): string
+getAddress(): string
+getItemNumber(): numeric
+getQuantity(): numeric
+setName(string name): void
+setAddress(string address): void
+setItemNumber(numeric item): void
+setQuantity(numeric amount): void
```

FIGURE 7-22: DISCOUNTS ON ORDERS BY QUANTITY

Quantity	Discount %
0–8	0
9–12	10
13–25	15
26 or more	20

FIGURE 7-23: USABLE—BUT INEFFICIENT—DISCOUNT ARRAY

```
discount[0] = 0
discount[1] = 0
discount[2] = 0
discount[3] = 0
discount[4] = 0
discount[5] = 0
discount[6] = 0
discount[7] = 0
discount[8] = 0
discount[9] = 10
discount[10] = 10
discount[11] = 10
discount[12] = 10
discount[13] = 10
discount[14] = 15
discount[15] = 15
...and so on
```

This approach has three drawbacks:

- It requires a very large array that uses a lot of memory.

- You must store the same value repeatedly. For example, each of the first nine elements receives the same value, 0, and each of the next four elements receives the same value, 10.

- Where do you stop adding array elements? Is a customer order quantity of 75 items enough? What if a customer orders 100 or 1,000 items? No matter how many elements you place in the array, there's always a chance that a customer will order more.

A better approach is to create just four discount array elements, one for each of the possible discount rates, as shown in Figure 7-24.

FIGURE 7-24: SUPERIOR DISCOUNT ARRAY

```
discount[0] = 0
discount[1] = 10
discount[2] = 15
discount[3] = 20
```

With the new four-element `discount` array, you need a parallel array to search for the appropriate level for the discount. At first, beginning programmers might consider creating an array named `discountRange` and testing whether the quantity ordered equals one of the four stored values. For example:

```
discountRange[0] = 0 through 8
discountRange[1] = 9 through 12
discountRange[2] = 13 through 25
discountRange[3] = 26 and higher
```

However, you cannot create an array like the one previously shown. Each element in any array is simply a single variable. A simple variable like `age` or `payRate` can hold 6 or 12, but it can't hold every value 6 *through* 12. Similarly, the `discountRange[0]` variable can hold a 0, 1, 8, or any other single value, but it can't hold 0 *through* 8; there is no such numeric value.

One solution to create a useable `discountRange` array is to create an array that holds only the low-end value of each range, as Figure 7-25 shows.

FIGURE 7-25: THE `discountRange` ARRAY USING LOW END OF EACH DISCOUNT RANGE

```
discountRange[0] = 0
discountRange[1] = 9
discountRange[2] = 13
discountRange[3] = 26
```

Using an array such as the one in Figure 7-25, you can compare each `CustomerOrder`'s quantity value with each `discountRange` array value in turn. You can start with the *last* range limit (`discountRange[3]`). If the quantity ordered is at least that value, 26, the loop is never entered and the customer gets the highest discount rate (`discount[3]`, or `20 percent`). If the quantity ordered is not at least `discountRange[3]`, that is, if it is less than `26`, then you reduce the subscript and check to see if the quantity is at least `discountRange[2]`, or 13. If so, the customer receives `discount[2]`, or 15 percent, and so on. Figure 7-26 shows a `determineDiscount()` method that accepts a CustomerOrder object and determines the appropriate discount rate. The appropriate rate is printed from within the method and also returned by the method so it can be used by a calling method.

FIGURE 7-26: FLOWCHART AND PSEUDOCODE FOR DISCOUNT DETERMINATION

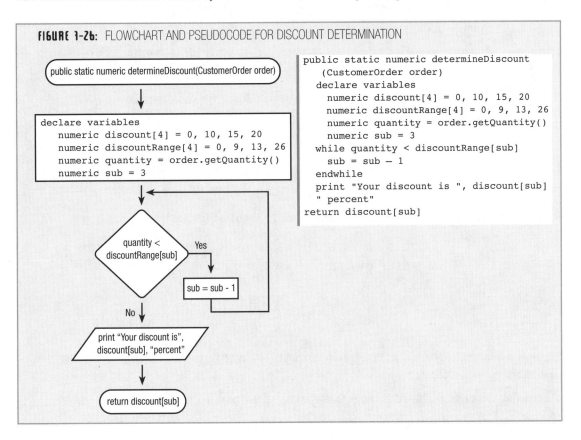

```
public static numeric determineDiscount
   (CustomerOrder order)
   declare variables
      numeric discount[4] = 0, 10, 15, 20
      numeric discountRange[4] = 0, 9, 13, 26
      numeric quantity = order.getQuantity()
      numeric sub = 3
   while quantity < discountRange[sub]
      sub = sub - 1
   endwhile
   print "Your discount is ", discount[sub]
   " percent"
return discount[sub]
```

> **TIP** ▫ ▫ ▫ ▫   An alternate approach is to store the high end of every range in an array. Then you start with the *lowest* element and check for values *less than or equal to* each array element value.

When using an array to store range limits, you use a loop to make a series of comparisons that would otherwise require many separate decisions. Your `determineDiscount()` method is written using fewer instructions than would be required if you did not use an array, and modifications to your method will be easier to make in the future.

CHAPTER SUMMARY

- ☐ An array is a series or list of variables in computer memory, all of which have the same name but are differentiated with special numbers called subscripts.

- ☐ When you declare an array, you declare a programming structure that contains multiple elements, each of which has the same name and the same data type. Each array element has a unique integer subscript indicating how far away the individual element is from the first element.

- ☐ You often can use a variable as a subscript to an array, replacing multiple nested decisions.

- ☐ You can declare and initialize all of the elements in an array using a single statement that provides a type, a name, and a quantity of elements for the array. You also can initialize array values within an initialization loop.

- ☐ Some arrays contain values that are determined during the execution of a program; other arrays are more useful when their final desired values are hard-coded when you write the program.

- ☐ You can load an array from a file. This step is often performed near the start of a program.

- ☐ Searching through an array to find a value you need involves initializing a subscript, using a loop to test each array element, and setting a flag when a match is found.

- ☐ In parallel arrays, each element in one array is associated with the element in the same relative position in the other array.

- ☐ When you need to compare a value to a range of values in an array, you can store either the low- or high-end value of each range for comparison.

KEY TERMS

An **array** is a series or list of variables in computer memory, all of which have the same name but are differentiated with special numbers called subscripts.

A **subscript**, also called an index, is a number that indicates the position of a particular item within an array.

An **index**, also called a subscript, is a number that indicates the position of a particular item within an array.

Each separate array variable is one **element** of the array.

The **size of the array** is the number of elements it can hold.

An **initialization loop** is a loop structure that provides initial values for every element in any array.

Populating an array is the act of assigning values to the array elements.

Hard-coded values are explicitly assigned.

Dynamic arrays, or **dynamically allocated** arrays, are arrays whose size is determined during program execution.

A **flag** is a variable that you set to indicate whether some event has occurred.

Parallel arrays are two or more arrays in which each element in one array is associated with the element in the same relative position in the other array or arrays.

Leaving a loop as soon as a match is found is called an **early exit**.

Magic numbers are numbers hard coded into a program without explanation; using them is a bad programming practice.

A **range of values** is any series of values.

REVIEW QUESTIONS

1. A subscript is a(n) _____.

   a. element in an array
   b. alternate name for an array
   c. number that indicates the position of a particular item within an array
   d. number that represents the highest value stored within an array

2. Each variable in an array must have the same _____ as the others.

   a. subscript
   b. data type
   c. value
   d. memory location

3. Each variable in an array is called a(n) _____.

   a. element
   b. subscript
   c. component
   d. data type

4. The subscripts of any array are always _____.

   a. characters
   b. fractions
   c. integers
   d. strings of characters

5. Suppose you have an array named `number`, and two of its elements are `number[1]` and `number[4]`. You know that _____.

   a. the two elements hold the same value
   b. the two elements are at the same memory location
   c. the array holds exactly four elements
   d. there are exactly two elements between those two elements

6. Suppose you want to write a program that reads customer records and prints a summary of the number of customers who owe more than $1,000 each, in each of 12 sales regions. Customer fields include `name`, `zipCode`, `balanceDue`, and `regionNumber`. At some point during record processing, you would add 1 to an array element whose subscript would be represented by _____.

   a. `name`
   b. `zipCode`
   c. `balanceDue`
   d. `regionNumber`

7. Arrays are most useful when you use a _____ as a subscript.

   a. numeric constant
   b. character
   c. variable
   d. file name

8. Suppose you create a program containing a seven-element array that contains the names of the days of the week. In the `housekeeping()` module, you display the day names using a subscript named `dayNum`. In the same program, you display the same array values again in the `finish()` module. In the `finish()` module, you _____ as a subscript to the array.

   a. must use `dayNum`
   b. can use `dayNum` but can also use another variable
   c. must not use `dayNum`
   d. must use a numeric constant

9. Declaring a numeric array sets its individual elements' values to _____.

   a. zero in every programming language
   b. zero in some programming languages
   c. consecutive digits in every programming language
   d. consecutive digits in some programming languages

10. Filling an array with values during a program's execution is known as _____ the array.

    a. populating
    b. colonizing
    c. initializing
    d. declaring

11. A hard-coded array is one whose final desired values are set _____.

    a. at the beginning of the program
    b. during the execution of the program
    c. by the end of the program
    d. to zero

12. When you create an array of whole values that you explicitly set upon creation, using numeric constants, the values are said to be _____.

   a. postcoded
   b. precoded
   c. soft-coded
   d. hard-coded

13. Many arrays contain values that change periodically. For example, a bank program that uses an array containing mortgage rates for various terms might change several times a day. The newest values are most likely _____.

   a. typed into the program by a programmer who then recompiles the program before it is used
   b. calculated by the program, based on historical trends
   c. read into the program from a file that contains the current rates
   d. typed in by a clerk each time the program is executed for a customer

14. A _____ is a variable that you set to indicate a true or false state.

   a. subscript
   b. flag
   c. counter
   d. banner

15. Two arrays in which each element in one array is associated with the element in the same relative position in the other array are _____ arrays.

   a. cohesive
   b. perpendicular
   c. hidden
   d. parallel

16. The highest subscript you should use with a 10-element array is _____.

   a. 8
   b. 9
   c. 10
   d. 11

17. If you perform an early exit from a loop while searching through an array for a match, you _____.

   a. quit searching as soon as you find a match
   b. quit searching before you find a match
   c. set a flag as soon as you find a match, but keep searching for additional matches
   d. repeat a search only if the first search was unsuccessful

18. In programming terminology, the values 0.25 through 0.40 represent a(n) _____ of values.

    a. assortment
    b. range
    c. diversity
    d. collection

19. Each element in a five-element array can hold _____ value(s).

    a. one
    b. five
    c. at least five
    d. an unlimited number of

20. After the annual dog show in which the Barkley Dog Training Academy awards points to each participant, the Academy assigns a status to each dog based on the following criteria:

Points Earned	Level of Achievement
0–5	Good
6–7	Excellent
8–9	Superior
10	Unbelievable

The Academy needs a program that compares a dog's points earned with the grading scale, in order to award a certificate acknowledging the appropriate level of achievement. Of the following, which set of values would be most useful for the contents of an array used in the program?

    a. 0, 6, 9, 10
    b. 5, 7, 8, 10
    c. 5, 7, 9, 10
    d. any of these

EXERCISES

1a. The city of Cary is holding a special census. The census takers collect one record for each citizen, containing the citizen's age, gender, marital status, and voting district. The voting district field contains a number from 1 through 22.

Design a `Citizen` class. Also design the logic of an application that would produce a count of the number of citizens residing in each of the 22 voting districts.

1b. The city of Redgranite is holding a special census. The census takers collect one record for each citizen.

Using the `Citizen` class from Exercise 1a, design an application that reads Citizen records and produces a count of the number of citizens in each of the following age groups: under 18, 18 through 30, 31 through 45, 46 through 64, and 65 and older.

2. The Midville Park District maintains records containing information about players on its soccer teams. Each record contains a player's first name, last name, and team number. The teams are:

```
Soccer teams
Team Number    Team Name
1              Goal Getters
2              The Force
3              Top Guns
4              Shooting Stars
5              Midfield Monsters
```

Design a `SoccerPlayer` class and the logic for creating a report that lists all players along with their team numbers and team names.

3. **Create the logic for an application that produces a count of the number of players registered for each team listed in Exercise 2.**

4. **An elementary school contains 30 classrooms numbered 1 through 30. Each classroom can contain any number of students up to 35. Each student takes an achievement test at the end of the school year and receives a score from 0 through 100. One record is created for each student in the school; each record contains a student ID, classroom number, and score on the achievement test.**

Design a `Student` class and the logic for an application that lists the total points scored for each of the 30 classrooms.

5. **Modify Exercise 4 so that each classroom's average of the test scores prints, rather than each classroom's total.**

6. **The school in Exercises 4 and 5 maintains a file containing the teacher's name for each classroom. Each record in this file contains a room number 1 through 30, and the last name of the teacher.**

Design a `Teacher` class. Modify Exercise 5 so that the correct teacher's name appears on the list with his or her class's average.

7. **A fast-food restaurant sells the following products:**

```
Fast-food items
Product         Price
Cheeseburger    2.49
Pepsi           1.00
Chips            .59
```

Design a Customer record that contains a customer number and item name. Also design the logic for an application that reads in a Customer record and prints either the correct price or the message "Sorry, we do not carry that" as output.

8. **Design the logic for an application for a company that wants a report containing a breakdown of payroll by department. Input records contain an employee's last name, first name, department number, hourly salary, and number of hours worked. Input records are organized in alphabetical order by employee, *not* in department number order.**

    The output is a list of the seven departments in the company (numbered 1 through 7) and the total gross payroll (rate times hours) for each department.

9. **Modify Exercise 8 so that the report lists department names as well as numbers. The department names are:**

    ```
    Department numbers and names
    Department Number          Department Name
    1                          Personnel
    2                          Marketing
    3                          Manufacturing
    4                          Computer Services
    5                          Sales
    6                          Accounting
    7                          Shipping
    ```

10. **Modify the report created in Exercise 9 so that it prints a line of information for each employee before printing the department summary at the end of the report. Each detail line must contain the employee's name, department number, department name, hourly wage, hours worked, gross pay, and withholding tax.**

    Withholding taxes are based on the following percentages of gross pay:

    ```
    Withholding taxes
    Weekly Salary          Withholding Percent
    0.00-200.00            10
    200.01-350.00          14
    350.01-500.00          18
    500.01-up              22
    ```

11. **The Perfect Party Catering Company keeps records concerning the events it caters.**

    Create an `Event` class that contains an event number, the event host's last name, and numeric month, day, and year values representing the event date. The `Event` class also contains the number of guests that will be attending the Event and a numeric meal code representing the entree that the event hosts will serve.

    Create a `Meal` class that contains the meal selection codes (such as 4), name of entree (such as "Roast beef"), and current price per guest (such as 19.50).

    Design the logic for an application that produces a report that reads up to 10 Meal records from a file and stores them in an array. Then the application reads Event records from a file, and lists each event number, host name, date, meal, guests, gross total price for the party, and price for the party after discount. Print the month name—for example, "October"—rather than "10". Print the meal selection—for example, "Roast beef"—rather than "4". The gross total price for the party is the price per guest for the meal, times the number of guests. The final price includes a discount based on the following table:

```
Discounts for large parties
Number of Guests    Discount
1-25                $0
26-50               $75
51-100              $125
101-250             $200
251 and over        $300
```

12. *Daily Life Magazine* **wants an analysis of the demographic characteristics of its readers. The Marketing Department has collected reader survey records containing the age, gender, marital status, and annual income of readers.**

Design a `Reader` class that contains fields for this information from the survey records.

a. Create the logic for a program that would produce a count of readers by age groups as follows: under 20, 20–29, 30–39, 40–49, and 50 and older.

b. Create the logic for a program that would produce a count of readers by gender within age group—that is, under 20 females, under 20 males, and so on.

c. Create the logic for a program that would produce a count of readers by income groups as follows: under $20,000, $20,000–$24,999, $25,000–$34,999, $35,000–$49,999, and $50,000 and up.

13. **Glen Ross Vacation Property Sales employs seven salespeople as follows:**

```
Salespeople
ID Number    Name
103          Darwin
104          Kratz
201          Shulstad
319          Fortune
367          Wickert
388          Miller
435          Vick
```

When a salesperson makes a sale, a record is created including the date, time, and dollar amount of the sale. The time is expressed in hours and minutes, based on a 24-hour clock. The sale amount is expressed in whole dollars. Design a `Sale` class that contains a sale's data.

Salespeople earn a commission that differs for each sale, based on the following rate schedule:

```
Commission rates
Sale Amount            Rate
$0-50,000              .04
$51,000-$125,000       .05
$126,000-$200,000      .06
$201,000 and up        .07
```

Design an application that produces each of the following reports:

a. A report listing each salesperson number, name, total sales, and total commissions
b. A report listing each month of the year as both a number and a word (for example, "01 January"), and the total sales for the month for all salespeople
c. A report listing total sales as well as total commissions earned by all salespeople for each of the following time frames, based on hour of the day: 00–05, 06–12, 13–18, and 19–23

CASE PROJECT

In earlier chapters, you developed classes needed for Cost Is No Object—a car rental service that specializes in lending antique and luxury cars to clients on a short-term basis. You created pseudocode for `Employee`, `Customer`, `Automobile`, and `RentalAgreement` classes including attributes and methods to get and set those attributes.

In Chapter 6, you improved the `Employee` class by adding the following fields as well as a get and set method for each:

- An employee ID number

- A first name

- A last name

- A street address

- A ZIP code

- A job description code

- An hourly pay rate

- An insurance plan code

Add three additional string fields to the `Employee` class:

- City

- State

- Job title

Create an application that continues to prompt the user for Employee data and writes the data to a file; the application continues until the user enters 0 for an ID number to indicate the desire to quit. While the ID number is not zero, prompt the user for a value for each Employee field and assign it to an Employee object, except *do not* prompt for city, state, job title, or hourly pay rate.

Any time the user enters an invalid field value, continue to reprompt the user for the same data. Only when a data item is valid, assign it to the appropriate field. Invalid field values are:

- An employee ID number that is greater than 999

- A ZIP code that is not in the list of allowed ZIP codes

- A job description code that is not between 10 and 19 inclusive

- An insurance plan code that is not 1 or 2

Determine the employee's city and state based on the ZIP code, as described in Table 7-2. Determine the Employee's job title based on the values in Table 7-3. Determine the Employee's hourly pay rate based on the values in Table 7-4. (Contract employees have an hourly rate of $0.)

TABLE 7-2: ZIP CODES FOR COST IS NO OBJECT

ZIP Code	City	State
53115	Delavan	WI
53125	Fontana	WI
53147	Lake Geneva	WI
53184	Walworth	WI
53585	Sharon	IL
60001	Alden	IL
60033	Harvard	IL
60034	Hebron	IL
61012	Capron	IL

TABLE 7-3: JOB TITLES FOR COST IS NO OBJECT

Job Code	Title
10	Desk clerk
11	Credit checker
12	Billing
13	Car cleaner
14	Chauffeur
15	Marketer
16	Accountant
17	Mechanic
18	CEO
19	Contract

TABLE 7-4: HOURLY PAY RATES FOR COST IS NO OBJECT

Job Code	Hourly Pay Rate
10–13	$9.00
14–15	$14.50
16–17	$20.00
18	$65.00
19	$0.0

When all the needed data has been entered correctly for an Employee, write the Employee record to a data file and prompt the user for the next ID number.

8

ADVANCED ARRAY CONCEPTS

After studying Chapter 8, you should be able to:

- ☐ Remain within array bounds
- ☐ Use a **for** loop to process arrays
- ☐ Declare an array of objects
- ☐ Pass arrays to methods
- ☐ Sort array elements
- ☐ Sort arrays of objects
- ☐ Use two-dimensional and multidimensional arrays
- ☐ Use a built-in **Arrays** class

REMAINING WITHIN ARRAY BOUNDS

Every array has a finite size. You can think of an array's size in one of two ways—either by the number of elements in the array, or by the number of bytes in the array. Arrays are always composed of elements of the same data type, and elements of the same data type always occupy the same number of bytes of memory, so the number of bytes in an array is always a multiple of the number of elements in an array. For example, in Java, integers occupy four bytes of memory, so an array of 10 integers occupies exactly 40 bytes.

In every programming language, when you access data stored in an array, it is important to use a subscript containing a value that accesses memory occupied by the array. For example, examine the `findItem()` method in Figure 8-1. The method accepts a numeric item number and searches an array to find its location. The logic makes a dangerous assumption: that every item number passed to the method is a valid item number. If the item number is valid, then on one of the first four passes through the while loop, a match is found, and a message indicating the item's location prints. However, if an invalid item number is passed to the method, for example 110, the method will never find a match. The value of **x** will just continue to increase until it reaches a value higher than the number of elements in the array. At that point, one of two things will happen. When you use a subscript value that is higher than the number of elements in an array, some programming languages will stop execution of the program and issue an error message. Other programming languages will not issue an error message but will continue to search through computer memory beyond the end of the array. Either way, the program doesn't end elegantly. When you use a subscript that is not within the range of acceptable subscripts, your subscript is said to be **out of bounds**. Submitting an incorrect item number from a customer's order is a frequent error; a good program should be able to handle the mistake and not allow the subscript to go out of bounds.

FIGURE 8-1: A `findItem()` METHOD THAT MIGHT GO OUT OF BOUNDS

```
public void findItem(numeric itemNum)
     constant numeric NUM_PRODUCTS = 4
     numeric validItem[NUM_PRODUCTS] =
        101, 103, 307, 405
     numeric x
     x = 0
     while itemNum not = validItem[x]
        x = x + 1
     endwhile
     print "Item was found in position ", x
return
```

You can improve the `findItem()` module by adding a test that ensures the subscript used to access the array does not become larger than the size of the array. For example, if an array contains four elements, then the useable subscript values are 0, 1, 2, and 3. The highlighted segments in Figure 8-2 shows one method that ensures that the subscript used with the array does not exceed its bounds and that an appropriate message is displayed when the subscript becomes too large.

FIGURE 8-2: THE `findItem()` MODULE ENSURING ARRAY BOUNDS ARE OBSERVED

```
public void findItem(numeric itemNum)
    constant numeric NUM_PRODUCTS = 4
    numeric validItem[NUM_PRODUCTS] =
        101, 103, 307, 405
    numeric x
    x = 0
    while x < NUM_PRODUCTS AND
        itemNum not = validItem[x]
        x = x + 1
    endwhile
    if x = NUM_PRODUCTS then
        print "Item was not found"
    else
        print "Item was found in position ", x
    endif
return
```

Every time you use an array, you should keep its size in mind. For example, when a user's input value is used to access an array, you should always test the size of the value to make sure it is within bounds before using the value. If the value of the variable used as a subscript is too low (below zero) or too high (the size of the array or larger), you should either not access the array or force the value to a useable value with an assignment statement.

USING A FOR LOOP TO PROCESS ARRAYS

Figure 8-3 contains a `showItems()` method that displays all the elements in a `validItem` array. In the high-lighted `while` loop, the variable `x` is initialized, compared with the number of array elements, and while `x` continues to be within range, an array element is printed and `x` is increased.

FIGURE 8-3: PRINTING AN ARRAY USING A `while` LOOP

```
public void showItems()
    constant numeric NUM_PRODUCTS = 4
    numeric validItem[NUM_PRODUCTS] =
        101, 103, 307, 405
    numeric x
    x = 0
    while x < NUM_PRODUCTS
        print validItem[x]
        x = x + 1
    endwhile
return
```

In Chapter 6, you learned about the `for` loop—a loop that, in a single statement, initializes a loop control variable, compares it to a limit, and increments it. The `for` loop is a particularly convenient tool when working with arrays because you frequently need to process every element of an array from beginning to end. As with a `while` loop, when you use a `for` loop, you must be careful to stay within array bounds, remembering that the highest useable array sub-script is one less than the size of the array. Figure 8-4 shows a `for` loop that correctly prints the `validItem` array. Notice that `x` is incremented through one less than the number of products because with a four-item array, the sub-scripts you can use are 0, 1, 2, and 3.

FIGURE 8-4: PRINTING AN ARRAY USING A `for` LOOP

```
public void showItems()
    constant numeric NUM_PRODUCTS = 4
    numeric validItem[NUM_PRODUCTS] =
       101, 103, 307, 405
    numeric x
    for x = 0 to NUM_PRODUCTS - 1
      print validItem[x]
    endfor
return
```

The loop in the `showItems()` method in Figure 8-4 is slightly inefficient because, as it executes four times, the subtraction operation that deducts 1 from **NUM_PRODUCTS** occurs each time. Four subtraction operations do not consume much computer power or time, but in a loop that processes thousands or millions of array elements, the pro-gram's efficiency would be compromised. Figure 8-5 shows a superior solution. A new constant, **ARRAY_LIMIT** is calculated once, then used repeatedly in the comparison operation to determine when to stop cycling through the array.

FIGURE 8-5: PRINTING AN ARRAY USING A MORE EFFICIENT `for` LOOP

```
public void showItems()
    constant numeric NUM_PRODUCTS = 4
    numeric validItem[NUM_PRODUCTS] =
       101, 103, 307, 405
    numeric x
    constant numeric ARRAY_LIMIT = NUM_PRODUCTS - 1
    for x = 0 to ARRAY_LIMIT
      print validItem[x]
    endfor
return
```

TIP ▫ ▫ ▫ ▫ In Java, C++, and C#, the `for` loop looks the same. To control a loop in which x varies from zero to one less than NUM_PRODUCTS, you can write the following:

`for(x = 0; x < NUM_PRODUCTS; x++)`

The keyword `for` is followed by parentheses. The parentheses contain three sections, sep-arated with semicolons. The first section sets x to a starting value. The middle section makes a comparison; the `for` loop continues to execute while this expression is true. The last section executes when the body of the loop is complete; usually it alters the loop con-trol variable. In Java, C++, and C#, x++ means "add one to x".

DECLARING AN ARRAY OF OBJECTS

You can declare arrays of numbers, and you also can declare arrays of strings. For example, the following array contains the names of the days of the week:

```
string days[7] = "Sunday", "Monday", "Tuesday", "Wednesday",
        "Thursday", "Friday", "Saturday"
```

TIP □ □ □ □ When you provide initial values for an array, many programming languages allow you to omit the number in the brackets. Instead, the value is assumed from the number of items in the list. For example, the following statements have identical meanings:
```
numeric nums[] = 14, 21
numeric nums[2] = 14, 21
```

You can declare arrays that hold elements of any type, including objects. For example, assume you create the **Employee** class shown in Figure 8-6. This class has two data fields (**empNum** and **empSal**), and a **get()** and **set()** method for each field.

FIGURE 8-6: THE **Employee** CLASS

```
public class Employee
    private numeric empNum
    private numeric empSal

    public numeric getEmpNum()
    return empNum

    public numeric getEmpSal()
    return empSal

    public void setEmpNum(numeric e)
        empNum = e
    return

    public void setEmpSal(numeric s)
        empSal = s
    return
endClass
```

You can create separate **Employee** objects with unique names, such as **Employee painter, electrician,** or **plumber,** but for many applications it is far more convenient to create an array of **Employee** objects. The syntax to declare an array named **emp** that holds seven **Employee** objects varies slightly between languages, but the statement is similar to the following, including the data type (the class), the array name, and the size:

```
Employee emp[7]
```

TIP □ □ □ □ Although the syntax differs in various programming languages, declaring an array always includes the size. For example, in Java, you write: **Employee[] emp = new Employee[7];** but in C++ you write **Employee emp[7];**.

Alternatively, if you have declared a symbolic constant such as `constant int NUM_EMPLOYEES = 7`, you can write:

```
Employee emp[NUM_EMPLOYEES]
```

These statements reserve enough computer memory for seven `Employee` objects named `emp[0]` through `emp[6]`.

When a class contains only a nondefault constructor—that is, when the only constructors available for a class require one or more arguments—then you must provide those values when you create an array just as you must when you declare an individual object. For example, if the only constructor available for the `Employee` class requires both an employee number and salary as arguments, then the declaration of the array is similar to the following pseudocode:

```
Employee emp[NUM_EMPLOYEES] = {101, 12.45}, {103, 7.50},
       {119, 13.25}, {213, 15.00}, {218, 8.40},
       {395, 16.00}, {405, 9.00}
```

The declaration includes seven pairs of constructor values. The syntax differs among languages, but the pairs usually can be grouped using punctuation such as curly braces.

To use a method that belongs to an object that is part of an array, you insert the appropriate subscript notation after the array name and before the dot that precedes the method name. For example, to print data for seven `Employee`s stored in the `emp` array, you can write the following:

```
numeric MAX = NUM_EMPLOYEES - 1
for x = 0 to MAX
    print emp[x].getEmpNum(), " ", emp[x].getEmpSal()
endfor
```

TIP □ □ □ □ | You learned to use a `for` loop in Chapter 6.

Pay attention to the syntax of the `Employee` objects' method calls, such as `emp[x].getEmpNum()`. Although you might be tempted to place the subscript at the end of the expression after the method name, as in `emp.getEmpNum[x]`, you cannot—the values in `x` (0 through 6) refer to a particular `emp`, each of which has access to a single `getEmpNum()` method. Placement of the bracketed subscript so it follows `emp` means the method "belongs" to a particular `emp`.

PASSING ARRAYS TO METHODS

You might want to pass an array from one method to another on many occasions—for example, when the array is filled with values in one method, but those values are referenced, altered, or displayed in another method. You have already seen that you can use any individual array element in the same manner as you use any single variable of the same type. That is, if you declare a numeric array as numeric `someNums[12]`, you can subsequently print `someNums[0]`, or add one to `someNums[1]`, or work with any element just as you do for any singly declared number. Similarly, you can pass a single array element to a method in exactly the same manner as you pass a variable.

Examine the `PassArrayElement` application class shown in Figure 8-7 and the output shown in Figure 8-8. The application creates an array of four numbers and prints them. Then, the application calls the `methodGetsOneNumber()` method four times, passing each element in turn. The method prints the number, changes the number to 999, and then prints the number again. Finally, back in the `main()` method, the four numbers are printed again.

FIGURE 8-7: THE `PassArrayElement` CLASS

```
public class PassArrayElement
   public static void main()
      constant numeric NUM_ELEMENTS = 4
      constant numeric MAX = NUM_ELEMENTS - 1
      numeric someNums[NUM_ELEMENTS] = 5, 10, 15, 20
      numeric x
      print "At start of main: "
      for x = 0 to MAX
         print someNums[x]
      endfor
      for x = 0 to MAX
         methodGetsOneNumber(someNums[x])
      endfor
      print "At end of main: "
      for x = 0 to MAX
         print someNums[x]
      endfor
      return
   public static void methodGetsOneNumber(numeric one)
      print "At start of method one is: ", one
      one = 999
      print "and at end of method one is: ",  one
   return
endClass
```

FIGURE 8-8: OUTPUT OF THE `PassArrayElement` APPLICATION

```
At start of main:
5
10
15
20
At start of method one is: 5
and at end of method one is: 999
At start of method one is: 10
and at end of method one is: 999
At start of method one is: 15
and at end of method one is: 999
At start of method one is: 20
and at end of method one is: 999
At end of main:
5
10
15
20
```

As you can see in Figure 8-8, after the four numbers print in `main()`, each is passed to the method in turn where it retains its original value, and then is changed to 999. At the end of the program, after each number has been processed by the `methodGetsOneNumber()` method, when the logic returns to the `main()` method, the numbers that were changed in the method remain unaltered. In other words, any change made to a local variable in a method affects only the local variable and not the original array element in the calling method. The variable named `one` is local to the `methodGetsOneNumber()` method, and any changes to variables passed into the method are not permanent and are not reflected in the array in the `main()` program. Each variable named `one` in the `methodGetsOneNumber()` method holds only a copy of the array element passed into the method. The individual array elements are **passed by value**; that is, a copy is made and used within the receiving method.

The outcome is quite different when you pass an entire array to a method. Arrays, like all objects, are **passed by reference**; this means that the receiving method receives the actual memory address of the array, and has access to and the ability to alter the actual values in the array elements. The class shown in Figure 8-9 creates an array of four numbers. After the values print, the entire array is passed to a method named `methodGetsArray()`. Within the method, the numbers print, and Figure 8-10 shows that they retain their values from `main()`.

FIGURE 8-9: THE `PassArray` CLASS

```
public class PassArray
  public static void main()
    constant numeric NUM_ELEMENTS = 4
    constant numeric MAX = NUM_ELEMENTS - 1
    numeric someNums[NUM_ELEMENTS] = 5, 10, 15, 20
    numeric x
    print "At start of main: "
    for x = 0 to MAX
      print someNums[x]
    endfor
    methodGetsArray(someNums, MAX)
    print "At end of main: "
    for x = 0 to MAX
      print someNums[x]
    endfor
  return
  public static void methodGetsArray(numeric arr[], numeric max)
    numeric x
    print "At start of method arr holds: "
    for x = 0 to max
      print arr[x]
    endfor
    for x = 0 to max
      arr[x] = 888
    endfor
    print "and at end of method arr holds: "
    for x = 0 to max
      print arr[x]
    endfor
  return
endClass
```

Within the method, after the array values print, the value 888 is assigned to each number, and the numbers display again. Even though the `methodGetsArray()` method is a void method (meaning nothing is returned to the `main()` method), when the program prints the array for the second time within `main()`, all of the values have been changed to 888. Because arrays are passed by reference, the `methodGetsArray()` method "knows" the address of the array declared in `main()` and makes its changes directly to the original array that was declared in the `main()` method.

FIGURE 8-10: OUTPUT OF THE `PassArray` APPLICATION

```
At start of main:
5
10
15
20
At start of method array holds:
5
10
15
20
and at end of method array holds:
888
888
888
888
At end of main:
888
888
888
888
```

The array named `someNums` is passed to the `methodGetsArray()` method in the first highlighted statement in Figure 8-9. No brackets are used with the array name; the array name itself represents the starting memory address where the array elements reside. You might be tempted to pass the array to the method with a statement such as the following:

```
methodGetsArray(someNums,[NUM_ELEMENTS], MAX)
```

This statement would be in error because it would attempt to send the fourth (the value of **NUM_ELEMENTS**) element of the array to the method. Element 4 of the array is not within the array bounds—only elements 0 through 3 are. Not only is element 4 undefined for this array, but the method is not prepared to receive a single numeric element; it is written to receive a memory address that represents the start of the array.

Notice in the highlighted portion of the `methodGetsArray()` method header, the array name is followed by brackets. The brackets indicate that the value being passed is not simply numeric; instead, it is a numeric array. Notice also that the brackets following the passed array name are empty. Although in most programming languages you could place a number in the brackets and the program would still execute, any number you might place there is meaningless. When you pass an array name to a method, you are actually passing a memory address. Using a subscript with the array name determines the distance from the start of the array you will access; any number in the brackets in the method header signifies nothing. For example, in the loop that displays the array, you first access the number that is zero numbers away from the start of the array, then the number that is one number away, and so on. In the `methodGetsArray()` method, it is only by limiting the value of `x` by comparing it to `max` that you ensure the array bounds are not violated. In the header of a method that receives an array, do not use a number within the brackets following the local array name—leaving the number out shows you understand the process, and is less confusing to other programmers.

In Figure 8-9, the `methodGetsArray()` method receives the `max` value as well as the array address. Using this value, the method knows how many times to loop to process the array. Passing the array size makes the method more flexible than using a constant number such as 4 within the method. If the application changes to use an array of a different size, no changes will have to be made to this method. Instead, if the array size in `main()` is altered, the adjusted value of `NUM_ELEMENTS` from `main()` will automatically be passed into the method.

In the `PassArray` class, when the constant `MAX` is passed to the `methodGetsArray()` method, the value is no longer constant. In most languages, you could place the appropriate constant keyword for the language in front of the max declaration in the method header to indicate the variable will not be alterable within the method.

SORTING ARRAY ELEMENTS

Sorting is the process of arranging a series of objects in some logical order. When you place objects in order, beginning with the object that has the lowest value, you are sorting in **ascending order**; conversely, when you start with the object that has the largest value, you are sorting in **descending order**.

The simplest possible sort involves two values that are out of order. To place the values in order, you must swap the two values. Suppose that you have two variables—`valA` and `valB`—and further suppose that `valA = 16` and `valB = 2`. To exchange the values of the two variables, you cannot simply use the following code:

```
valA = valB
valB = valA
```

If `valB` is 2, after you execute `valA = valB`, both variables hold the value 2. The value 16 that was held in `valA` is lost. When you execute the second assignment statement, `valB = valA`, each variable still holds the value 2.

The solution that allows you to retain both values is to employ a variable to hold `valA`'s value temporarily during the swap:

```
temp = valA
valA = valB
valB = temp
```

Using this technique, `valA`'s value (16) is assigned to the `temp` variable. The value of `valB` (2) is then assigned to `valA`, so `valA` and `valB` are equivalent. Then, the `temp` value (16) is assigned to `valB`, so the values of the two variables finally are swapped.

If you want to sort any two values, `valA` and `valB`, in ascending order so that `valA` is always the lower value, you use the following `if` statement to make the decision whether to swap. If `valA` is more than `valB`, you want to switch the values. If `valA` is not more than `valB`, you do not want to switch the values.

```
if valA > valB then
    temp = valA
    valA = valB
    valB = temp
endif
```

Sorting two values is a fairly simple task; sorting more values (`valC`, `valD`, `valE`, and so on) is more complicated. Without the use of an array, sorting a series of numbers is a daunting task; the task becomes manageable when you know how to use an array.

As an example, you might have a list of five numbers that you want to place in ascending numeric order. One approach is to use a method popularly known as a bubble sort. A **bubble sort** is a type of sort in which you continue to compare pairs of items, swapping them if they are out of order, so that the smallest items "bubble" to the top of the list, eventually creating a sorted list.

TIP ☐ ☐ ☐ ☐ | Many sorting techniques are more efficient than the bubble sort, but the bubble sort is one of the easiest to understand, and is useful in helping you master array manipulation.

To use a bubble sort, you place the original, unsorted values in an array, such as the following:

```
numeric someNums[5] = 88, 33, 99, 22, 54
```

You compare the first two numbers in the array; if they are not in ascending order, you swap them. You compare the second and third numbers; if they are not in ascending order, you swap them. You continue down the list. Generically, for any `someNums[x]`, if the value of `someNums[x]` is larger than `someNums[x + 1]`, you want to swap the two values.

With the numbers 88, 33, 99, 22, and 54, the process proceeds as follows:

1. Compare 88 and 33. They are out of order. Swap them. The list becomes 33, 88, 99, 22, 54.
2. Compare the second and third numbers in the list—88 and 99. They are in order. Do nothing.
3. Compare the third and fourth numbers in the list—99 and 22. They are out of order. Swap them. The list becomes 33, 88, 22, 99, 54.
4. Compare the fourth and fifth numbers—99 and 54. They are out of order. Swap them. The list becomes 33, 88, 22, 54, 99.

When you reach the bottom of the list, the numbers are not in ascending order, but the largest number, 99, has moved to the bottom of the list. This feature gives the bubble sort its name—the "heaviest" value has sunk to the bottom of the list as the "lighter" values have started to bubble to the top.

Assuming b and `temp` both have been declared as numeric variables, and **ARRAY_SIZE** has been declared with a value of 5, the code so far is as follows:

```
for b = 0 to ARRAY_SIZE - 2
    if someNums[b] > someNums[b + 1] then
        temp = someNums[b]
        someNums[b] = someNums[b + 1]
        someNums[b + 1] = temp
    endif
endfor
```

Notice that the `for` statement tests every value of b from 0 through 3. The array `someNums` contains five elements. The subscripts in the array range in value from 0 through 4. Within the `for` loop, each `someNums[b]` is compared to `someNums[b + 1]`, so the highest legal value for b is 3 when array element b (3) is compared to array element b + 1 (4). For a sort on any size array, the value of b must remain no more than the array's length minus 2—in other words, b must be less than the array's length minus one.

The list of numbers that began as 88, 33, 99, 22, 54 is currently 33, 88, 22, 54, 99. You must perform the entire comparison-swap procedure again.

1. Compare the first two values—33 and 88. They are in order. Do nothing.
2. Compare the second and third values—88 and 22. They are out of order. Swap them so the list becomes 33, 22, 88, 54, 99.
3. Compare the third and fourth values—88 and 54. They are out of order. Swap them so the list becomes 33, 22, 54, 88, 99.
4. Compare the fourth and fifth values—88 and 99. They are in order. Do nothing.

After this second pass through the list, the numbers are 33, 22, 54, 88, and 99—close to ascending order, but not quite. You can see that with one more pass through the list, the values 22 and 33 will swap, and the list is finally placed in order. To fully sort the worst-case list, one in which the original numbers are descending (as out-of-ascending order as they could possibly be), you need to go through the list four times making comparisons and swaps. You always need to pass through the list as many times as its length minus one; in other words, you can count from zero to the array size minus two. Figure 8-11 shows the entire procedure.

FIGURE 8-11: ASCENDING BUBBLE SORT OF THE **someNums** ARRAY ELEMENTS

```
for a = 0 to ARRAY_SIZE - 2
  for(b = 0 to ARRAY_SIZE -2
    if someNums[b] > someNums[b + 1]
        temp = someNums[b]
        someNums[b] = someNums[b + 1]
        someNums[b + 1] = temp
    endif
  endfor
endfor
```

TIP ▫ ▫ ▫ ▫   A list might be in order before passing through it as many times as its length minus one. For example, the following list of numbers would be in order after only one pass: 1, 2, 3, 5, 4, 6, 7. However, unless you revise the code in Figure 8-11 to determine whether the list is in order "early", you must pass through the list the full number of times.

TIP ▫ ▫ ▫ ▫   To place the list in descending order, you need to make only one change in the method in Figure 8-11: You change the greater than sign (>) in `if someNums[b] > someNums[b + 1]` to a less than sign (<).

In the code in Figure 8-11, it would be more efficient to declare a new variable and assign the value of `ARRAY_SIZE - 2` to it instead of repeating the subtraction operation on each pass through both loops. In addition, when you use a bubble sort to sort any array into ascending order, the largest value "falls" to the bottom of the array after you have compared each pair of values in the array one time. The second time you go through the array making comparisons, there is no need to check the last pair of values. The largest value is guaranteed to already be at the bottom of the array. You can make the sort process even more efficient by using a new variable for the inner `for` loop and reducing the value by one on each cycle through the array. Figure 8-12 shows how you can use new variables named `passesToMake` to control the outer `for` loop and `comparisonsToMake` to control how many comparisons are made in the inner loop during each pass through the list of values to be sorted. The `passesToMake` value remains the same throughout the procedure, but the `comparisonsToMake` value is decremented by one on each pass through the list.

FIGURE 8-12: MORE EFFICIENT ASCENDING BUBBLE SORT OF THE **someNums** ARRAY ELEMENTS

```
numeric passesToMake = ARRAY_SIZE - 2
numeric comparisonsToMake = ARRAY_SIZE - 2
for a = 0 to passesToMake
    for b = 0 to comparisonsToMake
        if someNums[b] > someNums[b+ 1] then
            temp = someNums[b]
            someNums[b] = someNums[b + 1]
            someNums[b + 1] = temp
        endif
    endfor
    comparisonsToMake = comparisonsToMake - 1
endfor
```

SORTING ARRAYS OF OBJECTS

You can sort arrays of objects in much the same way that you sort arrays of primitive types. The major difference occurs when you make the comparison that determines whether you want to swap two array elements. When you construct an array of a primitive element type, you compare the two array elements to determine whether they are out of order. When array elements are objects, you usually want to sort based on a particular object field.

Assume you have created a simple `Employee` class, as shown in Figure 8-13. (Figure 8-6 showed a different, briefer `Employee` class. The class shown in Figure 8-13 contains more fields and methods.) The class holds four data fields, a constructor, and get and set methods for the fields.

FIGURE 8-13: AN EXPANDED **Employee** CLASS

```
public class Employee
    private numeric empNum
    private string lastName
    private string firstName
    private numeric salary

    public int getEmpNum()
    return empNum

    public void setEmpNum(numeric emp)
        empNum = emp
    return

    public string getLastName()
    return lastName

    public void setLastName(string name)
        lastName = name
    return

    public string getFirstName()
    return firstName

    public void setFirstName(string name)
        firstName = name
    return

    public numeric getSalary()
    return salary

    public void setSalary(numeric sal)
        salary = sal
    return
endClass
```

You can write a program that contains an array of **Employee** objects using the statement **Employee someEmps[5]**. Assume that after you assign employee numbers and salaries to the **Employee** objects, you want to sort the **Employee**s in **empSal** order. You can pass the array and its length to a **bubbleSort()** method that is prepared to receive **Employee** objects. Figure 8-14 shows the method.

Examine Figure 8-14 carefully and notice that the **bubbleSort()** method is very similar to the **bubbleSort()** method you use for an array of any primitive type, but there are three major differences:

- The **bubbleSort()** method header shows that it receives an array of type **Employee**.
- The **temp** variable created for swapping is type **Employee**. The **temp** variable will hold an **Employee** object, not just one number or one field.
- The comparison for determining whether a swap should occur uses method calls to the **getEmpSal()** method to compare the returned salary for each **Employee** object in the array with the salary of the adjacent **Employee** object.

FIGURE 8-14: THE `bubbleSort()` METHOD THAT SORTS `Employee` OBJECTS BY THEIR SALARIES

```
public static void bubbleSort(Employee array[], numeric len)
   numeric a
   numeric b
   Employee temp
   numeric passes = len - 2
   numeric max = len - 2
   for a = 0 to passes
      for b = 0 to max
         if array[b].getEmpSal() > array[b + 1].getEmpSal() then
            temp = array[b]
            array[b] = array[b + 1]
            array[b + 1] = temp
         endif
      endfor
      max = max - 1
   endfor
return
```

TIP ▫▫▫▫ Note that even though only employee salaries are compared, you do not swap employee salaries. You do not want to substitute one employee's salary for another's. Instead, you swap the entire `Employee` object so that each `Employee` object's `empNum` and `empSal` are swapped as a unit.

USING TWO-DIMENSIONAL AND MULTIDIMENSIONAL ARRAYS

When you declare an array such as `numeric someNumbers[3]`, you can envision the three declared numbers as a column of numbers in memory, as shown in Figure 8-15. In other words, you can picture the three declared numbers stacked one on top of the next. An array that you can picture as a column of values, and whose elements you can access using a single subscript, is a **one-dimensional** or **single-dimensional array**.

FIGURE 8-15: VIEW OF A SINGLE-DIMENSIONAL ARRAY IN MEMORY

| someNumbers[0] |
| someNumbers[1] |
| someNumbers[2] |

TIP ▫▫▫▫ You can think of the single dimension of a single-dimensional array as the height of the array.

Most object-oriented programming (OOP) languages also support two-dimensional arrays. **Two-dimensional arrays** have both rows and columns of values, as shown in Figure 8-16. You must use two subscripts when you access an element in a two-dimensional array. When mathematicians use a two-dimensional array, they often call it a **matrix** or a **table**; you might have used a two-dimensional array called a spreadsheet.

FIGURE 8-16: VIEW OF A TWO-DIMENSIONAL ARRAY IN MEMORY

someNumbers[0] [0]	someNumbers[0] [1]	someNumbers[0] [2]	someNumbers[0] [3]
someNumbers[1] [0]	someNumbers[1] [1]	someNumbers[1] [2]	someNumbers[1] [3]
someNumbers[2] [0]	someNumbers[2] [1]	someNumbers[2] [2]	someNumbers[2] [3]

TIP ▫ ▫ ▫ ▫   You can think of the two dimensions of a two-dimensional array as height and width.

When you declare a one-dimensional array, you type a set of square brackets after the array type. To declare a two-dimensional array, many languages require you to type two sets of brackets after the array type. For example, the array in Figure 8-16 can be declared as `numeric someNumbers[3][4]`, creating an array named `someNumbers` that holds three rows and four columns.

In many OOP languages, if you do not provide initial values for a numeric array, then each element is zero by default. However, just as you can assign values to a one-dimensional array when you create it or elements later, you can assign other values to a two-dimensional array when you create it or elements later. For example, `someNumbers[0][0] = 14` assigns the value 14 to the element of the `someNumbers` array that is in the first column of the first row. Alternatively, you can initialize a two-dimensional array with values when it is created as in the following pseudocode:

```
numeric someNumbers[3][4] = {8, 9, 10, 11},
                            {1, 3, 12, 15},
                            {5, 9, 44, 99}
```

In this example, the values that are assigned to each row are enclosed in braces to help you picture the placement of each number in the array. The first row of the array holds the four integers 8, 9, 10, and 11. Similarly, 1, 3, 12, and 15 make up the second row, and 5, 9, 44, and 99 are the values in the third row. The value of `someNumbers[0][0]` is 8. The value of `someNumbers[0][1]` is 9. The value of `someNumbers[2][3]` is 99. The value within the first pair of brackets following the array name always refers to the row; the value within the second pair of brackets refers to the column.

As an example of how useful two-dimensional arrays can be, assume you own an apartment building with four floors—a basement, which you refer to as floor zero, and three other floors numbered one, two, and three. In addition, each of the floors has studios (with no bedroom) and one- and two-bedroom apartments. The monthly rent for each type of apartment is different—the higher the floor, the higher the rent (the view is better), and the rent is higher for apartments with more bedrooms. Table 8-1 shows the rental amounts.

TABLE 8-1: RENTS CHARGED

Floor	Zero Bedrooms	One Bedroom	Two Bedrooms
0	400	450	510
1	500	560	630
2	625	676	740
3	1,000	1,250	1,600

To determine a tenant's rent, you need to know two pieces of information: the floor on which the tenant rents an apartment and the number of bedrooms in the apartment. Within a rent-determining application, you can declare an array of rents using the following code:

```
numeric rents[4][3] =  (400, 450, 510},
                       {500, 560, 630},
                       {625, 676, 740},
                       {1000, 1250, 1600}
```

Assuming you declare two variables to hold the floor number and bedroom count as `numeric floor` and `numeric bedrooms`, any tenant's rent is `rents[floor] [bedrooms]`.

Besides one- and two-dimensional arrays, many programming languages also support **multidimensional arrays**, which might contain any number of dimensions. For example, if you own an apartment building with a number of floors and different numbers of bedrooms available in apartments on each floor, you can use a two-dimensional array to store the rental fees. If you own several apartment buildings, you might want to employ a third dimension to store the building number. An expression such as `rents[building][floor][bedrooms]` refers to a specific rent figure for a building whose building number is stored in the `building` variable, and whose floor and bedroom numbers are stored in the `floor` and `bedrooms` variables. Specifically, `rents[5][1][2]` refers to a two-bedroom apartment on the first floor of building 5 (which is the sixth building in an array where the first building is referenced with a 0 subscript).

USING A BUILT-IN ARRAYS CLASS

When you fully understand the power of arrays, you will want to use them to store all kinds of objects. Frequently, you will want to perform similar tasks with different arrays—for example, filling them with values and sorting their elements. Many OOP languages provide an **Arrays class**, which contains many useful methods for manipulating arrays. One of the advantages of using modern object-oriented languages is the vast libraries of classes containing useful built-in methods that are available to you. The **Arrays** class is just one of many examples.

Table 8-2 shows some of the typically included, useful methods of the **Arrays** class. The most useful **Arrays** class would contain an overloaded version of each method for each appropriate data type. For example, you would want a version of the **sort()** method to sort numeric, string, and object elements.

TABLE 8-2: TYPICAL USEFUL METHODS OF THE **Arrays** CLASS

Method	Purpose
`static numeric binarySearch(type a[], type key)`	Searches the specified array for the specified key value using the binary search algorithm
`static boolean equals(type a[], type a2[])`	Returns `true` if the two specified arrays of the same type are equal to one another
`static void fill (type a[], type val)`	Assigns the specified value to each element of the specified array
`static void sort (type a[])`	Sorts the specified array into ascending numerical order

If you are using an object-oriented language that does not provide a built-in **Arrays** class to perform common array-based tasks, you could write one yourself. Doing so would require a lot of code-writing up front, but the future availability of useful methods to handle common array tasks would be well worth the effort. The **ArraysDemo** application in Figure 8-17 demonstrates how some of the methods in the **Arrays** class can be used to manipulate lists of items stored in arrays. In the **ArraysDemo** class, the **myScores** array is created to hold five numbers. Then, a message, the array, and the array size are passed to a **display()** method. The first line of the output in Figure 8-18 shows that the original array is filled with 0s at creation. After the first display, the **Arrays.fill()** method is called in the first highlighted statement in Figure 8-17. Because the arguments are the name of the array and the number 8, when the array is displayed a second time, the output is all 8s. In the application, two of the array elements are changed to 6 and 3, and the array is displayed again. Finally, in the second highlighted statement, the **Arrays.sort()** method is called. The output in Figure 8-18 shows that when the **display()** method executes the fourth time, the array elements have been sorted in ascending order.

FIGURE 8-17: THE `ArraysDemo` APPLICATION

```
public class ArraysDemo
   public static void main()
     final numeric SIZE = 5
     numeric myScores[SIZE]
     display("Original array:", myScores, SIZE)
     Arrays.fill(myScores, 8)
     display("After filling with 8s:", myScores, SIZE)
     myScores[2] = 6
     myScores[4] = 3
     display("After changing two values:", myScores, SIZE)
     Arrays.sort(myScores)
     display("After sorting:", myScores, SIZE)
   return
   public static void display(string message,
     numeric array[], numeric sz)
     print message
     for x = 0 to sz - 1
         print array[x], " "
     endfor
   return
endClass
```

FIGURE 8-18: OUTPUT OF THE `ArraysDemo` APPLICATION

```
Original array:
0 0 0 0 0
After filling with 8s:
8 8 8 8 8
After changing two values:
8 8 6 8 3
After sorting:
3 6 8 8 8
```

CHAPTER SUMMARY

☐ When you access data stored in an array, it is important to use a subscript containing a value that accesses memory occupied by the array. When you use a subscript that is not within the defined range of acceptable subscripts, your subscript is said to be out of bounds.

☐ The `for` loop is a particularly convenient tool when working with arrays because you frequently need to process every element of an array from beginning to end.

☐ You can declare arrays that hold elements of any type, including objects. When a class contains only a nondefault constructor, that is, when the only constructors available for a class require one or more arguments, then you must provide those values when you create an array just as you must when you declare an individual object. To use a method that belongs to an object that is part of an array, you insert the appropriate subscript notation after the array name and before the dot that precedes the method name

☐ Individual array elements are passed to methods by value, but arrays, like all objects, are passed by reference; this means that the receiving method receives the actual memory address of the array, and has access to and the ability to alter the actual values in the array elements.

☐ Sorting is the process of arranging a series of objects in some logical order. When you place objects in order, beginning with the object that has the lowest value, you are sorting in ascending order; conversely, when you start with the object that has the largest value, you are sorting in descending order. A bubble sort is a type of sort in which you continue to compare pairs of items, swapping them if they are out of order, so that the smallest items "bubble" to the top of the list, eventually creating a sorted list.

☐ You can sort arrays of objects in much the same way that you sort arrays of primitive types. When array elements are objects, you usually want to sort based on a particular object field.

☐ An array that you can picture as a column of values, and whose elements you can access using a single subscript, is a one-dimensional or single-dimensional array. Most object-oriented programming (OOP) languages also support two-dimensional arrays, which have rows and columns of values.

☐ Many OOP languages provide an `Arrays` class, which contains many useful methods for manipulating arrays. If you are using an object-oriented language that does not provide a built-in `Arrays` class to perform common array-based tasks, you could write one yourself. Doing so would require a lot of code-writing up front, but the future availability of useful methods to handle common array tasks would be well worth the effort.

KEY TERMS

An array subscript is **out of bounds** if it is not within the range of acceptable subscripts.

Individual array elements are **passed by value**; that is, a copy is made and used within the receiving method.

Arrays, like all objects, are **passed by reference**; this means that the receiving method receives the actual memory address of the array, and has access to and the ability to alter the actual values in the array elements.

Sorting is the process of arranging a series of objects in some logical order.

Ascending order is order from lowest to highest.

Descending order is order from highest to lowest.

A **bubble sort** is a type of sort in which you continue to compare pairs of items, swapping them if they are out of order, so that the smallest items "bubble" to the top of the list, eventually creating a sorted list.

A **one-dimensional** or **single-dimensional array** is one that you can picture as a column of values, and whose elements you can access using a single subscript.

Two-dimensional arrays have both rows and columns. You must use two subscripts when you access an element in a two-dimensional array.

A **matrix** is a two-dimensional array.

A **table** is a two-dimensional array.

Multidimensional arrays can have any number of dimensions.

A built-in `Arrays` **class** contains many useful methods for manipulating arrays.

REVIEW QUESTIONS

1. **Which of the following is true?**
   a. Every array can hold numbers.
   b. Every array has a finite size.
   c. An array with 10 elements supports subscripts 0 through 10.
   d. An array with several elements might have some that are numeric and some that are strings.

2. **When a subscript exceeds the acceptable values for an array _____.**
   a. execution stops and an error message displays
   b. the application continues to access succeeding memory locations
   c. the result depends on the programming language
   d. in every programming language, the result is unpredictable

3. **When you use a subscript that is not within the range of acceptable subscripts, your subscript is said to be _____.**
   a. improper
   b. in the twilight zone
   c. off balance
   d. out of bounds

4. **The _____ loop is particularly useful for working with arrays.**
   a. continuous
   b. infinite
   c. for
   d. extended

5. When an array is declared as `numeric numbers[8]`, which of the following is true?

   a. The highest useable subscript is 8.
   b. The array contains 8 elements.
   c. both of these
   d. none of these

6. You can declare arrays of _____.

   a. numbers
   b. strings
   c. objects
   d. all of the above

7. What does the following statement declare? `Product inventory[1000]`

   a. 1,000 numbers in an array named `Product`
   b. 1,000 `Product` objects in an array named `inventory`
   c. A class named `inventory` that contains 1,000 fields
   d. A class named `Product` that contains strings representing 1,000 `inventory` items

8. Assume `Student` is a class that contains fields for an ID number, last name, and grade level. It also contains get and set methods for each field and a constructor that requires a numeric ID number argument. Which of the following declares an array of three `Student` objects?

   a. `numeric Student[3] = 1234, 2345, 3456`
   b. `Student students[3]`
   c. `Student students[3] = 1234, 2345, 3456`
   d. two of the above

9. Assume `Student` is a class that contains fields for an ID number, last name, and grade level. It also contains a nonstatic `public getGPA()` method that returns a `Student`'s grade point average. Which of the following prints the grade point average of the second `Student` in an array declared as `Student stu[3]`?

   a. `print Student[1]`
   b. `print stu[1]`
   c. `print stu.getGpa()[1]`
   d. `print stu[1].getGpa()`

10. Assume you have a class named `Business` that contains a name, address, number of employees, and annual revenue figure for a `Business`. The class contains a nonstatic, `public getName()` method that returns the name of the `Business`. You have declared an array as `Business bus[50]`. Which of the following prints the name of the last `Business` in the array?

    a. `print Business[50].getName()`
    b. `print bus[50].getName()`
    c. both of these
    d. none of these

11. Assume you have a class named `Business` that contains a name, address, number of employees, and annual revenue figure for a business. The class contains a nonstatic, `public` `setEmployeeCount()` method that accepts a numeric argument that is assigned to a field named `numEmps`, which holds the number of workers employed by the `Business`. You have declared an array as `Business bus[50]`. Which of the following sets the number of employees for the first `Business` in the array to 250?

    a. `bus[250].setEmployeeCount()`
    b. `bus[0].setEmployeeCount(250)`
    c. `bus[1].setEmployeeCount(250)`
    d. `bus.setEmployeeCount(250)`

12. Assume you have a class named `Business` that contains a name, address, number of employees, and annual revenue figure for a business. You have declared an array as `Business bus[50]`. Assume you write an application containing a method called `computeTaxes()`. You want to pass the first element of the `bus` array to the method. Which of the following is a suitable method header?

    a. `public void computeTaxes(Business b)`
    b. `public void computeTaxes(Business b[])`
    c. `public void computeTaxes(Business b[0])`
    d. `public void computeTaxes(Business[50])`

13. Assume you have a class named `Business` that contains a name, address, number of employees, and annual revenue figure for a business. You have declared an array as `Business bus[50]`. Assume you write an application containing a method called `computeTaxes()`. You want to pass the first element of the `bus` array to the method. Which of the following is a suitable method call?

    a. `computeTaxes(bus)`
    b. `computeTaxes(Business bus[])`
    c. `computeTaxes(Business bus[0])`
    d. `computeTaxes(bus[0])`

14. Assume you have a class named `Business` that contains a name, address, number of employees, and annual revenue figure for a business. You have declared an array as `Business bus[50]`. Assume you write an application containing a method called `computeTaxes()`. You want to pass all the elements of the `bus` array at once to the method. Which of the following is the best method header?

    a. `public void computeTaxes(Business bus)`
    b. `public void computeTaxes(Business bus[])`
    c. `public void computeTaxes(Business bus[0])`
    d. `public void computeTaxes(Business bus[50])`

15. **When a variable is passed to a method by value, the method _____.**

    a. receives a copy of the variable
    b. has access to the original value in the calling method
    c. might do either a or b; it's unpredictable
    d. issues a warning but executes

16. **When you pass an entire array to a method, you _____.**

    a. pass by reference
    b. pass the memory address of the array
    c. both of these
    d. none of these

17. **Arranging items from the one with the highest value to the one with lowest value places them in _____ order.**

    a. ascending
    b. descending
    c. cascading
    d. reference

18. **How does a bubble sort begin its operation on an array list?**

    a. Each element in a list is compared with an average value and placed above or below that point.
    b. Each element in a list is compared with the value in the middle position and placed above or below that point.
    c. Each element in a list is compared with the one following it, and their values are exchanged if they are out of order.
    d. The first and last elements in a list are compared, and then exchanged if they are out of order. Then the second and second-to-last items are compared, and so on.

19. **Assume you declare an array as** `numeric values[5][12]`. **Which of the following is true?**

    a. The array contains five columns.
    b. The array contains 44 elements (4 times 11).
    c. The array contains 12 rows.
    d. The array cannot contain strings.

20. **Assume you declare an array as follows:**

    ```
    string names[2][4] = {"Amy", "Brian", "Carol", "Dan"},
                     {"Emily", "Frank", "Georgette", "Hank"}
    ```

    Which of the following is true?

    a. "Carol" is in location [1][3].
    b. "Emily" is in location [2][1].
    c. "Georgette" is in location [1][2].
    d. Two of these are true.

EXERCISES

1. **Professor Zak allows students to drop the two lowest scores on the ten 100-point quizzes she gives during the semester. Based on this information, complete the following tasks.**

   Create a usable Student class that contains ID number, last name, first name, and 10 quiz scores. Write an application that allows the professor to enter records for 20 students. The output lists each student ID, name, and total points for the eight highest-scoring quizzes.

2. **The Hinner College Foundation holds an annual fundraiser for which the foundation director maintains records. Based on this information, complete the following tasks.**

   Design a useable class that contains a donor name and contribution amount. Develop the logic for a program that sorts the donations by amounts in descending order. Assume that there are never more than 300 donors. Output lists the five highest donation amounts.

3. **The Spotless Reputation Dry Cleaning Store maintains customer records with data fields for first name, last name, address, and annual cleaning bill in dollars. At the end of the year, the store manager sends a $25 coupon to each of the 100 customers with the highest annual purchases. Based on this information, complete the following task.**

   Develop the logic that sorts up to 1,000 customer records by annual purchase amount and prints the names and address for the top 100 customers.

4. **The village of Ringwood has taken a special census. Every census record contains a household ID number, number of occupants, and income. Ringwood has exactly 75 households. Based on this information, complete the following task.**

   Village statisticians are interested in the median household size and the median household income. Develop the logic for a program that determines these figures.

5. **The village of Marengo has taken a special census and collected records that each contains a household ID number, number of occupants, and income. The exact number of household records has not yet been determined, but you know that there are fewer than 1,000 households in Marengo. Based on this information, complete the following task.**

   Develop the logic for a program that determines the median household size and the median household income.

6. The MidAmerica Bus Company charges fares to passengers based on the number of travel zones they cross. Additionally, discounts are provided for multiple passengers traveling together. Ticket fares are shown in the following table.

	Zones Crossed			
Passengers	1	2	3	4
1	7.50	10.00	12.00	12.75
2	14.00	18.50	22.00	23.00
3	20.00	21.00	32.00	33.00
4	25.00	27.50	36.00	37.00

Develop a class that holds a travel party's last name, number in the party, and zones crossed. Design the logic for an application that reads in travel party records and displays the travel party data as well as the ticket charge per person, and ticket charge per party.

7. Complete the following tasks:

a. In golf, par is a number that represents a standard number of strokes a player will need to complete a hole. Instead of using an absolute score, players can compare their scores on a hole to the par figure and determine whether they are above or below par. Families can play nine holes of miniature golf at the Family Fun Miniature Golf Park. So that family members can compete fairly, the course provides a different par for each hole based on the player's age. The par figures are shown in the following table.

	Holes								
Age	1	2	3	4	5	6	7	8	9
4 and under	8	8	9	7	5	7	8	5	8
5–7	7	7	8	6	5	6	7	5	6
8–11	6	5	6	5	4	5	5	4	5
12–15	5	4	4	4	3	4	3	3	4
16 and over	4	3	3	3	2	3	2	3	3

Design a class that holds a player's name, age, and nine-hole score. Develop the logic for an application that prints a page for each player containing the player's name and score on each of the nine holes with one of the phrases "Over par", "Par", or "Under par" next to each score.

b. Modify the program in Exercise 7a so that at the end of each golfer's report the golfer's total score displays. Include the figure indicating how many strokes over or under par the player is for the entire course.

8. The It's Greek To Me Translation Service pays its translators a per-page rate based on two criteria—number of pages to be translated and years of service the translator has provided. The salary schedule exists as follows:

Years of Service	Pages in Document			
	1–10	11–20	21–40	41 or more
1	1.50	1.75	2.00	2.20
2	2.00	2.25	2.95	3.30
3	2.50	3.00	3.50	4.00
4	3.50	4.25	5.00	5.65
5 or more	5.50	6.75	8.25	11.00

Create a class to hold translator employee records including ID numbers, last and first names, and year hired. Calculate a years-of-service field by subtracting the year hired from the current year.

Create a Job class that holds an Employee, a number of pages to be translated, and the per-page rate for the Job.

Develop the logic for an application program that reads a file of Jobs and displays each Job's employee's ID number, name, and pay rate for the Job.

9. The Roadmaster Driving School allows students to sign up for any number of driving lessons. The school allows up to four attempts to pass the driver's license test, otherwise the student's tuition is returned. The school maintains an archive containing student records for those who have successfully passed the licensing test over the last 10 years. Each record contains a student ID number, name, number of driving lessons completed, and the number of the attempt on which the student passed the licensing test. The records are stored in alphabetical order by student name. The school administration is interested in examining the correlation between the number of lessons taken and the number of attempts required to pass the test. Based on this information, complete the following task.

Develop the logic for a program that would produce a table for the school. Each row represents the number of lessons taken: 0–9, 10–19, 20–29, and 30 or more. Each column represents the number of test attempts in order to pass—1 through 4.

10. The Stevens College Testing Center creates a record each time a student takes a placement test. Students can take a test in any of twelve subject areas: English, Math, Biology, Chemistry, History, Sociology, Psychology, Art, Music, Spanish, German, or Computer Science. Each record contains the date the test was taken, the student's ID number, the test subject area, and a percent score on the test. Records are maintained in the order they are entered as the tests are taken. Based on this information, complete the following task.

The college would like a report that lists each of the twelve tests along with a count of the number of students who have received scores in each of the following categories: at least 90 percent, 80 through 89 percent, 70 through 79 percent, and below 70 percent. Develop the logic that produces the report.

CASE PROJECT

In earlier chapters you developed classes needed for Cost is No Object—a car rental service that specializes in lending antique and luxury cars to clients on a short-term basis. You created pseudocode for `Employee`, `Customer`, `Automobile`, and `RentalAgreement` classes including attributes and methods to get and set those attributes.

In Chapters 6 and 7, you improved the `Employee` class by adding several fields and methods.

Create an application in which you create an array of 20 `Employee` objects. In turn, pass each `Employee` object to a method that accepts an `Employee`, prompts the user for necessary data, and returns a "filled" `Employee` object to the array.

Pass the `Employee` array to a method that counts the number of Employees in each of the 10 job description categories and displays a count of each.

Pass the `Employee` array to a method that counts the number of employees in each of the two insurance plans and displays a count of each.

Pass the `Employee` array to a method that sorts the Employees in ascending ID number order and display a list of the first and last names of the Employees in ID number order.

9

EVENT-DRIVEN PROGRAMMING WITH GRAPHICAL USER INTERFACES

After studying Chapter 9, you should be able to:

- ☐ Understand the principles of event-driven programming
- ☐ Describe the actions that GUI components can initiate
- ☐ Design graphical user interfaces
- ☐ Modify the attributes of GUI components
- ☐ List the steps to developing an event-driven application
- ☐ Understand multithreading
- ☐ Create animation

UNDERSTANDING EVENT-DRIVEN PROGRAMMING

From the 1950s, when businesses began to use computers to help them perform many jobs, right through the 1960s and 1970s, almost all interactive dialogs between people and computers took place on the command line. The **command line** is the location on your computer screen at which you type entries to communicate with the computer's operating system. An **operating system** is the software that you use to run a computer and manage its resources. Interacting with a computer operating system was difficult because the user had to know the exact syntax (that is, the correct sequence of words and symbols that form the operating system's command set) to use when typing commands, and had to spell and type those commands accurately. Figure 9-1 shows a command line in the Windows operating system.

FIGURE 9-1: A COMMAND LINE SCREEN

TIP □ □ □ □ The command line also is called the **command prompt**. People who use the Disk Operating System (DOS) operating system also call the command line the **DOS prompt**.

TIP □ □ □ □ If you use the Windows operating system on a PC, you can locate the command prompt by clicking Start, pointing to Programs (or All Programs in Windows XP) then Accessories, and then clicking Command Prompt.

TIP □ □ □ □ Although you frequently use the command line to communicate with the operating system, you also sometimes communicate with software through the command line. For example, when you issue a command to execute some applications, you can include data values that the program uses.

Fortunately for today's computer users, operating system software is available that allows them to use a mouse or other pointing device to select pictures, or **icons**, on the screen. This type of environment is a **graphical user interface**, or **GUI**. Computer users can expect to see a standard interface in the GUI programs they use. Rather than memorizing difficult commands that must be typed at a command line, GUI users can select options from menus and click buttons to make their preferences known to a program. Users can select objects that look like their real-world counterparts and get the expected results. For example, users may select an icon that looks like a pencil when they want to write a memo, or they may drag an icon shaped like a folder to another icon that resembles a recycling bin when they want to delete a file. For example, Figure 9-2 shows a Windows program named Paint in which icons representing pencils, paint cans, and so on appear on clickable buttons. Performing an operation on an icon (for example, clicking or dragging it) causes an **event**—an occurrence that generates a message sent to an object.

FIGURE 9-2: A GUI APPLICATION CONTAINING BUTTONS AND ICONS

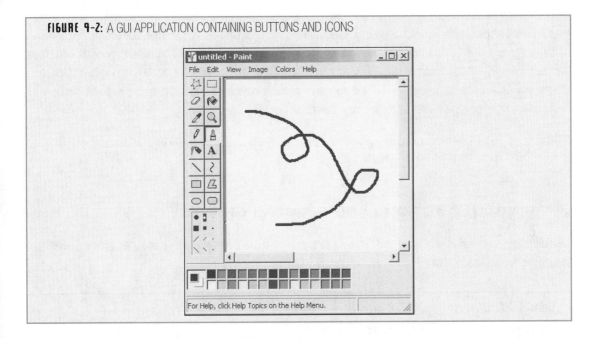

TIP □ □ □ □ You first learned about built-in GUI components and the libraries that contain them in Chapter 2.

GUI programs are called **event-based** or **event-driven** because actions occur in response to user-initiated events such as clicking a mouse button. When you program with event-driven languages, the emphasis is on the objects that the user can manipulate, such as buttons and menus, and on the events that the user can initiate with those objects, such as clicking or double-clicking. The programmer writes instructions within modules that correspond to each type of event.

For the programmer, event-driven programs require unique considerations. The program logic you have developed within many of the methods of this book is procedural; each step occurs in the order the programmer determines. In a procedural application, if you issue a prompt and a statement to read the user's response, you have no control over how much time the user takes to enter a response, but you do control the sequence of events—the processing goes no further until the input is completed. In contrast, with event-driven programs, the user might initiate any number of events in any order. For example, if you use an event-driven word-processing program, you have dozens of choices at your disposal at any moment. You can type words, select text with the mouse, click a button to change text to bold or to italics, choose a menu item, and so on. With each word-processing document you create, you choose options in any order that seems appropriate at the time. The word-processing program must be ready to respond to any event you initiate.

Within an event-driven program, a component from which an event is generated is the **source** of the event. A button that a user can click is an example of a source; a text field that one can use to enter text is another source. An object that is "interested in" an event you want it to respond to is a **listener**. It "listens for" events so it knows when to respond. Not all objects can receive all events—you probably have used programs in which clicking many areas of the screen has no effect at all. If you want an object, such as a button, to be a listener for an event such as a mouse click, you must write the appropriate program statements.

Although event-based programming is relatively new, the instructions that programmers write to correspond to events are still simply sequences, selections, and loops. Event-driven programs still declare variables, use arrays, and contain all the attributes of their procedural-program ancestors. An event-based program might contain components with labels like "Sort Records," "Merge Files," or "Total Transactions." The programming logic you use when writing code for each of these processes is the same logic you have learned throughout this book. Writing event-driven programs simply involves thinking of possible events as the modules that constitute the program.

TIP ◻ ◻ ◻ ◻ | In object-oriented languages, the procedural modules that depend on user-initiated events are often called *scripts*.

USER-INITIATED ACTIONS AND GUI COMPONENTS

To understand GUI programming, you need to have a clear picture of the possible events a user can initiate. These include the events listed in Table 9-1.

TABLE 9-1: COMMON USER-INITIATED EVENTS

Event	Description
Key press	Pressing a key on the keyboard
Mouse point	Placing the mouse pointer over an area on the screen
Mouse click or left mouse click	Pressing the left mouse button
Right mouse click	Pressing the right mouse button
Mouse double-click	Pressing the left mouse button two times in rapid sequence
Mouse drag	Holding the left mouse button down while moving the mouse over the desk surface

You also need to be able to picture common GUI components. Some are listed in Table 9-2. Figure 9-3 shows a screen that contains several common GUI components.

When you program in a language that supports event-driven logic, you do not create the GUI components you need from scratch. Instead, you call prewritten methods that draw the GUI components on the screen for you. The components themselves are constructed using preexisting classes complete with names, attributes, and methods. In some programming language environments, you write statements that call the methods that create the GUI objects; in others, you can drag GUI objects onto your screen from a toolbar. Either way, you do not worry about the details of constructing the components. Instead, you concentrate on the actions that you want to take place when a user initiates an event from one of the components. Thus, GUI components are excellent examples of the best principles of object-oriented programming (OOP)—they represent objects with attributes and methods that operate like black boxes, making them easy for you to use.

TABLE 9-2: COMMON GUI COMPONENTS

GUI Components	Description
Label	A rectangular area that displays text
Text field	A rectangular area into which the user can type a line of text
Button	A rectangular object you can click; usually it appears to press inward like a push button
Check box	A label positioned beside a square; you can click the square to display or remove a check mark—allows the user to turn an option (or multiple options) on or off
Option buttons	A group of check-box-type objects in which the options are mutually exclusive; when the user selects any one option, the others are turned off—when they are square, they are often called a check box group, when they are round rather than square, they often are called a set of radio buttons
List box	When the user clicks a list arrow, a menu of options appears; when the user selects an option from the list, the selected item replaces the original item in the display—all other items are unselected (with some list boxes, the user can make multiple selections)
Toolbar	A strip of icons that activate menu items

FIGURE 9-3: ILLUSTRATION OF COMMON GUI COMPONENTS

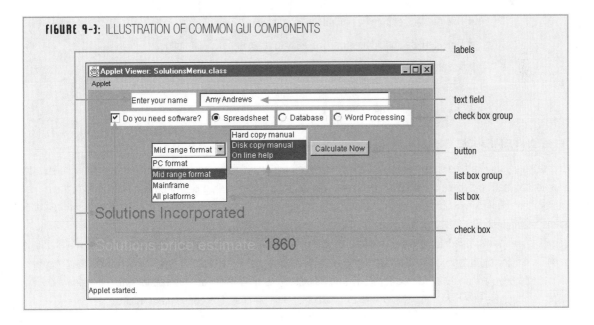

 GUI components are often referred to as *widgets*, which is short for *windows gadgets*. Originally, "widget" comes from the 1924 play "Beggar on Horseback", by George Kaufman and Marc Connelly. In the play, a young composer gets engaged to the daughter of a rich businessman, and foresees spending his life doing pointless work in a bureaucratic big business manufacturing widgets, which represent a useless item whose purpose is never explained.

When you use already created GUI components, you are instantiating objects, each of which belongs to a prewritten class. For example, you might use a `Button` class object when you want the user to be able to click a button to make a selection. Depending on the programming language you use, the `Button` class might contain attributes or properties such as `color` and `label` and methods such as `setLabel()`, in which you define the words that appear on the `Button`'s surface, and `click()`, in which you define the actions that will take place when a user clicks the `Button` object. To create a `Button` object, you might write a statement similar to `Button myProgramButton`, in which `Button` represents the type and `myProgramButton` represents the object you create.

DESIGNING GRAPHICAL USER INTERFACES

You should consider several general design principles when creating a program that will use a GUI:

- The interface should be natural and predictable.
- The interface should be attractive, easy to read, and nondistracting.
- To some extent, it's helpful if the user can customize your applications.
- The program should be forgiving.
- The GUI is only a means to an end.

THE INTERFACE SHOULD BE NATURAL AND PREDICTABLE

The GUI program interface should represent objects like their real-world counterparts. In other words, it makes sense to use an icon that looks like a recycling bin when you want to allow a user to drag files or other components to the bin to delete them. Using a recycling bin icon is "natural" in that people use one in real life when they want to discard real-life items; dragging files to the bin is also "natural" because that's what people do with real-life items they discard. Using a recycling bin for discarded items is also predictable, because a number of other programs, with which users are already familiar, employ the recycling bin icon. Some icons may be natural, but if they are not predictable as well, then they are not as effective. An icon that depicts a recycling truck is just as "natural" as far as corresponding to real-world recycling, but because other programs do not use a truck icon for this purpose, it is not as predictable.

GUIs should also be predictable in their layout. For example, with most GUI programs, you use a menu bar at the top of the screen, and the first menu item is almost always *File*. If you design a program interface in which the menu runs vertically down the right side of the screen, or in which *File* is the last menu option instead of the first, you will confuse the people who use your program. Either they will make mistakes when using it, or they may give up using it entirely. It doesn't matter if you can prove that your layout plan is more efficient than the standard one—if you do not use a predictable layout, your program will meet rejection from users in the marketplace.

TIP ▫ ▫ ▫ ▫ Many studies have proven that the Dvorak keyboard layout is more efficient for typists than the QWERTY keyboard layout that most of us use. The QWERTY keyboard layout gets its name from the first six letter keys in the top row. With the Dvorak layout, which gets its name from its inventor, the most frequently used keys are in the home row, allowing typists to complete many more keystrokes per minute. However, the Dvorak keyboard has not caught on with the computer-buying public because it is not predictable.

TIP ▫ ▫ ▫ ▫ Stovetops often have an unnatural interface, making unfamiliar stoves more difficult for you to use. Most stovetops have four burners arranged in two rows, but the knobs that control the burners frequently are placed in a single horizontal row. Because there is not a natural correlation between the placement of, for example, the left front burner and its control, you are more likely to select the wrong knob when adjusting the burner's flame or heating element.

THE INTERFACE SHOULD BE ATTRACTIVE, EASY TO READ, AND NONDISTRACTING

If your interface is attractive, people are more likely to use it. If it is easy to read, they are less likely to make mistakes and more likely to want to use it. And if the interface is easy to read, it will more likely be considered attractive. When it comes to GUI design, fancy fonts and weird color combinations are the signs of amateur designers. In addition, you should make sure that unavailable screen options are either sufficiently dimmed or removed, so the user does not waste time clicking components that aren't functional.

TIP ▫ ▫ ▫ ▫ Dimming a component is also called *graying* the component. Dimming a component provides another example of predictability—users with computer experience do not expect to be able to use a dimmed component.

Screen designs should not be distracting. When there are too many components on a screen, users can't find what they're looking for. When a text field or button is no longer needed, it should be removed from the interface. You also want to avoid distracting users with overly creative design elements. When users click a button to open a file, they might be amused the first time a file name dances across the screen, or the speakers play a tune. But after one or two experiences with your creative additions, users find that intruding design elements simply hamper the actual work of the program.

TIP ▫ ▫ ▫ ▫ GUI programmers sometimes refer to screen space as *real estate*. Just as a plot of real estate becomes unattractive when it supports no open space, your screen becomes unattractive when you fill the limited space with too many components.

TO SOME EXTENT, IT'S HELPFUL IF THE USER CAN CUSTOMIZE YOUR APPLICATIONS

Every user works in his or her own way. If you are designing an application that will use numerous menus and toolbars, it's helpful if users can position the components in the order that's easiest for them to work with. Users appreciate being able to change features like color schemes. Allowing a user to change the background color in your application may seem frivolous to you, but to users who are color-blind or visually impaired, it might make the difference in whether they use your application at all.

TIP ⬚ ⬚ ⬚ ⬚   The screen design issues that make programs easier to use for individuals with physical limitations are known as **accessibility** issues.

THE PROGRAM SHOULD BE FORGIVING

Perhaps you have had the inconvenience of accessing a voice mail system in which you selected several sequential options, only to find yourself at a dead end with no recourse but to hang up and redial the number. Good program design avoids equivalent problems. You should always provide an escape route to accommodate users who have made bad choices or changed their minds. By providing a Back button or functional Escape key, you provide more functionality to your users.

THE GUI IS ONLY A MEANS TO AN END

The most important principle of GUI design is to remember always that any GUI is only an interface. Using a mouse to click items and drag them around is not the point of any business programs except those that train people how to use a mouse. Instead, the point of a graphical interface is to help people be more productive. To that end, the design should help the user see what options are available, allow the use of components in the ordinary way, and not force the user to concentrate on how to interact with your application. The real work of any GUI program is done after the user clicks a button or makes a list box selection. Then actual program tasks take place.

MODIFYING THE ATTRIBUTES OF GUI COMPONENTS

When you design a program with premade or preprogrammed graphical components, you will want to change their appearance to customize them for the current application. Each programming language provides its own means of changing components' appearances, but all involve changing the values stored in the components' attribute fields. Some common changes include setting the following items:

- Setting the size of the component
- Setting the color of the component
- Setting the screen location of the component
- Setting the font for any text contained in or on the component
- Setting the component to be visible or invisible
- Setting the component to be dimmed or undimmed, sometimes called enabled or disabled

You must learn the exact names of the methods and what type of arguments you are allowed to use in each programming language you learn, but all languages that support creating event-driven applications allow you to set components' attributes. With some languages, you set attributes by coding assignment statements, such as `myButton.text = "Push here"`. With other languages, to change an attribute, you might call a module and send an argument, using a statement such as `myButton.setText("Push here")`. With other languages, you can access a properties list for every GUI object you create, and simply type the needed text into a table of attributes.

THE STEPS TO DEVELOPING AN EVENT-DRIVEN APPLICATION

In Chapter 1, you first learned the steps to developing a computer program. They are:

1. Identify the objects, design the classes, and establish communication.
2. Plan the logic.
3. Code the program.
4. Translate the program into machine language.
5. Test the program.
6. Put the program into production.

When you develop an event-driven application, you expand on the initial design step, including three new substeps as follows:

1a. Create storyboards.
1b. Define the objects.
1c. Define the connections between the screens the user will see.

For example, suppose you want to create a simple, interactive program that determines premiums for prospective insurance customers. The users should be able to use a graphical interface to select a policy type—health or auto. Next, the users answer pertinent questions, such as how old they are, whether they smoke, and what their driving records are like. Although most insurance premium amounts would be based on more characteristics than these, assume that policy rates are determined using the factors shown in Table 9-3. The final output of the program is a second screen that shows the semiannual premium amount for the chosen policy.

TABLE 9-3: INSURANCE PREMIUMS BASED ON CUSTOMER CHARACTERISTICS

Health Policy Premiums	Auto Policy Premiums
Base rate: $500	Base rate: $750
Add $100 if over age 50	Add $400 if more than 2 tickets
Add $250 if smoker	Subtract $200 if over age 50

CREATING STORYBOARDS

A **storyboard** represents a picture or sketch of a screen the user will see when running a program. Filmmakers have long used storyboards to illustrate key moments in the plots they are developing; similarly, GUI storyboards represent "snapshot" views of the screens the user will encounter during the run of a program. If the user could view up to four screens during the insurance premium program, then you would draw four storyboard cells, or frames.

Figure 9-4 shows two storyboard sketches for the insurance program. They represent the introductory screen at which the user selects a premium type and answers questions, and the final screen that displays the semiannual premium.

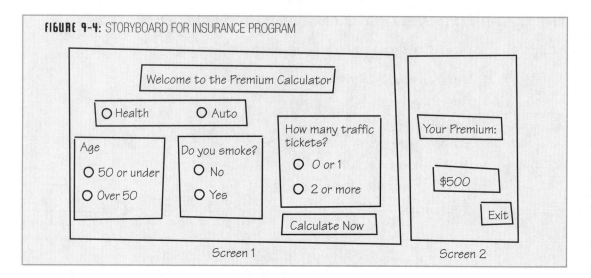

FIGURE 9-4: STORYBOARD FOR INSURANCE PROGRAM

DEFINING THE OBJECTS IN AN OBJECT DICTIONARY

An event-driven program may contain dozens, or even hundreds, of objects. To keep track of them, programmers often use an object dictionary. An **object dictionary** is a list of the objects used in a program, including which screens they are used on and whether any code, or script, is associated with them.

Figure 9-5 shows an object dictionary for the insurance premium program. The type and name of each object to be placed on a screen is listed in the left column. The second column shows the screen number on which the object appears. The next column names any variables that are affected by an action on the object. The right column indicates whether any code or script is associated with the object. For example, the label named `welcomeLabel` appears on the first screen. It has no associated actions—it does not call any methods nor change any variables; it is just a label. The `calculateButton`, however, does cause execution of a method named `calcRoutine()`. This method calculates the semiannual premium amount and stores it in the `premiumAmount` variable. Depending on the programming language you use, you might need to name `calcRoutine()` something similar to `calculateButton.click()` to identify it as the module that executes when the user clicks the `calculateButton`.

TIP ☐ ☐ ☐ ☐ | Some organizations also include the disk location where an object is stored as part of the object dictionary.

FIGURE 9-5: OBJECT DICTIONARY FOR INSURANCE PREMIUM PROGRAM

Object Name	Screen Number	Variables Affected	Script?
Label welcomeLabel	1	none	none
Choice healthOrAuto	1	policyType	none
Choice age	1	ageOfInsured	none
Choice smoker	1	insuredIsSmoker	none

FIGURE 9-5: OBJECT DICTIONARY FOR INSURANCE PREMIUM PROGRAM (CONTINUED)

Object Name	Screen Number	Variables Affected	Script?
Choice tickets	1	numTickets	none
Button calculateButton	1	premiumAmount	calcRoutine()
Label yourPremium	2	none	none
Text field premAmtField	2	none	none
Button exitButton	2	none	exitRoutine()

DEFINING THE CONNECTIONS BETWEEN THE USER SCREENS

The insurance premium program is a small one, but with larger programs you may need to draw the connections between the screens to show how they interact. Figure 9-6 shows an interactivity diagram for the screens used in the insurance premium program. An **interactivity diagram** shows the relationship between screens in an interactive GUI program. Figure 9-6 shows that the first screen calls the second screen, and the program ends.

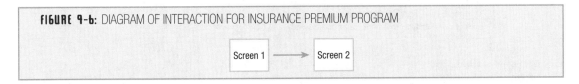

FIGURE 9-6: DIAGRAM OF INTERACTION FOR INSURANCE PREMIUM PROGRAM

Figure 9-7 shows how a diagram might look for a more complicated program in which the user has several options available at Screens 1, 2, and 3. Notice how each of these three screens may lead to different screens, depending on the options the user selects at any one screen.

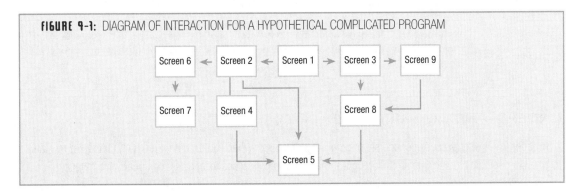

FIGURE 9-7: DIAGRAM OF INTERACTION FOR A HYPOTHETICAL COMPLICATED PROGRAM

PLANNING THE LOGIC

In an event-driven program, you design the screens, define the objects, and define how the screens will connect. Then you can plan the logic for each of the modules (or methods or scripts) that the program will use. For example, given the program requirements shown in Table 9-3, you can write the pseudocode for the `calcRoutine()` of the insurance premium program, as shown in Figure 9-8. The `calcRoutine()` does not execute until the user clicks the `calculateButton`. At that point, the user's choices are sent to the method and used to calculate the premium amount.

FIGURE 9-8: PSEUDOCODE FOR `calcRoutine()`

```
public static numeric calcRoutine(string policyType, numeric ageOfInsured,
    string insuredIsSmoker, numeric numTickets)
      numeric premiumAmount
      if policyType = "H" then
          premiumAmount = 500
          if ageOfInsured > 50 then
              premiumAmount = premiumAmount + 100
          endif
          if insuredIsSmoker = "Y" then
              premiumAmount = premiumAmount + 250
          endif
      else
          premiumAmount = 750
          if numTickets > 2 then
              premiumAmount = premiumAmount + 400
          endif
          if ageOfInsured > 50 then
              premiumAmount = premiumAmount - 200
          endif
      endif
return premiumAmount
```

The pseudocode in Figure 9-8 should look very familiar to you—it uses decision-making logic you have used since the early chapters of this book. The basic structures of sequence, selection, and looping will continue to serve you well, whether you are programming in a procedural or event-driven environment.

TIP ☐ ☐ ☐ ☐ | With some OOP languages, you must **register**, or sign up, components that will react to events initiated by other components. The details of how this is accomplished vary among languages.

UNDERSTANDING MULTITHREADING

A **thread** is the flow of execution of one set of program statements. When you execute a program statement by statement, from beginning to end, you are following a thread. Many applications follow a single thread; this means that at any one time the application executes only a single program statement.

Single-thread programs contain statements that execute in very rapid sequence, but only one statement executes at a time. When a computer contains a single central processing unit (CPU, or processor), it can execute only one computer instruction at a time, regardless of its processor speed. When you use a computer with multiple CPUs, the computer can execute multiple instructions simultaneously.

Some OOP languages, for example Java, allow you to launch, or start, multiple threads, no matter which type of processing system you use. Using multiple threads of execution is known as **multithreading**. As already noted, if you use a computer system that contains more than one CPU (such as a very large mainframe or supercomputer), multiple threads can execute simultaneously. Figure 9-9 illustrates how multithreading executes in a multiprocessor system.

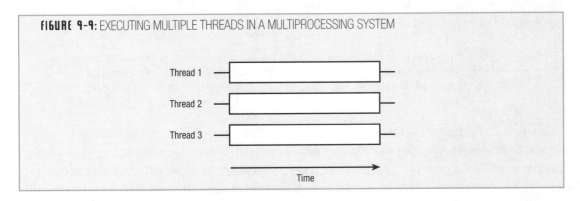

FIGURE 9-9: EXECUTING MULTIPLE THREADS IN A MULTIPROCESSING SYSTEM

If you use a computer with a single processor, the multiple threads share the CPU's time, as shown in Figure 9-10. The CPU devotes a small amount of time to one task, and then devotes a small amount of time to another task. The CPU never actually performs two tasks at the same instant. Instead, it performs a piece of one task, and then a piece of another task. The CPU performs so quickly that each task seems to execute without interruption.

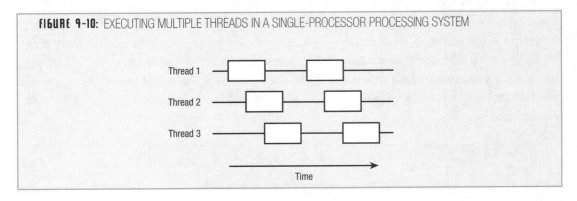

FIGURE 9-10: EXECUTING MULTIPLE THREADS IN A SINGLE-PROCESSOR PROCESSING SYSTEM

Perhaps you have seen an expert chess player participate in chess games with several opponents at once. The chess player makes a move on the first playing board, and then moves to the second board against a second opponent, while the first opponent analyzes his next move. The master can move to the third board, make a move, and return to the first board before the first opponent is even ready to respond. To the first opponent, it might seem as though the expert player is devoting all of her time to him. Because the expert is so fast, she can play other opponents in the first opponent's "downtime." Executing multiple threads on a single CPU works in a similar way. The CPU transfers its attention from thread to thread so quickly that the tasks don't even "miss" the CPU's attention.

You use multithreading to improve the performance of your programs. Multithreaded programs often run faster, but what is more important is that they are more user-friendly. With a multithreaded program, your user can continue to click buttons while your program is reading a data file. With multithreading, an animated figure can appear on one part of the screen while the user makes menu selections on another part of the screen. When you use the Internet, multithreading increases in importance. For example, you can begin to read a long text file or listen to an audio file while the file is still downloading. Web users are likely to abandon a site if downloading a file takes too long. When you use multithreading to perform concurrent tasks, you are more likely to retain visitors to your Web site—this is particularly important if your site sells a product or service.

TIP ▫ ▫ ▫ ▫ | Programmers sometimes use the terms "thread of execution" or "execution context" to describe a thread. They also describe a thread as a lightweight process because it is not a full-blown program. Rather, a thread must run within the context of a full, heavyweight program.

Object-oriented languages often contain a built-in **Thread** class that contains methods to help handle multiple threads. For example, one often-needed method is a **sleep()** method that can pause program execution for a specified amount of time. Computer instruction processing speed is so rapid that sometimes you have to slow processing down for human consumption. An application that frequently requires **sleep()** method calls is computer animation.

CREATING ANIMATION

Many object-oriented languages contain built-in classes that contain methods you can use to draw geometric figures on the screen. The methods typically have names like drawLine(), drawCircle(), drawRectangle(), and so on. You place figures on the screen based on a graphing coordinate system. Typically, any component you place on the screen has a horizontal, or **x-axis**, position as well as a vertical, or **y-axis**, position in a screen window. The upper-left corner of any display is position 0,0. The first, or **x-coordinate**, value increases as you travel from left to right across the window. The second, or **y-coordinate**, value increases as you travel from top to bottom. Figure 9-11 shows three screen coordinate positions. The more to the right a spot is, the higher its x-coordinate value, and the lower a spot is, the higher its y-coordinate value.

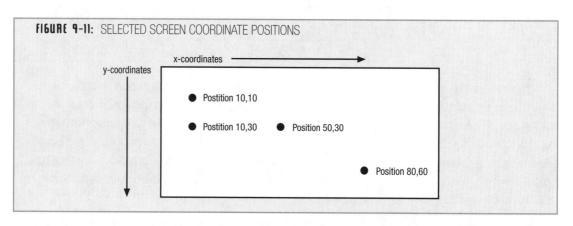

FIGURE 9-11: SELECTED SCREEN COORDINATE POSITIONS

x-coordinates

y-coordinates

● Postition 10,10

● Postition 10,30 ● Position 50,30

● Position 80,60

Cartoonists create animated films by drawing a sequence of frames or cells. These individual drawings are shown to the audience in rapid succession to give the illusion of natural movement. You create computer animation using the same techniques. If you display computer images as fast as your CPU can process them, you might not be able to see anything. Most computer animation employs a `Thread` class `sleep()` method to pause for short periods of time between animation cells, so the human brain has time to absorb each image's content.

Artists often spend a great deal of time creating the exact images they want to use in an animation sequence. As a much simpler example, Figure 9-12 shows pseudocode for a `MovingCircle` class, which, as its name implies, moves a circle across the screen. The class contains data fields to hold x- and y-coordinates that identify the location at which a circle appears. The constants `SIZE`, and `INCREASE` respectively define the size of the first circle drawn and the relative increase in size and position of each subsequent circle. The `MovingCircle` class assumes you are working with a language that provides a `drawCircle()` method that takes care of the details of creating a circle when it is given parameters for horizontal and vertical positions and circle size. Assuming you are working with a language that provides a `sleep()` method that accepts a pause time in milliseconds, the `SLEEP_TIME` constant provides a 100-millisecond time gap before the production of each new circle.

FIGURE 9-12: THE `MovingCircle` CLASS

```
public class MovingCircle
{
  private numeric x = 20
  private numeric y = 20
  private constant numeric SIZE = 40
  private constant numeric INCREASE = SIZE / 10
  private constant numeric SLEEP_TIME = 100
  public static void main()
      while(true)
        repaintScreen()
      endwhile
  return
  public static void repaintScreen()
      drawCircle(x, y, SIZE)
      x = x + INCREASE
      y = y + INCREASE
      Thread.sleep(SLEEP_TIME)
  return
endClass
```

The `main()` method in the `MovingCircle` class executes a continuous loop. A similar technique is used in many languages that support GUI interfaces. Program execution will cease only when the user quits the application by clicking a window's close button on the screen, for example. In the `repaintScreen()` method of the `MovingCircle` class, a circle is drawn at the x, y position, then `x` and `y` are both increased. The application sleeps for one-tenth of a second (the `SLEEP_TIME` value), and then the `repaintScreen()` method draws a new circle more to the right, further down, and a little larger. The effect is a moving circle that leaves a trail of smaller circles behind it as it moves diagonally across the screen. Figure 9-13 shows the output as a Java version of the application executes.

FIGURE 9-13: OUTPUT OF THE `MovingCircle` APPLICATION

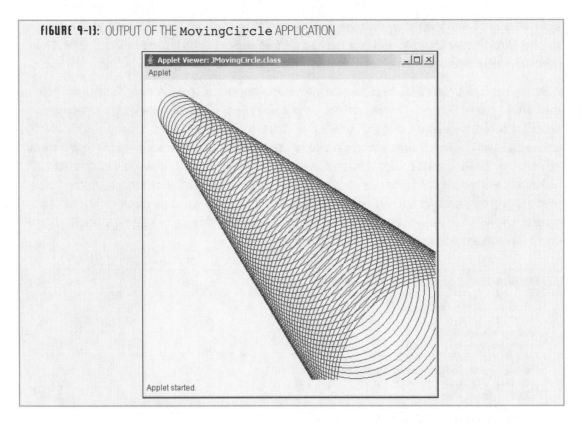

Although an object-oriented language might make it easy for you to draw geometric shapes, you also can substitute a variety of more sophisticated, predrawn animated images to achieve the graphic effects you want within your programs. An image is loaded in a separate thread of execution; this allows program execution to continue while the image loads. This is a great advantage because loading a large image can be time consuming.

TIP □ □ □ □ Many animated images are available on the Web for you to use freely. Use your search engine to search for keywords such as gif files, jpeg files, and animation to find sources for shareware files.

CHAPTER SUMMARY

☐ Interacting with a computer operating system from the command line is difficult; it is easier to use an event-driven graphical user interface (GUI), in which users manipulate objects such as buttons and menus. Within an event-driven program, a component from which an event is generated is the source of the event. A listener is an object that is "interested in" an event to which you want it to respond.

☐ The possible events a user can initiate include a key press, mouse point, click, right-click, double-click, and drag. Common GUI components include labels, text fields, buttons, check boxes, check box groups, option buttons, lists, and toolbars. GUI components are excellent examples of the best principles of object-oriented programming (OOP)—they represent objects with attributes and methods that operate like black boxes.

☐ When you create a program that will use a GUI, the interface should be natural, predictable, attractive, easy to read, and nondistracting. It's helpful if the user can customize your applications. The program should be forgiving, and you should not forget that the GUI is only a means to an end.

☐ You can modify the attributes of GUI components. For example, you can set the size, color, screen location, font, visibility, and enabled status of the component.

☐ Developing an event-driven application is more complicated than developing a standard procedural program. You must understand the problem, create storyboards, define the objects, define the connections between the screens the user will see, plan the logic, code the program, translate the program into machine language, test the program, and put the program into production.

☐ A thread is the flow of execution of one set of program statements. Many applications follow a single thread; using multiple threads of execution is known as multithreading.

☐ Many object-oriented languages contain built-in classes that contain methods you can use to draw geometric figures on the screen. Typically, any component you place on the screen has a horizontal, or x-axis, position as well as a vertical, or y-axis, position in a screen window. You create computer animation by drawing a sequence of images, which are shown in rapid succession.

KEY TERMS

The **command line** is the location on your computer screen at which you type entries to communicate with the computer's operating system.

An **operating system** is the software that you use to run a computer and manage its resources.

The command line also is called the **command prompt**.

The **DOS prompt** is the command line in the DOS operating system.

Icons are small pictures on the screen that the user can select with a mouse.

A **graphical user interface**, or **GUI**, allows users to interact with an operating system by clicking on icons to select options.

An **event** is an occurrence that generates a message sent to an object.

GUI programs are called **event-based** or **event-driven** because actions occur in response to user-initiated events such as clicking a mouse button.

A component from which an event is generated is the **source** of the event.

A **listener** is an object that is "interested in" an event to which you want it to respond.

The screen design issues that make programs easier to use for individuals with physical limitations are known as **accessibility** issues.

A **storyboard** represents a picture or sketch of a screen the user will see when running a program.

An **object dictionary** is a list of the objects used in a program, including which screens they are used on and whether any code, or script, is associated with them.

An **interactivity diagram** shows the relationship between screens in an interactive GUI program.

In some object-oriented programming languages, you **register**, or sign up, components that will react to events initiated by other components.

A **thread** is the flow of execution of one set of program statements.

Multithreading is using multiple threads of execution.

The **x-axis** represents horizontal positions in a screen window.

The **y-axis** represents vertical positions in a screen window.

The **x-coordinate** value increases as you travel from left to right across a window.

The **y-coordinate** value increases as you travel from top to bottom across a window.

REVIEW QUESTIONS

1. As opposed to using a command line, an advantage to using an operating system that employs a GUI is _____.

   a. you can interact directly with the operating system
   b. you do not have to deal with confusing icons
   c. you do not have to memorize complicated commands
   d. all of the above

2. When users can initiate actions by clicking a mouse on an icon, the program is said to be _____ -driven.

   a. event
   b. prompt
   c. command
   d. incident

3. **A component from which an event is generated is the _____ of the event.**

   a. base
   b. icon
   c. listener
   d. source

4. **An object that responds to an event is a _____.**

   a. source
   b. listener
   c. transponder
   d. snooper

5. **All of the following are user-initiated events except _____.**

   a. key press
   b. key drag
   c. right mouse click
   d. mouse drag

6. **All of the following are typical GUI components except _____.**

   a. label
   b. text field
   c. list box
   d. button box

7. **GUI components operate like _____.**

   a. black boxes
   b. procedural functions
   c. looping structures
   d. command lines

8. **Which is *not* a principle of good GUI design?**

   a. The interface should be predictable.
   b. The fancier the screen design, the better.
   c. The program should be forgiving.
   d. The user should be able to customize your applications.

9. **Which of the following aspects of a GUI layout is most predictable and natural for the user?**

   a. A menu bar appears running down the right side of the screen.
   b. *Help* is the first option on a menu.
   c. Saving a file is represented by a dollar sign icon.
   d. Pressing *Esc* allows the user to cancel a selection.

10. In most GUI programming environments, you can change all of the following attributes of most components except their _____.

    a. color
    b. screen location
    c. size
    d. You can change all of these attributes.

11. Depending on the programming language you use, to change a screen component's attributes, you might _____.

    a. use an assignment statement
    b. call a module
    c. enter a value into a list of properties
    d. all of the above

12. When you create an event-driven application, which of the following must be done before defining the objects you will use?

    a. Plan the logic.
    b. Create storyboards.
    c. Test the program.
    d. Code the program.

13. A _____ is a sketch of a screen the user will see when running a program.

    a. flowchart
    b. hierarchy chart
    c. storyboard
    d. tale timber

14. A list of objects used in a program is an object _____.

    a. thesaurus
    b. glossary
    c. index
    d. dictionary

15. A diagram that shows the connections between the various screens a user might see during a program's execution is a(n) _____ diagram.

    a. interactivity
    b. help
    c. cooperation
    d. communication

16. In OOP, the flow of execution of one set of program statements is a _____.

    a. thread
    b. string
    c. path
    d. route

17. When a computer contains a single CPU, it can execute _____ computer instruction(s) at a time.

    a. one
    b. several
    c. an unlimited number of
    d. from several to thousands, depending on the processor speed

18. Typically, any component you place on the screen has a horizontal, or _____, position as well as a vertical position in a screen window.

    a. x-axis
    b. y-axis
    c. v-axis
    d. h-axis

19. You create computer animation by _____.

    a. drawing an image and setting its animation property to true
    b. drawing a single image and executing it on a multiprocessor system
    c. drawing a sequence of frames that are shown in rapid succession
    d. Animation is not used in computer applications.

20. You can use sophisticated, predrawn animated images to achieve the graphic effects you want within your programs _____.

    a. by loading them in a separate thread of execution
    b. only by subscribing to expensive imaging services
    c. only with multiprocessing systems
    d. two of the above

EXERCISES

1. Take a critical look at three GUI applications with which you are familiar—for example, a spreadsheet, a word-processing program, and a game. Describe how well each conforms to the GUI design guidelines listed in this chapter.

2. Select one element of poor GUI design in a program with which you are familiar. Describe how you would improve the design.

3. Select a GUI program that you have never used before. Describe how well it conforms to the GUI design guidelines listed in this chapter.

4. Design the storyboards, interactivity diagram, object dictionary, and any necessary scripts for an interactive program for customers of Sunflower Floral Designs.

   Allow customers the option of choosing a floral arrangement ($25 base price), cut flowers ($15 base price), or a corsage ($10 base price). Let the customer choose roses, daisies, chrysanthemums, or irises as the dominant flower. If the customer chooses roses, add $5 to the base price. After the customer clicks an "Order Now" button, display the price of the order.

5. **Design the storyboards, interactivity diagram, object dictionary, and any necessary scripts for an interactive program for customers of Toby's Travels.**

   Allow customers the option of at least five trip destination options and four means of transportation, each with a unique price. After the customer clicks the "Plan Trip Now" button, display the price of the trip.

6. **Design the storyboards, interactivity diagram, object dictionary, and any necessary scripts for an interactive program for customers of The Mane Event Hair Salon.**

   Allow customers the option of choosing a haircut ($15), coloring ($25), or perm ($45). After the customer clicks a "Select" button, display the price of the service.

CASE PROJECT

In earlier chapters, you developed classes needed for Cost Is No Object—a car rental service that specializes in lending antique and luxury cars to clients on a short-term basis. You created pseudocode for `Employee`, `Customer`, `Automobile`, and `RentalAgreement` classes including attributes and methods to get and set those attributes.

Design an interactive application that displays the following:

- A main screen containing at least the company name, an animated image, and two buttons. One button allows the rental agent to proceed to a data entry screen where the agent can enter customer data (name, address, and so on), and the other allows the agent to enter rental agreement data.

- A customer data entry screen.

- A rental agreement data entry screen.

Create storyboards, define the objects you need, and define the connections between the screens the user will see.

10

MODELING WITH UML

After studying Chapter 10, you should be able to:

- Understand the need for system modeling
- Describe the UML
- Work with use case diagrams
- Use class and object diagrams
- Use sequence and collaboration diagrams
- Use statechart diagrams
- Use activity diagrams
- Use component and deployment diagrams
- Decide which UML diagrams to use

UNDERSTANDING THE NEED FOR SYSTEM MODELING

Computer programs often stand alone to solve a user's specific problem. For example, a program might exist only to print paychecks for the current week. Most computer programs, however, are part of a larger system. Your company's payroll system might consist of dozens of programs, including programs that produce employee paychecks, apply raises to employee records, alter employee deduction options, and print W2 forms at the end of the tax year. Each program you write as part of a system might be related to several others. Some programs depend on input from other programs in the system or produce output to be fed into other programs. Similarly, an organization's accounting, inventory, and customer ordering systems all consist of many interrelated programs. Producing a set of programs that operate together correctly requires careful planning. **System design** is the detailed specification of how all the parts of a system will be implemented and coordinated.

TIP □ □ □ □ | Usually, system design refers to computer system design, but even a noncomputerized manual system can benefit from good design techniques.

Many textbooks cover the theories and techniques of system design. If you continue to study in a Computer Information Systems program at a college or university, you probably will be required to take a semester-long course in system design. Explaining all the techniques of system design is beyond the scope of this book. However, some basic principles parallel those you have used throughout this book in designing individual programs:

- Large systems are easier to understand when you break them down into subsystems.
- Good modeling techniques are increasingly important as the size and complexity of systems increase.
- Good models promote communication among technical and nontechnical workers while ensuring good business solutions.

In other words, developing a model for a single program or an entire business system requires organization and planning. In this chapter, you will learn the basics of one popular design tool, the UML, which is based on these principles. The UML allows you to envision systems with an object-oriented perspective, breaking a system into subsystems, focusing on the big picture, and hiding the implementation details. Additionally, the UML provides a means for programmers and businesspeople to communicate about system design. Understanding the UML's principles helps you design a variety of system types and talk about systems with the people who will use them.

TIP □ □ □ □ | In addition to modeling a system before creating it, system analysts sometimes model an existing system to get a better picture of its operation. Creating a model for an existing system is called **reverse engineering**.

WHAT IS UML?

UML stands for Unified Modeling Language. The **UML** is a standard way to specify, construct, and document systems that use object-oriented methods. (The UML is a modeling language, not a programming language. The systems you develop using the UML probably will be implemented later in object-oriented programming (OOP) languages such as

Java, C++, C#, or Visual Basic.) As with flowcharts, pseudocode, hierarchy charts, and class diagrams, the UML has its own notation that consists of a set of specialized shapes and conventions. You can use the UML's shapes to construct different kinds of software diagrams and model different kinds of systems. Just as you can use a flowchart or hierarchy chart to diagram real-life activities, organizational relationships, or computer programs, you also can use the UML for many purposes, including modeling business activities, organizational processes, or software systems.

TIP ▫ ▫ ▫ ▫ | The UML was created at Rational Software by Grady Booch, Ivar Jacobson, and Jim Rumbaugh. The Object Management Group (OMG) adopted the UML as a standard for software modeling in 1997. The OMG includes more than 800 software vendors, developers, and users who seek a common architectural framework for OOP. You can view or download the entire UML specification and usage guidelines from the OMG at *www.omg.org/uml/*.

TIP ▫ ▫ ▫ ▫ | You can purchase compilers for most programming languages from a variety of manufacturers. Similarly, you can purchase a variety of tools to help you create UML diagrams, but the UML itself is vendor-independent.

When you draw a flowchart or write pseudocode, your purpose is to illustrate the individual steps in a process. When you draw a hierarchy chart, you use more of a "big picture" approach. As with a hierarchy chart, you use the UML to create top-view diagrams of business processes that let you hide details and focus on functionality. This approach lets you start with a generic view of an application and introduce details and complexity later. UML diagrams are useful as you begin designing business systems, when customers who are not technically oriented must accurately communicate with the technical staff members who will create the actual systems. The UML was intentionally designed to be nontechnical so that developers, customers, and implementers (programmers) could all "speak the same language." If business and technical people can agree on what a system should do, the chances improve that the final product will be useful.

The UML provides nine different diagram types that you can use to model systems. Each of the diagram types lets you see a business process from a different angle, and appeals to a different type of user. Just as an architect, interior designer, electrician, and plumber use different diagram types to describe the same building, different computer users appreciate different perspectives. For example, a business user will most value a system's use case diagrams because they illustrate who is doing what. On the other hand, programmers will find class and object diagrams more useful because they help explain details of how to build classes and objects into applications. The nine UML diagram types are:

- Use case diagrams
- Class diagrams
- Object diagrams
- Sequence diagrams
- Collaboration diagrams
- Statechart diagrams
- Activity diagrams
- Component diagrams
- Deployment diagrams

TIP ▫ ▫ ▫ ▫ | You can categorize UML diagrams as those that illustrate the dynamic, or changing, aspects of a system and those that illustrate the static, or steady, aspects of a system. Dynamic diagrams include use case, sequence, collaboration, statechart, and activity diagrams. Static diagrams include class, object, component, and deployment diagrams.

TIP ▫ ▫ ▫ ▫ | Statechart diagrams are sometimes referred to as *state chart diagrams*, and sometimes as *state machine diagrams*.

TIP ▫ ▫ ▫ ▫ | Although many sources list nine types of UML diagrams, the Object Management Group (OMG) defines twelve. Structural diagrams include the Class diagram, Object diagram, Component diagram, and Deployment diagram. Behavior diagrams include the Use case diagram, Sequence diagram, Activity diagram, Collaboration diagram, and Statechart diagram. According to the OMG, a third category is Model Management Diagrams, which include Packages, Subsystems, and Models. For more information, visit *www.omg.org*.

Each of the nine basic UML diagram types supports multiple variations, and explaining them all would require an entire textbook. This chapter presents an overview and simple examples of each type of diagram, which will provide a good foundation for the further study of the UML.

USING USE CASE DIAGRAMS

The **use case diagram** shows how a business works from the perspective of those who approach it from the outside, or those who actually use the business. This category includes many types of users—for example, employees, customers, and suppliers. Although users also can be governments, private organizations, machines, or other systems, it is easiest to think of them as people, so users are called actors and are represented by stick figures in use case diagrams. The actual use cases are represented by ovals.

Use cases do not necessarily represent all the functions of a system; they are the system functions or services that are visible to the system's actors. In other words, they represent the cases by which an actor uses and presumably benefits from the system. Determining all the cases for which users interact with systems helps you divide a system logically into functional parts.

Establishing use cases usually follows from analyzing the main events in a system. For example, from a librarian's point of view, two main events are `acquireNewBook()` and `checkOutBook()`. Figure 10-1 shows a use case diagram for these two events.

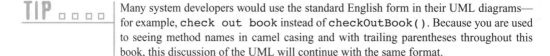

TIP ▫ ▫ ▫ ▫ | Many system developers would use the standard English form in their UML diagrams—for example, `check out book` instead of `checkOutBook()`. Because you are used to seeing method names in camel casing and with trailing parentheses throughout this book, this discussion of the UML will continue with the same format.

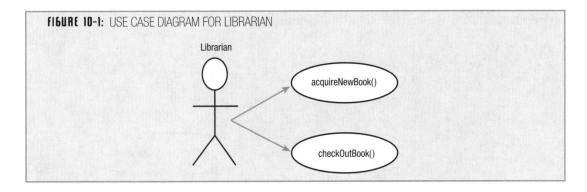

FIGURE 10-1: USE CASE DIAGRAM FOR LIBRARIAN

In many systems there are variations in use cases. The three possible types of variations are:

- Extend
- Include
- Generalization

An **extend** is a use case variation that shows functions beyond those found in a base case. For example, checking out a book for a new library patron who doesn't have a library card is slightly more complicated than checking out a book for an existing patron. Each variation in the sequence of actions required in a use case is a **scenario**. Each use case has at least one main scenario, but might have several more that are extensions or variations of the main one. Figure 10-2 shows how you would diagram the relationship between the use case `checkOutBook()` and the more specific scenario `checkOutBookForNewPatron()`. Extended use cases are shown in an oval with a dashed arrow pointing to the more general base case.

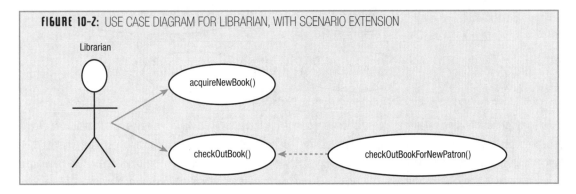

FIGURE 10-2: USE CASE DIAGRAM FOR LIBRARIAN, WITH SCENARIO EXTENSION

For clarity, you can add "<<extend>>" near the line that shows a relationship extension. Such a feature, which adds to the UML vocabulary of shapes to make them more meaningful for the reader, is called a **stereotype**. Figure 10-3 includes a stereotype.

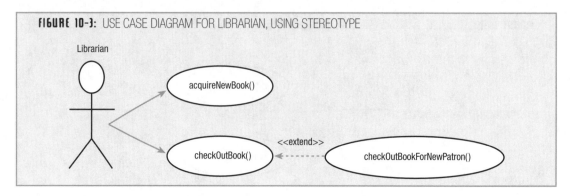

FIGURE 10-3: USE CASE DIAGRAM FOR LIBRARIAN, USING STEREOTYPE

In addition to extend relationships, use case diagrams can also show include relationships. You use an **include** relationship when a case can be part of multiple use cases. This concept is very much like that of a subroutine or submodule. You show an include use case in an oval with a dashed arrow pointing to the subroutine use case. For example, `issueLibraryCard()` might be a function of `checkOutBook()` when the patron is new, but it might also be a function of `registerNewPatron()`, which occurs when a patron registers at the library but does not want to check out books yet. See Figure 10-4.

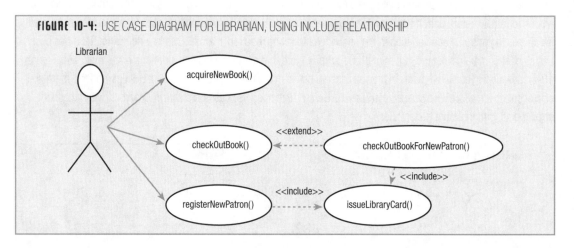

FIGURE 10-4: USE CASE DIAGRAM FOR LIBRARIAN, USING INCLUDE RELATIONSHIP

You use a **generalization** when a use case is less specific than others, and you want to be able to substitute the more specific case for a general one. For example, a library has certain procedures for acquiring new materials, whether they are videos, tapes, CDs, paperbacks, or hardcover books. However, the procedures might become more specific during a particular acquisition—perhaps the librarian must procure plastic cases for circulating videos or assign locked storage locations for CDs. Figure 10-5 shows the generalization `acquireNewItem()` with two more specific situations: acquiring videos and CDs. The more specific scenarios are attached to the general scenario with open-headed dashed arrows.

Many use case diagrams show multiple actors. For example, Figure 10-6 shows that a library clerk cannot perform as many functions as a librarian; the clerk can check out books and register new patrons but cannot acquire new materials.

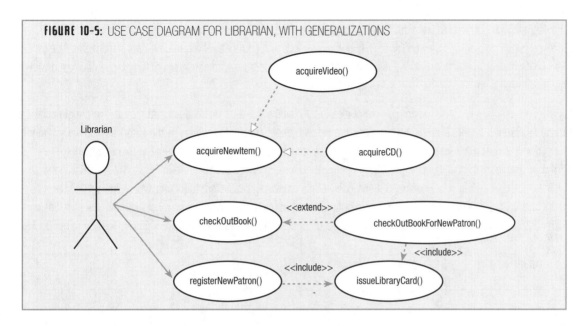

FIGURE 10-5: USE CASE DIAGRAM FOR LIBRARIAN, WITH GENERALIZATIONS

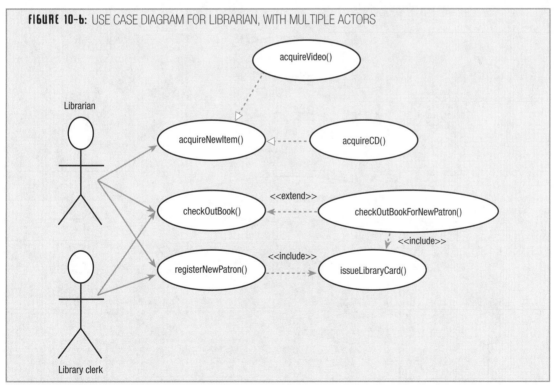

FIGURE 10-6: USE CASE DIAGRAM FOR LIBRARIAN, WITH MULTIPLE ACTORS

While designing an actual library system, you could add many more use cases and actors to the use case diagram. The purpose of such a diagram is to encourage discussion between the system developer and the library staff. Library staff members do not need to know any of the technical details of the system that the analysts will eventually create, and they certainly do not need to understand computers or programming. However, by viewing the use cases, the library staff can visualize activities they perform while doing their jobs and correct the system developer if inaccuracies exist. The final software products developed for such a system are far more likely to satisfy users than those developed without this design step.

A use case diagram is only a tool to aid communication. No single "correct" use case diagram exists; you might correctly represent a system in several ways. For example, you might choose to emphasize the actors in the library system, as shown in Figure 10-7, or to emphasize system requirements, as shown in Figure 10-8. Diagrams that are too crowded are neither visually pleasing nor very useful. Therefore, the use case diagram in Figure 10-7 shows all the specific actors and their relationships, but purposely omits more specific system functions, while Figure 10-8 shows many actions that are often hidden from users but purposely omits more specific actors. For example, the activities carried out to `manageNetworkOutage()`, if done properly, should be invisible to library patrons checking out books.

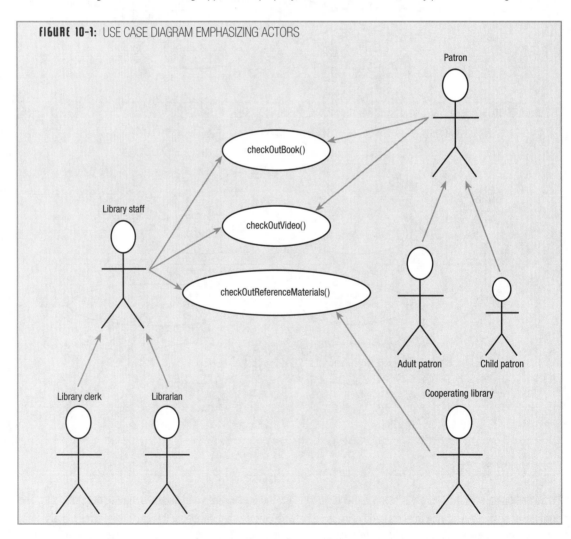

FIGURE 10-7: USE CASE DIAGRAM EMPHASIZING ACTORS

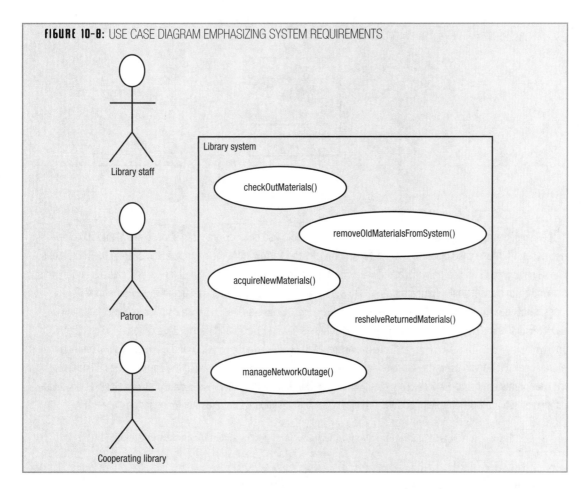

FIGURE 10-8: USE CASE DIAGRAM EMPHASIZING SYSTEM REQUIREMENTS

In Figure 10-8, the relationship lines between the actors and use cases have been removed because the emphasis is on the system requirements, and too many lines would make the diagram confusing. When system developers omit parts of diagrams for clarity, they refer to the missing parts as **elided**. For the sake of clarity, eliding extraneous information is perfectly acceptable. The main purpose of UML diagrams is to facilitate clear communication.

USING CLASS AND OBJECT DIAGRAMS

You use a class diagram to illustrate the names, attributes, and methods of a class or set of classes. Class diagrams are more useful to a system's programmers than to its users because they closely resemble code the programmers will write. A class diagram illustrating a single class contains a rectangle divided into three sections: the top section contains the name of the class, the middle section contains the names of the attributes, and the bottom section contains the names of the methods. Figure 10-9 shows the class diagram for a `Book` class. Each `Book` object contains an `idNum`, `title`, and `author`. Each `Book` object also contains methods to create a `Book` when it is acquired, and to retrieve or get `title` and `author` information when the `Book`'s `idNum` is supplied.

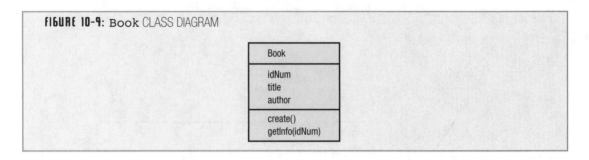

FIGURE 10-9: Book CLASS DIAGRAM

TIP □ □ □ □ You first used class diagrams in Chapter 2.

In the last section, you learned how to use generalizations with use case diagrams to show general and more specific use cases. With use case diagrams, you drew an open-headed arrow from the more specific case to the more general one. Similarly, you can use generalizations with class diagrams to show more general (or parent) classes and more specific (or child) classes that inherit attributes from parents. For example, Figure 10-10 shows **Book** and **Video** classes that are more specific than the general **LibraryItem** class. All **LibraryItem** objects contain an **idNum** and **title**, but each **Book** item also contains an **author**, and each **Video** item also contains a **runningTime**. The **Book** and **Video** classes each contain a **create()** and **getInfo()** method that is more specific than and overrides the more general **LibraryItem** methods with the same names. In addition, **Video** items contain a **rewind()** method not found in the more general **LibraryItem** class. Child classes contain all the attributes of their parents and usually contain additional attributes not found in the parent.

TIP □ □ □ □ You will learn more about inheritance and parent and child classes in Chapter 11.

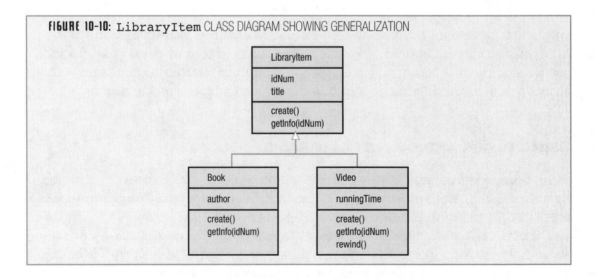

FIGURE 10-10: LibraryItem CLASS DIAGRAM SHOWING GENERALIZATION

Class diagrams can include symbols that show the relationships between objects. You can show two types of relationships:

- An association relationship
- A whole-part relationship

An **association relationship** describes the connection or link between objects. You represent an association relationship between classes with a straight line. Frequently you include information about the arithmetical relationship or ratio (called **cardinality** or **multiplicity**) of the objects. For example, Figure 10-11 shows the association relationship between a `Library` and the `LibraryItem`s it lends. Exactly one `Library` object exists, and it can be associated with any number of `LibraryItem`s from 0 to infinity, represented by an asterisk. Figure 10-12 adds the `Patron` class to the diagram and shows how you indicate that any number of `Patron`s can be associated with the `Library`, but that each `Patron` can borrow only up to five `LibraryItem`s at a time, or currently might not be borrowing any. Additionally, each `LibraryItem` can be associated with at most one `Patron`, but at any given time might not be on loan.

FIGURE 10-11: CLASS DIAGRAM WITH ASSOCIATION RELATIONSHIP

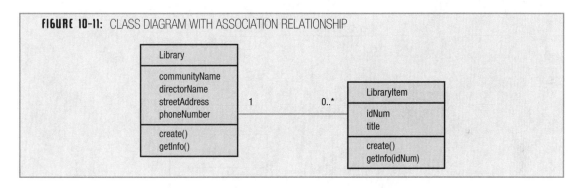

FIGURE 10-12: CLASS DIAGRAM WITH SEVERAL ASSOCIATION RELATIONSHIPS

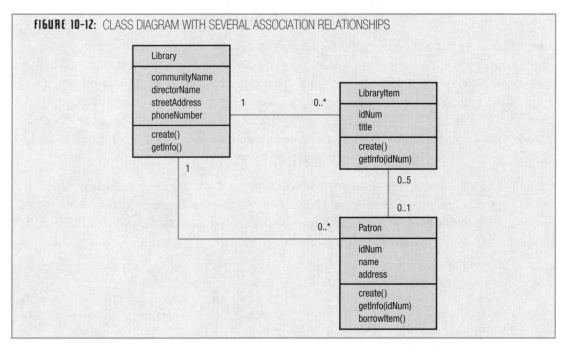

A **whole-part relationship** describes an association in which one or more classes make up the parts of a larger whole class. For example, 50 states "make up" the United States, and 10 departments might "make up" a company. This type of relationship is also called an **aggregation**, and is represented by an open diamond at the "whole part" end of the line that indicates the relationship. You also can call a whole-part relationship a **has-a relationship** because the phrase describes the association between the whole and one of its parts; for example, "The company has a Personnel Department." Figure 10-13 shows a whole-part relationship for a `Library`.

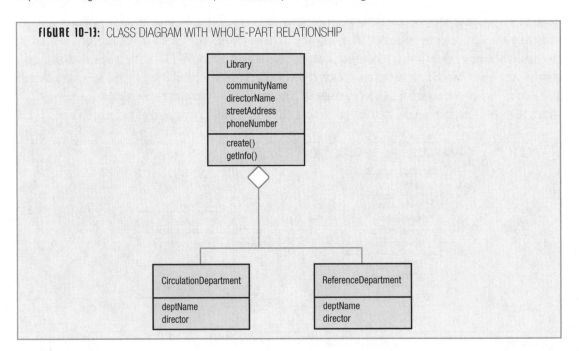

FIGURE 10-13: CLASS DIAGRAM WITH WHOLE-PART RELATIONSHIP

Object diagrams are similar to class diagrams, but they model specific instances of classes. You use an object diagram to show a snapshot of an object at one point in time, so you can more easily understand its relationship to other objects. Imagine looking at the travelers in a major airport. If you try to watch them all at once, you see a flurry of activity, but it is hard to understand all the tasks (buying a ticket, checking luggage, and so on) a traveler must accomplish to take a trip. However, if you concentrate on one traveler and follow his or her actions through the airport from arrival to takeoff, you get a clearer picture of the required activities. An object diagram serves the same purpose; you concentrate on a specific instance of a class to better understand how a class works.

Figure 10-14 contains an object diagram showing the relationship between one `Library`, `LibraryItem`, and `Patron`. Notice the similarities between Figures 10-12 and 10-14. If you need to describe the relationship between three classes, you can use either model—a class diagram or an object diagram—interchangeably. You simply use the model that seems clearer to you and your intended audience.

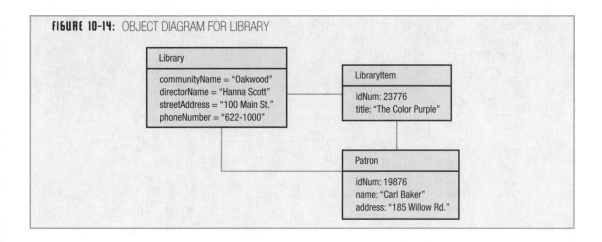

FIGURE 10-14: OBJECT DIAGRAM FOR LIBRARY

USING SEQUENCE AND COLLABORATION DIAGRAMS

You use a **sequence diagram** to show the timing of events in a single use case. A sequence diagram makes it easier to see the order in which activities occur. The horizontal axis (x-axis) of a sequence diagram represents objects, and the vertical axis (y-axis) represents time. You create a sequence diagram by placing objects that are part of an activity across the top of the diagram along the x-axis, starting at the left with the object or actor that begins the action. Beneath each object on the x-axis you place a vertical dashed line that represents the period of time the object exists. Then you use horizontal arrows to show how the objects communicate with each other over time.

For example, Figure 10-15 shows a sequence diagram for a scenario that a librarian can use to create a book checkout record. The librarian begins a `create()` method with `Patron idNum` and `Book idNum` information. The `BookCheckOutRecord` object requests additional `Patron` information (such as name and address) from the `Patron` object with the correct `Patron idNum,` and additional `Book` information (such as title and author) from the `Book` object with the correct `Book idNum`. When the `BookCheckOutRecord` contains all the data it needs, a completed record is returned to the librarian.

TIP □ □ □ □   In Figures 10-15 and 10-16, patronInfo and bookInfo represent group items that contain all of a Patron's and Book's data. For example, patronInfo might contain an idNum, lastName, firstName, address, and phoneNumber, all of which have been defined as attributes of that class.

A **collaboration diagram** emphasizes the organization of objects that participate in a system. It is similar to a sequence diagram, except that it contains sequence numbers to represent the precise order in which activities occur. Figure 10-16 shows the same sequence of events as Figure 10-15, but the steps to creating a `BookCheckOutRecord` are clearly numbered. Decimal numbered steps (1.1, 1.2, and so on) represent substeps of the main steps. Checking out a library book is a fairly straightforward event, so a sequence diagram sufficiently illustrates the process. Collaboration diagrams become more useful with more complicated systems.

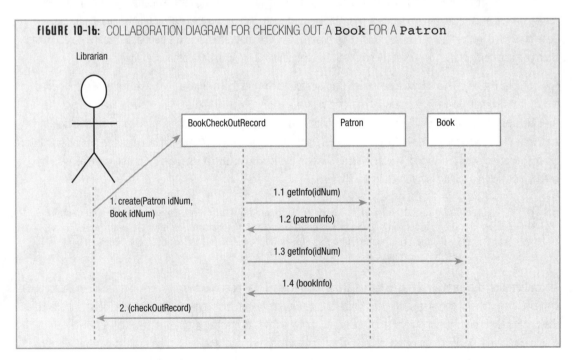

FIGURE 10-15: SEQUENCE DIAGRAM FOR CHECKING OUT A **Book** FOR A **Patron**

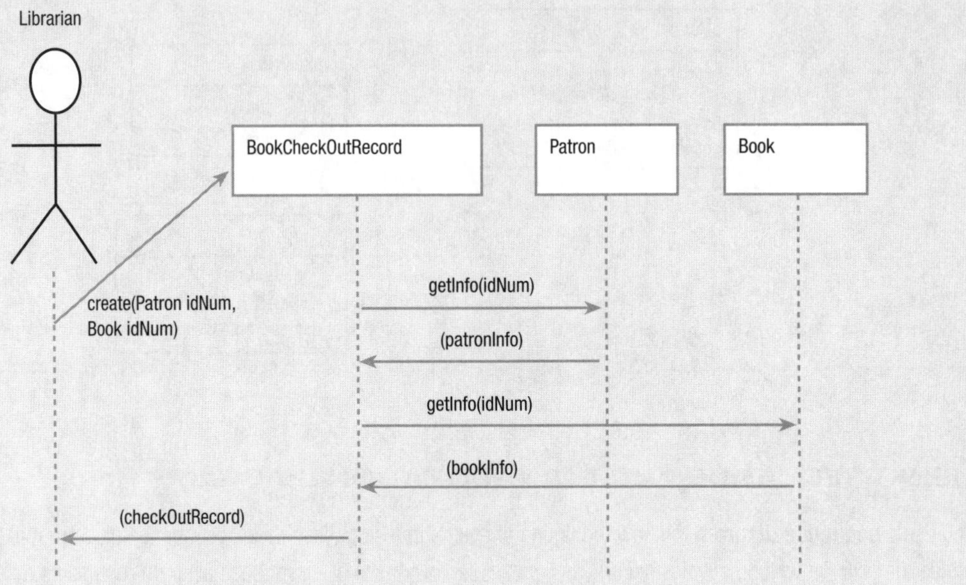

FIGURE 10-16: COLLABORATION DIAGRAM FOR CHECKING OUT A **Book** FOR A **Patron**

USING STATECHART DIAGRAMS

A **statechart diagram** shows the different statuses of or changes of behavior in a class or object at different points in time. You use a statechart diagram to illustrate aspects of a system that show interesting changes in behavior as time passes. Conventionally, you use rounded rectangles to represent each state and labeled arrows to show the sequence in which events affect the states. A solid dot indicates the start and stop states for the class or object. Figure 10-17 contains a statechart diagram you can use to describe the states of a `Book`.

TIP ◻ ◻ ◻ ◻ | So that your diagrams are clear, you should use the correct symbol in each UML diagram you create, just as you should use the correct symbol in each program flowchart. However, if you create a flowchart and use a rectangle for an input or output statement where a parallelogram is conventional, others will still understand your meaning. Similarly, with UML diagrams, the exact shape you use is not nearly as important as the sequence of events and relationships between objects.

FIGURE 10-17: STATECHART DIAGRAM FOR **Book** CLASS

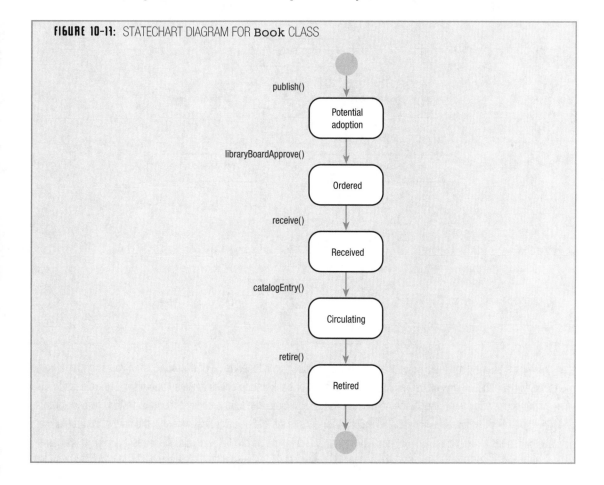

USING ACTIVITY DIAGRAMS

The UML diagram that most closely resembles a conventional flowchart is an activity diagram. In an **activity diagram**, you show the flow of actions of a system, including branches that occur when decisions affect the outcome. Conventionally, activity diagrams use flowchart start and stop symbols (called lozenges) to describe actions, and solid dots to represent start and stop states. Like flowcharts, activity diagrams use diamonds to describe decisions. Unlike the diamonds in flowcharts, the diamonds in UML activity diagrams usually are empty; the possible outcomes are documented along the branches emerging from the decision symbol. As an example, Figure 10-18 shows a simple activity diagram with a single branch.

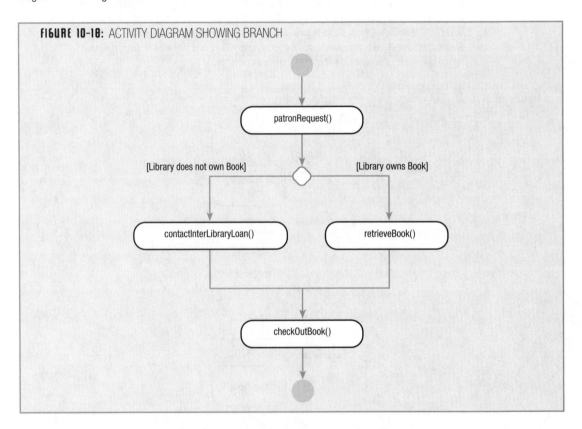

FIGURE 10-18: ACTIVITY DIAGRAM SHOWING BRANCH

Many real-life systems contain activities that are meant to occur simultaneously. For example, when you apply for a home mortgage with a bank, a bank officer might perform a credit or background check while an appraiser determines the value of the house you are buying. When both activities are complete, the loan process continues. UML activity diagrams use forks and joins to show simultaneous activities. A fork is similar to a decision, but whereas the flow of control follows only one path after a decision, a fork defines a branch in which all paths are followed simultaneously. A join, as its name implies, reunites the flow of control after a fork. You indicate forks and joins with thick straight lines. Figure 10-19 shows how you might model the way an interlibrary loan system processes book requests. When a request is received, simultaneous searches begin at three local libraries that are part of the library system.

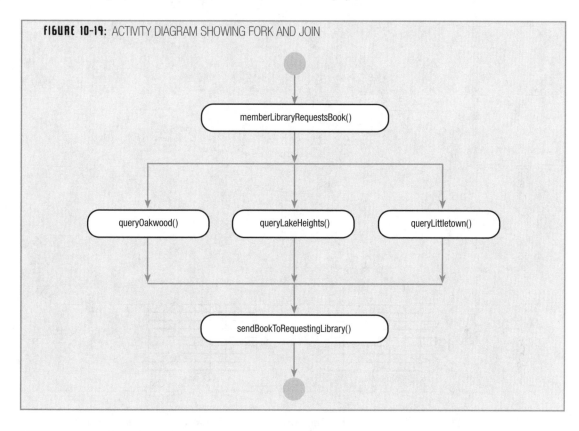

FIGURE 10-19: ACTIVITY DIAGRAM SHOWING FORK AND JOIN

TIP ▫ ▫ ▫ ▫ | A fork does not have to indicate strictly simultaneous activity. The actions in the branches for a fork might only be concurrent or interleaved.

USING COMPONENT AND DEPLOYMENT DIAGRAMS

Component and deployment diagrams model the physical aspects of systems. You use a **component diagram** when you want to emphasize the files, database tables, documents, and other components that a system's software uses. You use a **deployment diagram** when you want to focus on a system's hardware. You can use a variety of icons in each type of diagram, but each icon must convey meaning to the reader. Figures 10-20 and 10-21 show component and deployment diagrams that illustrate aspects of a library system. Figure 10-20 contains icons that symbolize paper and Internet requests for library items, the library database, and two tables that constitute the database. Figure 10-21 shows some commonly used icons that represent hardware components.

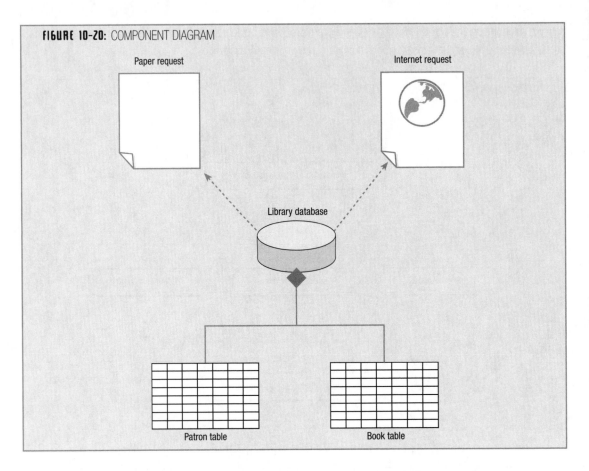

FIGURE 10-20: COMPONENT DIAGRAM

Paper request

Internet request

Library database

Patron table

Book table

TIP ▫ ▫ ▫ ▫

In Figure 10-20, notice the filled diamond connecting the two tables to the database. Just as it does in a class diagram, the diamond aggregation symbol shows the whole-part relationship of the tables to the database. You use an open diamond when a part might belong to several wholes (Door and Wall objects belong to many House objects), but you use a filled diamond when a part can belong to only one whole at a time (the Patron table can belong only to the Library database). You can use most UML symbols in multiple types of diagrams.

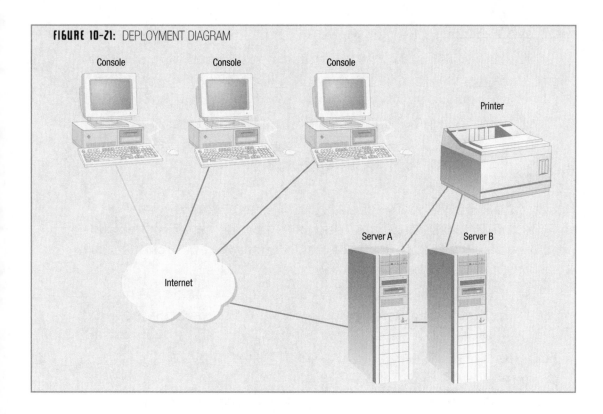

FIGURE 10-21: DEPLOYMENT DIAGRAM

DECIDING WHICH UML DIAGRAMS TO USE

Each of the nine UML diagram types provides a different view of a system. Just as a portrait artist, psychologist, and neurosurgeon each prefer a different conceptual view of your head, the users, managers, designers, and technicians of computer and business systems each prefer specific system views. Very few systems require diagrams of all nine types; you can illustrate the objects and activities of many systems by using a single diagram, or perhaps one that is a hybrid of two or more basic types. No view is superior to the others; you can achieve the most complete picture of any system by using several views. The most important reason you use any UML diagram is to communicate clearly and efficiently with the people for whom you are designing a system.

CHAPTER SUMMARY

☐ System design is the detailed specification of how all the parts of a system will be implemented and coordinated. Good designs make systems easier to understand. The Unified Modeling Language (UML) provides a means for programmers and businesspeople to communicate about system design.

☐ The UML is a standard way to specify, construct, and document systems that use object-oriented methods. The UML has its own notation, with which you can construct software diagrams that model different kinds of systems. The UML provides nine diagram types that you use at the beginning of the design process.

☐ A use case diagram shows how a business works from the perspective of those who approach it from the outside, or those who actually use the business. The diagram often includes actors, represented by stick figures, and use cases, represented by ovals. Use cases can include variations such as extend relationships, include relationships, and generalizations.

☐ You use a class diagram to illustrate the names, attributes, and methods of a class or set of classes. A class diagram of a single class contains a rectangle divided into three sections: the name of the class, the names of the attributes, and the names of the methods. Class diagrams can show generalizations and the relationships between objects. Object diagrams are similar to class diagrams, but they model specific instances of classes at one point in time.

☐ You use a sequence diagram to show the timing of events in a single use case. The horizontal axis (x-axis) of a sequence diagram represents objects, and the vertical axis (y-axis) represents time. A collaboration diagram emphasizes the organization of objects that participate in a system. It is similar to a sequence diagram, except that it contains sequence numbers to represent the precise order in which activities occur.

☐ A statechart diagram shows the different statuses of a class or object at different points in time.

☐ In an activity diagram, you show the flow of actions of a system, including branches that occur when decisions affect the outcome. UML activity diagrams use forks and joins to show simultaneous activities.

☐ You use a component diagram when you want to emphasize the files, database tables, documents, and other components that a system's software uses. You use a deployment diagram when you want to focus on a system's hardware.

☐ Each of the nine UML diagram types provides a different view of a system. Very few systems require diagrams of all nine types; the most important reason to use any UML diagram is to communicate clearly and efficiently with the people for whom you are designing a system.

KEY TERMS

System design is the detailed specification of how all the parts of a system will be implemented and coordinated.

Reverse engineering is the process of creating a model of an existing system.

The **UML** is a standard way to specify, construct, and document systems that use object-oriented methods. UML is an acronym for Unified Modeling Language.

The **use case diagram** is a UML diagram that shows how a business works from the perspective of those who approach it from the outside, or those who actually use the business.

An **extend** is a use case variation that shows functions beyond those found in a base case.

Each variation in the sequence of actions required in a use case is a **scenario**.

A feature that adds to the UML vocabulary of shapes to make them more meaningful for the reader is called a **stereotype**.

An **include** relationship is a use case variation that you use when a case can be part of multiple use cases in a UML diagram.

You use a **generalization** in a UML diagram when a use case is less specific than others, and you want to be able to substitute the more specific case for a general one.

When system developers omit parts of UML diagrams, for clarity, they refer to the missing parts as **elided**.

An **association relationship** describes the connection or link between objects in a UML diagram.

Cardinality and **multiplicity** refer to the arithmetic relationships between objects.

A **whole-part relationship** describes an association in which one or more classes make up the parts of a larger whole class. This type of relationship is also called an **aggregation**. You also can call a whole-part relationship a **has-a relationship** because the phrase describes the association between the whole and one of its parts.

Object diagrams are UML diagrams that are similar to class diagrams, but they model specific instances of classes.

A **sequence diagram** is a UML diagram that shows the timing of events in a single use case.

A **collaboration diagram** is a UML diagram that emphasizes the organization of objects that participate in a system.

A **statechart diagram** is a UML diagram that shows the different statuses of or changes of behavior in a class or object at different points in time.

An **activity diagram** is a UML diagram that shows the flow of actions of a system, including branches that occur when decisions affect the outcome.

A **component diagram** is a UML diagram that emphasizes the files, database tables, documents, and other components that a system's software uses.

A **deployment diagram** is a UML diagram that focuses on a system's hardware.

REVIEW QUESTIONS

1. **The detailed specification of how all the parts of a system will be implemented and coordinated is called _____.**
    a. programming
    b. paraphrasing
    c. system design
    d. structuring

2. **The primary purpose of good modeling techniques is to _____.**

   a. promote communication
   b. increase functional cohesion
   c. reduce the need for structure
   d. reduce dependency between modules

3. **The Unified Modeling Language provides standard ways to do all of the following to business systems except to _____ them.**

   a. construct
   b. document
   c. describe
   d. destroy

4. **The UML is commonly used to model _____.**

   a. business activities
   b. organizational processes
   c. software systems
   d. all of the above

5. **The UML was intentionally designed to be _____.**

   a. low-level and detail-oriented
   b. used with Visual Basic
   c. nontechnical
   d. inexpensive

6. **The UML diagrams that show how a business works from the perspective of those who actually use the business, such as employees or customers, are _____ diagrams.**

   a. collaboration
   b. use case
   c. statechart
   d. class

7. **Which of the following is an example of a relationship that would be portrayed as an extend relationship in a use case diagram for a hospital?**

   a. the relationship between the head nurse and the floor nurses
   b. admitting a patient who has never been admitted before
   c. serving a meal
   d. scheduling the monitoring of patients' vital signs

8. **The people shown in use case diagrams are called _____.**

   a. workers
   b. clowns
   c. actors
   d. relatives

9. One aspect of use case diagrams that makes them difficult to learn about is that _____.

    a. they require programming experience to understand
    b. they use a technical vocabulary
    c. there is no single right answer for any case
    d. all of the above

10. The arithmetic association relationship between a college student and college courses would be expressed as _____.

    a. 1   0
    b. 1   1
    c. 1   0..*
    d. 0..* 0..*

11. In the UML, object diagrams are most similar to _____ diagrams.

    a. use case
    b. activity
    c. class
    d. sequence

12. In any given situation, the primary reason you make a decision to use one type of UML diagram over another is that the one you choose is _____.

    a. shorter
    b. clearer
    c. more detailed
    d. closest to the programming language you will use to implement the system

13. A whole-part relationship can be described as a(n) _____ relationship.

    a. parent-child
    b. is-a
    c. has-a
    d. creates-a

14. The timing of events is best portrayed in a(n) _____ diagram.

    a. sequence
    b. use case
    c. collaboration
    d. association

15. A collaboration diagram is closest to a(n) _____ diagram.

    a. activity
    b. use case
    c. deployment
    d. sequence

16. A(n) _____ diagram shows the different statuses of a class or object at different points in time.

    a. activity

    b. statechart

    c. sequence

    d. deployment

17. The UML diagram that most closely resembles a conventional flowchart is a(n) _____ diagram.

    a. activity

    b. statechart

    c. sequence

    d. deployment

18. You use a _____ diagram when you want to emphasize the files, database tables, documents, and other components that a system's software uses.

    a. statechart

    b. component

    c. deployment

    d. use case

19. The UML diagram that focuses on a system's hardware is a(n) _____ diagram.

    a. deployment

    b. sequence

    c. activity

    d. use case

20. When using UML to describe a single system, most designers would use _____.

    a. a single type of diagram

    b. at least three types of diagrams

    c. most of the available types of diagrams

    d. all nine types of diagrams

EXERCISES

1. **Complete the following tasks:**

    a. Develop a use case diagram for a convenience food store. Include an actor representing the store manager and use cases for `orderItem()`, `stockItem()`, and `sellItem()`.

    b. Add more use cases to the diagram you created in Exercise 1a. Include two generalizations for `stockItem()`: `stockPerishable()` and `stockNonPerishable()`. Also include an extension to `sellItem()` to `checkCredit()` when a customer purchases items using a credit card.

    c. Add a customer actor to the use case diagram you created in Exercise 1b. Show that the customer participates in `sellItem()` but not in `orderItem()` or `stockItem()`.

2. Develop a use case diagram for a department store credit card system. Include at least two actors and four use cases.

3. Develop a use case diagram for a college registration system. Include at least three actors and five use cases.

4. Develop a class diagram for a `Shape` class. Include generalizations for child classes `Rectangle`, `Circle`, and `Triangle`.

5. Develop a class diagram for a `BankLoan` class. Include generalizations for child classes `Mortgage`, `CarLoan`, and `EducationLoan`.

6. Develop a class diagram for a college registration system. Include at least three classes that cooperate to achieve student registration.

7. Develop a sequence diagram that shows how a clerk at a mail-order company places a customer `Order`. The `Order` accesses `Inventory` to check availability. Then the `Order` accesses `Invoice` to produce a customer invoice that returns to the clerk.

8. Develop a statechart diagram that shows the states of a `CollegeStudent` from `PotentialApplicant` to `Graduate`.

9. Develop a statechart diagram that shows the states of a `Book` from `Concept` to `Publication`.

10. Develop an activity diagram that illustrates how to build a house.

11. Develop an activity diagram that illustrates how to prepare dinner.

12. Develop the UML diagram of your choice that illustrates some aspect of your life.

13. Complete the following tasks:

    a. Develop the UML diagram of your choice that best illustrates some aspect of a place you have worked.

    b. Develop a different UML diagram type that illustrates the same functions as the diagram you created in Exercise 13a.

CASE PROJECT

In earlier chapters you developed classes needed for Cost Is No Object—a car rental service that specializes in lending antique and luxury cars to clients on a short-term basis. You created pseudocode for `Employee`, `Customer`, `Automobile`, and `RentalAgreement` classes including attributes and methods to get and set those attributes. Now, you can create the following:

- Develop a use case diagram that includes an actor representing a rental agent and use cases for `addVehicleToFleet()`, `acceptCustomerInfo()`, and `createRentalAgreement()`. Include two generalizations for `createRentalAgreement()`: `rentAntiqueCar()`, and `rentLuxuryCar()`. Also include an extension to `acceptCustomerInfo()` to `checkCredit()` when a customer rents a vehicle using a credit card. Add a customer actor to the use case diagram, showing that the customer participates in `acceptCustomerInfo()` and `createRentalAgreement()`, but not in `addVehicleToFleet()`.

- Develop a sequence diagram that shows how a rental agent completes a rental agreement. The clerk accepts customer information, performs a credit check, accepts information regarding this rental (type of vehicle desired, start and stop dates of rental), checks vehicle availability, and so on.

- Develop a statechart diagram that shows the states of an `Automobile` from potential purchase to fleet member, to rented vehicle, through sold or destroyed vehicle.

OBJECT CONCEPTS: POLYMORPHISM AND INHERITANCE

After studying Chapter 11, you should be able to:

- ☐ Understand blocks and scope
- ☐ Overload methods and constructors without ambiguity
- ☐ Learn about the `this` reference
- ☐ Use inheritance to extend classes
- ☐ Override superclass methods
- ☐ Understand how to use superclass constructors
- ☐ Learn about information hiding
- ☐ Understand how inheritance promotes good software design

UNDERSTANDING BLOCKS AND SCOPE

Within any class or method, a set of statements that act as a unit constitute a **block**. For example, all the statements between the method header and the method's return statement are a block. Similarly, in a single-alternative `if` statement, all the code between the `if` and the `endif` is a block, and a dual-alternative `if` contains two blocks: the first runs from the `if` to the `else`, and the second runs from the `else` to the `endif`. Additionally, all the statements from a `while` to its `endwhile` create a block.

> **TIP** □ □ □ □   In Java, C++, and C#, blocks are always contained between pairs of curly braces. In these languages you can create blocks anywhere you want by enclosing the desired statements between braces.

For example, the method shown in Figure 11-1 contains two blocks. The first block contains another, so it is an **outside block**. It begins immediately after the method declaration and ends at the end of the method. The second block, or **inside block** (which is highlighted), contains two executable statements: the declaration of `anotherNumber` and a `print` statement. The inside block is **nested**, or contained entirely within, the outside block. A block can exist entirely within another block, or entirely outside and separate from another block, but blocks can never overlap. For example, you already know that when a method contains an `if` statement that starts an inner block, the `endif` must occur before the return from the method. As another example, when two `if` statements occur before any `endif`, the first `endif` encountered completes the second `if` statement, making the inner `if` block fall entirely within the outer `if` block. Another way to state this concept is that whenever you encounter the end of any block, it always is the end of the most recently started block.

FIGURE 11-1: A METHOD WITH NESTED BLOCKS

```
public static void methodWithNestedBlocks()
      numeric aNumber = 10
      print "In outer block, aNumber is ", aNumber
      if aNumber > 0 then
            numeric anotherNumber = 512
            print "In inner block, aNumber is ", aNumber,
                  " and another number is ", anotherNumber
      endif
      print "In outer block, aNumber is ", aNumber
return
```

When you declare a variable within a method, the variable is local to that method and cannot be accessed outside that method. Similarly, when you declare a variable within a block, you cannot refer to that variable outside the block. The portion of a program within which you can refer to a variable is the variable's **scope**. A variable comes into existence, or **comes into scope**, when you declare it. A variable ceases to exist, or **goes out of scope**, at the end of the block in which it is declared.

> **TIP** □ □ □ □   Although you can create as many variables and blocks as you need within any program, it is not wise to do so without a reason. The use of unnecessary variables and blocks increases the likelihood of improper use of variable names and scope.

TIP ☐ ☐ ☐ ☐ | In some older programming languages, notably C, you were required to declare all variables in a method prior to any executable statements. Although most newer languages do not require this, many programmers still prefer to follow this convention. Only declare variables later in a method if you have a good reason to do so.

In the `methodWithNestedBlocks()` method shown in Figure 11-1, the variable `aNumber` exists from the point of its declaration until the end of the method. This means `aNumber` exists both in the outer block and in the inner block, and can be used anywhere in the method. The variable `anotherNumber` comes into existence within the inner block; `anotherNumber` ceases to exist when the inner block ends, and cannot be used beyond its block. Figure 11-2 shows the output when the method in Figure 11-1 is called from another method.

FIGURE 11-2: OUTPUT PRODUCED BY APPLICATION THAT USES `methodWithNestedBlocks()`

```
In outer block, aNumber is 10
In inner block, aNumber is 10 and another number is 512
In outer block, aNumber is 10
```

Figure 11-3 shows a method containing some invalid statements. The first assignment `aNumber = 75` is invalid because `aNumber` has not been declared yet. Similarly, Invalid statement 2, `anotherNumber = 489`, is invalid because `anotherNumber` has not been declared yet, and Invalid statement 3 is invalid because `anotherNumber` still has not been declared. After you declare `anotherNumber`, you can use it for the remainder of the block, but Invalid statement 4 is outside the block in which `anotherNumber` was declared, and by the time Invalid statement 4 executes, it has gone out of scope. The last statement in Figure 11-3, `aNumber = 29`, does not work because it falls outside the block in which `aNumber` was declared; it actually falls outside the entire `methodWithInvalidStatements()` method.

Within a method, you can declare a variable with the same name multiple times, as long as each declaration is in its own, nonoverlapping block. For example, the two highlighted declarations of variables named `someVar` in Figure 11-4 are valid because each variable is contained within its own block. The first instance of `someVar` has gone out of scope before the second instance comes into scope. Figure 11-5 shows the output created—the first output statement displays `someVar` as 7 because that is the definition of `someVar` within the `if` block, but the next four print operations that execute in the loop use the value of `someVar` that is local to that block.

FIGURE 11-3: THE `methodWithInvalidStatements()` METHOD

```
public static void methodWithInvalidStatements()
    aNumber = 75                              ◄──────  Invalid statement  1
    numeric aNumber = 22
    aNumber = 6
    anotherNumber = 489                       ◄──────  Invalid statement  2
    if aNumber > 0 then
        anotherNumber = 165                   ◄──────  Invalid statement  3
        numeric anotherNumber = 99
        anotherNumber = 2
        aNumber = 50
    endif
    anotherNumber = 34                        ◄──────  Invalid statement  4
return
aNumber = 29                                  ◄──────  Invalid statement  5
```

FIGURE 11-4: THE `twoDeclarations()` METHOD

```
public static void twoDeclarations()
    numeric  x = 0
    if x < 10 then
        numeric someVar = 7
        print someVar
    endif
    while  x < 4
        numeric someVar = 845
        print someVar
        x  =  x + 1
    endwhile
return
```

FIGURE 11-5: OUTPUT OF THE `twoDeclarations()` METHOD

```
7
845
845
845
845
```

You cannot declare the same variable name more than once within a block, even if a block contains other blocks. When you declare a variable more than once in a block, you are attempting to **redeclare the variable**—an illegal action. For example, in Figure 11-6, the second declaration of `aValue` causes an error because you cannot declare the same variable twice within the outer block of the method. By the same reasoning, the third declaration of `aValue` is also invalid, even though it appears within a new block. The block that contains the third declaration is entirely within the outside block, so the first declaration of `aValue` has not gone out of scope.

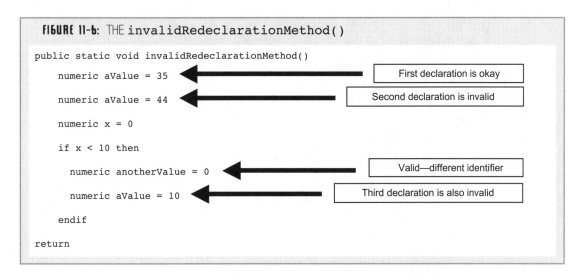

FIGURE 11-6: THE `invalidRedeclarationMethod()`

```
public static void invalidRedeclarationMethod()
    numeric aValue = 35          ◄─────────────    First declaration is okay
    numeric aValue = 44          ◄─────────────    Second declaration is invalid
    numeric x = 0
    if x < 10 then
       numeric anotherValue = 0  ◄─────────────    Valid—different identifier
       numeric aValue = 10       ◄─────────────    Third declaration is also invalid
    endif
return
```

You can declare a variable within one method of a class, and use the same variable name within another method of the class. In this case, the variable used inside the method resides in its own location in computer memory, and when you use its name within the method in which it is declared, it takes precedence over, or **overrides**, the first variable. In other words, a locally declared variable always masks or hides another variable with the same name elsewhere in the class. For example, consider the class in Figure 11-7. In the `main()` method of the `OverridingVariable` class, `aNumber` is declared and assigned the value 10. When the application calls `firstMethod()`, a new variable is declared with the same name, but a different memory address and a new value. The new variable exists only within `firstMethod()` where it is displayed holding the value 77. After `firstMethod()` executes and the logic returns to the `main()` method, the original `aNumber` is displayed, containing 10. When `aNumber` is passed to `secondMethod()`, a copy is made within the method. This copy has the same identifier as the original `aNumber`, but a different memory address. So, within `secondMethod()`, when the value is changed to 862 and displayed, it has no effect on the original variable in `main()`. When the logic returns to `main()` after `secondMethod()`, the original value is displayed again. Examine the output in Figure 11-8 to understand the sequence of events.

FIGURE 11-7: THE `OverridingVariable` CLASS

```
public class OverridingVariable
    public static void main()
        numeric aNumber = 10
        print "In main(), aNumber is ", aNumber
        firstMethod()
        print "Back in main(), aNumber is ", aNumber
        secondMethod(aNumber)
        print "Back in main() again, aNumber is ", aNumber
    return
    public static void firstMethod()
        numeric aNumber = 77
        print "In firstMethod(), aNumber is ", aNumber
    return
    public static void secondMethod(numeric aNumber)
        aNumber = 862
        print "In secondMethod(), aNumber is ", aNumber
    return
endClass
```

FIGURE 11-8: OUTPUT OF THE `OverridingVariable` APPLICATION

```
In main(), aNumber is 10
In firstMethod(), aNumber is 77
Back in main(), aNumber is 10
In secondMethod(), aNumber is 862
Back in main() again, aNumber is 10
```

TIP ▫ ▫ ▫ ▫ | Object-oriented programmers also use the term "override" when a child class contains a field or method that has the same name as one in the parent class. You will learn more about inheritance later in this chapter.

TIP ▫ ▫ ▫ ▫ | You are familiar with local names overriding names defined elsewhere. If someone in your household is named "Eric," and someone in the house next door is named "Eric," members of your household who talk about "Eric" are referring to the local in-house version. They would add a qualifier such as "Eric Johnson" or "Eric next door" to refer to the nonlocal version.

When they have the same name, variables within methods of a class also override class instance variables. Figure 11-9 shows an `Employee` class that contains two instance variables and three `void` methods. The `setValues()` method provides values for the two class instance fields. Whenever the method named `methodThatUsesInstanceAttributes()` is used with an `Employee` object, the instance values for `empNum` and `empPayRate` are used. However, when the other method, `methodThatUsesLocalVariables()`, is used with an `Employee` object, the local variable values within the method, 33333 and 555.55, override the class's instance variables. Figure 11-10 shows a short application that declares an `Employee` object and uses each method; Figure 11-11 shows the output.

FIGURE 11-9: THE `Employee` CLASS

```
public class Employee
   private numeric empNum
   private numeric empPayRate
   public void setValues()
      empNum = 111
      empPayRate = 22.22
   return
   public void methodThatUsesInstanceAttributes()
      print "Employee number is ", empNum
      print "Pay rate is ", empPayRate
   return
   public void methodThatUsesLocalVariables()
      numeric empNum = 33333
      numeric empPayRate = 555.55
      print "Employee number is ", empNum
      print "Pay rate is ", empPayRate
   return
endClass
```

FIGURE 11-10: THE `TestEmployeeMethods` APPLICATION

```
public class TestEmployeeMethods
   public static void main()
      Employee aWorker
      aWorker.setValues()
      aWorker.methodThatUsesInstanceAttributes()
      aWorker.methodThatUsesLocalVariables()
   return
endClass
```

FIGURE 11-11: OUTPUT OF THE `TestEmployeeMethods` APPLICATION

```
Employee number is 111
Pay rate is 22.22
Employee number is 33333
Pay rate is 555.55
```

When you write programs, you might choose to avoid confusing situations that arise when you give the same name to a class instance field and a local method variable. But, if you do use the same name, be aware that within the method, the method's local variable overrides the instance variable.

TIP ▯ ▯ ▯ ▯ | Programmers frequently use the same name for a class instance field and an argument to a method simply because it is the "best name"; in these cases, the programmer must use the `this` reference, which you will learn about later in this chapter.

It is important to understand the impact that blocks and methods have on your variables. Variables and fields with the same names represent different memory locations when they are declared within different scopes. After you understand the scope of variables, you can more easily locate the source of many errors within your programs.

OVERLOADING A METHOD

Overloading involves using one term to indicate diverse meanings, or writing multiple methods with the same name, but with different arguments. Overloading methods is an object-oriented programming (OOP) technique that did not exist in earlier languages. When you use the English language, you overload words all the time. When you say "open the door," "open your eyes," and "open a computer file," you are talking about three very different actions using very different methods, and producing very different results. However, anyone who speaks English fluently has no trouble understanding your meaning because the verb *open* is understood in the context of the noun that follows it.

When you overload a method, you write multiple methods with a shared name. The compiler understands your meaning based on the arguments you use with the method. For example, suppose you create a class method to apply a simple interest rate to a bank balance. The method is named `calculateInterest()`; it receives two numeric arguments—the balance and the interest rate—and displays the multiplied result. Figure 11-12 shows the method.

FIGURE 11-12: THE `calculateInterest()` METHOD WITH TWO `double` ARGUMENTS

```
public void calculateInterest(numeric bal, numeric rate)
    numeric interest
    interest = bal * rate
    print "Simple interest on $", bal, " at ", rate,
        "% rate is ", interest
return
```

When an application calls the `calculateInterest()` method and passes two numeric values, as in `calculateInterest(1000.00, 0.04)`, the interest is calculated correctly as 4 percent of $1,000.00. Assume, however, that different users want to calculate interest using different argument types. Some users who want to indicate an interest rate of 4 percent might using one of several string constants—perhaps "low", representing 2 percent, "medium", representing 4 percent, or "high", representing 6 percent. In this case, you can overload the `calculateInterest()` method so there are two versions—one that accepts two numbers and another that accepts a number and a string. For example, in addition to the `calculateInterest()` method shown in Figure 11-12, you could add the method shown in Figure 11-13.

If an application calls the method `calculateInterest()` using two numeric arguments—for example, `calculateInterest(1000.00, 0.04)`—the first version of the method, the one shown in Figure 11-12, executes. However, if a string is used as the second parameter in a call to `calculateInterest()`—as in `calculateInterest(1000.00, "medium")`—the second version of the method, the one shown in Figure 11-13, executes. In this second example, the string is used to determine the rate for calculating the interest earned.

 As you learned in Chapter 3, the arguments to methods must appear in the correct order. For example, if you attempted to pass a string followed by a number to the calculateInterest() method in Figure 11-13, the method call would fail. Of course, you could create a third overloaded version of the method that accepted the data types you wanted.

> **FIGURE 11-13:** THE `calculateInterest()` METHOD WITH A `numeric` ARGUMENT AND A STRING
>   ARGUMENT
>
> ```
> public void calculateInterest(numeric bal, string rate)
>    numeric interest, rateAsPercent
>    if rate = "low" then
>       rateAsPercent = .02
>    else
>       if rate = "medium" then
>          rateAsPercent = .04
>       else
>          rateAsPercent = .06
>       endif
>    endif
>    interest = bal * rateAsPercent
>    print "Simple interest on $", bal, " at ", rate,
>          "% rate is ", interest
> return
> ```

Of course, you could use methods with different names to solve the dilemma of producing an accurate interest figure—for example, `calculateInterestUsingNumbers()` and `calculateInterestUsingAString()`. However, it is easier and more convenient for programmers who use your methods to remember just one method name that they can use in the form that is most appropriate for their programs. It is a convenience to be able to use one reasonable name for tasks that are functionally identical except for argument types.

LEARNING ABOUT AMBIGUITY

When an application contains just one version of a method, you can call the method using a parameter of the correct data type. When you properly overload a method, you can call it providing different argument lists, and the appropriate version of the method executes. Sometimes, when you overload methods, you risk creating an **ambiguous** situation—one in which the compiler cannot determine which method to use. Consider the following overloaded `calculateInterest()` method declarations:

```
public void calculateInterest(numeric bal, numeric rate)
public void calculateInterest(numeric rate, numeric bal)
```

A programmer who inserts these methods into an application seems to be attempting to allow a client to use the method in two ways—by passing the balance first and by passing the rate first. However, the compiler does not attempt to make sense of parameter name; only the data types matter. If an application called the `calculateInterest()` method with two numeric arguments, the compiler would not be able to distinguish between the methods above.

Note that you can overload methods correctly by providing different argument lists for methods with the same name. Methods with identical names that have identical argument lists, but different return types, are not overloaded—they are illegal. For example, methods with the following headers cannot coexist within a program:

```
public numeric aMethod(numeric x)
public void aMethod(numeric x)
```

The compiler determines which of several versions of a method to call based on argument lists. If those two methods could exist within a class, when the method call **aMethod(17)** was made, the compiler would not know which method to execute because both methods take a numeric argument.

TIP ☐ ☐ ☐ ☐ | An overloaded method is not ambiguous on its own—it only becomes ambiguous if you create an ambiguous situation. A program containing a potentially ambiguous situation will run problem-free if you do not make any ambiguous method calls.

TIP ☐ ☐ ☐ ☐ | The compiler determines which version of a method to call by the method's signature. A method's **signature** is the combination of the method name and the number, types, and order of arguments.

OVERLOADING CONSTRUCTORS

In Chapter 3, you learned that OOP languages automatically provide a constructor method when you create a class. You also learned that you can write your own constructor method, and that you often do so when you want to ensure that fields within classes are initialized to some appropriate default value. In Chapter 3, you learned about automatically written default constructors that do not require arguments. However, when you write your own constructor methods, the constructors you write can receive arguments. Such arguments are often used for initialization purposes when the values that you want to assign to objects upon creation might vary.

For example, consider the **Employee** class with just one data field shown in Figure 11-14. Its constructor method assigns 999 to the **empNum** of each potentially instantiated **Employee** object. Any time an **Employee** object is created using a statement such as **Employee partTimeWorker**, even if no other data-assigning methods are ever used, you ensure that the **partTimeWorker Employee**, like all **Employee** objects, will have an initial **empNum** of 999.

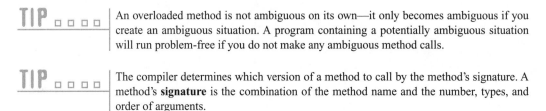

FIGURE 11-14: THE **Employee** CLASS WITH CONSTRUCTOR THAT INITIALIZES **empNum** FIELD

```
public class Employee
    private numeric empNum
    Employee()
       empNum = 999
    return
endClass
```

TIP ☐ ☐ ☐ ☐ | You can use a **setEmpNum()** method to assign values to individual **Employee** objects after construction, but a constructor method assigns the values at the time of creation.

Alternatively, you might choose to create **Employee** objects with initial **empNum** values that differ for each **Employee**. To accomplish this when the object is instantiated, you can pass an employee number to the constructor. Figure 11-15 shows an **Employee** class containing a constructor that receives an argument. With this constructor, an argument is passed using a statement, such as **Employee partTimeWorker(881)**. When the constructor executes, the number that is a parameter within the method call is passed to `Employee()` where argument `num` assumes the value. Then `num` is assigned to the `empNum` within the constructor method.

FIGURE 11-15: THE `Employee` CLASS WITH CONSTRUCTOR THAT ACCEPTS A VALUE

```
public class Employee
     private numeric empNum
     Employee(numeric num)
          empNum = num
     return
```

When you create an `Employee` class with a constructor such as the one shown in Figure 11-15, every `Employee` object you create must have an integer argument. In other words, with this new version of the class, the statement `Employee partTimeWorker` no longer works. After you write a constructor for a class, you no longer receive the automatically written default constructor. If a class's only constructor requires an argument, you must provide an argument for every object of the class that you create.

Fortunately, as with any other method, you can overload constructors. Overloading constructors provides you with a way to create objects with or without initial arguments, as needed. For example, in addition to using the provided constructor method shown in Figure 11-15, you can create a second constructor method for the `Employee` class; Figure 11-16 shows an `Employee` class containing two constructors. When you use this class to create an `Employee` object, you have the option of creating the object either with or without an initial `empNum` value. When you create an `Employee` object with the statement `Employee aWorker`, the constructor with no arguments is called, and the `Employee` object receives an initial `empNum` value of 999. When you create an `Employee` object with `Employee anotherWorker(7677)`, the constructor version that requires a numeric parameter is used, and the `anotherWorker Employee` receives an initial `empNum` of 7677.

FIGURE 11-16: THE `Employee` CLASS CONTAINING TWO CONSTRUCTORS

```
public class Employee
   private numeric empNum
   Employee(numeric num)
      empNum = num
   return
   Employee()
      empNum = 999
   return
endClass
```

TIP ▢ ▢ ▢ ▢   You can use constructor arguments to initialize field values, but you can also use arguments for any other purpose. For example, you could use the presence or absence of an argument simply to determine which of two possible constructors to call, yet not make use of the argument within the constructor method. As long as the constructor argument lists differ, there is no ambiguity in which constructor method to call.

LEARNING ABOUT THE this REFERENCE

When you start creating classes, the classes can become large very quickly. Besides data fields, each class can have many methods, including several overloaded versions. On paper, a single class might require several pages of coded statements.

When you instantiate an object from a class, memory is reserved for each instance field in the class. For example, if a class contains 20 data fields, then when you create one object from that class, enough memory is reserved to hold the 20 values for that object. When you create 200 objects of the same class, the computer reserves enough memory for 4,000 data fields—20 for each of the 200 objects. In many applications, the computer memory requirements can become substantial. Fortunately, it is not necessary to store a separate copy of each variable and method for each instantiation of a class.

Usually, you want each instantiation of a class to have its own data fields. If an `Employee` class contains fields for employee number, name, and salary, every individual `Employee` object needs a unique number, name, and salary value. (When you want each object to have a unique field value, you do not define the field as `static`.) However, when you create a method for a class, any object can use the same method. Whether the method performs a calculation, sets a field value, or constructs an object, the instructions are the same for each instantiated object. Not only would it take an enormous amount of memory to store a separate copy of a method for every class object, but memory would also be wasted because you would be storing methods with the same contents for each object. Luckily, in OOP languages, just one copy of each method in a class is stored, and all instantiated objects can use that copy.

When you use a nonstatic method, you use the object name, a dot, and the method name—for example, `aWorker.getEmpNum()`. When you execute the `aWorker.getEmpNum()` method, you are running the general, shared `Employee` class `getEmpNum()` method; `aWorker` has access to the method because `aWorker` is a member of the `Employee` class. However, within the `getEmpNum()` method, when you access the `empNum` *field*, you access `aWorker`'s private, individual copy of the `empNum` field. Because many `Employee` objects might exist, but just one copy of the method exists no matter how many `Employee`s there are, when you call `aWorker.getEmpNum()`, the compiler must determine *whose* copy of the `empNum` value should be returned by the single `getEmpNum()` method.

The compiler accesses the correct object's field because you implicitly pass a reference to `aWorker` to the `getEmpNum()` method. A **reference** is a variable that can hold an object's memory address. The reference passed to an object's instance method is implicit because it is automatically understood without actually being written. The reference to an object that is automatically passed to any object's nonstatic instance method is called the **this reference**. For example, the two `getEmpNum()` methods shown in Figure 11-17 perform identically. The first method simply uses the `this` reference without you being aware of it; the second method uses the `this` reference explicitly.

TIP □ □ □ □ | C++ programmers call the `this` reference a **this pointer**. A pointer is a variable that holds a memory address. C++ programmers also use a pointer symbol constructed from a hyphen and a greater-than sign, as in `this->empNum`.

FIGURE 11-17: TWO VERSIONS OF THE `GetEmpnum()` METHOD, WITH AND WITHOUT AN EXPLICIT `this` REFERENCE

```
public numeric getEmpNum()
return empNum

public numeric getEmpNum()
return this.empNum
```

Usually, you neither want nor need to refer to the `this` reference within the methods you write, but the `this` reference is always there, working behind the scenes, so that the data field for the correct object can be accessed.

TIP □ □ □ □ | Recall that methods associated with individual objects are instance methods. Only instance methods implicitly receive a `this` reference.

On a few occasions, you must use the `this` reference to make your classes work correctly; one example is shown in the `Student` class in Figure 11-18. Within the constructor for this class, the parameter names `stuNum` and `gpa` are identical to the class field names. Within the constructor, `stuNum` and `gpa` refer to the locally declared names—the ones in the method header—not the class field names. The statement `stuNum = stuNum` accomplishes nothing—it assigns the local variable value to itself, and the class attribute is never assigned a value. (In most object-oriented languages, the value of the class `stuNum` field would be 0.)

FIGURE 11-18: A `Student` CLASS WHOSE CONSTRUCTOR DOES NOT WORK AS EXPECTED

```
public class Student
   private numeric stuNum
   private numeric gpa
   public Student(numeric stuNum, numeric gpa)
      stuNum = stuNum
      gpa = gpa
   return
   public void showStudent()
      print "Student #", stuNum, " gpa is ", gpa
   return
endClass
```

Figure 11-19 shows a modified `Student` class. The only difference between this class and the one in Figure 11-18 is the explicit use of the `this` reference within the constructor. When the `this` reference is used with a field name in a class method, the reference is to the class field instead of to the local variable declared within the method. When you instantiate a `Student` object with a statement such as `Student onePupil(1234, 3.2)`, the `onePupil` object will possess the correct values as assigned.

FIGURE 11-19: THE `Student` CLASS USING THE EXPLICIT `this` REFERENCE WITHIN THE CONSTRUCTOR

```
public class Student
   private numeric stuNum
   private numeric gpa
   public Student(numeric stuNum, numeric gpa)
      this.stuNum = stuNum
      this.gpa = gpa
   return
   public void showStudent()
      print "Student #", stuNum, " gpa is ", gpa
   return
endClass
```

LEARNING ABOUT THE CONCEPT OF INHERITANCE

In object-oriented languages, **inheritance** is a mechanism that enables one class to inherit, or assume, both the behavior and the attributes of another class. Inheritance allows you to apply your knowledge of a general category to more specific objects. You are familiar with the concept of inheritance from all sorts of nonprogramming situations.

TIP ▫ ▫ ▫ ▫ | In Chapter 2, you first learned about inheritance, in which a class object can inherit all the attributes of an existing class. You can create a functional new class simply by indicating how it is different from the class from which it is derived.

When you use the term inheritance, you might think of genetic inheritance. You know from biology that your blood type and eye color are the product of inherited genes; you can say that many facts about you—your attributes or "data fields"—are inherited. Similarly, you often can credit your behavior to inheritance. For example, your attitude toward saving money might be the same as your grandma's, and the odd way that you pull on your ear when you are tired might match what your Uncle Steve does—thus, your methods are inherited, too.

You also might choose plants and animals based on inheritance. You plant impatiens next to your house because of your shady street location; you adopt a Doberman Pinscher because you need a watchdog. Every individual plant and pet has slightly different characteristics, but within a species, you can count on many consistent inherited attributes and behaviors. Similarly, the classes you create in OOP languages can inherit data and methods from existing classes. When you create a class by making it inherit from another class, you are provided with data fields and methods automatically.

From the first chapter of this book, you have been creating classes and instantiating objects that are members of those classes. For example, consider the simple `Employee` class shown in Figure 11-20. The class contains two data fields, `empNum` and `empSal`, and four methods, a `get` and `set` method for each field. Figure 11-21 shows a class diagram for the `Employee` class.

TIP ▫ ▫ ▫ ▫ | You first learned how to create and read class diagrams in Chapter 2.

FIGURE 11-20: THE **Employee** CLASS

```
public class Employee
   private numeric empNum
   private numeric empSal

   public numeric getEmpNum()
   return empNum

   public numeric getEmpSal()
   return empSal

   public void setEmpNum(numeric num)
     empNum = num
   return

   public void setEmpSal(numeric sal)
      empSal = sal
   return
endClass
```

FIGURE 11-21: THE **Employee** CLASS DIAGRAM

```
Employee

-empNum: numeric

-empSal: numeric

+getEmpNum(): numeric

+getEmpSal(): numeric

+setEmpNum(numeric num): void

+setEmpSal(numeric sal): void
```

After you create the **Employee** class, you can create specific **Employee** objects, such as **Employee receptionist** and **Employee deliveryPerson**. These **Employee** objects can eventually possess different numbers and salaries, but because they are **Employee** objects, you know that each **Employee** has *some* number and salary.

Suppose you hire a new **Employee** named **serviceRep**. Suppose further that a **serviceRep** object requires an employee number and a salary, but a **serviceRep** object also requires a data field to indicate territory served. You can create a class with a name such as **EmployeeWithTerritory**, and provide the class three fields (`empNum`, `empSal`, and `empTerritory`) and six methods (`get` and `set` methods for each of the three fields). However, when you do this, you are duplicating much of the work that you have already done for the `Employee` class. The wise, efficient alternative is to create the class `EmployeeWithTerritory` so it inherits all the attributes and methods of `Employee`. Then, you can add just the one field and two methods that are additions within `EmployeeWithTerritory` objects. Figure 11-22 shows a class diagram of this relationship; the arrow that extends from the `EmployeeWithTerritory` class and points to the `Employee` class shows the inheritance relationship.

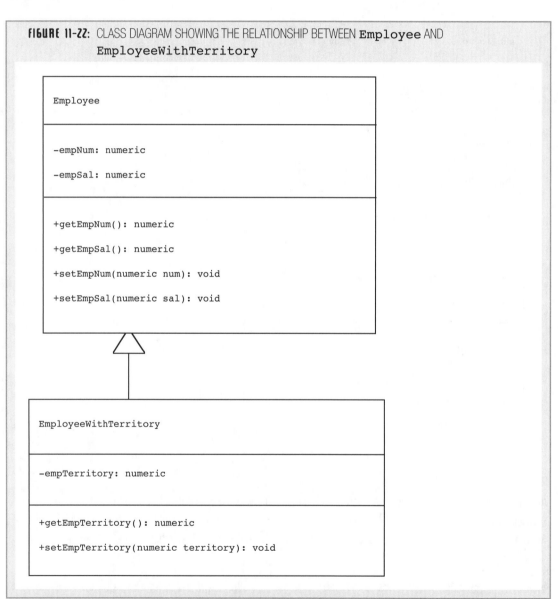

FIGURE 11-22: CLASS DIAGRAM SHOWING THE RELATIONSHIP BETWEEN **Employee** AND **EmployeeWithTerritory**

When you use inheritance to create the `EmployeeWithTerritory` class, you:

- Save time because the `Employee` fields and methods already exist

- Reduce errors because the `Employee` methods already have been used and tested

- Reduce the amount of new learning required to use the new class because you have used the `Employee` methods on simpler objects and already understand how they work

The ability to use inheritance in object-oriented programs makes programs easier to write, less error-prone, and more quickly understood. Imagine that besides creating `EmployeeWithTerritory`, you also want to create several other specific `Employee` classes (perhaps `EmployeeEarningCommission`, including a commission rate, or `DismissedEmployee`, including a reason for dismissal). By using inheritance, you can develop each new class correctly and more quickly.

TIP ▫ ▫ ▫ ▫ | The concept of inheritance is useful because it makes class code reusable. Each method already written and tested in the original class becomes part of the new class that inherits it.

A class that is used as a basis for inheritance, such as `Employee`, is a **base class**. When you create a class that inherits from a base class (such as `EmployeeWithTerritory`), it is a **derived class**. When confronted with two classes that inherit from each other, you can tell which class is the base class and which is the derived class by using the two classes in a sentence with the phrase "is a." A derived class always "is a" case or example of the more general base class. For example, a `Tree` class can be a base class to an `Evergreen` class. An `Evergreen` "is a" `Tree`, so `Tree` is the base class; however, it is not true for all `Tree`s that "a `Tree` is an `Evergreen`." Similarly, an `EmployeeWithTerritory` "is an" `Employee`—but not the other way around—so `Employee` is the base class.

You can use the terms **superclass** and **subclass** as synonyms for base class and derived class, respectively. Thus, `Evergreen` can be called a subclass of the `Tree` superclass. You can also use the terms **parent class** and **child class**. An `EmployeeWithTerritory` is a child to the `Employee` parent. Use the pair of terms with which you are most comfortable; all of these terms are used interchangeably throughout this book.

As an alternative way to discover which of two classes is the base class or subclass, you can try saying the two class names together. When people say their names together, they state the more specific name before the all-encompassing family name, as in "Ginny Kroening". Similarly, with classes, the order that "makes more sense" is the child-parent order. "Evergreen Tree" makes more sense than "Tree Evergreen", so `Evergreen` is the child class.

Finally, you usually can distinguish superclasses from their subclasses by size. Although it is not required, in general a subclass is larger than a superclass because it usually has additional fields and methods. A subclass description might look small, but any subclass contains all the fields and methods of its superclass, as well as the new, more specific fields and methods you add to that subclass.

TIP ▢ ▢ ▢ ▢ | Some OOP languages, such as C++, allow a subclass to inherit from more than one parent class. For example, you might create an InsuredItem class that contains data fields pertaining to each possession for which you have insurance and an Automobile class that contains data fields such as vehicle identification number, make, model, and year of an Automobile. When you create an InsuredAutomobile class for a car rental agency, you might want to include InsuredItem information and methods, as well as Automobile information and methods. The capability to inherit from more than one class is called **multiple inheritance**.

EXTENDING CLASSES

You achieve inheritance in different ways when writing code in different programming languages. For example, when you create a child class in Java, you use the keyword `extends` between the child class name and its parent's name. In C++ and C#, you place a single colon between the two names to achieve inheritance. In each language the meaning is the same—the new class derives from an existing class. In pseudocode, you can use any means you prefer to indicate inheritance; this book uses the phrase `derivesFrom`. For example, the class header `public class EmployeeWithTerritory derivesFrom Employee` creates a superclass-subclass relationship between `Employee` and `EmployeeWithTerritory`. Each `EmployeeWithTerritory` automatically receives the data fields and methods of the superclass `Employee`; you then add new fields and methods to the newly created subclass. Figure 11-23 shows an `EmployeeWithTerritory` class.

FIGURE 11-23: THE `EmployeeWithTerritory` CLASS

```
public class EmployeeWithTerritory derivesFrom Employee
   private numeric empTerritory

   public numeric getEmpTerritory()
   return empTerritory

   public void setEmpTerritory(numeric num)
       empTerritory = num
   return
endClass
```

When you write a statement that instantiates an object, such as `EmployeeWithTerritory northernRep`, you can use any of the following statements to get field values for the `northernRep` object:

- `northernRep.getEmpNum()`
- `northernRep.getEmpSal()`
- `northernRep.getEmpTerritory()`

The `northernRep` object has access to all three `get` methods—two methods that it inherits from `Employee,` and one method that belongs to `EmployeeWithTerritory`.

Similarly, any of the following statements are legal:

- `northernRep.setEmpNum(915)`
- `northernRep.setEmpSal(210.00)`
- `northernRep.setEmpTerritory(5)`

The `northernRep` object has access to all the `Employee` class `set` methods, as well as its own new `set` method.

Inheritance is a one-way proposition; a child inherits from a parent, not the other way around. When you instantiate an `Employee` object, as in `Employee aClerk`, the `Employee` object does not have access to the `EmployeeWithTerritory` methods. `Employee` is the parent class, and `aClerk` is an object of the parent class. It makes sense that a parent class object does not have access to its child's data and methods. When you create the parent class, you do not know how many future subclasses it might have, or what their data or methods might look like. In addition, subclasses are more specific. An `Orthodontist` class and `Periodontist` class are children of the `Dentist` parent class. You do not expect all members of the general parent class `Dentist` to have the `Orthodontist`'s `applyBraces()` method or the `Periodontist`'s `deepClean()` method. However, `Orthodontist` objects and `Periodontist` objects have access to the more general `Dentist` methods `takeXRays()` and `billPatients()`.

TIP ▫ ▫ ▫ ▫ Sometimes, a parent class is so general that you never intend to create any specific instances of the class. For example, you might never create an object that is "just" an `Employee`; each `Employee` is more specifically a `SalariedEmployee`, `HourlyEmployee`, or `ContractEmployee`. A class such as `Employee` that you create only to extend from, but not to instantiate objects from, is an abstract class. An **abstract class** is one from which you cannot create any concrete objects, but from which you can inherit.

OVERRIDING SUPERCLASS METHODS

When you create a subclass by extending an existing class, the new subclass contains data and methods that were defined in the original superclass. In other words, any child class object can use all the nonprivate members of its parent. Sometimes, however, those superclass data fields and methods are not entirely appropriate for the subclass objects; in those cases, you want to override the parent class methods.

When you use the English language, you often use the same method name to indicate diverse meanings. For example, if you think of `MusicalInstrument` as a class, you can think of `play()` as a method of that class. If you think of various subclasses such as `Guitar` and `Drum`, you know that you carry out the `play()` method quite differently for each subclass. Using the same method name to indicate different implementations is called **polymorphism**, a term that means "many forms"; many forms of action take place, even though you use the same word to describe the action. In other words, many forms of the same word exist, depending on the object associated with the word.

You first learned the term "polymorphism" in Chapter 2. Polymorphism is one of the basic principles of OOP. If a programming language does not support polymorphism, the language is not considered object-oriented.

For example, suppose you create an `Employee` superclass containing data fields, such as `firstName`, `lastName`, `socialSecurityNumber`, `dateOfHire`, `rateOfPay`, and so on, and the methods contained in the `Employee` class include the usual collection of `set` and `get` methods. If your standard time period for payment to each `Employee` object is weekly, your `printRateOfPay()` method might include a statement such as `print "Pay is ", rateOfPay, " per week"`.

Imagine your company has a few `Employee`s who are not paid weekly. Maybe some are paid by the hour, and others are `Employee`s whose work is contracted on a job-to-job basis. Because each `Employee` type requires different paycheck-calculating procedures, you might want to create subclasses of `Employee`, such as `HourlyEmployee` and `ContractEmployee`.

When you call the `printRateOfPay()` method for an `HourlyEmployee` object, you want the display to include the phrase "per hour", as in "Pay is $8.75 per hour". When you call the `printRateOfPay()` method for a `ContractEmployee`, you want to include "per contract", as in "Pay is $2,000 per contract". Each class—the `Employee` superclass and the two subclasses—requires its own `printRateOfPay()` method. Fortunately, if you create separate `printRateOfPay()` methods for each class, each class's objects use the appropriate method for that class. When you create a method in a child class that has the same name and argument list as a method in its parent class, you **override the method** in the parent class. When you use the method name with a child object, the child's version of the method is used.

It is important to note that each subclass method overrides any method in the parent class that has both the same name and argument list. If the parent class method has the same name but a different argument list, the subclass method does not override the parent class version; instead, the subclass method overloads the parent class method and any subclass object has access to both versions. You learned about overloading methods in Chapter 3.

You also saw the term "override" earlier in this chapter, when you learned that a variable declared within a block overrides another variable with the same name declared outside the block.

If you could not override superclass methods, you could always create unique names for each subclass method, such as `printRateOfPayForHourly()` and `printRateOfPayForContractual()`, but the classes you create are easier to write and understand if you use one reasonable name for methods that do essentially the same thing. Because you are attempting to print the rate of pay for each object, `printRateOfPay()` is an excellent method name for all the object types.

Object-oriented programmers use the term "polymorphism" when discussing any operation that has multiple meanings. For example, the plus sign (+) is polymorphic because you can use it to add numbers or to indicate a positive value. As another example, methods with the same name but different argument lists are polymorphic because the method call operates differently depending on the arguments. When developers refer to polymorphism, they most often mean **subtype polymorphism**—the ability of one method name to work appropriately for different subclass objects of the same parent class.

UNDERSTANDING HOW CONSTRUCTORS ARE CALLED DURING INHERITANCE

When you create any object, as in `SomeClass anObject`, you are calling a class constructor method that has the same name as the class itself. When you instantiate an object that is a member of a subclass, you are actually calling at least two constructors: the constructor for the base class and the constructor for the extended, derived class. When you create any subclass object, the superclass constructor must execute first, and *then* the subclass constructor executes.

When a superclass contains a default constructor, the execution of the superclass constructor when a subclass object is instantiated often is transparent. However, you should realize that when you create an object such as `HourlyEmployee clerk` (where `HourlyEmployee` is a subclass of `Employee`), *both* the `Employee()` and `HourlyEmployee()` constructors execute.

When you create a class and do not provide a constructor, object-oriented languages automatically supply you with a default constructor—one that never requires arguments. When you write your own constructor, you replace the automatically supplied version. Depending on your needs, a constructor you create for a class might require arguments. When you use a class as a superclass, and the class has only constructors that require arguments, you must be certain that any subclasses provide the superclass constructor with the arguments it needs.

TIP ▫ ▫ ▫ ▫ | Don't forget that a class can have many constructors. As soon as you create at least one constructor for a class, you no longer can use the automatically supplied version.

When a superclass has a default constructor, you can create a subclass with or without its own constructor. This is true whether the default constructor is the automatically supplied one or one you have written. However, when a superclass contains only constructors that require arguments, you must include at least one constructor for each subclass you create. Your subclass constructors can contain any number of statements, but it must call the superclass constructor. This is accomplished slightly differently in different programming languages, but the principle is the same—a parent constructor must be fully executed before the child class constructor can operate. When a superclass requires parameters upon instantiation, even if you have no other reason to create a subclass constructor, you must write the subclass constructor so it can call its superclass's constructor.

TIP ▫ ▫ ▫ ▫ | If a superclass has multiple constructors, but one is a default constructor, you do not have to create a subclass constructor unless you want to. If the subclass contains no constructor, all subclass objects use the superclass default constructor when they are instantiated.

LEARNING ABOUT INFORMATION HIDING

The `Student` class shown in Figure 11-24 is an example of a typical class. Within the `Student` class, as with most classes from which you create objects, the keyword `private` precedes each data field, and the keyword `public` precedes each method. As a matter of fact, the four `get` and `set` methods are `public` within the `Student` class specifically because the data fields are `private`. Without the `public` `get` and `set` methods, there would be no way to access the `private` data fields.

FIGURE 11-24: THE Student CLASS

```
public class Student
    private numeric idNum
    private numeric gpa

    public numeric getIdNum()
    return idNum

    public numeric getGpa()
    return gpa

    public void setIdNum(numeric num)
        idNum = num
    return

    public void setGpa(numeric gradePoint)
        gpa = gradePoint
    return
endClass
```

When an application is a client of the `Student` class (that is, it instantiates a `Student` object), the client cannot directly alter the data in any `private` field. For example, when you write a `main()` method that creates a `Student` as `Student someStudent`, you cannot change the `Student`'s `idNum` with a statement such as `someStudent.idNum = 812`. The `idNum` of the `someStudent` object is not accessible in the `main()` method that uses the `Student` object because `idNum` is `private`. Only methods that are part of the `Student` class itself are allowed to alter `Student` data. To alter a `Student`'s `idNum`, you must use a `public` method, as in `someStudent.setIdNum(812)`.

The concept of keeping data private is known as **information hiding**. When you employ information hiding, your data can be altered only by the methods you choose and only in ways that you can control. For example, you might want the `setIdNum()` method to check to make certain the `idNum` is within a specific range of values. If a class other than the `Student` class itself could alter `idNum`, `idNum` could be assigned a value that the `Student` class couldn't control.

TIP ▢ ▢ ▢ ▢ | You first learned about information hiding and using the `public` and `private` keywords in Chapter 2. You might want to review these concepts.

When a class serves as a superclass to other classes you create, your subclasses inherit all the data and methods of the superclass. The methods in a subclass can use all of the data fields and methods that belong to its parent, with one exception: `private` members of the parent class are not accessible with a child class's methods. If you could use `private` data outside its class, you would lose the advantages of information hiding. For example, if you want the `Student` class data field `idNum` to be `private`, you don't want any outside classes using the field. If a new class could simply extend your `Student` class and get to its data fields without going through the proper channels, information hiding would not be operating.

Sometimes, you want to access parent class data from within a subclass. For example, suppose you create two child classes that extend the `Student` class: `PartTimeStudent` and `FullTimeStudent`. If you want the subclass methods to be able to directly access `idNum` and `gpa`, those data fields cannot be `private`. However, if you don't want other, nonchild classes to access those data fields, they cannot be `public`. To solve this problem, you can create the fields using the modifier `protected`. Using the keyword **`protected`** provides you with an intermediate level of security between `public` and `private` access. If you create a `protected` data field or method, it can be used within its own class or in any classes extended from that class, but it cannot be used by "outside" classes. In other words, `protected` members are those that can be used by a class and its descendants.

TIP □ □ □ □ | A child class always can access its parent's `private` data fields by using `public` methods defined in the parent class, just as any other class can. You only need to make parent class fields `protected` if you want child classes to be able to access `private` data directly.

USING INHERITANCE TO ACHIEVE GOOD SOFTWARE DESIGN

When an automobile company designs a new car model, the company does not build every component of the new car from scratch. The company might design a new feature completely from scratch; for example, at some point someone designed the first air bag. However, many of a new car's features are simply modifications of existing features. The manufacturer might create a larger gas tank or more comfortable seats, but even these new features still possess many properties of their predecessors in the older models. Most features of new car models are not even modified; instead, existing components, such as air filters and windshield wipers, are included on the new model without any changes.

Similarly, you can create powerful computer programs more easily if many of their components are used either "as is" or with slight modifications. Inheritance does not give you the ability to write any programs that you could not write without it, because you *could* create every part of a program from scratch. Inheritance simply makes your job easier. Professional programmers constantly create new class libraries for use with OOP languages. Having these classes available to extend makes programming large systems more manageable. When you create a useful, extendable superclass, you and other future programmers gain several advantages:

- Subclass creators save development time because much of the code needed for the class has already been written.
- Subclass creators save testing time because the superclass code has already been tested and probably used in a variety of situations. In other words, the superclass code is reliable.
- Programmers who create or use new subclasses already understand how the superclass works, so the time it takes to learn the new class features is reduced.
- When you create a new subclass, neither the superclass source code nor the superclass byte-code is changed. The superclass maintains its integrity.

When you consider classes, you must think about the commonalities between them, and then you can create super-classes from which to inherit. You might be rewarded professionally when you see your own superclasses extended by others in the future.

CHAPTER SUMMARY

☐ Within any class or method, a set of statements that act as a unit constitute a block. An inner block can be nested within an outer block. A variable comes into existence, or comes into scope, when you declare it. A variable ceases to exist, or goes out of scope, at the end of the block in which it is declared. Within a method, you can declare a variable with the same name multiple times, as long as each declaration is in its own, nonoverlapping block. You cannot declare the same variable name more than once within a block, even if a block contains other blocks. A locally declared variable always overrides another variable with the same name elsewhere in the class.

☐ Overloading involves using one term to indicate diverse meanings, or writing multiple methods with the same name, but with different arguments. The compiler understands your meaning based on the arguments you use with the method.

☐ When you overload methods, you risk creating an ambiguous situation—one in which the compiler cannot determine which method to use. Methods with identical names that have identical argument lists, but different return types, are not overloaded—they are illegal.

☐ If a class's only constructor requires an argument, you must provide an argument for every object of the class that you create. Fortunately, as with any other method, you can overload constructors. Overloading constructors provides you with a way to create objects with or without initial arguments, as needed.

☐ When you instantiate an object from a class, memory is reserved for each instance field in the class. However, when you create a method for a class, any object can use the same method. Within methods, the compiler accesses the correct object's fields because you implicitly pass a reference to the method. The reference to an object that is passed to any object's nonstatic class method is called the `this` reference.

☐ In object-oriented languages, inheritance is a mechanism that enables one class to inherit, or assume, both the behavior and the attributes of another class. When you use inheritance you save time, reduce errors, and reduce the amount of new learning required to use the new class. A class that is used as a basis for inheritance is a base class. When you create a class that inherits from a base class, it is a derived class. You can use the terms superclass and subclass as synonyms for base class and derived class, respectively. You can also use the terms parent class and child class.

☐ You achieve inheritance in different ways when writing code in different programming languages. In each language the new class derives from an existing class. Inheritance is a one-way proposition; a child inherits from a parent, not the other way around.

☐ When you create a subclass by extending an existing class, the new subclass contains data and methods that were defined in the original superclass. In other words, any child class object can use all the nonprivate members of its parent. Sometimes, however, those superclass data fields and methods are not entirely appropriate for the subclass objects; in those cases, you want to override the parent class methods. Using the same method name to indicate different implementations is called polymorphism, a term that means "many forms"; many forms of action take place, even though you use the same word to describe the action. When you create a method in a child class that has the same name and argument list as a method in its parent class, you override the method in the parent class. When you use the method name with a child object, the child's version of the method is used.

☐ When you instantiate an object that is a member of a subclass, you are actually calling at least two constructors: the constructor for the base class and the constructor for the extended, derived class.

☐ The concept of keeping data private is known as information hiding. When you employ information hiding, your data can be altered only by the methods you choose and only in ways that you can control. When a class serves as a superclass to other classes you create, your subclasses inherit all the data and methods of the superclass. The methods in a subclass can use all of the data fields and methods that belong to its parent, with one exception: `private` members of the parent class are not accessible with a child class's methods. If you want the subclass methods to be able to directly access superclass fields, you can create the fields using the modifier `protected`.

☐ You can create powerful computer programs more easily if many of their components are used either "as is" or with slight modifications. Professional programmers constantly create new class libraries for use with object-oriented programming (OOP) languages. Having these classes available to extend makes programming large systems more manageable.

KEY TERMS

A **block** is a set of statements that act as a unit within any class or method.

An **outside block** contains another block.

An **inside block** is contained within another block.

An inside block is **nested**, or contained entirely within, an outside block.

A variable's **scope** is the portion of a program within which you can refer to it.

A variable comes into existence, or **comes into scope**, when you declare it.

A variable ceases to exist, or **goes out of scope**, at the end of the block in which it is declared.

To **redeclare the variable** is an attempt to declare it more than once within a block—an illegal action.

When a variable **overrides** another, it takes precedence over it.

Overloading involves using one term to indicate diverse meanings, or writing multiple methods with the same name, but with different arguments.

An **ambiguous** situation is one in which the compiler cannot determine which method to use.

A method's **signature** is the combination of the method name and the number, types, and order of arguments.

A **reference** is a named variable that holds an object's memory address.

The **this reference** is a reference to an object that is automatically passed to any object's nonstatic instance method.

C++ programmers call the **this** reference a **this pointer**.

In object-oriented languages, **inheritance** is a mechanism that enables one class to inherit, or assume, both the behavior and the attributes of another class.

A **base class** is a class that is used as a basis for inheritance.

A **derived class** is a class that inherits from a base class.

You can use the terms **superclass** and **subclass** as synonyms for base class and derived class, respectively.

You can use the terms **parent class** and **child class** as synonyms for base class and derived class, respectively.

Multiple inheritance is the capability of inheriting from more than one class.

An **abstract class** is one from which you cannot create any concrete objects, but from which you can inherit.

Polymorphism is the process of using the same method name to indicate different implementations.

When you create a method in a child class that has the same name and argument list as a method in its parent class, you **override the method** in the parent class.

Subtype polymorphism is the ability of one method name to work appropriately for different subclass objects of the same parent class.

Information hiding is the concept of keeping data private.

Using the keyword **protected** provides you with an intermediate level of security between **public** and **private** access; **protected** members are those that can be used by a class and its descendants.

REVIEW QUESTIONS

1. **In program code, when a block exists within another block, the blocks are _____.**
   a. structured
   b. nested
   c. sheltered
   d. illegal

2. **The portion of a program within which you can reference a variable is the variable's _____.**
   a. range
   b. space
   c. domain
   d. scope

3. **If you declare a variable as an instance variable within a class, and declare and use the same variable name within a method of the class, then within the method, _____.**
   a. the variable used inside the method takes precedence
   b. the class instance variable takes precedence

    c. the two variables refer to a single memory address

    d. an error will occur

4. **Nonambiguous, overloaded methods must have the same _____.**

    a. name

    b. number of arguments

    c. argument names

    d. type of argument

5. **If a method is written to receive a numeric argument, and you pass a string to the method, then the method will _____.**

    a. work correctly; the number will be promoted to a string

    b. work correctly; the string will remain a string

    c. execute, but any output will be incorrect

    d. not work; an error message will be issued

6. **A constructor _____ overloaded.**

    a. can be

    b. cannot be

    c. must be

    d. is always automatically

7. **Usually, you want each instantiation of a class to have its own copy of _____.**

    a. the data fields

    b. the class methods

    c. both of the above

    d. none of the above

8. **If you create a class that contains one method, and instantiate two objects, you usually store _____ for use with the objects.**

    a. one copy of the method

    b. two copies of the method

    c. two different methods containing two different `this` references

    d. data only (the methods are not stored)

9. **As an alternative way to discover which of two classes is the base class or subclass, _____.**

    a. look at the class size

    b. try saying the two class names together

    c. use polymorphism

    d. Both a and b are correct.

10. **Employing inheritance reduces errors because** _____.

    a. the new classes have access to fewer data fields
    b. the new classes have access to fewer methods
    c. you can copy methods that you already created
    d. many of the methods you need have already been used and tested

11. **A base class can also be called a** _____.

    a. child class
    b. subclass
    c. derived class
    d. superclass

12. **Which of the following choices most closely describes a parent class/child class relationship?**

    a. Rose/Flower
    b. Present/Gift
    c. Dog/Poodle
    d. Sparrow/Bird

13. **Which of the following statements is false?**

    a. A child class inherits from a parent class.
    b. A parent class inherits from a child class.
    c. Both of the preceding statements are false.
    d. Neither of the preceding statements is false.

14. **When a subclass method has the same name and argument types as a superclass method, the subclass method can** _____ **the superclass method.**

    a. override
    b. overuse
    c. overload
    d. overcompensate

15. **When you instantiate an object that is a member of a subclass, the** _____ **constructor executes first.**

    a. subclass
    b. child class
    c. extended class
    d. parent class

16. **The process of using the same method name to indicate different implementations is** _____.

    a. inheritance
    b. constructing
    c. masking
    d. polymorphism

17. **If a superclass constructor requires arguments, its subclass _____.**

    a. must contain a constructor
    b. must not contain a constructor
    c. must contain a constructor that requires arguments
    d. must not contain a constructor that requires arguments

18. **The concept of keeping data private is known as _____.**

    a. polymorphism
    b. information hiding
    c. data deception
    d. concealing fields

19. **If you create a data field or method that is _____, it can be used within its own class or in any classes extended from that class.**

    a. `public`
    b. `protected`
    c. `private`
    d. both a and b

20. **Inheritance gives a programmer the ability to _____.**

    a. write programs that could not otherwise be written
    b. develop programs more quickly
    c. both of these
    d. none of these

EXERCISES

1. **Create a class named `Commission` that includes two numeric variables: a sales figure and a commission rate.**

   Also create two overloaded methods named `computeCommission()`. The first method takes two numeric arguments representing sales and rate, multiplies them, and then displays the results. The second method takes a single argument representing sales. When this method is called, the commission rate is assumed to be 7.5 percent and the results are displayed.

2. **Create a class named `Pay` that includes five `numeric` variables that hold hours worked, rate of pay per hour, withholding rate, gross pay, and net pay.**

   Also create three overloaded `computeNetPay()` methods. When `computeNetPay()` receives values for hours, pay rate, and withholding rate, it computes the gross pay and reduces it by the appropriate withholding amount to produce the net pay. (Gross pay is computed as hours worked, multiplied by pay per hour.) When `computeNetPay()` receives two arguments, they represent the hours and pay rate, and the withholding rate is assumed to be 15 percent. When `computeNetPay()` receives one argument, it represents the number of hours worked, the withholding rate is assumed to be 15 percent, and the hourly rate is assumed to be 5.65.

3. **Create a class named** Household **that includes data fields for the number of occupants and the annual income, as well as methods named** setOccupants(), setIncome(), getOccupants(), **and** getIncome() **that set and return those values, respectively.**

Also create a constructor that requires no arguments and automatically sets the number of the occupants field to 1 and the income field to 0. Create an additional overloaded constructor for the Household class that receives a numeric argument and assigns the value to the occupants field. Create a third overloaded constructor for the Household class that receives two arguments, the values of which are assigned to the occupants and income fields, respectively.

4. **Create a class named** Box **that includes integer data fields for length, width, and height.**

Also create three constructors that require one, two, and three arguments, respectively. When one argument is used, assign it to length, assign zeros to height and width, and print "Line created". When two arguments are used, assign them to length and width, assign zero to height, and print "Rectangle created". When three arguments are used, assign them to the three variables and print "Box created".

5. **Complete the following tasks:**

a. Create a class named Book that contains data fields for the title and number of pages. Include get and set methods for these fields.

b. Next create a subclass named Textbook, which contains an additional field that holds a grade level for the Textbook and additional methods to get and set the grade level field.

c. Write an application that demonstrates using objects of each class.

6. **Complete the following tasks:**

a. Create a class named Square that contains data fields for height, width, and surfaceArea, and a method named computeSurfaceArea().

b. Create a child class named Cube. Cube contains an additional data field named depth, and a computeSurfaceArea() method that overrides the parent method.

c. Write an application that instantiates a Square object and a Cube object and displays the surface areas of the objects.

7. **Complete the following tasks:**

a. Create a class named Order that performs order processing of a single item. The class has four fields: customer name, customer number, quantity ordered, and unit price. Include set and get methods for each field. The set methods prompt the user for values for each field. This class also needs a method to compute the total price (quantity multiplied by unit price) and a method to display the field values.

b. Create a subclass named ShippedOrder that overrides computePrice() by adding a shipping and handling charge of $4.00.

c. Write an application named UseOrder that instantiates an object of each of these classes. Prompt the user for data for the Order object, and display the results; then prompt the user for data for the ShippedOrder object, and display the results.

8. **Complete the following tasks:**

   a. Create a class named `Year` that contains a data field that holds the number of months in a year and the number of days in a year. Include a `get` method that displays the number of days and a constructor that sets the number of months to 12 and the number of days to 365.

   b. Create a subclass named `LeapYear`. `LeapYear`'s constructor overrides `Year`'s constructor and sets the number of days to 366.

   c. Write an application named `UseYear` that instantiates one object of each class and displays their data.

   d. Add a method named `daysElapsed()` to the `Year` class you created in Exercise 8a. The `daysElapsed()` method accepts two arguments representing a month and a day; it returns a number indicating the number of days that have elapsed since January 1 of that year. For example, on March 3, 61 days have elapsed (31 in January, 28 in February, and 2 in March). Create a `daysElapsed()` method for the `LeapYear` class that overrides the method in the `Year` class. For example, on March 3 in a `LeapYear`, 62 days have elapsed (31 in January, 29 in February, and 2 in March).

   e. Write an application named `UseYear2` that prompts the user for a month and day, and calculates the days elapsed in a `Year` and in a `LeapYear`.

9. **Complete the following tasks:**

   a. Create a class named `HotelRoom` that includes an integer field for the room number and a `double` field for the nightly rental rate. Include `get` methods for these fields and a constructor that requires an integer argument representing the room number. The constructor sets the room rate based on the room number; rooms numbered 299 and below are $69.95 per night, and all others are $89.95 per night.

   b. Create an extended class named `Suite` whose constructor requires a room number and adds a $40.00 surcharge to the regular hotel room rate based on the room number.

   c. Write an application named `UseHotelRoom` that creates an object of each class, and demonstrates using all the methods.

10. **Complete the following tasks:**

   a. Create a class named `Package` with data fields for weight in ounces, shipping method, and shipping cost. The shipping method is a character: "A" for air, "T" for truck, or "M" for mail. The `Package` class contains a constructor that requires arguments for weight and shipping method. The constructor calls a `calculateCost()` method that determines the shipping cost based on the following table:

Weight (Lb)	Air	Truck	Mail
1 to 8	2.00	1.50	.50
9 to 16	3.00	2.35	1.50
17 and over	4.50	3.25	2.15

   The Package class also contains a `display()` method that displays the values in all four fields.

b. Create a subclass named `InsuredPackage` that adds an insurance cost to the shipping cost based on the following table:

Shipping Cost Before Insurance	Additional Cost ($)
0 to 1.00	2.45
1.01 to 3.00	3.95
3.01 and over	5.55

c. Write an application named `UsePackage` that instantiates at least three objects of each type (`Package` and `InsuredPackage`) using a variety of weights and shipping method codes. Display the results for each `Package` and `InsuredPackage`.

11. **Complete the following tasks:**

a. Create a class named `CollegeCourse` that includes data fields that hold the department (for example, "ENG"), the course number (for example, 101), the credits (for example, 3), and the fee for the course (for example, $360). All of the fields are required as arguments to the constructor, except for the fee, which is calculated at $120 per credit hour. Include a `display()` method that displays the course data.

b. Create a subclass named `LabCourse` that adds $50 to the course fee. Override the parent class `display()` method to indicate that the course is a lab course and to display all the data.

c. Write an application named `UseCourse` that prompts the user for course information. If the user enters a class in any of the following departments, create a `LabCourse`: BIO, CHM, CIS, or PHY. If the user enters any other department, create a `CollegeCourse` that does not include the lab fee. Then display the course data.

CASE PROJECT

In earlier chapters you developed classes needed for Cost Is No Object—a car rental service that specializes in lending antique and luxury cars to clients on a short-term basis. You created pseudocode for `Employee`, `Customer`, `Automobile`, and `RentalAgreement` classes including attributes and methods to get and set those attributes. Now, you can create the following:

☐ Create a superclass named `Person` from which both `Employee` and `Customer` can descend. Include attributes and methods that any `Person` should possess—for example, a name and address. Then rewrite the `Employee` and `Customer` classes to descend from `Person` including only attributes and methods appropriate for each subclass.

☐ Create at least two subclasses that descend from `Employee` (for example, `PartTimeEmployee`) adding new fields and methods as appropriate. Override at least one parent method.

☐ Create at least two subclasses that descend from **Customer** (for example,
PreferredCustomer) adding new fields and methods as appropriate. Override at least one
parent method.

☐ Create at least two subclasses that descend from **Automobile** (for example, **LuxuryCar**)
adding new fields and methods as appropriate. Override at least one parent method.

12

EXCEPTION HANDLING

After studying Chapter 12, you should be able to:

- ☐ Learn about exceptions
- ☐ Understand the limitations of traditional error handling
- ☐ Try code and catch **Exception**s
- ☐ Throw and catch multiple **Exception**s
- ☐ Use the **finally** block
- ☐ Understand the advantages of exception handling
- ☐ Specify the **Exception**s a method can throw
- ☐ Trace **Exception**s through the call stack
- ☐ Create your own **Exception**s

LEARNING ABOUT EXCEPTIONS

An **exception** is an unexpected or error condition that occurs while a program is running. The programs you write can generate many types of potential exceptions, such as when you do the following:

- You issue a command to read a file from a disk, but the file does not exist there.
- You attempt to write data to a disk, but the disk is full or unformatted.
- Your program asks for user input, but the user enters invalid data.
- The program attempts to divide a value by zero, access an array with a subscript that is too large, or calculate a value that is too large for the answer's variable type.

These errors are called exceptions because, presumably, they are not usual occurrences; they are "exceptional." The object-oriented techniques to manage such errors comprise the group of methods known as **exception handling**. Sometimes, computer programs generate errors from which the programmer cannot possibly recover. For example, a power failure might interrupt production of your paycheck. Exception handling does not deal with these kinds of errors; its concern is predictable errors.

TIP ▫ ▫ ▫ ▫ | Providing for exceptions involves an oxymoron; you must expect the unexpected.

For example, Figure 12-1 contains a `dividingMethod()` method that displays the result of dividing two arguments. When this method executes, it's possible that an attempt will be made to divide by zero. Dividing by zero is an error in every programming language because it is an operation that is not defined mathematically. Of course, you never should write a method that purposely divides a value by zero. However, this situation certainly could occur by accident—for example, if the variable used as a divisor gets its value as the result of user input.

FIGURE 12-1: THE `dividingMethod()` METHOD

```
public static void dividingMethod(numeric number, numeric divisor)
     numeric result
     result = number / divisor
     print "Result is ", result
return
```

When you execute the method in Figure 12-1, the method fails if the divisor value is zero. Typically, the application that calls this method terminates, control returns to the operating system, and an error message is generated. The method has generated an exception; the error message might even use the term. For example, in Java you see a message indicating an object that is an `ArithmeticException` has been created.

TIP ▫ ▫ ▫ ▫ | In Java, an `ArithmeticException` is a type of `Exception`; it is a member of a class (`RuntimeException`) that is a child class of a built-in class named `Exception`. In some languages—for example, C++—when you want to create your own `Exception` classes, you do so from scratch. In others—for example, Java and C#—you extend an already created class. You will learn how to create `Exception` classes later in this chapter.

When a method in an object-oriented program causes an exception such as dividing by zero, the method **throws the exception**; you can picture the program tossing out an exception object that "someone else" (another method or the operating system) might handle. Just because a program throws an `Exception`, you don't necessarily have to deal with it. In the `dividingMethod()` method, you can simply let the offending program terminate. However, the program termination is abrupt and unforgiving. When a program divides two numbers (or performs a less trivial task such as balancing a checkbook), the user might be annoyed if the program ends abruptly. However, if the program is used for air-traffic control or to monitor a patient's vital statistics during surgery, an abrupt conclusion could be disastrous. You can handle exceptions either in a traditional manner or in an object-oriented manner. Object-oriented exception-handling techniques provide more elegant (and safer) solutions.

The `Exception`s automatically created and thrown differ in various programming languages, but some typical examples are:

- `ArithmeticException` or `DivideByZeroException`, thrown when an attempt to divide by 0 occurs
- `ArrayTypeMismatchException`, thrown when you attempt to store an object that is the wrong data type in an array
- `IndexOutOfRangeException`, thrown when you attempt to access an array with an invalid subscript
- `NullReferenceException`, thrown when an object reference does not correctly refer to a created object
- `OutOfMemoryException`, thrown when you attempt to allocate new memory for an object, but insufficient memory is available
- `OverflowException`, thrown when an arithmetic operation produces a result for which the value is greater than the assigned memory location can accommodate

UNDERSTANDING THE LIMITATIONS OF TRADITIONAL ERROR HANDLING

Programmers had to deal with error conditions long before object-oriented methods were conceived. Probably the most often used error-handling solution has been to make a decision before working with a potentially error-causing value. For example, you can change the `dividingMethod()` method to avoid division if the divisor is zero, as shown in Figure 12-2.

FIGURE 12-2: THE `dividingMethod()` METHOD USING A TRADITIONAL ERROR-HANDLING TECHNIQUE

```
public static void dividingMethod(numeric number, numeric divisor)
    numeric result
    if divisor not = 0 then
        result = number / divisor
        print "Result is ", result
    endif
return
```

In the method in Figure 12-2, the division operation and printing the resulting message only occur when the **divisor** value is not zero. Otherwise, the method simply ends. A more user-friendly method might also include an **else** clause that displays a message explaining why the division did not take place. As another workable alternative, if the divisor is 0, you could force it to 1 or some other acceptable value before dividing, avoiding the error. Another possibility would be to insert a loop into the method and continuously prompt the user to enter a **divisor** value; the loop would execute until the user entered a value other than zero. In short, there are many ways you could avoid the abrupt termination of the **dividingMethod()** method other than having it halt and exit the program.

A drawback to using one of these approaches is that any client of the **dividingMethod()** method must accept the method's chosen way of handling the error. If the method prompts the user for a new value, then the method is not useful in an application that gets its values from a file instead of a user. On the other hand, if the method forces the divisor to 1, it is not useful in an application where that answer would be wrong and displaying a message would be more appropriate. In short, using a traditional error-handling method to avoid dividing by zero prevents the error, but makes the method inflexible. Programmers might have to write multiple versions of the method to fit different clients' needs.

Exception handling provides a more elegant solution for handling error conditions. In object-oriented terminology, you "try" a procedure that might cause an error. A method that detects an error condition "throws an exception," and, if you choose to create one, the block of code that processes the error "catches the exception."

TRYING CODE AND CATCHING EXCEPTIONS

When you create a segment of code in which something might go wrong, you place the code in a **try block**, which is a block of code you attempt to execute while acknowledging that an exception might occur. A **try** block consists of the keyword **try**, followed by any number of statements, some that might cause exceptions. If a statement does cause an exception, the remaining statements in the **try** block do not execute and the try block is abandoned. For pseudocode purposes, you can end a **try** block with a sentinel such as **endtry**.

You must code at least one **catch** block immediately following a **try** block. A **catch block** is a segment of code that can handle an exception that might be thrown by the **try** block that precedes it. A **throw statement** is one that sends an **Exception** out of a method so it can be handled elsewhere. Each **catch** block can "catch" one type of exception—that is, one object that is an object of type **Exception** or one of its child classes. You create a **catch** block by typing the following elements:

- The keyword **catch**
- An opening parenthesis
- An **Exception** type
- A name for an instance of the **Exception** type
- A closing parenthesis

- Statements that take the action you want to use to handle the error condition
- For pseudocode purposes, an `endcatch` statement

TIP □ □ □ □ In some object-oriented programming (OOP) languages, notably C++, you can throw a number or string as well as an `Exception`.

Figure 12-3 shows the general format of a method that includes a highlighted `try...catch` pair.

FIGURE 12-3: FORMAT OF `try...catch` PAIR

```
returnType methodName(optional arguments)
    optional statements prior to code that is tried
    try
        statement or statements that might generate an
           exception
    endtry
    catch(Exception someException)
        actions to take if exception occurs
    endcatch
    optional statements that occur after try, whether catch
      block executes or not
return
```

TIP □ □ □ □ A catch block looks a lot like a method named `catch()` that takes an argument that is some type of `Exception`. However, it is not a method; it has no return type, and you can't call it directly.

TIP □ □ □ □ Some programmers refer to a `catch` block as a `catch` clause.

In Figure 12-3, `someException` represents an object of the `Exception` class or any of its subclasses. If an `Exception` occurs during the execution of the `try` block, the statements in the `catch` block execute. If no `Exception` occurs within the `try` block, the `catch` block does not execute. Either way, the statements following the `catch` block execute normally.

Figure 12-4 shows a rewritten `dividingMethod()` method with a `try` block containing code that attempts division. When the illegal division by zero takes place, an `ArithmeticException`, an object containing information about the error, is automatically created by the object-oriented language application. When the `ArithmeticException` is created and thrown, the `catch` block (that follows and contains an `ArithmeticException` argument) executes.

FIGURE 12-4: THE `dividingMethod()` METHOD WITH A `try...catch` PAIR

```
public static void dividingMethod(numeric number, numeric divisor)
    numeric result
    try
        result = number / divisor
        print "Result is ", result
    endtry
    catch(ArithmeticException mistake)
        print "Cannot divide by zero"
    endcatch
return
```

In the application in Figure 12-4, the `throw` occurs automatically when the division-by-zero error occurs; the programmer did not have to write any statement containing the word `throw`; the `throw` operation occurred implicitly. Later in this chapter, you will see methods in which the programmer explicitly throws an exception. Additionally, in this application, the `throw` and `catch` operations reside in the same method. Actually, this is not much different than including an `if...else` pair to handle the mistake. Later in this chapter, you will learn that `throws` and their corresponding `catches` frequently reside in separate methods.

In the method in Figure 12-4, the variable `mistake` in the `catch` block is an object of type `ArithmeticException`. The object is not used within the `catch` block, but it could be. For example, perhaps the `ArithmeticException` class contains a method named `getMessage()` that returns a string containing details about the cause of the error. In that case, you could place a statement such as `print mistake.getMessage()` in the `catch` block.

THROWING AND CATCHING MULTIPLE EXCEPTIONS

You can place as many statements as you need within a `try` block, and you can `catch` as many `Exception`s as you want. If you `try` more than one statement, only the first error-generating statement `throws` an `Exception`. As soon as the `Exception` occurs, the logic transfers to the `catch` block, which leaves the rest of the statements in the `try` block unexecuted.

When a program contains multiple `catch` blocks, they are examined in sequence until a match is found for the type of `Exception` that occurred. Then, the matching `catch` block executes and each remaining `catch` block is bypassed.

For example, consider the application in Figure 12-5. The `main()` method in the `TwoMistakes` class `throws` two types of `Exception`s: `ArithmeticException`s and `IndexOutOfBoundsException`s. (An `IndexOutOfBoundsException` occurs when an array subscript is not within the allowed range.)

FIGURE 12-5: THE `TwoMistakes` CLASS

```
public class TwoMistakes
    public static void main()
        numeric num[3] = 4, 0, 0
        try
            num[2] = num[0] / num[1]
            num[2] = num[3] / num[0]
        endtry
        catch(ArithmeticException e)
            print "Arithmetic error"
        endcatch
        catch(IndexOutOfBoundsException e)
            print "Out of bounds error"
        endcatch
    return
endClass
```

The `TwoMistakes` class declares a numeric array with three elements. In the `main()` method, the `try` block executes, and at the first statement within the `try` block (highlighted), an `Exception` occurs because the divisor in the division problem, `num[1]`, is zero. The `try` block is abandoned and the logic transfers to the first `catch` block (highlighted). Division by zero causes an `ArithmeticException`, and because the first `catch` block receives an `ArithmeticException`, which has the local name `e`, the message "Arithmetic error" displays. In this example, the second `try` statement is never attempted, and the second `catch` block is skipped.

If you make any one of several minor changes to the class in Figure 12-5, you can force the second `catch` block, the one with the `IndexOutOfBoundsException` argument, to execute. For example, you can force the division in the `try` block to succeed by substituting a nonzero value for the divisor in the first arithmetic statement of the first highlighted statement in the `try` block, as shown in Figure 12-6. Alternatively, you could reverse the positions of the two arithmetic statements or comment out the first statement. With any of these changes, division by zero does not take place. In the code in Figure 12-6, the first statement in the `try` block succeeds, and the logic proceeds to the second statement in the `try` block. This highlighted statement attempts to access element 3 (the fourth element) of a three-element array (whose subscripts should only be 0, 1, or 2), so it `throws` an `IndexOutOfBoundsException`. The `try` block is abandoned, and the first `catch` block is examined and found unsuitable because it does not catch an `IndexOutOfBoundsException`. The program logic proceeds to the second `catch` block (highlighted), whose `Exception` argument type is a match for the thrown `Exception`, so the message "Out of bounds error" appears.

FIGURE 12-6: THE `TwoMistakes2` CLASS

```
public class TwoMistakes2
    public static void main()
        numeric num[3] = 4, 0, 0
        try
            num[2] = num[0] / 10
            num[2] = num[3] / num[0]
        endtry
        catch(ArithmeticException e)
            print "Arithmetic error"
        endcatch
        catch(IndexOutOfBoundsException e)
            print "Out of bounds error"
        endcatch
    return
endClass
```

Sometimes, you want to execute the same code no matter which `Exception` type occurs. For example, within the `TwoMistakes2` application in Figure 12-6, each of the two `catch` blocks prints a unique message. If both the `ArithmeticException` class and the `IndexOutOfBoundsException` class descend from the same base class, `Exception`, then you can use a single `catch` block to accept both types of objects. For example, Figure 12-7 shows a rewritten `TwoMistakes` class that uses a single generic `catch` block (highlighted) that can `catch` any type of `Exception`.

FIGURE 12-7: THE `TwoMistakes3` APPLICATION

```
public class TwoMistakes3
    public static void main()
        numeric num[3] = 4, 0, 0
        try
            num[2] = num[0] / 10
            num[2] = num[3] / num[0]
        endtry
        catch(Exception e)
            print "Error!"
        endcatch
    return
endClass
```

The `catch` block in Figure 12-7 accepts a more generic `Exception` argument type than that thrown by either of the potentially error-causing `try` statements, so the generic `catch` block can act as a "catch-all" block. When either an arithmetic or array error occurs, the thrown exception is "promoted" to an `Exception` error in the `catch` block. Through inheritance, `ArithmeticException`s and `IndexOutOfBoundsException`s are `Exception`s.

When you list multiple `catch` blocks following a `try` block, you must be careful that some `catch` blocks don't become unreachable. **Unreachable code** statements are program statements that can never execute under any circumstances. For example, if two successive `catch` blocks catch an `IndexOutOfBoundsException` and an ordinary `Exception`, the `IndexOutOfBoundsException` errors will cause the first `catch` to execute and other Exceptions will "fall through" to the more general Exception catch block. However, if you reverse the sequence of the catch blocks so that the code that catches general Exception objects is first, even IndexOutOfBoundsExceptions will be caught by the Exception catch. The IndexOutOfBoundsException catch block is unreachable because the Exception catch block is in its way and the class will not compile.

TIP □ □ □ □ | Programmers also call unreachable code **dead code**.

USING THE finally BLOCK

When you have actions you must perform at the end of a try...catch sequence, in several languages you can use a **finally block**. The code within a finally block executes whether or not the preceding try block identifies an Exception. Usually, you use a finally block to perform cleanup tasks that must happen whether or not any Exceptions occurred, and whether or not any Exceptions that occurred were caught. Figure 12-8 shows the format of a try...catch sequence that uses a finally block.

FIGURE 12-8: FORMAT OF try...catch...finally SEQUENCE

```
try
   statements to try
endtry
catch(Exception e)
   actions that occur if exception was thrown
endcatch
finally
   actions that occur whether catch block executed or not
endfinally
```

Compare Figure 12-8 to Figure 12-3 shown earlier in this chapter. When the try code works without error in Figure 12-3, control passes to the statements at the end of the method. Also, when the try code fails and throws an Exception, and the Exception is caught, the catch block executes and control again passes to the statements at the end of the method. At first glance, it seems as though the statements at the end of the method always execute. However, the last set of statements in Figure 12-3 might never execute for at least two reasons:

- An unplanned Exception might occur.
- The try or catch block might contain a statement that terminates the program.

Any try block might throw an Exception for which you did not provide a catch block. After all, Exceptions occur all the time without your handling them, as one would if you attempted division by zero without try and catch blocks. In the case of an unhandled Exception, program execution stops immediately, the Exception is sent to the operating system for handling, and the current method is abandoned. Likewise, if the try block contains an exit() statement (or the statement that stops program execution in the programming language you are using), execution stops immediately.

When you include a `finally` block, you are assured that the `finally` statements will execute before the method is abandoned, even if the method concludes prematurely. For example, programmers often use a `finally` block when the program uses data files that must be closed. Consider the pseudocode in Figure 12-9, which represents part of the logic for a typical file-handling program:

FIGURE 12-9: PSEUDOCODE THAT TRIES READING A FILE AND HANDLES AN `Exception`

```
try
        Open the file
        Read the file
        Place the file data in an array
        Calculate an average from the data
        Display the average
endtry
catch(IOException e)
        Issue an error message
        System exit
endcatch
finally
        If the file is open, close it
endfinally
```

The pseudocode in Figure 12-9 represents an application that opens a file; if a file does not exist when you open it, object-oriented languages automatically throw an input/output exception. (This pseudocode assumes the class that contains input/output error information is called `IOException`.) However, because the application uses an array (see the statement "Place the file data in an array"), it is possible that even though the file opened successfully, an uncaught `IndexOutOfBoundsException` might occur. In such an event, close the file before proceeding. By using the `finally` block, you ensure that the file is closed because the code in the `finally` block executes before control returns to the operating system. The code in the `finally` block executes no matter which of the following outcomes of the `try` block occurs:

- The `try` ends normally.

- The `catch` executes.

- An `Exception` causes the method to abandon prematurely—perhaps the array is not large enough to hold the data, or calculating the average results in division by zero. These `Exceptions` would not allow the `try` block to finish, nor would they cause the `catch` block to execute.

TIP ☐ ☐ ☐ ☐ You can avoid using a `finally` block, but you would need repetitious code. For example, instead of using the `finally` block in the pseudocode in Figure 12-9, you could insert the statement "If the file is open, close it" as both the last statement in the `try` block and the second-to-last statement in the `catch` block, just before `System exit`. However, writing code just once in a `finally` block is clearer and less prone to error.

TIP ☐ ☐ ☐ ☐ C++ does not provide a `finally` block, but it does provide a default "catch all" block that can catch any previously uncaught exceptions.

UNDERSTANDING THE ADVANTAGES OF EXCEPTION HANDLING

Before the inception of OOP languages, potential program errors were handled using somewhat confusing, error-prone methods. For example, a traditional, non-object-oriented, procedural program might perform three methods that depend on each other using code that provides error checking similar to the pseudocode in Figure 12-10.

The following pseudocode represents an application in which the logic must pass three tests before a final result can be displayed. It performs `methodA()`; it then performs `methodB()` only if `methodA()` is successful. Similarly, `methodC()` executes only when `methodA()` and `methodB()` are both successful. When any method fails, the program sets an appropriate `errorCode` to 'A', 'B', or 'C'. (Presumably, the `errorCode` is used later in the application.) The logic in Figure 12-10 is difficult to follow, and the application's purpose and intended outcome—to print the `finalResult`—is lost in the maze of `if` statements. Also, you can easily make coding mistakes within such a program because of the complicated nesting and indenting.

FIGURE 12-10: PSEUDOCODE REPRESENTING TRADITIONAL ERROR CHECKING

```
call methodA()
if methodA() worked then
    call methodB()
    if methodB() worked then
        call methodC()
        if methodC() worked then
            everything's okay so print finalResult
        else
            set errorCode to 'C'
        endif
    else
        set errorCode to 'B'
    endif
else
    set errorCode to 'A'
endif
```

Compare the same program logic using the object-oriented, error-handling technique shown in Figure 12-11. Using the `try...catch` object-oriented technique provides the same results as the traditional method, but the statements of the program that do the "real" work (calling methods A, B, and C, and printing `finalResult`) are placed together where their logic is easy to follow. The `try` steps should usually work without generating errors; after all, the errors are "exceptions." It is convenient to see these business-as-usual steps in one location. The unusual, exceptional events are grouped and moved out of the way of the primary action.

TIP ▫ ▫ ▫ ▫ | In Figure 12-11, each of the methods, `methodA()`, `methodB()`, and `methodC()` must throw a different type of error that can only be caught by the appropriate catch block.

FIGURE 12-11: PSEUDOCODE REPRESENTING OBJECT-ORIENTED EXCEPTION HANDLING

```
try
    call methodA() and maybe throw an exception
    call methodB() and maybe throw an exception
    call methodC() and maybe throw an exception
    everything's okay, so display finalResult
endtry
catch(methodA()'s type of error)
    set errorCode to 'A'
endcatch
catch(methodB()'s type of error)
    set errorCode to 'B'
endcatch
catch(methodC()'s type of error)
    set errorCode to 'C'
endcatch
```

Besides clarity, an advantage to object-oriented exception handling is the flexibility it allows in the handling of error situations. When a method you write **throws** an **Exception**, the same method can **catch** the **Exception**, although it is not required to do so, and in most object-oriented programs it will not. Often, you won't want a method to handle its own **Exception**. In many cases, you want the method to check for errors, but you do not want to require a method to handle an error if it finds one. Another advantage to object-oriented exception handling is that you gain the ability to appropriately deal with **Exceptions** as you decide how to handle them. When you write a method, it can call another, **catch** a thrown **Exception**, and you can decide what you want to do. Just as a police officer can deal with a speeding driver differently depending on circumstances, you can react to **Exceptions** specifically for your current purposes.

Methods are flexible partly because they are reusable—that is, a well-written method might be used by any number of applications. Each calling application might need to handle the error differently, depending on its purpose. For example, an application that uses a method that divides values might need to terminate if division by zero occurs. A different program simply might want the user to reenter the data to be used, and a third program might want to force division by one. The method that contains the division statement can throw the error, but each calling program can assume responsibility for handling the error detected by the method in an appropriate way.

For example, Figure 12-12 shows a **PriceList** class used by a company to hold a list of prices for items it sells. For simplicity, there are only four prices and a single method that displays the price of a single item. The **displayPrice()** method accepts an argument to use as the array subscript, and because the subscript could be out of bounds, the method might throw an exception.

FIGURE 12-12: THE **PriceList** CLASS

```
public class PriceList
    private numeric price[4] = 15.99, 27.88, 34.56, 45.89
    public static void displayPrice(numeric item)
        print "The price is $", price[item]
    return
endClass
```

TIP □ □ □ □ | In Java, if a method throws an Exception that it will not catch, but that will be caught by a different method, you must also use the keyword throws, followed by an Exception type in the method header.

Figures 12-13 and 12-14 show two applications in which programmers have chosen to handle the exception differently. In the first class, PriceListApplication1, the programmer has chosen to handle the exception in the highlighted catch block by displaying a price of $0. In the second class, PriceListApplication2, the programmer has chosen to continue using an input dialog box in the highlighted catch block to prompt the user for a new item number until it is within the correct range. Other programmers could choose still different actions, but they all can use the flexible displayPrice() method because it throws the error but doesn't limit the calling method's choice of recourse.

FIGURE 12-13: THE PriceListApplication1 CLASS

```
public class PriceListApplication1
   public static void main()
      numeric item = 4
      try
            PriceList.displayPrice(item)
      endtry
      catch(IndexOutOfBoundsException e)
            print "Price is $0"
      endcatch
   return
endClass
```

FIGURE 12-14: THE PriceListApplication2 CLASS

```
public class PriceListApplication2
   public static void main()
      numeric item = 4
      try
            PriceList.displayPrice(item)
      endtry
      catch(IndexOutOfBoundsException e)
            while item < 0 OR item > 3
                print "Please reenter a value 0, 1, 2 or 3"
                read item
            endwhile
                PriceList.displayPrice(item)
      endcatch
   return
endClass
```

SPECIFYING THE EXCEPTIONS A METHOD CAN THROW

When you write a method that might throw an Exception, such as the displayPrice() method in Figure 12-12, you can type an **exception specification clause**, which is a declaration of a method's possible throw types.

TIP ☐ ☐ ☐ ☐ The syntax used for an exception specification clause differs slightly in different programming languages. For example, in Java you might type `throws IndexOutOfBoundsException` after the `displayPrice()` method header to indicate the type of `Exception` that might be thrown. The syntax is similar in C++; you would type `throw(IndexOutOfBoundsException)` as part of the method header, using `throw` instead of `throws`, and including parentheses.

Every method you write has the potential to throw an **Exception**. Some **Exception**s can occur anywhere at any time—for example, if the system runs out of memory. However, for most methods that you write, you do not use a `throws` clause. For example, you have not needed to use a `throws` clause in any of the many programs you have seen while working through this book; however, in those methods, if you divided by zero or went beyond an array's bounds, an **Exception** was thrown. Most of the time, you let the language handle any **Exception** by shutting down the program. Imagine how unwieldy your programs would become if you were required to provide instructions for handling every possible error, including equipment failures and memory problems. Most exceptions never have to be explicitly thrown or caught, nor must you include a `throws` clause in the headers of methods that automatically throw these **Exception**s.

However, if you write a method that explicitly throws an **Exception** that is not caught within a method, you can use a `throws` clause in the header of the method. (As a matter of fact, Java requires that you do.) Using the `throws` clause does not mean that the method *will* throw an **Exception**—everything might go smoothly. Instead, it means the method *might* throw an **Exception**. You include the `throws` clause in the method header so applications that use your methods are notified of the potential for an **Exception**. To be able to use a method to its full potential, you must know the method's name and three additional pieces of information:

- The method's return type
- The type and number of arguments the method requires
- The type and number of **Exception**s the method `throws`

To use a method, you must first know what types of arguments are required by the method. You can call a method without knowing its return type, but if you do so, you can't benefit from any value that the method returns. (Also, if you use a method without knowing its return type, you probably don't understand the purpose of the method.) Likewise, you can't make sound decisions about what to do in case of an error if you don't know what types of **Exception**s a method might throw. A method's header, including its name, any arguments, and any `throws` clause, is called the **method's signature**.

 When a method might throw more than one **Exception** type, you can specify a list of potential **Exception**s in the method header by separating them. For example, Java and C++ both use commas for this purpose. As an alternative, you could specify that the method might throw an object of the general **Exception** parent class that would cover all specific instances.

 In C++, you can throw objects that are basic data types, such as numbers and strings, as well as **Exception** class objects.

TRACING EXCEPTIONS THROUGH THE CALL STACK

When one method calls another, the computer's operating system must keep track of where the method call came from, and program control must return to the calling method when the called method is completed. For example, if `methodA()` calls `methodB()`, the operating system has to "remember" to return to `methodA()` when `methodB()` ends. Likewise, if `methodB()` calls `methodC()`, then while `methodC()` executes, the computer must "remember" to return to `methodB()`, and eventually to `methodA()`. The memory location known as the **call stack** is where the computer stores the list of method locations to which the system must return.

When a method `throws` an `Exception` and the method does not `catch` it, the `Exception` is thrown to the next method up the call stack, or in other words, to the method that called the offending method. Figure 12-15 shows how the call stack works. If `methodA()` calls `methodB()`, and `methodB()` calls `methodC()`, and `methodC()` `throws` an `Exception`, the application first looks for a `catch` block in `methodC()`. If none exists, it looks for the same thing in `methodB()`. If `methodB()` does not have a `catch` block, the application looks to `methodA()`. If `methodA()` cannot `catch` the `Exception`, it is thrown to the operating system, which displays a message at the command prompt or GUI.

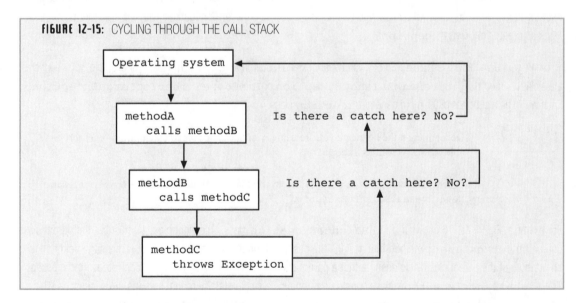

FIGURE 12-15: CYCLING THROUGH THE CALL STACK

In most OOP languages, the messages displayed when an exception is thrown include a list of the methods through which the exception passed. Using this list of error messages, you could track down the location where the error was generated.

The technique of cycling through the methods in the stack has great advantages because it allows methods to handle `Exceptions` wherever the programmer has decided it is most appropriate—including allowing the operating system to handle the error. However, when a program uses several classes, this system's disadvantage is that the programmer finds it difficult to locate the original source of an `Exception`. Even when you catch an `Exception` instead of allowing it to be thrown to the operating system, object-oriented languages contain an **Exception** class method with a name similar to **printStackTrace()** that allows you to display a list of methods in the call stack so you can determine the location of the **Exception**. Often, you do not want to place a **printStackTrace()** method call in a finished program. The typical application user has no interest in the cryptic messages that display. However, while you are developing an application, printing a list of the method calls in the stack can be a useful tool for diagnosing your application's problems.

CREATING YOUR OWN EXCEPTIONS

Many (but not all) OOP languages provide many built-in exception types. For example, Java and C# each provide dozens of categories of **Exception**s that you can use in your programs. Those who create the built-in **Exception**s that are part of a programming language cannot predict every condition that might be an **Exception** in your applications. For example, you might want to declare an **Exception** when your bank balance is negative or when an outside party attempts to access your e-mail account. Most organizations have specific rules for exceptional data; for example, an employee number must not exceed three digits, or an hourly salary must not be less than the legal minimum wage. Of course, you can handle these potential error situations with **if** statements, but you also can create your own **Exception**s.

To create your own throwable **Exception**, you usually extend a built-in **Exception** class. For example, you might create a class named **NegativeBankBalanceException** or **EmployeeNumberTooLargeException**. Each would be a subclass of the more general **Exception** class.

TIP ▫ ▫ ▫ ▫ Depending on the language you are using, you might be able to extend from other throwable classes as well as **Exception**.

TIP ▫ ▫ ▫ ▫ When you create an **Exception**, it's conventional to end its name with **Exception**, as in **NegativeBankBalanceException**.

For example, Figure 12-16 shows a **HighBalanceException** class. This example assumes that the parent class contains a **setMessage()** method that assigns the passed string to an error **Exception** message field that is an attribute of the parent class. Also assume that a parent class **getMessage()** method can retrieve the message. The **HighBalanceException** class constructor contains a single statement that sets the error message. This string would be retrieved if you called the **getMessage()** method using a **HighBalanceException** object.

FIGURE 12-16: THE **HighBalanceException** CLASS

```
public class HighBalanceException derivesFrom Exception
    public HighBalanceException()
        setMessage("Customer balance is high");
    return
endClass
```

Figure 12-17 shows a `CustomerAccount` class that uses a `HighBalanceException`. The `CustomerAccount` class contains an account number, a balance, and a constant that stores a limit for customer credit. It also contains a highlighted `HighBalanceException` object named `anError`; this object might be thrown if the customer balance exceeds the credit limit constant. The `CustomerAccount` constructor header indicates that it might throw a `HighBalanceException` (see the second highlighted statement in the figure), and if the balance used as an argument to the constructor exceeds the limit, the instance of the `HighBalanceException` class is thrown (see the final highlighted statement in the figure).

FIGURE 12-17: THE `CustomerAccount` CLASS

```
public class CustomerAccount
    private numeric acctNum
    private numeric balance
    public constant numeric HIGH_CREDIT_LIMIT = 20000.00
    HighBalanceException anError
    public CustomerAccount(numeric num, numeric bal) throws
      HighBalanceException
        acctNum = num
        balance = bal
        if balance > HIGH_CREDIT_LIMIT then
            throw anError
        endif
    return
endClass
```

Figure 12-18 shows an application that instantiates a `CustomerAccount`. In this application, a user is prompted for an account number and balance. After those values are entered, an attempt is made to construct a `CustomerAccount` in a `try` block (as shown in the first highlighted section). If the attempt is successful—that is, if the `CustomerAccount` constructor does not throw an `Exception`—the `CustomerAccount` information is displayed. However, if the `CustomerAccount` constructor does throw a `HighBalanceException`, the `catch` block receives it (as shown in the second highlighted section) and displays two messages. The `catch` block in this class demonstrates that you can decide to create your own message in the `catch` block, or use the message that is part of every `HighBalanceException`—the one that was set in the `Exception` class constructor in Figure 12-16. A different application could take any number of different actions in its `catch` block; for example, it could display only one of the messages or a different message, construct a new `CustomerAccount` object with a lower balance, or construct a different type of object—perhaps a child of `CustomerAccount` called `PreferredCustomerAccount` that allows a higher balance.

FIGURE 12-18: THE `UseCustomerAccount` CLASS

```
public class UseCustomerAccount
    public static void main()
        numeric num
        numeric balance
        print "Enter account number"
        read num
        print "Enter balance due"
        read balance
        try
            CustomerAccount newAccount(num, balance);
            print "Customer #", num,
                " has a balance of $", balance
        endtry
        catch(HighBalanceException hbe)
            print "Customer #", num, " has a balance
                higher than the credit limit"
            print hbe.getMessage()
        endcatch
    return
endClass
```

TIP ☐ ☐ ☐ ☐   In Figure 12-18, `balance` is a local variable in the `main()` method. When `balance` is passed to the `CustomerAccount` constructor, its value is assigned to `bal` as defined in the header of the `CustomerAccount` class.

TIP ☐ ☐ ☐ ☐   In the `catch` block in the `main()` method in the `UseCustomerAccount` class in Figure 12-18, the `getMessage()` method is used with the `hbe` object. Because the `hbe` object is a `HighBalanceException`, which is an `Exception`, and because the `HighBalanceException` class in Figure 12-16 contains no `getMessage()` method, you know that the `HighBalanceException` inherits the `getMessage()` method from the more general `Exception` class.

You should not create an excessive number of special **Exception** types for your classes, especially if the language with which you are working already contains an **Exception** that will **catch** the error. Extra **Exception** types add complexity for other programmers who use your classes. However, when appropriate, specialized **Exception** classes provide an elegant way for you to handle error situations. They enable you to separate your error code from the usual, nonexceptional sequence of events, they allow errors to be passed up the stack and traced, and they allow clients of your classes to handle exceptional situations in the manner most suitable for their application.

CHAPTER SUMMARY

☐ An exception is an unexpected or error condition. The object-oriented techniques to manage such errors comprise the group of methods known as exception handling.

☐ Exception handling provides an elegant solution for handling error conditions. In object-oriented terminology, you "try" a procedure that might cause an error. A method that detects an error condition or `Exception` "throws an exception," and the block of code that processes the error "catches the exception."

☐ When you create a segment of code in which something might go wrong, you place the code in a `try` block, which is a block of code you attempt to execute while acknowledging that an exception might occur. You must code at least one catch block immediately following a `try` block. A `catch` block is a segment of code that can handle an exception that might be thrown by the `try` block that precedes it.

☐ You can place as many statements as you need within a `try` block, and you can `catch` as many `Exception`s as you want. If you try more than one statement, only the first error-generating statement `throws` an `Exception`. As soon as the `Exception` occurs, the logic transfers to the `catch` block, which leaves the rest of the statements in the `try` block unexecuted. When a program contains multiple `catch` blocks, they are examined in sequence until a match is found for the type of `Exception` that occurred. Then, the matching `catch` block executes and each remaining `catch` block is bypassed.

☐ When you have actions you must perform at the end of a `try...catch` sequence, in some languages you can use a `finally` block. The code within a `finally` block executes whether or not the preceding `try` block identifies an `Exception`. Usually, you use a `finally` block to perform cleanup tasks that must happen whether or not any `Exception`s occurred, and whether or not any `Exception`s that occurred were caught.

☐ Besides clarity, an advantage to object-oriented exception handling is the flexibility it allows in the handling of error situations. Each calling application might need to handle the same error differently, depending on its purpose.

☐ When you write a method that might throw an `Exception` that is not caught within the method, you can type a `throws` clause after the method header to indicate the type of `Exception` that might be thrown. A method's header, including its name, any arguments, and any `throws` clause, is called the method's signature.

☐ When one method calls another, the computer's operating system must keep track of where the method call came from, and program control must return to the calling method when the called method is completed. The memory location known as the call stack is where the computer stores the list of method locations to which the system must return.

     ❑ Those who create the built-in **Exception**s that are part of a programming language cannot predict every condition that might be an **Exception** in your applications, so you can create your own **Exception**s. Usually you accomplish this by creating a subclass on a built-in **Exception** class.

KEY TERMS

An **exception** is an unexpected or error condition that occurs while a program is running.

Exception handling is an object-oriented technique for managing errors.

Throwing an exception is the process of tossing out an exception object that another method or the operating system might handle.

When you create a segment of code in which something might go wrong, you place the code in a **try** block, which is a block of code you attempt to execute while acknowledging that an exception might occur.

A **catch** block is a segment of code that can handle an exception that might be thrown by the **try** block that precedes it.

A **throw statement** is one that sends an **Exception** out of a method so it can be handled elsewhere.

Unreachable code statements are program statements that can never execute under any circumstances.

Programmers also call unreachable code **dead code**.

When you have actions you must perform at the end of a **try...catch** sequence, you can use a **finally** block.

An **exception specification clause** is a declaration of a method's possible throw types.

A **method's signature** is the method's header, including its name, any arguments, and any **throws** clause.

The memory location known as the **call stack** is where the computer stores the list of method locations to which the system must return.

REVIEW QUESTIONS

1. **In object-oriented programming terminology, an unexpected or error condition is a(n)**
   _____.
   a. anomaly
   b. aberration
   c. deviation
   d. exception

2. **A programmer can recover from _____ errors.**
   a. all
   b. some
   c. only unpredictable
   d. no

3. **When a program might generate an exception, you _____.**

   a. must write statements to handle it
   b. must write a class to handle it
   c. can choose to handle it or not
   d. cannot handle it; the operating system must do so

4. **Exceptions automatically created and thrown in object-oriented languages typically include exceptions that occur when all of the following occur except when _____.**

   a. you attempt to access an array element using an illegal subscript
   b. you attempt to store an object in an array that is an incorrect data type
   c. when an arithmetic operation produces a result for which the value is greater than the assigned memory location can accommodate
   d. when you store an employee's Social Security number containing only eight digits instead of nine

5. **In object-oriented terminology, you _____ a procedure that might not complete correctly.**

   a. `try`
   b. `catch`
   c. `handle`
   d. `encapsulate`

6. **A method that detects an error condition or `Exception` _____ an `Exception`.**

   a. tries
   b. catches
   c. handles
   d. throws

7. **A `try` block can include all of the following elements except _____.**

   a. the keyword `try`
   b. the keyword `catch`
   c. statements that might cause `Exceptions`
   d. statements that cannot cause `Exceptions`

8. **The segment of code that handles or takes appropriate action following an exception is a _____ block.**

   a. `try`
   b. `catch`
   c. `throws`
   d. `handles`

9. **You _____ within a `try` block.**

   a. must place only a single statement
   b. can place any number of statements
   c. must place at least two statements
   d. must place a `catch` block

10. If you `try` three statements and include three `catch` blocks, and the second statement that is tried throws an `Exception`, _____.

    a. the first `catch` block executes

    b. the first two `catch` blocks execute

    c. only the second `catch` block executes

    d. the first matching `catch` block executes

11. When a `try` block does not generate an `Exception` and you have included multiple `catch` blocks, _____.

    a. they all execute

    b. only the first one executes

    c. only the first matching one executes

    d. no `catch` blocks execute

12. The `catch` block that begins `catch (Exception e)` can catch `Exception`s of type _____.

    a. `IndexOutOfBoundsException`

    b. `ArithmeticException`

    c. both of the above

    d. none of the above

13. The code within a `finally` block executes when the `try` block _____.

    a. identifies one or more `Exception`s

    b. does not identify any `Exception`s

    c. either a or b

    d. neither a nor b

14. An advantage to using a `try...catch` block is that exceptional events are _____.

    a. eliminated

    b. reduced

    c. integrated with regular events

    d. isolated from regular events

15. Which methods can `throw` an `Exception`?

    a. only methods with a `throws` clause

    b. only methods with a `catch` block

    c. only methods with both a `throws` clause and a `catch` block

    d. any method

16. A method can _____.

    a. check for errors but not handle them

    b. handle errors but not check for them

    c. either of the above

    d. neither of the above

17. **You must know three pieces of information to use a method to its full potential, but you don't need to know _____.**

    a. the method's return type

    b. the type of arguments the method requires

    c. the number of statements within the method

    d. the type of `Exceptions` the method `throws`

18. **The memory location where the computer stores the list of method locations to which the system must return is known as the _____.**

    a. registry

    b. call stack

    c. chronicle

    d. archive

19. **You can get a list of the methods through which an `Exception` has traveled by displaying the method's _____.**

    a. constructor

    b. `getMessage()` value

    c. stack trace

    d. `path`

20. **To create your own `Exception` class from which you create objects that you can throw, in most object-oriented languages you must create _____.**

    a. a subclass of an existing `Exception` class

    b. an overloaded constructor for the existing `Exception` class

    c. a new class that does not descend from any class

    d. additional methods for the class that will throw the new `Exception` type

EXERCISES

1. **Design an application in which you declare an array of five numbers and store five values in the array. Write a `try` block in which you loop to display each successive element of the array, increasing a subscript by one on each pass through the loop. Create a `catch` block that catches an automatically created `ArrayIndexOutOfBoundsException` and displays the message, "Now you've gone too far."**

2. **Create a class named `ArithmeticOperations` that contains public methods named `add()`, `subtract()`, `multiply()`, and `divide()`. Each of the methods accepts two numeric arguments and returns a number that represents the result of the appropriate arithmetic operation. Design an application that prompts the user for two numbers and tries each of the `ArithmeticOperations` methods. Catch the automatically generated `NumberFormatException` that is thrown when a method's argument is not numeric, and the `ArithmeticException` that is thrown when the `divide()` method attempts division by zero. Display an appropriate message when an `Exception` is caught.**

3. Design an application that prompts the user to enter a number to use as an array size, and then attempt to declare an array using the entered size. If the array is created successfully, display an appropriate message. Assume you are working with a language that generates a `NegativeArraySizeException` if you attempt to create an array with a negative size, and a `NumberFormatException` if you attempt to create an array using a nonnumeric value for the size. Use a `catch` block that executes if the array size is nonnumeric or negative, displaying a message that indicates the array was not created.

4. Design an application that throws and catches an automatically generated `ArithmeticException` when you attempt to take the square root of a negative value. Prompt the user for an input value and try a `squareRoot()` method that accepts a numeric argument and returns its square root. (You do not need to design the implementation of the `squareRoot()` method.) The application either displays the square root or catches the thrown `Exception` and displays an appropriate message.

5. Complete the following tasks:

   a. Design an `EmployeeException` class whose constructor receives a `String` that consists of an employee's ID and pay rate. Include a `getMessage()` method that returns a string that contains the employee's data.

   b. Create an `Employee` class with two numeric fields, `idNum` and `hourlyWage`. The `Employee` constructor requires values for both fields. Upon construction, throw an `EmployeeException` if the `hourlyWage` is less than $6.00 or more than $50.00.

   c. Write an application that establishes an array of 20 `Employees`. Prompt the user for ID numbers and hourly rates for each `Employee`. Display an appropriate message when an `Employee` is successfully created as well as when one is not.

6. Complete the following tasks:

   a. Create an `IceCreamConeException` class whose constructor receives a `String` that consists of an ice cream cone's flavor and an integer representing the number of scoops in the `IceCreamCone`. Create a `getMessage()` method that returns a string containing the `IceCreamCone` information.

   b. Create an `IceCreamCone` class with two fields—`flavor` and `scoops`. The `IceCreamCone` constructor calls two data-entry methods—`setFlavor()` and `setScoops()`. The `setScoops()` method `throws` an `IceCreamConeException` when the scoop quantity exceeds three.

   c. Write an application that establishes an array of 10 `IceCreamCone` objects and handles the `Exceptions` that occur as a user enters data.

   d. Create an `IceCreamCone2` class in which you modify the `IceCreamCone setFlavor()` method to ensure that the user enters a valid flavor. Allow at least four flavors of your choice. If the user's entry does not match a valid flavor, throw an `IceCreamConeException`.

   e. Write an application that establishes an array of 10 `IceCreamCone` objects and demonstrates the handling of the new `Exception`.

7. Write an application that displays a series of five student ID numbers that you store in an array: 1023, 1045, 2134, 2768, and 3478. Ask the user to enter a numeric test score for each student. Create a `ScoreException` class, and throw a `ScoreException` if the user does not enter a valid score (greater than or equal to 0 and less than or equal to 100). `Catch` the `ScoreException` and then display an appropriate message. In addition, if an exception is thrown, store a zero for the student's score. At the end of the application, display all the student IDs and scores.

8. Write an application that displays a series of 10 student ID numbers that you have stored in an array: 1023, 1045, 2134, 2768, 3478, 3712, 4198, 4367, 5510, and 5672. Ask the user to enter a test letter grade for each student. Create an `Exception` class named `GradeException` that contains an array of valid grade letters ('A', 'B', 'C', 'D', 'F', and 'I') you can use to determine whether a grade input from the application is valid. In your application, throw a `GradeException` if the user does not enter a valid letter grade. `Catch` the `GradeException` and then display an appropriate message. In addition, store an 'I' (for Incomplete) for any student for whom an exception is caught. At the end of the application, display all the student IDs and grades.

CASE PROJECT

In earlier chapters, you developed classes needed for Cost Is No Object—a car rental service that specializes in lending antique and luxury cars to clients on a short-term basis. You created pseudocode for `Person`, `Employee`, `PartTimeEmployee`, `Customer`, `PreferredCustomer`, `Automobile`, `RentalAgreement`, and other classes, each including attributes and methods to get and set those attributes.

In Chapter 5, you modified the `RentalAgreement` class to contain all the attributes and methods associated with one rental contract. Specifically, a `RentalAgreement` contains the following:

- ☐ Contract number

- ☐ Customer ID number

- ☐ Automobile vehicle identification number

- ☐ Starting date for the rental agreement stored as three separate fields—month, day, and year

- ☐ Length, in days, for the rental agreement

- ☐ Expected ending date for the rental agreement stored as three separate fields—month, day, and year

- ☐ Indicator of whether the customer has elected to buy the optional insurance policy

- ☐ A get method for each field that returns the field's value

In the `RentalAgreement` class you modified in Chapter 5, you included set methods that either assign a value to one or more of the class fields or display an error message as follows:

- ☐ `void setContractNumber(numeric number)`—Ensures that the contract number is between 10000 and 99999 inclusive

☐ `void setCustomerIDNumber(numeric number)`—Ensures that the customer ID is between 100 and 999 inclusive

☐ `void setVehicleIdentificationNumber(numeric number)`—Ensures that the vehicle identification number is between 100 and 999 inclusive

☐ `void setStartingDate(numeric month, numeric day, numeric year)`—Ensures that the starting date for the rental agreement is not prior to today's date, and the month is between 1 and 12 inclusive; also ensures that the date is appropriate for the month (for example, that June is between 1 and 30 inclusive)

☐ `void setAgreementLength(numeric days)`—Ensures that the length of the agreement is between 1 and 30 days inclusive; also calculates the ending month, day, and year based on the starting date and length of the agreement

☐ `void setInsuranceIndicator(string insuranceIndicator)`—Ensures that the insurance indicator is "Y" or "N" (for "Yes" or "No")

Now you can create the following:

☐ Design a `RentalAgreementException` class. The class contains a string field that holds an error message. The constructor accepts a string message that it can return with a `getMessage()` method.

☐ Modify the `RentalAgreement` class so that each set method throws a `RentalAgreementException` containing an appropriate message if any of the method's arguments are out of range, as listed in the preceding method descriptions.

☐ Design an application that creates an array of 10 `RentalAgreement` objects. In a loop, prompt the user to enter the needed data for each object. If a `RentalAgreementException` is thrown, display the `RentalAgreementException`'s message, and end the application.

☐ Design a second application that creates an array of 10 `RentalAgreement` objects. In a loop, prompt the user to enter the needed data for each object. If a `RentalAgreementException` is thrown after the user enters data for any field, display the `RentalAgreementException`'s message, and continue to prompt the user for data until a valid value for the erroneous field is entered. After all the objects are entered, display all 10 `RentalAgreement` objects.

☐ Design a third application that creates an array of 10 `RentalAgreement` objects. In a loop, prompt the user to enter the needed data for each object. If a `RentalAgreementException` is thrown after the user enters data for any field, force the user to reenter all the data for that object, continuing until there are 10 completely valid objects. After all the objects are entered, display all 10 `RentalAgreement` objects.

APPENDIX A

SOLVING DIFFICULT STRUCTURING PROBLEMS

In Chapter 4 you learned that you can solve any logical problem using only the three standard structures—sequence, selection, and looping. Often it is a simple matter to modify an unstructured program method to make it adhere to structured rules. Sometimes, however, it is a challenge to structure a more complicated method. Still, no matter how complicated, large, or poorly structured a problem is, the same tasks can *always* be accomplished in a structured manner.

Consider the flowchart segment in Figure A-1. Is it structured?

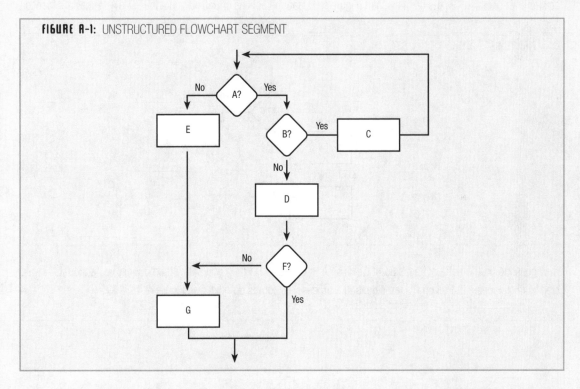

FIGURE A-1: UNSTRUCTURED FLOWCHART SEGMENT

No, it's not. To straighten out the flowchart segment, making it structured, you can use the "spaghetti" method. Using this method, you untangle each path of the flowchart as if you were attempting to untangle strands of spaghetti in a bowl. The objective is to create a new flowchart segment that performs exactly the same tasks as the first, but using only the three structures—sequence, selection, and loop.

To begin to untangle the unstructured flowchart segment, you start at the beginning with the decision labeled A, shown in Figure A-2. This step must represent the beginning of either a selection or a loop, because a sequence would not contain a decision.

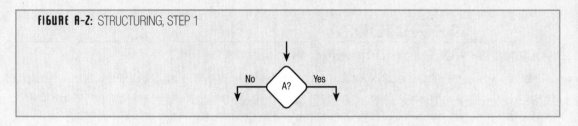

FIGURE A-2: STRUCTURING, STEP 1

If you follow the logic on the No, or left, side of the question in the original flowchart, you can pull up on the left branch of the decision. You encounter process E, followed by G, followed by the end, as shown in Figure A-3. Compare the "No" actions after Decision A in the first flowchart (Figure A-1), and the actions after Decision A in Figure A-3; they are identical.

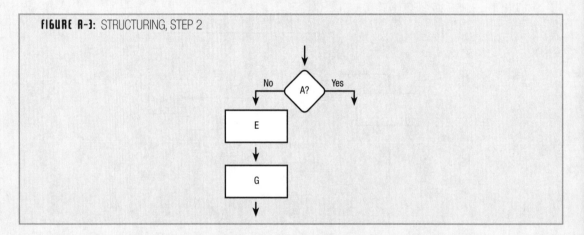

FIGURE A-3: STRUCTURING, STEP 2

Now continue on the right, or Yes, side of Decision A in Figure A-1. When you follow the flowline, you encounter a decision symbol, labeled B. Pull on B's left side, and a process, D, comes up next. See Figure A-4.

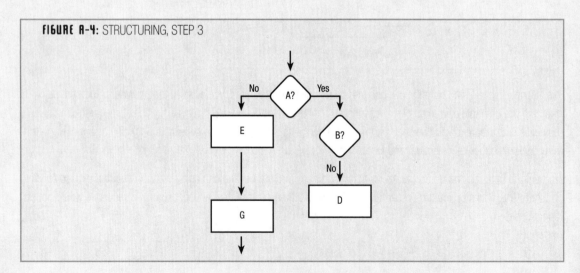

FIGURE A-4: STRUCTURING, STEP 3

After Step D in the original diagram, a decision labeled F comes up. Pull on its left, or No, side and get a process, G, and then the end. When you pull on F's right, or Yes, side in the original flowchart, you simply reach the end, as shown in Figure A-5. Notice in Figure A-5 that the G process now appears in two locations. When you improve unstructured flowcharts so that they become structures, you often must repeat steps. This eliminates crossed lines and difficult-to-follow spaghetti logic.

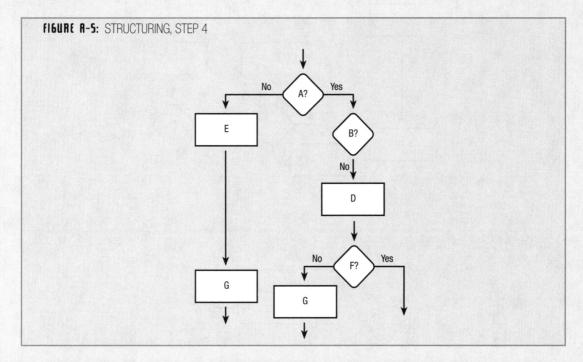

FIGURE A-5: STRUCTURING, STEP 4

The biggest problem in structuring the original flowchart segment from Figure A-1 follows the right, or Yes, side of the B decision. When the answer to B is Yes, you encounter process C, as shown in both Figures A-1 and A-6. The structure that begins with Decision C looks like a loop because it doubles back, up to Decision A. However, the rules of a structured loop say that it must have the appearance shown in Figure A-7: a question, followed by a structure, returning right back to the question. In Figure A-1, if the path coming out of C returned right to B, there would be no problem; it would be a simple, structured loop. However, as it is, Question A must be repeated. The spaghetti technique says if things are tangled up, start repeating them. So repeat an A decision after C, as Figure A-6 shows.

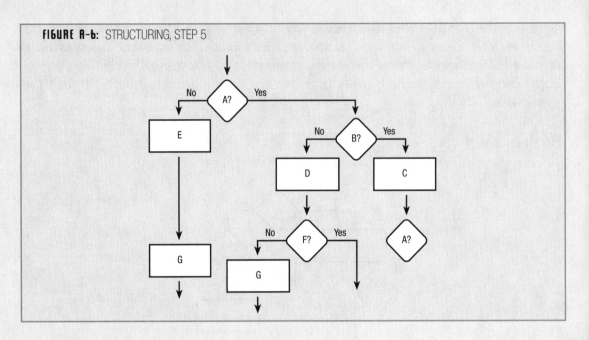

FIGURE A-6: STRUCTURING, STEP 5

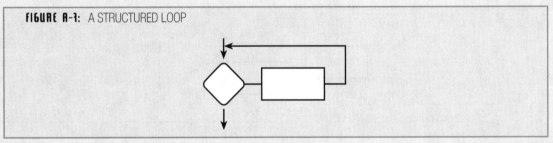

FIGURE A-7: A STRUCTURED LOOP

In the original flowchart segment in Figure A-1, when A is Yes, Question B always follows. So, in Figure A-8, after A is Yes, B is Yes, Step C executes, and A is asked again, when A is Yes, B repeats. In the original, when B is Yes, C executes, so in Figure A-8, on the right side of B, C repeats. After C, A occurs. On the right side of A, B occurs. On the right side of B, C occurs. After C, A should occur again, and so on. Soon you should realize that, in order to follow the steps in the same order as in the original flowchart segment, you will repeat these same steps forever. See Figure A-8.

FIGURE A-8: STRUCTURING, STEP 6, WHICH NEVER ENDS

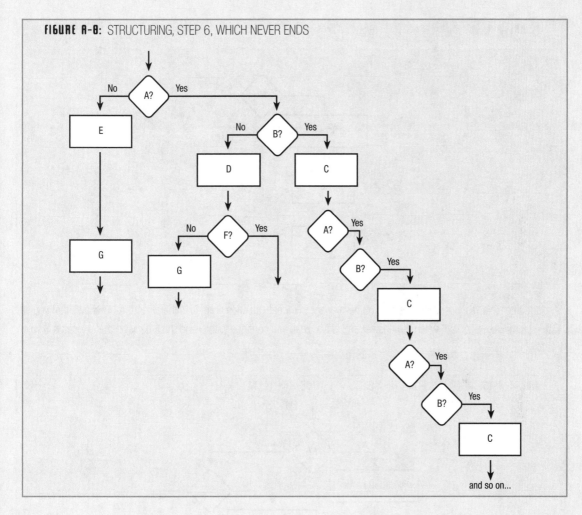

If you continue with Figure A-8, you will never be able to end; every C is always followed by another A, B, and C. Sometimes, in order to make a program segment structured, you have to add an extra flag variable to get out of an infinite mess. A flag is a variable that you set to indicate a true or false state. Typically, a variable is called a flag when its only purpose is to tell you whether some event has occurred. You can create a flag variable named `shouldRepeat` and set the value of `shouldRepeat` to "Yes" or "No," depending on whether it is appropriate to repeat Decision A. When A is No, the `shouldRepeat` flag should be set to "No" because, in this situation, you never want to repeat Question A again. See Figure A-9.

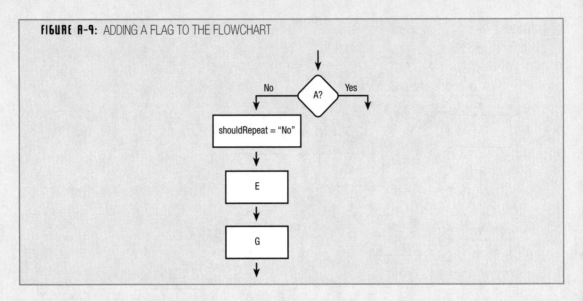

FIGURE A-9: ADDING A FLAG TO THE FLOWCHART

Similarly, after A is Yes, but when B is No, you never want to repeat Question A again, either. Figure A-10 shows that you set `shouldRepeat` to "No" when the answer to B is No. Then you continue with D and the F decision that executes G when F is No.

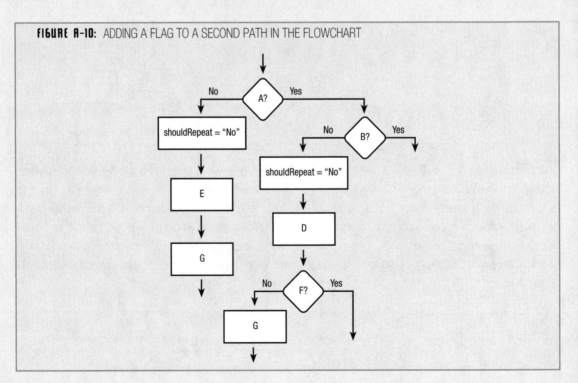

FIGURE A-10: ADDING A FLAG TO A SECOND PATH IN THE FLOWCHART

However, in the original flowchart segment in Figure A-1, when the B decision result is Yes, you *do* want to repeat A. So when B is Yes, perform the process for C and set the `shouldRepeat` flag equal to "Yes", as shown in Figure A-11.

FIGURE A-11: ADDING A FLAG TO A THIRD PATH IN THE FLOWCHART

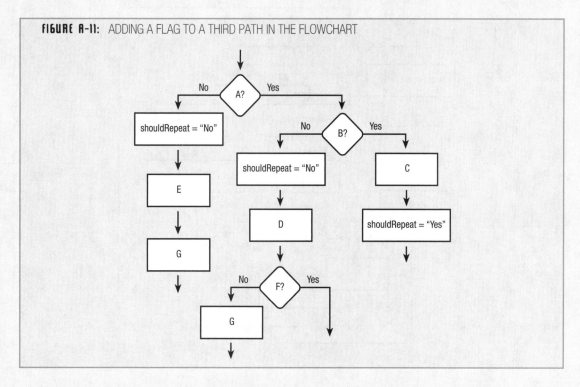

Now all paths of the flowchart can join together at the bottom with one final question: Is `shouldRepeat` equal to "Yes"? If it isn't, exit; but if it is, extend the flowline to go back to repeat Question A. See Figure A-12. Take a moment to verify that the steps that would execute following Figure A-12 are the same steps that would execute following Figure A-1.

- When A is No, E and G always execute.
- When A is Yes and B is No, D and Decision F always execute.
- When A is Yes and B is Yes, C always executes and A repeats.

TIP □ □ □ □ | Figure A-12 contains three nested selection structures. In Figure A-12 notice how the F decision begins a complete selection structure whose Yes and No paths join together when the structure ends. This F selection structure is within one path of the B decision structure; the B decision begins a complete selection structure, the Yes and No paths of which join together at the bottom. Likewise, the B selection structure resides entirely within one path of the A selection structure.

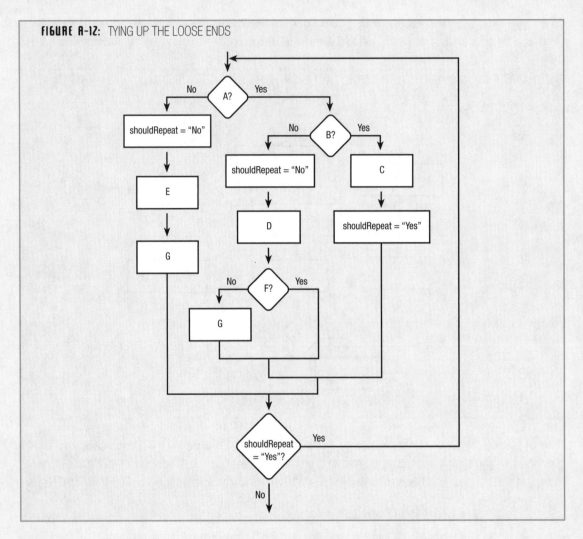

FIGURE A-12: TYING UP THE LOOSE ENDS

The flowchart segment in Figure A-12 performs identically to the original spaghetti version in Figure A-1. However, is this new flowchart segment structured? There are so many steps in the diagram, it is hard to tell. You may be able to see the structure more clearly if you create a method named `aThroughG()`. If you create the method shown in Figure A-13, then the original flowchart segment can be drawn as in Figure A-14.

FIGURE A-13: THE `aThroughG()` MODULE

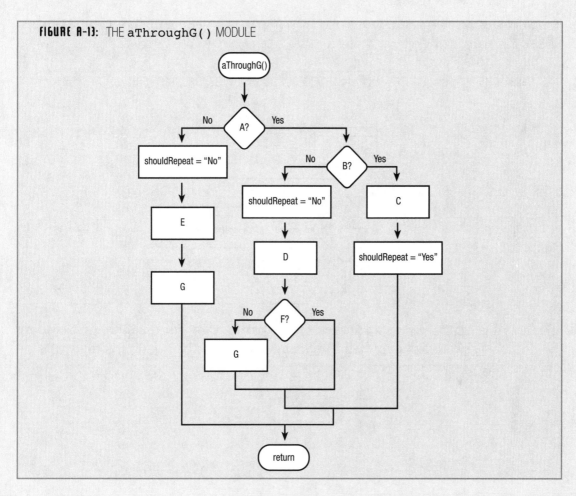

FIGURE A-14: LOGIC IN FIGURE A-12, SUBSTITUTING A MODULE FOR STEPS A THROUGH G

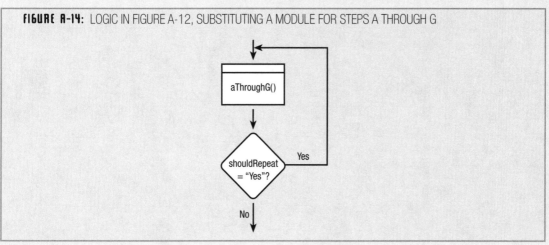

Now you can see that the completed flowchart segment in Figure A-14 is a `do until` loop. If you prefer to use a `while` loop, you can redraw Figure A-14 to perform a sequence followed by a `while` loop, as shown in Figure A-15.

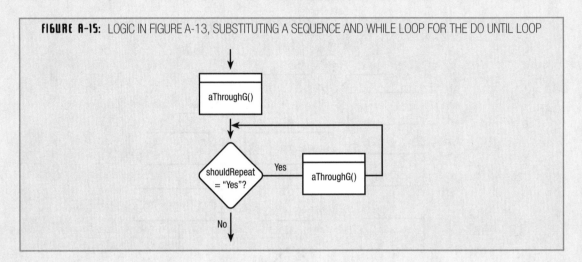

FIGURE A-15: LOGIC IN FIGURE A-13, SUBSTITUTING A SEQUENCE AND WHILE LOOP FOR THE DO UNTIL LOOP

It has taken some effort, but any logical problem can be made to conform to structured rules. It may take extra steps, including repeating specific steps and using some flag variables, but every logical problem can be solved using the three structures: sequence, selection, and loop.

APPENDIX B

UNDERSTANDING NUMBERING SYSTEMS AND COMPUTER CODES

The numbering system with which you are most familiar is the decimal system—the system based on ten digits, 0 through 9. When you use the decimal system, there are no other symbols available; if you want to express a value larger than 9, you must resort to using multiple digits from the same pool of ten, placing them in columns.

When you use the decimal system, you analyze a multicolumn number by mentally assigning place values to each column. The value of the rightmost column is 1, the value of the next column to the left is 10, the next column is 100, and so on, multiplying the column value by 10 as you move to the left. There is no limit to the number of columns you can use; you simply keep adding columns to the left as you need to express higher values. For example, Figure B-1 shows how the value 305 is represented in the decimal system. You simply sum the value of the digit in each column after it has been multiplied by the value of its column.

FIGURE B-1: REPRESENTING 305 IN THE DECIMAL SYSTEM

Column value:	100	10	1
Number:	3	0	5
Evaluation:	3*100	+0*10	+5*1

The **binary numbering system** works in the same way as the decimal numbering system, except that it uses only two digits, 0 and 1. When you use the binary system, if you want to express a value greater than 1, you must resort to using multiple columns, because no single symbol is available that represents any value other than 0 or 1. However, instead of each new column to the left being 10 times greater than the previous column, when you use the binary system, each new column is only two times the value of the previous column. For example, Figure B-2 shows how the number 9 is represented in the binary system, and Figure B-3 shows how the value 305 is represented. Notice that in both figures that show binary numbers, as well as in the decimal system, it is perfectly acceptable—and often necessary—to write a number containing 0 as some of the digits. As with the decimal system, when you use the binary system, there is no limit to the number of columns you can use—you use as many as it takes to express a value.

FIGURE B-2: REPRESENTING 9 IN THE BINARY SYSTEM

Column value:	8	4	2	1
Number:	1	0	0	1

Conversion to decimal: 1*8 = 8
                        +0*4 = 0
                        +0*2 = 0
                        +1*1 = 1
                        ─────────
              Total: 9

FIGURE B-3: REPRESENTING 305 IN THE BINARY SYSTEM

Column value:	256	128	64	32	16	8	4	2	1
Number:	1	0	0	1	1	0	0	0	1

```
Conversion to decimal:            1* 256 =  256

                            +    0* 128 =    0

                            +    0*  64 =    0

                            +    1*  32 =   32

                            +    1*  16 =   16

                            +    0*   8 =    0

                            +    0*   4 =    0

                            +    0*   2 =    0

                            +    1*   1 =    1
                                       _____

                  Total:                     305
```

TIP ▫ ▫ ▫ ▫   Mathematicians call decimal numbers **base 10 numbers** and binary numbers base 2 numbers.

Every computer stores every piece of data it ever uses as a set of 0s and 1s. Each 0 or 1 is known as a **bit**, which is short for **bi**nary digi**t**. Every computer uses 0s and 1s because all values in a computer are stored as electronic signals that are either on or off. This two-state system is most easily represented using just two digits.

Every computer uses a set of binary digits to represent every character it can store. If computers used only one binary digit to represent characters, then only two different characters could be represented, because the single bit could be only 0 or 1. If they used only two digits, then only four characters could be represented—one that used each of the four codes 00, 01, 10, and 11, which in decimal values are 0, 1, 2, and 3, respectively. Many computers use sets of eight binary digits to represent each character they store, because using eight binary digits provides 256 different combinations. One combination can represent an "A", another a "B", and still others "a" and "b", and so on. Two hundred fifty-six combinations are enough so that each capital letter, small letter, digit, and punctuation mark used in English has its own code; even a space has a code. For example, in some computers 01000001 represents the character "A". The binary number 01000001 has a decimal value of 65, but this numeric value is not important to ordinary computer users; it is simply a code that stands for "A". The code that uses 01000001 to mean "A" is the **American Standard Code for Information Interchange**, or **ASCII**.

TIP ▫ ▫ ▫ ▫   A set of eight bits is called a byte. Half a byte, or four bits, is a **nibble**.

The ASCII code is not the only computer code; it just is typical, and it is the one used in most personal computers. The **Extended Binary Coded Decimal Interchange Code**, or **EBCDIC**, is an eight-bit code that is used in IBM mainframe computers. In these computers, the principle is the same—every character is stored as a series of binary digits. The only difference is that the actual values used are different. For example, in EBCDIC, an "A" is 11000001, or 193.

Another code used by languages such as Java and C# is Unicode; with this code, 16 bits are used to represent each character. The character "A" in Unicode has the same decimal value as the ASCII "A", 65, but it is stored as 0000000001000001. Using 16 bits provides many more possible combinations than using only eight—65,536 to be exact. With Unicode, not only are there enough available codes for all English letters and digits, but also for characters from many international alphabets.

Ordinary computer users seldom think about the numeric codes behind the letters, numbers, and punctuation marks they enter from their keyboards or see displayed on a monitor. However, they see the consequence of the values behind letters when they see data sorted in alphabetical order. When you sort a list of names, "Andrea" comes before "Brian," and "Caroline" comes after "Brian" because the numeric code for "A" is lower than the code for "B", and the numeric code for "C" is higher than the code for "B" no matter whether you are using ASCII, EBCDIC, or Unicode.

Table B-1 shows the decimal and binary values behind the most commonly used characters in the ASCII character set—the letters, numbers, and punctuation marks you can enter from your keyboard using a single key press.

TIP □ □ □ □ | Most of the values not included in Table B-1 have a purpose. For example, the decimal value 7 represents a bell—a dinging sound your computer can make, often used to notify you of an error or some other unusual condition.

TIP □ □ □ □ | Each binary number in Table B-1 is shown containing two sets of four digits; this convention makes the long eight-digit numbers easier to read.

TABLE B-1: DECIMAL AND BINARY VALUES FOR COMMON ASCII CHARACTERS

Decimal Number	Binary Number	ASCII Character	
32	0010 0000		Space
33	0010 0001	!	Exclamation point
34	0010 0010	"	Quotation mark, or double quote
35	0010 0011	#	Number sign, also called an octothorpe or a pound sign
36	0010 0100	$	Dollar sign
37	0010 0101	%	Percent
38	0010 0110	&	Ampersand
39	0010 0111	'	Apostrophe, single quote
40	0010 1000	(	Left parenthesis
41	0010 1001	)	Right parenthesis
42	0010 1010	*	Asterisk
43	0010 1011	+	Plus sign
44	0010 1100	,	Comma
45	0010 1101	-	Hyphen or minus sign

TABLE B-1: DECIMAL AND BINARY VALUES FOR COMMON ASCII CHARACTERS (CONTINUED)

Decimal Number	Binary Number	ASCII Character	
46	0010 1110	.	Period or decimal point
47	0010 1111	/	Slash or front slash
48	0011 0000	0	0
49	0011 0001	1	1
50	0011 0010	2	2
51	0011 0011	3	3
52	0011 0100	4	4
53	0011 0101	5	5
54	0011 0110	6	6
55	0011 0111	7	7
56	0011 1000	8	8
57	0011 1001	9	9
58	0011 1010	:	Colon
59	0011 1011	;	Semicolon
60	0011 1100	<	Less-than sign
61	0011 1101	=	Equal sign
62	0011 1110	>	Greater-than sign
63	0011 1111	?	Question mark
64	0100 0000	@	At sign
65	0100 0001	A	A
66	0100 0010	B	B
67	0100 0011	C	C
68	0100 0100	D	D
69	0100 0101	E	E
70	0100 0110	F	F
71	0100 0111	G	G
72	0100 1000	H	H
73	0100 1001	I	I
74	0100 1010	J	J
75	0100 1011	K	K
76	0100 1100	L	L

TABLE B-1: DECIMAL AND BINARY VALUES FOR COMMON ASCII CHARACTERS (CONTINUED)

Decimal Number	Binary Number	ASCII Character	
77	0100 1101	M	M
78	0100 1110	N	N
79	0100 1111	O	O
80	0101 0000	P	P
81	0101 0001	Q	Q
82	0101 0010	R	R
83	0101 0011	S	S
84	0101 0100	T	T
85	0101 0101	U	U
86	0101 0110	V	V
87	0101 0111	W	W
88	0101 1000	X	X
89	0101 1001	Y	Y
90	0101 1010	Z	Z
91	0101 1011	[	Opening or left bracket
92	0101 1100	\	Backslash
93	0101 1101	]	Closing or right bracket
94	0101 1110	^	Caret
95	0101 1111	_	Underline or underscore
96	0110 0000	`	Grave accent
97	0110 0001	a	a
98	0110 0010	b	b
99	0110 0011	c	c
100	0110 0100	d	d
101	0110 0101	e	e
102	0110 0110	f	f
103	0110 0111	g	g
104	0110 1000	h	h
105	0110 1001	i	i
106	0110 1010	j	j
107	0110 1011	k	k
108	0110 1100	l	l

TABLE B-1: DECIMAL AND BINARY VALUES FOR COMMON ASCII CHARACTERS (CONTINUED)

Decimal Number	Binary Number	ASCII Character	
109	0110 1101	m	m
110	0110 1110	n	n
111	0110 1111	o	o
112	0111 0000	p	p
113	0111 0001	q	q
114	0111 0010	r	r
115	0111 0011	s	s
116	0111 0100	t	t
117	0111 0101	u	u
118	0111 0110	v	v
119	0111 0111	w	w
120	0111 1000	x	x
121	0111 1001	y	y
122	0111 1010	z	z
123	0111 1011	{	Opening or left brace
124	0111 1100			Vertical line or pipe
125	0111 1101	}	Closing or right brace
126	0111 1110	~	Tilde

APPENDIX C

USING A LARGE DECISION TABLE

In Chapter 5 you learned to use a simple decision table, but real-life problems often require many decisions. A complicated decision process is represented in the following situation. Suppose your employer sends you a memo outlining a year-end bonus plan with complicated rules. Appendix C will walk you through the process of solving this problem by using a large decision table.

```
To: Programming staff
From: The boss
I need a report listing every employee and the
bonus I plan to give him or her. Everybody gets
at least $100. All the employees in Department 2
get $200, unless they have more than 5 dependents.
Anybody with more than 5 dependents gets $1000
unless they're in Department 2. Nobody with an ID
number greater than 800 gets more than $100 even
if they're in Department 2 or have more than 5
dependents.
P.S. I need this by 5 o'clock.
```

Drawing the flowchart or writing the pseudocode for the `mainLoop()` for this task may seem daunting. You can use a decision table to help you manage all the decisions, and you can begin to create one by listing all the possible decisions you need to make to determine an employee's bonus. They are:

- $empDept = 2$?
- $empDepend > 5$?
- $empIdNum > 800$?

Next, determine how many possible Boolean value combinations exist for the conditions. In this case, there are eight possible combinations, shown in Figure C-1. An employee can be in Department 2, have over five dependents, and have an ID number greater than 800. Another employee can be in Department 2, have over five dependents, but have an ID number that is 800 or less. Since each condition has two outcomes and there are three conditions, there are 2 * 2 * 2 , or eight possibilities. Four conditions would produce 16 possible outcome combinations, five would produce 32, and so on.

FIGURE C-1: POSSIBLE OUTCOMES OF BONUS CONDITIONS

Condition	Outcome							
empDept = 2	T	T	T	T	F	F	F	F
empDepend > 5	T	T	F	F	T	T	F	F
empIdNum > 800	T	F	T	F	T	F	T	F

TIP ☐ ☐ ☐ ☐ In Figure C-1, notice how the pattern of Ts and Fs varies in each row. The bottom row contains one T and F, repeating four times, the second row contains two of each, repeating twice, and the top row contains four of each without repeating. If a fourth decision was required, you would place an identical grid of T and Fs to the right of this one, then add a new top row containing eight Ts (covering all eight columns you see currently) followed by eight Fs (covering the new copy of the grid to the right).

Next, list the possible outcome values for the bonus amounts. If you declare a numeric variable named **bonus** by placing the statement **num bonus** in your list of variables at the beginning of the program, then the possible outcomes can be expressed as:

- bonus = 100
- bonus = 200
- bonus = 1000

Finally, choose one required outcome for each possible combination of conditions. For example, the first possible outcome is a $100 bonus. As Figure C-2 shows, you place Xs in the **bonus = 100** row each time **empIdNum > 800** is true, no matter what other conditions exist, because the memo from the boss said, "Nobody with an ID number greater than 800 gets more than $100, even if they're in Department 2 or have more than 5 dependents."

FIGURE C-2: DECISION TABLE FOR BONUSES, PART 1

Condition	Outcome							
empDept = 2	T	T	T	T	F	F	F	F
empDepend > 5	T	T	F	F	T	T	F	F
empIdNum > 800	T	F	T	F	T	F	T	F
bonus = 100	X		X		X		X	
bonus = 200								
bonus = 1000								

Next, place an X in the **bonus = 1000** row under all remaining columns (that is, those without a selected outcome) in which **empDepend > 5** is true *unless* the **empDept = 2** condition is true, because the memo stated, "Anybody with more than 5 dependents gets $1000 unless they're in Department 2." the first four columns of the decision table do not qualify, because the **empDept** value is 2; only the sixth column in Figure C-3 meets the criteria for the $1000 bonus.

FIGURE C-3: DECISION TABLE FOR BONUSES, PART 2

Condition	Outcome							
empDept = 2	T	T	T	T	F	F	F	F
empDepend > 5	T	T	F	F	T	T	F	F
empIdNum > 800	T	F	T	F	T	F	T	F
bonus = 100	X		X		X		X	
bonus = 200								
bonus = 1000						X		

Place Xs in the `bonus = 200` row for any remaining columns in which `empDept = 2` is true and `empDepend > 5` is false, because "All the employees in Department 2 get $200, unless they have more than 5 dependents." Column 4 in Figure C-4 satisfies these criteria.

FIGURE C-4: DECISION TABLE FOR BONUSES, PART 3

Condition	Outcome							
empDept = 2	T	T	T	T	F	F	F	F
empDepend > 5	T	T	F	F	T	T	F	F
empIdNum > 800	T	F	T	F	T	F	T	F
bonus = 100	X		X		X		X	
bonus = 200				X				
bonus = 1000						X		

Finally, fill any unmarked columns with an X in the `bonus = 100` row because, according to the memo, "Everybody gets at least $100." The only columns remaining are the second column and the last column on the right. See Figure C-5.

FIGURE C-5: DECISION TABLE FOR BONUSES, PART 4

Condition	Outcome							
empDept = 2	T	T	T	T	F	F	F	F
empDepend > 5	T	T	F	F	T	T	F	F
empIdNum > 800	T	F	T	F	T	F	T	F
bonus = 100	X	X	X		X		X	X
bonus = 200				X				
bonus = 1000						X		

The decision table is complete. When you count the Xs, you'll find there are eight possible outcomes. Take a moment and confirm that each bonus is the appropriate value based on the specifications in the original memo from the boss. Now you can start to plan the logic. If you choose to use a flowchart, you start by drawing the path to the first outcome, which occurs when `empDept = 2`, `empDepend > 5`, and `empIdNum > 800` are all true, and which corresponds to the first column in the decision table. See Figure C-6.

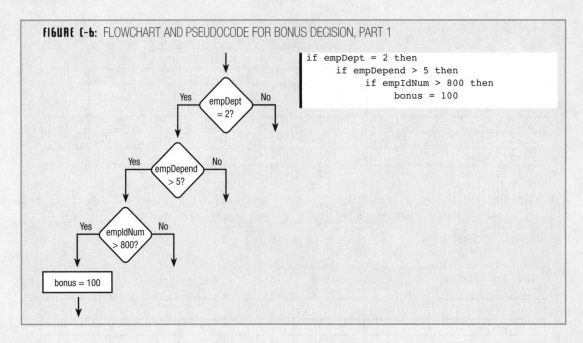

FIGURE C-6: FLOWCHART AND PSEUDOCODE FOR BONUS DECISION, PART 1

```
if empDept = 2 then
        if empDepend > 5 then
                if empIdNum > 800 then
                        bonus = 100
```

To continue creating the diagram started in Figure C-6, add the "false" outcome to the `empIdNum > 800` decision; this corresponds to the second column in the decision table. When an employee's department is 2, dependents greater than 5, and ID number not greater than 800, the employee's bonus should be $100. See Figure C-7.

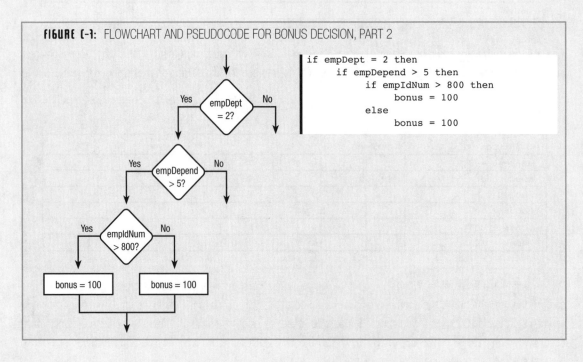

FIGURE C-7: FLOWCHART AND PSEUDOCODE FOR BONUS DECISION, PART 2

```
if empDept = 2 then
        if empDepend > 5 then
                if empIdNum > 800 then
                        bonus = 100
                else
                        bonus = 100
```

Continue the diagram in Figure C-7 by adding the "false" outcome when the empDepend > 5 decision is No and the empIdNum > 800 decision is Yes, which is represented by the third column in the decision table. In this case, the bonus is again $100. See Figure C-8.

FIGURE C-8: FLOWCHART AND PSEUDOCODE FOR BONUS DECISION, PART 3

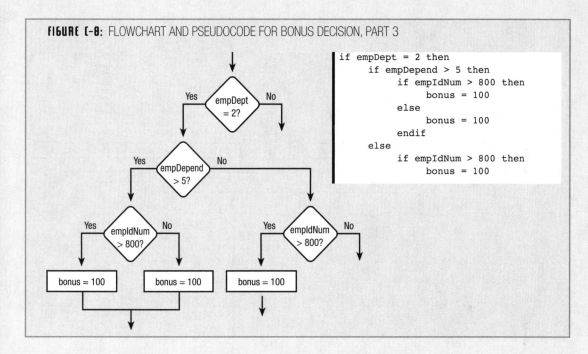

```
if empDept = 2 then
        if empDepend > 5 then
                if empIdNum > 800 then
                        bonus = 100
                else
                        bonus = 100
                endif
        else
                if empIdNum > 800 then
                        bonus = 100
```

Continue adding decisions until you have drawn all eight possible outcomes, as shown in Figure C-9.

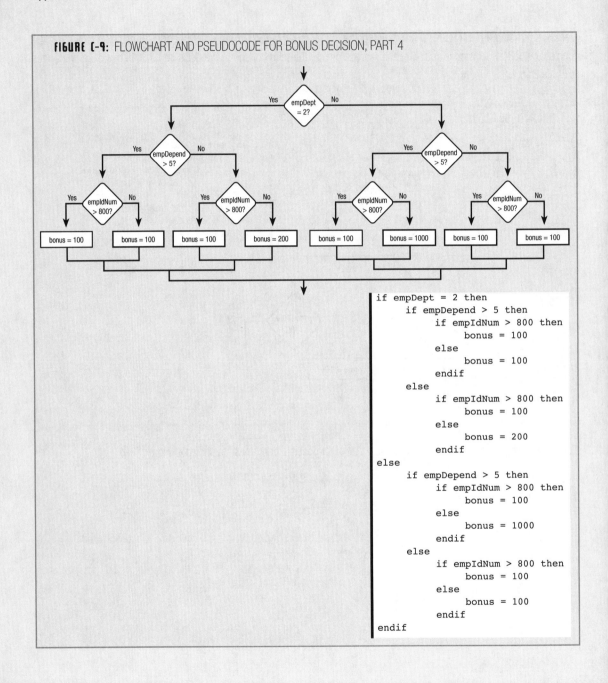

FIGURE C-9: FLOWCHART AND PSEUDOCODE FOR BONUS DECISION, PART 4

```
if empDept = 2 then
     if empDepend > 5 then
          if empIdNum > 800 then
               bonus = 100
          else
               bonus = 100
          endif
     else
          if empIdNum > 800 then
               bonus = 100
          else
               bonus = 200
          endif
else
     if empDepend > 5 then
          if empIdNum > 800 then
               bonus = 100
          else
               bonus = 1000
          endif
     else
          if empIdNum > 800 then
               bonus = 100
          else
               bonus = 100
          endif
endif
```

The logic shown in Figure C-9 correctly assigns a bonus to any employee, no matter what combination of characteristics the employee's record holds. However, you can eliminate many of the decisions shown in Figure C-9; you can eliminate any decision that doesn't make any difference. For example, if you look at the far left side of Figure C-9, you see that when `empDept` is 2 and `empDepend` is greater than 5, the outcome of `empIdNum > 800` does not matter; the bonus value is 100 either way. You might as well eliminate the selection. Similarly, on the far right, the question `empIdNum` makes no difference. Finally, many programmers prefer the True, or Yes, side of a flowchart decision always to appear on the right side. The result is Figure C-10.

FIGURE C-10: COMPLETE FLOWCHART AND PSEUDOCODE FOR BONUS DECISION

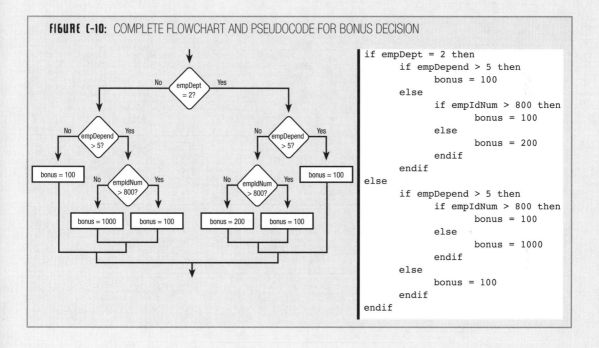

```
if empDept = 2 then
        if empDepend > 5 then
                bonus = 100
        else
                if empIdNum > 800 then
                        bonus = 100
                else
                        bonus = 200
                endif
        endif
else
        if empDepend > 5 then
                if empIdNum > 800 then
                        bonus = 100
                else
                        bonus = 1000
                endif
        else
                bonus = 100
        endif
endif
```

■■■■■GLOSSARY

abstract class—A class that is created only to be a parent; a class from which you cannot create any concrete objects, but from which you can inherit.

abstraction—The programming feature that allows you to use a method name to encapsulate a series of statements.

access specifier—The adjective that defines the type of access that outside classes will have to an attribute or method. Also called an **access modifier**.

accessibility issues—The screen design issues that make programs easier to use for individuals with physical limitations.

accessor method—A method that retrieves values.

accumulator—A variable that you use to gather or accumulate values.

activity diagram—A UML diagram that shows the flow of actions of a system, including branches that occur when decisions affect the outcome.

actual parameter—An argument in a method call.

ambiguous situation—A situation in which the compiler cannot determine which method to use.

AND decision—A decision in which two conditions must both be true for an action to take place.

annotation symbol—A three-sided box attached to a flowchart by a dashed line. It is used when you want to provide details for a step, though the details take a lot of room, not easily fitting within a flowchart symbol.

application software—The programs you apply to a task.

argument—A data item sent to methods. Also called a **parameter**.

array—A series or list of variables in computer memory, all of which have the same name but are differentiated with special numbers called subscripts.

Arrays class—A built-in class that contains many useful methods for manipulating arrays.

ascending order—Order from lowest to highest.

assignment operator—The equal sign; it always requires the name of a memory location on its left side.

assignment statement—A statement that stores the result of any calculation performed on its right side to the named location on its left side.

association relationship—An association that describes the connection or link between objects in a UML diagram.

attribute—A characteristic that defines an object as part of a class; a feature an object "has".

base 10 numbers — The decimal numbering system, which is based on ten digits, 0–9.

base class—A class that is used as a basis for inheritance. Also called a **superclass** or **parent class**.

behavior of an object—An action an object "does".

bit — A binary digit.

binary numbering system — A numbering system that uses only two digits, 0 and 1.

black box—A device you can use without knowing how its contents operate.

block—A set of statements that act as a unit within any class or method.

Boolean expression—An expression that represents only one of two states, usually expressed as true or false.

bubble sort—A type of sort in which you continue to compare pairs of items, swapping them if they are out of order, so that the smallest items "bubble" to the top of the list, eventually creating a sorted list.

call—To execute a method.

call stack—The memory location where the computer stores the list of method locations to which the system must return.

called method—A method that is invoked by another method.

calling method—A method that invokes the called method.

camel casing—The format for naming variables in which multiple-word variable names are run together, and each new word within the variable name begins with an uppercase letter.

cardinality—The arithmetic relationships between objects. Also called **multiplicity**.

cascading if statement—A series of nested if statements.

case structure—A structure in which there are several distinct possible values for a single variable you are testing, and each requires a different course of action; it provides a convenient alternative to using a series of decisions when you must make choices based on the value stored in a single variable.

catch block—A segment of code that can handle an exception that might be thrown by the `try` block that precedes it.

central processing unit (CPU)—The hardware component that processes data.

character constant—In most programming languages, a character constant holds a single character. In this book, "character constant" is used synonymously with "string constant" to mean one or more characters enclosed within quotation marks. If a working program contains the statement `lastName = "Lincoln"` then `"Lincoln"` is a character or string constant.

character variable—In most programming languages, a variable that holds a single character value. If a working program contains the statement `lastName = "Lincoln"` then `lastName` is a character or string variable. In this book, "character variable" is used synonymously with "string variable" and "text variable".

class—A category of things. It defines the characteristics of its objects and the methods that can be applied to its objects.

class definition—A set of program statements that tell you the characteristics of the class's objects and the methods that can be applied to its objects.

class diagram—A tool used to describe a class; it consists of a rectangle divided into three sections.

class header—The first line written in a class definition, the class header contains the word class and the class identifier.

client—A program that uses a class object.

close a file—To make a file no longer available for reading.

code—To write the statements in a programming language.

collaboration diagram—A UML diagram that emphasizes the organization of objects that participate in a system.

come into scope—To allow a variable to come into existence, which happens when you declare it.

command line—The location on your computer screen at which you type entries to communicate with the computer's operating system. Also called the **command prompt**.

compiler—Software that translates a high-level language into machine language and tells you if you have used a programming language incorrectly. Similar to an interpreter, though a compiler translates all the statements in a program prior to executing any statements.

component diagram—A UML diagram that emphasizes the files, database tables, documents, and other components that a system's software uses.

constructor—A method that establishes an object.

conversion—The entire set of actions an organization must take to switch over to using a new program or set of programs.

counter—Any numeric variable you use to count the number of times an event has occurred.

data—Facts.

data hiding—Another name for information hiding, the concept that other classes should not alter an object's attributes.

data modeling—The act of identifying all the objects you want to manipulate and how they relate to each other.

dead path—A logical path that can never be traveled. Also called an **unreachable path**.

decision table—A problem-analysis tool that lists conditions, combinations of outcomes when those conditions are tested, and possible actions based on the outcomes.

decrement—To decrease a variable by a constant value, frequently 1.

default constructor—A constructor that requires no arguments; the compiler automatically creates a default constructor when you create a class.

default value—In a decision or if statement, a value that is assigned after all test conditions are found to be false. In assigning values to variables, an automatically supplied value.

definite loop—A loop for which you definitely know the repetition factor.

deployment diagram—A UML diagram that focuses on a system's hardware.

derived class—A class that inherits from a base class. Also called a **subclass** or **child class**.

descendent class—A class that inherits the attributes of another class. Also called a **child class**, **derived class**, or **subclass**.

descending order—Order from highest to lowest.

do until loop—A loop in which a procedure executes at least once; then, depending on the answer to the controlling question, the loop may or may not execute additional times.

DOS prompt—The command line in the DOS operating system.

dual-alternative if—A structure that defines one action to be taken when the tested condition is true, and another action to be taken when it is false.

dual-alternative selection—A selection that offers two actions, each associated with one of two possible outcomes. Also called an **if-then-else** or **binary** structure.

dynamic array—An array whose size is determined during program execution. Also called **dynamically-allocated arrays**.

early exit—To leave a loop as soon as a match is found.

element—A variable that is part of an array.

elided—Part of a UML diagram omitted for clarity.

else clause—The part of a decision that holds the action or actions that execute only when the Boolean expression in the decision is false.

encapsulation—The process of combining all of an object's attributes and methods into a single package.

event—An occurrence that generates a message sent to an object.

event-based program—A GUI program in which actions occur in response to user-initiated events such as clicking a mouse button. Also called an **event-driven program**.

exception—An unexpected or error condition that occurs while a program is running.

exception handling—An object-oriented technique for managing errors.

exception specification clause—A declaration of a method's possible throw types.

execute—To have a computer use a written and compiled program. *See also* run.

extend—A use case variation that shows functions beyond those found in a base case.

external storage—Permanent storage outside the main memory of the machine, on a device such as a floppy disk, hard disk, or magnetic tape.

field—A data item within, or attribute of, an object.

`finally` **block**—A block of code containing actions that must be performed at the end of a `try...catch` sequence.

flag—A variable that you set to indicate whether some event has occurred.

floating-point—A data type for values that are fractional numeric variables and contain a decimal point.

flowchart—A pictorial representation of the logical steps it takes to solve a problem.

flowline—A line or arrow that connects the steps in a flowchart.

for statement—A statement that can be used to code definite loops. It contains a loop control variable that it automatically initializes, evaluates, and increments. Also called a **for loop**.

formal parameter—A variable in the method declaration that accepts the values from the actual parameters.

garbage value—An unknown value in an uninitialized variable.

generalization—An element you use in a UML diagram when a use case is less specific than others, and you want to be able to substitute the more specific case for a general one.

go out of scope—To have a variable cease to exist, which happens at the end of the block in which it is declared.

graphical user interface (GUI)—The part of a program or system that allows users to interact with that program by clicking icons to select options.

hard-coded—Values that are explicitly assigned.

hardware—The equipment of a computer system.

high-level programming language—A programming language that is English-like, as opposed to a low-level programming language.

icon—A small picture on the computer screen that the user can select with a pointing device.

identifier—The name of a programming object—a class, method, or variable.

if clause—The part of a decision that holds the action that results when a Boolean expression in a decision is true.

if-then-else—Another name for a selection structure.

implementation hiding—A principle of object-oriented programming that describes the encapsulation of method details within a class.

include relationship—A use case variation that you use when a case can be part of multiple use cases in a UML diagram.

increment—To add a constant value to a variable, frequently 1.

indeterminate loop—A loop for which you cannot predetermine the number of executions. Also called an **indefinite loop**.

index—A number that indicates the position of a particular item within an array.

infinite loop—A loop that never stops executing.

information hiding—The concept of keeping data private so that other classes cannot alter an object's attributes—outside classes should only be allowed to make a request that an attribute be altered; then it is up to the class methods to determine whether the request is appropriate.

inheritance—In object-oriented languages, a mechanism that enables one class to inherit, or assume, both the behavior and the attributes of another class.

initialization loop—A loop structure that provides initial values for every element in any array.

initialize—To provide a variable with a value when you create it, which is part of defining a variable.

inner loop—When one loop appears inside another, the loop that is contained within another loop is the inner loop.

input device—A hardware device such as a keyboard or mouse; through these devices, data enter the computer system. Data can also enter a system from storage devices such as magnetic disks and CDs.

input statement—A statement that reads data in from an input device such as a keyboard or file on disk. By convention, those who create flowcharts use a parallelogram to display input statements.

inside block—A block contained within another block.

instance—An existing object of a class.

instance method—A method that operates correctly for each separate instance of a class.

instantiate—To create a class object.

integer—A value that is a whole number numeric variable.

interactivity diagram—A drawing that shows the relationship between screens in an interactive GUI program.

interface—In a method, the part that includes the method's return type, name, and arguments; it is the part that a client sees and uses. In Graphical User Interfaces, the user-friendly boundary between the user and internal mechanisms of the device.

internal storage—Temporary storage within the computer; also called memory, main memory, or primary memory.

interpreter—Software that translates a high-level language into machine language and tells you if you have used a programming language incorrectly. Similar to a compiler, though, an interpreter translates one statement at a time, executing each statement as soon as it is translated.

invoke—To execute a method.

is-a—A phrase to test whether an object is an instance of a class.

library—A collection of classes that serve related purposes. Also called a **package**.

listener—An object that is "interested in" an event to which you want it to respond.

local variable—A variable known only within the boundaries of a method.

logic—Instructions given to the computer in a specific sequence, without leaving any instructions out or adding extraneous instructions.

logical AND operator—A symbol that you use to combine decisions so that two (or more) conditions must be true for an action to occur.

logical error—An error that occurs when incorrect instructions are performed, or when instructions are performed in the wrong order.

logical NOT operator—A symbol that reverses the meaning of a Boolean expression.

logical OR operator—A symbol that you use to combine decisions when any one condition can be true for an action to occur.

loop—A structure that repeats actions while some condition continues.

loop body—The set of statements that executes within a loop.

loop control variable—A variable that determines whether a loop will continue.

loop structure—A structure in which you ask a question; if the answer requires an action, you perform the action and ask the original question again.

low-level programming language—A programming language not far removed from machine language, as opposed to a high-level programming language.

lozenge—A racetrack-shaped symbol that marks the beginning or end of a method in a flowchart.

machine language—A computer's on-off circuitry language; the low-level language made up of 1s and 0s that the computer understands.

magic number—A number that is hard coded into a program without explanation; using them is a bad programming practice.

main loop—A basic set of instructions that is repeated for every record.

matrix—A two-dimensional array.

method—A program module that contains a series of statements that carry out a task.

method call—A statement that invokes a procedure, that is, causes the procedure to execute.

method declaration—The first line of a method. Also called the **header**.

method header—The first line in a method.

method's type—A method's return type.

mnemonic—A memory device; variable identifiers act as mnemonics for hard-to-remember memory addresses.

multidimensional array—An array that has any number of dimensions.

multiple inheritance—The capability of inheriting from more than one class.

multithreading—To use multiple threads of execution.

mutator method—A method that sets values.

nested block—A block that is contained entirely within another block.

nested decision—A decision "inside of" another decision. An AND decision requires a nested decision. Also called a **nested if**.

nested loops—Loops within loops.

nesting—To place a structure within another structure.

nonstatic method—A method that exists to be used with an object created from a class.

null case—A branch of a decision in which no action is taken.

numeric constant—A specific numeric value.

numeric variable—A variable that holds numeric values.

object diagram—A UML diagram similar to a class diagram that models specific instances of classes.

object dictionary—A list of the objects used in a program, including which screens they are used on and whether any code, or script, is associated with them.

object-oriented analysis (OOA)—Analyzing a system using an object-oriented approach.

object-oriented approach—Defining the objects needed to accomplish a task and developing the objects so that each maintains its own data and carries out tasks when another object requests them.

object-oriented design (OOD)—Designing a system using an object-oriented approach.

object-oriented programming (OOP)—A style of programming that focuses on an application's data and the methods you need to manipulate that data.

one-dimensional array—An array that you can picture as a column of values, and whose elements you can access using a single subscript. Also called a **single-dimensional array**.

open a file—To instruct the computer to find a stored file and prepare it for reading data into an application.

operating system—The software that you use to run a computer and manage its resources.

OR decision—A decision that contains two (or more) decisions; if at least one condition is met, the resulting action takes place.

original class—A class that has descendants. In other words, it is a class from which other classes are derived. Also called a **parent class**, **base class**, or **superclass**.

out of bounds—An array subscript is out of bounds if it is not within the range of acceptable subscripts.

outer loop—When one loop appears inside another, the loop that contains the other loop is the outer loop.

output device—A computer device such as a printer or monitor that lets people view, interpret, and work with information produced by a computer.

output statement—A statement that sends information to an output device such as a monitor or printer. By convention, those who create flowcharts use a parallelogram to display output statements.

outside block—A block that contains another block.

overload—To use one term to indicate diverse meanings, or write multiple methods with the same name, but with different arguments.

override a method—To create a method in a child class that has the same name and argument list as a method in its parent class.

override a variable—To allow one variable to take precedence over another variable.

parallel arrays—Two or more arrays in which each element in one array is associated with the element in the same relative position in the other array or arrays.

pass by reference—To have the receiving method receive the actual memory address of an array, allowing access to and the ability to alter the actual values in the array elements.

pass by value—To make a copy of individual array elements and use them within the receiving method.

pointer variable—A variable that holds a memory address.

polymorphism—The object-oriented feature that allows you to create multiple methods with the same name, which will act differently and appropriately when used with different types of objects; the process of using the same method name to indicate different implementations.

populate an array—To assign values to the array elements.

precedence—The quality of an operation that means it is evaluated before others.

primary key—A value that makes an object unique from all others; database designers frequently use this term.

priming read—The first read or data input statement that occurs before and outside of the loop that performs the rest of the input statements. Also called the **priming input**.

primitive data type—A simple data type, as opposed to a class type.

private access—A method modifier that indicates that data cannot be accessed by any method that is not part of the class.

procedural programming—A programming technique that focuses on the procedures that programmers create.

processing—To organize data items, check them for accuracy, or perform mathematical operations on them.

processing statement—A statement that works with and alters objects. In a flowchart, a processing statement appears in a rectangle.

programmer-defined type—A class.

programming language—A language such as Visual Basic, Pascal, COBOL, RPG, C#, C++, Java, or Fortran, used to write programs.

property—An attribute of prewritten graphical user interface (GUI) classes.

protected access—A level of access that provides you with an intermediate level of security between `public` and `private` access; `protected` members are those that can be used by a class and its descendants. You use the `protected` modifier when you want no outside classes to be able to use a data field, except classes that are children of the original class.

pseudocode—An English-like representation of the logical steps it takes to solve a problem.

public access—A method modifier that indicates that other programs and methods may use the methods that control access to the private data.

range check—A test in which you compare a variable to a series of values between limits.

range of values—A series of values that encompasses every value between a high and low limit.

redeclare a variable—To attempt to declare a variable more than once within a block, which is an illegal action.

reference—A named variable that holds an object's memory address.

register—To sign up components that will react to events initiated by other components in an object-oriented program.

relational comparison operators—The symbols that express Boolean comparisons. Examples include =, >, < >=, <=, and <>.

repetition—Another name for a loop structure. Also called **iteration**.

return a value—To send a data value from a called method back to the calling method.

reverse engineering—To create a model of an existing system.

run—To have a computer use a written and compiled program. *See also* execute.

save—To store a program on some nonvolatile medium.

scenario—Each variation in the sequence of actions required in a use case.

scope—The portion of a program within which you can refer to a variable.

selection structure—A structure in which you ask a question, and, depending on the answer, you take one of two courses of action. Then, no matter which path you follow, you continue with the next event. Also called a **decision**.

self-documenting program—A program in which the choice of variable names is clear so that the program code describes the program's purpose to the reader.

semantic errors—Logical errors in programs.

sentinel value—A limit, or ending, value.

sequence diagram—A UML diagram that shows the timing of events in a single use case.

sequence structure—A structure in which you perform an action or event, and then you perform the next action, in order. A sequence can contain any number of events, but there is no chance to branch off and skip any of the events.

signature—A method's header, including its name, any arguments, and any `throws` clause.

single-alternative if—A structure in which you take action on just one branch of the decision.

single-alternative selection—A selection in which action is required for only one outcome of the question. You call this form of the selection structure an **if-then**, because no "else" action is necessary. Also called a **unary** selection.

size of the array—The number of elements an array can hold.

software—Programs written by programmers that tell the computer what to do.

sort—To arrange a series of objects in some logical order.

source—A component from which an event is generated.

spaghetti code—Snarled, unstructured program logic.

stacking structures—To attach structures end-to-end.

state—A value of an object's attributes.

statechart diagram—A UML diagram that shows the different statuses of or changes of behavior in a class or object at different points in time.

static method—A method for which no object needs to exist.

stereotype—A feature that adds to the UML vocabulary of shapes to make them more meaningful for the reader.

storage device—Hardware such as magnetic disks, tapes, or compact discs, on which you can store output information.

storyboard—A picture or sketch of a screen the user sees when running a program.

string constant—One or more characters enclosed within quotation marks. If a working program contains the statement `lastName = "Lincoln"` then `"Lincoln"` is a character or string constant. In this book, "string constant" is used synonymously with "character constant".

string variable—A variable that holds character values. If a working program contains the statement `lastName = "Lincoln"` then `lastName` is a character or string variable. In this book, "string variable" is used synonymously with "character variable" and "text variable".

structure—A basic unit of programming logic; each structure is a sequence, selection, or loop.

structured method—A method that follows a specific set of rules for its logical design, including containing a single entry and exit point.

subscript—A number that indicates the position of a particular item within an array.

subtype polymorphism—The ability of one method name to work appropriately for different subclass objects of the same parent class.

summary report—A report that lists only totals, without individual detail records.

syntax—The rules of a language.

syntax error—An error in language or grammar.

system design—The detailed specification of how all the parts of a system will be implemented and coordinated.

system software—The programs that you use to manage your computer—operating systems such as Windows or Unix.

table—A two-dimensional array.

this reference—An object's memory address implicitly passed to a nonstatic, instance method. Also called the **this pointer**.

thread—The flow of execution of one set of program statements.

throw statement—A statement that sends an **Exception** out of a method so it can be handled elsewhere.

throwing an exception—the process of tossing out an exception object that another method or the operating system might handle.

trivial expression—A type of Boolean expression that always evaluates to the same result.

try block—A block of code you attempt to execute while acknowledging that an exception might occur.

two-dimensional array—An array that has both rows and columns. You must use two subscripts when you access an element in a two-dimensional array.

UML—A standard way to specify, construct, and document systems that use object-oriented methods. UML is an acronym for Unified Modeling Language.

undeclared variable—A variable that has not been provided with a data type or identifier.

undefined variable—A variable that has not been provided with a value before you attempt to use it.

unreachable code—Program statements that can never execute under any circumstances. Also called **dead code**.

use case diagram—A UML diagram that shows how a business works from the perspective of those who approach it from the outside, or those who actually use the business.

user-defined type—A class.

variable—A memory location, whose contents can vary, or differ, over time. Also called **field**.

variable declaration—A statement that names a variable and tells the computer which type of data to expect.

visual development environment—A development environment in which you can create programs by dragging components such as buttons and labels onto a screen and arranging them visually.

void—A data type that means a method returns nothing.

volatile—The characteristic of internal memory, which loses its contents every time the computer loses power.

while loop—A loop in which a process continues while some condition continues to be true. Also called a **while-do loop**.

whole-part relationship—An association in which one or more classes make up the parts of a larger whole class. This type of relationship is also called an **aggregation** or a **has-a relationship**.

work field—A variable used to hold a temporary calculation.

x-axis—The horizontal positions in a screen window.

x-coordinate—The value that increases as you travel from left to right across a window.

y-axis—The vertical positions in a screen window.

y-coordinate—The value that increases as you travel from top to bottom across a window.

■ ■ ■ ■INDEX